African Families at the Turn of the 21st Century

Edited by

Yaw Oheneba-Sakyi
California State University

and

Baffour K. Takyi
University of Akron

KENDALL/HUNT PUBLISHING COMPANY
4050 Westmark Drive   Dubuque, Iowa 52002

Case-Bound Text:
African Families at the Turn of the 21st Century, edited by Yaw Oheneba-Sakyi and Baffour K. Takyi, was originally published in hard cover by Praeger, an imprint of Greenwood Publishing Group, Inc., Westport, CT. Copyright © 2006, edited by Yaw Oheneba-Sakyi and Baffour K. Takyi. This paperback edition by arrangement with Greenwood Publishing Group, Inc. All rights reserved.

No part of this book may be reproduced or transmitted in any form or by any means electronic or mechanical including photocopying, reprinting, or on any information storage or retrieval system, without permission in writing from Greenwood Publishing Group.

Perfect-Bound Text:
On the cover:
folk image © Linda Webb 2007, used under license from Shutterstock, Inc.;
woman image © 2007, Lucian Coman, used under licese from Shutterstock, Inc.;
Africa image © Jiri Moucka 2007, used under license from Shutterstock, Inc.;
woman on computer © 2007, used under license from Shutterstock, Inc.;
children, woman walking images © Getty Images

Copyright Acknowledgments
The editors and publisher gratefully acknowledge permission for use of the following material:
Chapter 2: Excerpts from "Policy Shifts: State, Islam and Gender in Tunisia, 1930-1990s" by M.M. Charrad, published in *Social Politics* (Oxford University Press, vol. 4, no. 2, 1997), pp. 284-319. By permission of Oxford University Press.

Copyright © 2007 by Kendall/Hunt Publishing Company

ISBN 978-0-7575-4628-0

All rights reserved. No part of this publication may be reproduced, stored in a retrieval system, or transmitted, in any form or by any means, electronic, mechanical, photocopying, recording, or otherwise, without the prior written permission of Kendall/Hunt Publishing Company.

Printed in the United States of America
10 9 8 7 6 5 4 3 2 1

Contents

Preface — vii

Acknowledgments — xiii

Chapter 1 Introduction to the Study of African Families:
A Framework for Analysis — 1
Yaw Oheneba-Sakyi and Baffour K. Takyi

PART I NORTHERN AFRICA

Chapter 2 Continuity or Change: Family Law
and Family Structure in Tunisia — 27
Mounira M. Charrad and Allyson B. Goeken

Chapter 3 Diversity and Family: Examples from Egypt — 49
Bahira Sherif-Trask

Chapter 4 The Sudanese Family: Past Reflections
and Contemporary Realities — 69
Carolyn Fluehr-Lobban

PART II WESTERN AFRICA

Chapter 5 Senegalese Families: The Confluence of Ethnicity,
History, and Social Change — 83
Loretta E. Bass and Fatou Sow

Chapter 6 Structural Change and Continuity
in the Ivorian Family — 103
N'Dri Thérèse Assié-Lumumba

Chapter 7	The Family in Ghana: Past and Present Perspectives *Elizabeth Ardayfio-Schandorf*	129
Chapter 8	The Nigerian Family: Contrast, Convergence, Continuity, and Discontinuity *Obioma Nnaemeka*	153
PART III	CENTRAL AFRICA	
Chapter 9	Reflections on the Changing Family System in Cameroon *Chuks J. Mba and Martin W. Bangha*	171
PART IV	EASTERN AFRICA	
Chapter 10	Kenyan Families *Miroslava Prazak*	197
PART V	SOUTHERN AFRICA	
Chapter 11	Development, Family Change, and Community Empowerment in Malawi *Agnes M. Chimbiri*	227
Chapter 12	Family Life in Soweto, Gauteng, South Africa *Sylvia N. Moeno*	249
PART VI	CONCLUSION	
Chapter 13	The Study of African Families: Concluding Remarks *Baffour K. Takyi and Yaw Oheneba-Sakyi*	273

Appendix A: Contemporary Map of Africa — 279
Appendix B: Basic Information about Selected Countries — 280
Author Index — 283
Subject Index — 289
About the Contributors — 299

Preface

We are pleased to edit this volume on African families. As we begin the new millennium, there is no better time to publish a book that examines the historical processes that have shaped the essential elements of African families. In this volume, we examine trends in family research in Africa and reflect on the challenges that confront family life into the near future. With a population estimated at over 800 million people and a landmass nearly three and a half times the size of the United States, Africa is the world's second largest continent after Asia. More importantly, Africa is made up of 54 countries that encompass different ecological zones, and diverse ethnic groups, cultures, and subcultures within which about 1,000 different languages are spoken. In spite of this great diversity and heterogeneity, African societies share some common social and economic experiences.

At the center of the social and economic fabric of African societies is the institution of the family. Maintained through kinship networks and marriages, the family has played an important role in the processes of sustainable human development on the continent for generations. For much of Africa, the past centuries have seen significant changes in its institutions, including the family. For instance, between the 7th and the 11th centuries, the spread of Islam to North, West and East Africa and the Trans-Saharan trade with the Arabs resulted in significant transformations of family life. Then the Trans Atlantic Slave Trade with the Europeans beginning in the 17th century led to immense social disorganization with implications for the family. At the close of the 19th century, slavery had been abolished but a new phenomenon was emerging: the occupation of Africa by European countries and the imposition of colonialism.

Africa's link to the international community, via trade, occupation, colonial rule, and globalization, has altered, and continues to alter the continent's social institutions and the dynamics within families.

Against the backdrop of steady decay in the economies of several African countries since political independence, the last three decades have ushered in economic restructuring and globalization. Thus, African societies have found themselves at the receiving end of socioeconomic forces of contraction and expansion through global capitalism. With increasing modernization, rising levels of urbanization and migration, as well as widespread strains hastened by economic restructuring and the HIV/AIDS epidemic, many families in Africa have had to make rapid adjustments in both structure and function. For several decades, the dynamics and structure of family formations in Africa have been in stages of transition. At the same time that new types of family forms are emerging, the roles of respective family members are also changing.

This book has four main themes. First, because there is no recently published book on African families, we provide a historical context for understanding many different types of families in Africa. Second, the variety of topics and countries covered serve as a basis for those not familiar with the dynamics of African families to understand how family systems have changed and the consequences of changes in country-specific contexts. Third, we provide an overview of family processes in Africa that are scholarly in nature but at the same time are very readable for students and nonstudents alike. Fourth, unlike existing studies on African families that tend to focus on the English-speaking African countries, especially those in West and East Africa, we have tried to include selections from North Africa and also countries from Francophone Africa. Thus, our belief is that the book will be a significant addition to the limited scholarly work on family processes and dynamics in postcolonial Africa.

To allow our readers to compare information across countries, the book contains chapters that follow a standard outline with consistent order and parallel coverage of materials. In Chapter 1, we provide an overview of the historical processes that have shaped the essential elements of African families and reflect on the challenges that confront families on the continent at the beginning of the 21st century. We focus on the multiple heritage of Africa and analyze the similarities and variations in African families through the interplay of the indigenous, the Arabic/Islamic, and European/Christian cultures.

Chapters 2 through 12 represent 11 countries in Africa (one chapter for each country grouped into regions—Northern, Western, Central, Eastern and Southern). Because our major aim was to produce a volume that would be representative of the various geographic and cultural regions in Africa, we selected countries on the basis of ecological zones and culture areas, language families, ethnic variety, and levels of exposure to the Arabic/Islamic and European/Christian influences.

Three chapters are devoted to family life in the Arabic/Islamic world of North Africa. Mounira M. Charrad and Allyson B. Goeken examine family law reform pursued by Tunisia over the last half-century. The reforms have abolished polygyny, given men and women equal rights to divorce, increased women's right to custody of children, and to a lesser extent expanded women's inheritance rights. Considering change and continuity, the Tunisia chapter shows how family law and family structure in Tunisia reflect new realities at the same time that they retain distinctive features inherited from the past.

The analysis by Charrad and Goeken traces the development of family law reforms and the political forces that made them possible. Critical periods considered include colonization and nationalism, the formation of the national state, the consolidation of the postcolonial state, and the concomitant rise of Islamic fundamentalism and feminism with their contradictory demands with respect to the family. The chapter then outlines current trends in family structure and critically examines assumptions about the demise of extended kinship. Charrad and Goeken conclude that Tunisian families have experienced major changes even as they remain tied to extended kinship networks.

Bahira Sherif-Trask writes about the Egyptian family, pointing to the centrality of family despite class and regional differences. As is the case in many African countries, Sherif-Trask writes about the impact of modernization, urbanization, and globalization on the lives of individuals and their families. For example, she writes that an increasing number of women now work outside the home in contradiction to fundamentalist voices that advocate a return to more "traditional" gender roles. Egypt maintains a unique sense of identity despite a growing fundamentalist Islamic movement that calls for a greater sense of identification with the Muslim world of the Middle East. Still, most Egyptians continue to feel that family and extended kin provide for their security in an increasingly unfamiliar world.

As Africa's largest country, Sudan is a microcosm of the continent. It has also been through the crucible of civil war, ethnic cleansing, and numerous violations of women's and human rights as a result of the chronic warfare and civilian displacement. Nonetheless, as Carolyn Fluehr-Lobban points out, the Sudanese family has prevailed and women have been resilient in the face of multiple crises, even though the impact of these events has disproportionately fallen on them and their children. Sudanese history is full of strong women—from the ancient queens of Kush-Meroe to the many women who struggled for their rights and equality in the movement for independence and thereafter. African patriarchy in Sudan, whether in northern Muslim areas or southern Nilotic regions, remains intact even as women activists set their course for the 21st century.

West Africa is represented by both the Francophone world (Senegal and Côte d'Ivoire) and the Anglophone world (Ghana and Nigeria). From French-speaking West Africa, Loretta E. Bass and Fatou Sow examine how the confluence of ethnicity, history, and rapid social change have affected the Senegalese family, pointing, for instance, to the main piece of legislation regulating family functioning—the Senegalese Family Code. Drawing on Senegal's triple history of indigenous, Islamic, and colonial influences, the code also responds to more contemporary postcolonial realities such as population growth, women's empowerment, and urbanization.

N'Dri Thérèse Assié-Lumumba analyzes the historical background and the sociogeographic setting of contemporary family structures in Côte d'Ivoire. In spite of broad clusters of matrilineal societies in the eastern half of the country and patrilineal societies in the western half, the structural transformation of the family has been related over time to the heavy migration from neighboring countries, a phenomenon that was triggered by the capitalist economy set in motion by French colonial policies. Assié-Lumumba's analysis deals with the dynamics of the adoption and application of postcolonial family laws borrowed or inspired by the French legal traditions and to certain extent Islamic influence, alongside the enduring institutional practices of indigenous African family values. She also discusses gender equity in contemporary Ivorian family laws, pointing to new trends and the diversity of the contemporary family structures while retaining the African communal family ethos.

From Ghana, Elizabeth Ardayfio-Schandorf talks about the transformations that have occurred in family processes in the country since the precolonial era, drawing on the role of Islamic, Christian, and Western influences on family life in Ghana. The cumulative outcome of this triple heritage is that aspects of Islamic religion and culture converged with certain pertinent aspects of the Ghanaian traditional cultural domain and, therefore, found easy acceptance in some sections of Ghanaian family life. The European culture, on the other hand, totally revolutionalized marriage and the ways of doing things in the family that were in conflict with indigenous polygynous tendencies. Combinations of the penetration of these cultures have worked against the functions of indigenous families, especially those exposed to modernization. Growing emphasis on nuclear families in recent times is leading to the breaking of intergenerational ties with dire consequences for the Ghanaian family.

Writing about Nigeria, Obioma Nnaemeka focuses on the country's three major ethnic groups—Hausa-Fulani, Igbo, and Yoruba—and probes the differences and similarities among these groups in terms of cultural practices, gender relations, and family dynamics, and how these practices and realities are shaped and reshaped by geography, religion, and history. Arguing that the Nigerian family responds to the material, spiritual, and emotional needs of its members, Nnaemeka contends that the family also replicates many forms of inequalities, hierarchies, and privileges that breed domination, conflicts, and violence. The chapter proposes that a (re)conceptualization of the Nigerian family in times of change requires a reassessment of the tradition/modernity binary, not as a clear-cut oppositional paradigm but as a continuum that carries cultural residues of the old into the new. Of central concern is the institution of marriage and its unfolding over time in different regions of the country as people contend and negotiate with new and foreign contexts such as colonialism, Islam, and Christianity. Finally, the chapter examines the impact and consequences of internal and external migration on the Nigerian family, particularly the ways in which the mythologies and realities of the family are interrogated, challenged, and affirmed.

From the Central African region, Chuks J. Mba and Martin W. Bangha investigate the socioeconomic, cultural, and demographic evolution Cameroon has undergone as a result of the traditional and colonial past and the impact of contemporary global changes using primarily the postindependence censuses, nationally representative sample survey results, and other relevant small-scale studies. Being the only African country to be colonized by the Germans, British, and French, Cameroon is left to grapple with the problem of grafting a colonial cultural legacy onto a more or less heterogeneous traditional cultural heritage.

Mba and Bangha suggest that the drift toward the adoption of the modern European cultural value system gained currency with the expansion in education and health services. As the country continues to witness social and economic changes, it is important for the government to put in place a comprehensive and universal social security scheme to help families take care of their dependents. Additionally, the government should institute broad administrative reforms that will not only create jobs for graduates but also make working attractive in Cameroon.

Miroslava Prazak writes about family life in East Africa, focusing on Kenya. The chapter examines the dynamics of family-initiated adaptations to large-scale national and international forces that impinge on the everyday lives of individuals and their domestic groups in the precolonial and the postcolonial Kenya. Prazak traces the historical migrations of the peoples of Kenya, following the three major linguistic groups to their contemporary descendents who now make up the 43 main ethnic groups in the country. A brief look at the demographic issues highlights Kenya's exceptional population growth during the past 50 years and the fertility transition taking place today.

From the Southern African region, Agnes M. Chimbiri and Sylvia N. Moeno examine family life in Malawi and Soweto, Guateng, South Africa, respectively. Chimbiri presents a brief political history of Malawi, discusses its demographic, ethnic, religious, ecological, and socioeconomic profiles, and examines the conceptual issues related to shifts in development discourse since the 1950s. Based on the discussion in this chapter, Western values, faith-based cultural beliefs, and traditional beliefs will continue to coexist. Policies and program formulators and implementers, therefore, need to consider the impact that this coexistence has on family dynamics including its structure, function, and its members' roles.

The discussion in the Malawian chapter shows how families and communities have been rational in their responses to policies. They have chosen to adopt strategies that would ensure their survival in the changing world but have stuck to their traditional beliefs, norms, customs, and values. This means that the Western, Christian, and Islamic values have simply been laid over traditional values. They are merely a silver or gold coating that can fade at any time, while the traditional values remain intact. Thus, policies that aim to change people's behavior require a participatory approach that will make individuals, couples, families, and communities identify and appreciate the need for change.

From South Africa, Moeno examines family life in Soweto and points to the impact of apartheid legislation on the black majority in the country. In addition, the author points to the role of rural urban migration in destabilizing the South African black family. Moeno also examines a growing trend among young black South Africans to postpone marriage until a later age as a result of the extended family system, the low socioeconomic status of women in traditional society, and the accompanying poverty. Many upwardly mobile black families are customarily expected by their families to raise and educate the children of relatives and other close family members. Despite these challenges and the havoc that HIV/AIDS is having on families in South Africa, Moeno suggests that the South African family is resilient and may be able to weather some of the emerging "storms" facing the family.

The final chapter of this volume summarizes the predominant family systems and variations across the continent, reviews the main findings of the research on changes in family structures, and provides an analysis of public policies that will genuinely promote the well-being of contemporary African families into the new millennium.

Yaw Oheneba-Sakyi (Fresno, California)
Baffour K. Takyi (Akron, Ohio)
June 2005

Acknowledgments

This work is a joint effort and would not have been possible without expertise and assistance from many people who worked tireless to make this volume a reality. The book itself grew out of a chapter we wrote in the late 1990s about the changing African family, which was to be included in an edited volume on international families. For one reason or another, that volume was not published. Given the research and work that went into our chapter, we began to explore the possibilities of writing a compendium ourselves documenting transitions in the African family from colonial times through independence struggles to the postcolonial era. The Greenwood Publishing Group readily accepted our book proposal and we began work on this project in June 2000.

Using several sources, we invited scholars from Africa and the United States to contribute to the volume. The final selection of the authors for this book was based on their firsthand knowledge of family life in the particular country about which they are writing, their professional expertise, and their demonstrated ability to critically analyze African societies and cultures. Our goal was to produce a book that would provide information about African families from as many countries and religio-cultural and geographical areas as possible. We are indebted to our contributors, whose essays have enhanced our understanding of both the diversity and the commonality of African family forms and the cultural dynamics that ensure their survival.

Because both of us experienced job changes over the last three years, coupled with the difficulty of communicating with 14 different authors located across Africa and the United States, we must admit that the book has been delayed on several occasions. We would like to thank Suzanne I. Staszak-Silva, Jane Garry,

Jill-Marie McCormack, and Jim Lance, all of whom at some point served as our editorial assistants. We are grateful for their patience, time, and encouragement as we asked repeatedly for extensions over the years. Additionally, we thank the staff at Greenwood for guiding us through this long and involved process, especially Alexander Andrusyszyn, Bridget Austiguy-Preschel and Alexandra Goldmacher for their total commitment during the final stages of the preparation of this volume. We also wish to thank Nicholas Maier, our project manager at Stratford Publishing Services, for seeing through the production process.

A special thanks goes to Jesse Mann and Ferdinand Yomoah (graduate students at the University of Akron, Ohio) who gladly read some of the drafts. We also wish to express our thanks to JoLynne Blake (California State University, Fresno) for her technical assistance in formatting and final preparation of the manuscript. Our final thanks go to our friends and families who supported us as we labored to read and reread the articles that are included in the volume.

CHAPTER 1

Introduction to the Study of African Families: A Framework for Analysis

Yaw Oheneba-Sakyi and Baffour K. Takyi

INTRODUCTION

With a population of over 800 million people, Africa is the world's second largest continent after Asia. Although made up of over 50 countries, diverse ethnic groups, and cultures within which about 1,000 different languages are spoken, the centerpiece of the social and economic fabric of most African societies is the institution of the family. Sustained through kinship networks and marriages, the family has played an important role in the process of sustainable human development on the continent for generations.

The past centuries have seen significant changes in the institution of the African family. Between the 14th and the 18th centuries, the Trans-Saharan trade with the Arabs and the Trans-Atlantic Slave Trade with the Europeans led to immense social disorganization that tore families apart. At the close of the 19th century, the occupation of Africa by European countries and the imposition of colonialism further destabilized African family structures. Africa's link to the international community continues to alter the continent's social institutions and the relationships between family members.

This introductory chapter reflects the themes and approaches contained in the individual essays in this volume. We examine the notions of African families within the historical context of their experiences and contacts with outsiders. This historical framework helps us to understand the tenets of Arab occupation and European colonialism, and at the same time to comprehend the processes of modernization, urbanization, and globalization in the transformation of African families. We look at trends in family research in Africa beyond the usual, and stereotypical, ideals about the African extended family.

Furthermore, we focus on the concept of household, looking at what members of a household do rather than trying to fit them into Western sociological categories. In this perspective, African families are not defined primarily by biological ties that members of the household may have with each other, but as a dynamic social institution with members coming and going (see, e.g., Weisner, Bradley, & Kilbride, 1997). We challenge the notion that depicts African women as being subject to male domination. In fact, if one looks at the domestic scene, one finds that women do indeed have considerable influence and power in certain aspects of public life in African societies.

With increasing modernization, rural-urban migration, and economic restructuring, it is important to distinguish between African urban and rural households. While new types of family forms are emerging, roles and responsibilities of respective family members are also changing. Thus, we reflect on the challenges that confront contemporary families in Africa including civil unrest and economic hardships, as well as the HIV/AIDS epidemic, all of which have caused many families and households to make rapid adjustments in both structure and function.

THE HISTORICAL CONTEXT FOR ANALYZING AFRICAN FAMILIES

Throughout the 20th century, African families have undergone rapid changes inspired and directed by a complex interplay of both external and internal forces. To study how African families have been shaped historically, one needs to take a closer look at the juxtaposition of the African indigenous, the Arabic/Islamic, and European/Christian cultures within the larger global context of constantly shifting economic, social, and cultural forces.

The first scholar of African descent to draw attention to this multiple heritage of Africa was W. E. B. Du Bois with his publication of *The Negro* in 1915. Recognizing the combined presence of traditional Africa, Islamic Africa, and Euro-Christian Africa in a constantly changing global economy, Du Bois traced the earlier settlements in Africa across the Red Sea by the Semites and across the Mediterranean Sea by the Greeks, Phoenicians, and Romans thousands of years before Christ. These earlier contacts with outsiders were followed by the Portuguese in the 15th century and later the Spanish, French, Dutch, and English. In 1915, Du Bois wrote:

The intercourse of Africa with Arabia and other parts of Asia has been so close and long-continued that it is impossible to-day to disentangle the blood relationships.

Negro blood certainly appears in strong strain among the Semites, and the obvious mulatto groups in Africa, arising from ancient and modern mingling of Semite and Negro, has given rise to the term "Hamite," under cover of which millions of Negroids have been characteristically transferred to the "white" race by some eager scientists. (Du Bois, 2001, pp. 16–17)

In 1970, Nkrumah proposed an ideology of "philosophical consciencism" to provide the theoretical basis for raising the African consciousness of the experiences on the continent as a mingling of the Arabic-Islamic and Euro-Christian presence in the midst of the traditional African society (Nkrumah, 1970, p. 70).

Nkrumah's idea of philosophical consciencism was expanded by Mazrui in 1986, who gave it the new label "triple heritage." In his British Broadcasting Corporation (BBC) and Public Broadcasting Corporation (PBS) television documentary series *The Africans*, Mazrui journeyed into the soul of Africa, examining developments from ancient Egypt, matriarchal social systems, the slave trade, and colonialism, to contemporary issues such as apartheid, famine, political crises, and globalization.

The traditional face of Africa answers questions related to the basic principles of human life, human existence, and coping with everyday problems of life through the invocation of God. Most Africans invoke the power of God through intermediaries such as lesser gods, spirits of various types, sacred objects, and ancestors who are believed to possess supernatural powers to help the living with economic prosperity, good health, childbearing, and protection against evil (Skinner, 1986). Although variations exist among African societies as they adapt to different ecosystems and cultural realities, African indigenous cultures believe in the supremacy of the group. This concept often manifests itself in institutions such as the clan, through which family life events such as marriage, childbirth, motherhood, and social relations are organized (Nkrumah, 1970). The African indigenous heritage serves as the background against which the activities of the Arabic/Islamic and the European/Christian cultures take place.

Islam first entered North Africa from the Arabian peninsula around the 7th century, spreading to the East and West by the 11th century through the waging of jihads (holy wars), peaceful conversions, trading, occupation, and slave raiding (Skinner, 1986; Robinson, 2004). As a monotheistic religion, Islam provided theories and practices embedded in the Quran and the Shari'a (law of righteousness) that guided the way people made sense of their world. The areas that came under Islamic occupation also experienced Arabization, which in turn led to the introduction of Arabic characteristics into the African indigenous cultural landscape.

Although marriage practices such as arranged marriages, payment of bride wealth, birth rituals, and the practice of polygyny are common to both the African indigenous heritage and the Islamic culture, Asante (2003) contends that Africans and other non-Arabs are called on to submit to a strange God. He argues that the organization of Islam contributes to the "over-powering submissiveness... to the culture and religion of Arabs" through the use of the Arabic language as the language of God, taking a pilgrimage to Mecca, turning one's head in the direction of Mecca to pray, acceptance of Muhammad as the last important prophet, and use of Arab names and clothing (Asante, 2003, p. 7).

The resistance to and co-optation of Arab and Islamic influence in Africa manifested itself in the emergence of African Muslims with regional cultural traditions and practices (Diop, 1960; Robinson, 2004). Major changes that characterize African Muslim groups include the way property in the family devolves from one generation to another through preferential cousin marriage of the "father's brother's daughter," strong male dominance, and patrilineal kinship systems that weakened female economic self-reliance (Goody, 1976; Skinner, 1986; Lesthaeghe, 1989). In his discussion of the Muslim faith in African history, Robinson (2004) argues that

Arabic was the main language of revelation of God to Muhammad and consequently the language of the sacred book, the law, and prayer ... Arabic words spread into the languages of many more African societies, especially to describe religion, government, welfare, and trade. But most African Muslims continued to speak their own languages, the Swahili, Mankinda, and various Berber tongues, for instance, that had long been native to their regions. Male and female teachers in these societies soon developed ways of transmitting the faith, the Quran, and the prayers into vernaculars. (pp. 27–28)

The next external factor that profoundly influenced African family life was the infiltration of the Western European Christianity and culture into Africa beginning as early as the 15th century. Using the vehicles of trade, colonialism, and racist ideologies, Europe's interest in Africa peaked in the 1940s with total occupation of the continent by European countries. At the Berlin Conference of 1884–85, Britain, France, Belgium, Germany, Italy, and Portugal partitioned Africa and recognized each other's borders. And by the end of World War II, these European imperial powers occupied over 90 percent of the continent of Africa (Nkrumah, 1970; Mazrui, 1986; Khapoya, 1998).

Although Europeans did not introduce Christianity to Africa (the religion had existed for several thousands of years in Egypt, Sudan, and Ethiopia), their missionaries and colonial administrators introduced European education designed to expose a cadre of Africans to European ideals and cultural values, which were accepted as valid for African societies. The one major objective of European Christianity and colonialism was to instill a "conjugal" family model with a neolocal residence and a sense of individualism peculiar to Western Europe at the time (Lesthaeghe, 1989; Khapoya, 1998). The missionaries and colonizers sought to achieve this "ideal" family form for the

African by restricting the following social practices: polygyny, payment of bride wealth, ritual expressions of authority and rites of passage, postpartum sexual abstinence, and lineage systems of inheritance of land and property including widow inheritance.

European Christianity and its colonial ideology met resistance from the believers in indigenous African religions and Islam as well. The outcome of this resistance was the creation of African Christianity, a complex blend of European Christianity with African and Islamic religious traditions and cultural traditions. This blend produced a wide range of religious forms including African Independent Pentecostal churches, African Protestant churches, and African Roman Catholicism (Boahen, 1989). Thus, African Christians may share some common European traditions, yet in an attempt to recapture their true sense of "Africanity," they have a tendency to prefer African clergy and lifestyles; marry under traditional customs; tolerate polygyny; partake in African beliefs and practices concerning rites of passage, death, and burial; and use African names, saints, art, symbols, and musical instruments in religious services (Skinner, 1986). Accordingly, Lesthaeghe (1989) concludes that

the impact [of European Christianity] . . . is often shallow: the conjugal family model is seldom realized, and faith-healing, divinations, presence of spirits, and . . . witchcraft are still very common expressions of an older tradition . . . [and] . . . polygyny has survived to a remarkable extent despite the Christian ban. (p. 37)

The proper historical context for analyzing African families, then, is the infusion of foreign religions and cultures, specifically Islam and Christianity and their competing ideologies. This history serves as a guide to Africa's continual progress in the global context as the continent reacts and adjusts to new realities. Our approach to examining sociocultural changes helps us avoid the problem frequently encountered in the literature of the "traditional-modern" dichotomy. After all, the African "traditional" heritage does not begin and end somewhere before "modernity" (often linked to European expansionism) begins. Events such as the introduction of cash economy, formal schooling, modern medicine, rapid population growth and urbanization, and the quest for human and women's rights have occurred within the African indigenous social structures and institutions.

African family experiences have been neither homogeneous nor stable as evidenced by the fact that, during most of their postcolonial history, African societies have been characterized by increasing economic decline, political instability, poor health care, and illiteracy. Since the 1980s, several countries have been reforming their social, economic, and political systems along lines congruent with the World Bank and the International Monetary Bank (IMF) guidelines. In the last two decades, African countries have sought to strengthen female education, improve human rights and health care, and promote good governance and economic development.

THE STUDY OF AFRICAN FAMILIES

During the 18th and 19th centuries, the preoccupation with race/skin color and other physical traits as measures of "civilization" was strong and consistent among Western intellectuals and colonial authorities. For instance, in his *Lectures on the Philosophy of World History* (1822–28), Hegel argued that

The condition in which they [Africans] live is incapable of any development or culture, and their present existence is the same as it has always been. In face of enormous energy of sensuous arbitrariness which dominates their lives, morality has no determinate influence upon them. Anyone who wishes to study the most terrible manifestations of human nature will find them in Africa . . . For it is an unhistorical continent, with no movement or development of its own. (Quoted by Eze, 1997, p. 142)

As a result of the prevalence of Eurocentric beliefs, much of the earlier scholarly work on Africa was done by Western social scientists who were interested in studying "traditional" societies. This scholarship focused on such issues as inheritance, kinship patterns, residential arrangements, marital systems, polygyny, and mate selection—with limited understanding of the proper cultural and institutional context within which these practices occur (see, e.g., Rattray, 1923, 1929; Radcliffe-Brown & Forde, 1950; Lorimer, 1954; Goode, 1963; Goody, 1969). The conclusions and policy recommendations of these Western scholars often propelled colonial authorities to enact laws and sanctions for drastic changes in African cultural practices and family systems that were deemed so strange and unacceptable to the "civilized" Western world.

In an attempt to correct some of the misrepresentations of Africa by Western scholars, Du Bois conceived his *Encylopeadia Africana Project* (EAP) in 1909, perhaps making him the first "Afrocentric" scholar to examine the history and life of African peoples from their own perspective. The EAP (a 20-volume work in progress) will chronicle the history of peoples of African descent to be written mainly from the African point of view, by people who know and understand the history and culture of Africans. Due to the lack of necessary funds for collection and publication, the EAP project was not launched until 1962 when Du Bois moved to Ghana at the age of 93. Du Bois's many scholarly works including *The Suppression of the African Slave Trade to the United States* (1896); *The Philadelphia Negro: A Social Study* (1899); *The Souls of Black Folk* (1903); and *Black Folk, Then and Now* (1939) assess the social conditions of African peoples and their contributions to world civilization.

The response to racist attitudes and research that denied African history and devalued its culture ushered in a new agenda by African scholars themselves on the study of cultures and family life on the continent. With the coming of political independence around 1960, the noted African writer Chinua Achebe initiated the African Writers Series published by Heinemann. The series and other publications have been a venue for the exposure of some of the continent's best literary works including Achebe's own *Things Fall Apart* in

1958 and *No Longer At Ease* in 1960; Ngugi wa Thiong'o's *Weep Not Child* in 1964 and *A Grain of Wheat* in 1967; Wole Soyinka's *The Interpreters* in 1970; Ama Ata Aidoo's *No Sweetness Here and Other Stories* in 1971, *The Girl Who Can* in 2003, and *Changes* in 2004; Buchi Emecheta's *The Bride Price* in 1976 and *Joys of Motherhood* in 1980; Ayi Kwei Armah's *Two Thousand Seasons* in 1980 and *KMT: In The House of Life* in 2002; Okot p'Bitek's *Song of Lawino and Song of Ocol* in 1984; and Mariama Bâ's *So Long a Letter* in 1989. These works of fiction, nonfiction, short stories, poetry, and drama depict the full African experience including Arab and European colonization, marriage and relationships, the essence of womanhood, traditional rural life, urban life seduced by Western education, corruption, and resistance to postcolonial nondemocratic regimes.

But during the early 1960s, social demographic research was devoted primarily to understanding the social forces that shape reproductive-related behavior, mortality, and migration patterns. The aim was to examine how rapid population growth could be controlled. At that time, family researchers focused on what Africans knew about family planning and contraception (i.e., Knowledge, Attitudes, and Practice [KAP]). These studies were conducted under the auspices of the Population Council in New York and the African Family Studies Project directed by the Australian National University.

In the 1970s, the World Fertility Surveys (WFS) were conducted to gather information about demographic issues in some countries around the world, including several countries in Africa. Following the success of the WFS, the Demographic and Health Surveys (DHS) in the 1980s began conducting regular surveys on demographic trends and maternal and child health issues in participating countries. Thus, what we now know about the African family comes from analyses of these large data sets. Even here, given funding agencies and their interests, the research has been skewed primarily toward reproductive-related issues.

Since the 1980s, new scholarship has been devoted primarily to understanding the dynamic social forces that shape cultural beliefs, practices, and family life from the African peoples' points of view. Following the intellectual traditions of Du Bois, in recent years Asante has reconceptualized the study of the facts of African history and experience by peoples of African descent with the term *Afrocentricity*. In the revised and expanded edition of *Afrocentricity: The Theory of Social Change*, Asante (2003) defines Afrocentricity as:

a mode of thought and action in which the centrality of African interests, values, and perspectives predominate. In regards to theory, it is the placing of African people in the center of any analysis of African phenomena . . . a devotion to the idea that what is in the best interest of African consciousness is at the heart of ethical behavior. (p. 2)

Focusing on the different manifestations of social and economic change and what family change means to Africans themselves, Weisner, Bradley, and

Kilbride (1997) in collaboration with Ocholla-Ayayo, Akong'a, and Wandibba examine the crisis in contemporary African family life and discuss the adaptive responses of the changing family. Although their geographical focus is on western Kenya and eastern Uganda, the issues they raise about health, gender, children, the elderly, population growth, and the economics of family change mirror the rest of the continent.

The importance of using the household as a unit of analysis in the study of the African family is echoed by Weisner and colleagues (1997). In several of the essays produced in their edited collection, the authors emphasize the fact that the household as a coresidential and economic unit still functions under the umbrella of the institution of the family which binds together individual households. Oheneba-Sakyi's (1999) in-depth study in Ghana addresses the multiple links between reproduction, women's status, and the family, framing research questions, measures, and analyses in terms of the many roles women play in African households and in the economic and political spheres as well. It is very clear that the study of African families has shifted in focus and emphasis. But how have African families been conceptualized over the years?

CONCEPTUALIZATION OF AFRICAN FAMILIES

Western social scientists have conceptualized that family systems move from a so-called traditional type to a modern one (e.g., Goode, 1963; Pool, 1972). It has also been said that the differences between these two ideal types can easily be determined in terms of family distribution of power, decision making, communication, and division of labor in the household—whether activities are shared or one spouse exercises a dominant position at the expense of the other. The role of "modernization," commonly interpreted through formal education, European Christianity, urbanization, and industrialization, has often been stressed in the transformation from the traditional to the modern family. Indeed, in his book *World Revolution and Family Patterns* Goode (1963) saw this adjustment as a linear process and predicted that within a short period of time urbanized Africans who he labeled as "Europeanized, Western" would lead the rural folks who he labeled as "tribal" away from "tribal family patterns" toward "a conjugal system" (pp. 201–202). Thus, African families would be transformed into Western-style units of one wife, one husband, and a few children.

Given these expectations, we might ask the following questions with regard to the contemporary African family: Is there an "African" family type or several types in a transitional process? Where do these African family types fall along the continuum from traditional to modern? Does the use of bloodline to primarily define the family in Africa fully determine membership and obligations? How does the concept of household expand our understanding of the fluidity of family relations? What role does lineage still play in today's African family? Does the "nucleation" of the family diminish the traditional obligation of caring for aging parents and assisting in the education or job training of siblings, cousins, nieces and nephews, and others? How does the concept of the ancestral home as a reference point continue to provide the mechanism for social and economic networking among Africans living away from home?

CHARACTERISTICS OF THE AFRICAN FAMILY

The common characteristics of the African family focused on in this volume include mate selection and marriage, multiple marriage systems, childbearing, gender roles, and intergenerational relationship. We believe most African families have shown resilience in the face of challenges with regard to these characteristics and have continued to adapt their activities to changing circumstances.

Mate Selection and Marriage

One of the key findings about African societies is the existence of a profamily and marriage ideology (Bledsoe, 1990; Gage, 1998). Because African women and men are expected to marry and have children, it has been suggested that marriage is nearly universal, and voluntary celibacy is virtually nonexistent (Kayongo-Male & Onyango, 1984; Caldwell & Caldwell, 1987; van de Walle, 1993). While marriage is supposedly universal in Africa, there is an ongoing debate as to the mate selection process itself. Ethnographic studies, for instance, point to the influence of parents, and often members of the extended kin group, rather than the individual in the selection of a mate. The input of extended kin in mate selection is consistent with what has been reported in the literature regarding the dominant role of kin and lineage in the African family (see e.g., Caldwell et al., 1989; Lockwood, 1995). In relation to marriage, this view suggests that the concepts of romantic love and individuation, which are believed to serve as the basis of mate selection in Western societies, are less relevant to the realities of most African societies.

Family involvement in marriage negotiations and decision making is aimed at networking, keeping self-acquired property in the family, and ensuring the survival of the marriage (Rattray, 1929; Nukunya, 1969; Assimeng, 1981). Different kinship groups and corporate clans in Africa build alliances through the institution of marriage. Thus, marriage contracts are supposed to serve the emotional and financial interests of members of the families of the bride and the groom as well.

Up to about the 1950s, a system of marriage involving betrothals was used in some parts of Africa as another way of locating a prospective wife (Sarbah, 1904, p. 41, as quoted in Kuenyehia, 1978, p. 319; Goode, 1963; Gibbs, 1965; Fiawoo, 1978). Before marriageable age is attained, the family of the bride-to-be accepts money or token gifts with the understanding that in the future their daughter will become the wife of the party for whom the alliance is sought. In contrast to the ethnographic view there are studies that suggest that the traditional rules and norms which guided mate selection practices of earlier generations are less evident now due to the forces of social change. Given that African societies have undergone significant transformations since the colonial era, these researchers argue that current practices may be converging to the Euro-American model (see, e.g., Oppong, 1974, 1981; Aryee, 1985). Due in large part to structural changes such as urbanization, increased schooling, and economic independence of young adults, the role of kin in mate selection, the incidence of child betrothal, and arranged marriages in general have been on the decline in Africa (Goode, 1963; Oppong, 1983; Aryee, 1985). Examination of recent data on marriage processes in this volume will help to clarify developments in mate selection on the continent.

In spite of all the variations in marriage ceremonies in Africa, a common element in most marriages is the payment of bride wealth (Fortes, 1950; Nukunya, 1978; Lesthaeghe, 1989; Beckwith & Fisher, 1999). This practice involves complex negotiation of exchanges involving such items as money, drinks, kola nuts, jewelry, clothing, cattle, sheep, and goats. The bridegroom may also provide services to the prospective in-laws as a form of bride wealth payment. Seen as a legal bond uniting two families, the act provides protection and gives public recognition to the marriage, while also guaranteeing productive and reproductive services for the couple (Radcliffe-Brown & Forde, 1950; Fiawoo, 1978; Assimeng, 1981; Khapoya, 1998).

Marriage forms in Africa are significantly impacted by the extent to which both the individual and the family have adjusted to the influences of the triple heritage of Africanity, Arabic/Islamic, and European/Christian practices. Just as foreign cultural and religious beliefs have coexisted with Africanity, African Catholics and Protestants have lived with customary marriage practices such as payment of bride wealth, family involvement in mate selection, matri-/patri-focal residence, polygyny, and outside wifeship (Aryee, 1985). Furthermore, the marriage form that individuals decide to undertake may be a function of a combination of factors, including their economic situation (e.g., formal education, occupation, income, wealth), family background, and residential and geographical location.

Multiple Marriage Systems

In many parts of Africa, a multiplicity of marriage forms are recognized under the law. These include customary or traditional law marriages, marriage under Islamic rules and regulations, marriage under the ordinance (civil or church), consensual unions, polygynous marriages, and outside wifeships. The flexibility of marriage and the variety of marriage forms in African societies is often justified to sustain the universality of marriage, to continue the family lineage through reproduction, to keep family property, to protect and care for the economically vulnerable (women, children, and the elderly), and to ensure the stability of the family.

1. *Customary or Traditional Law Marriage.* Among several African groups, marriage under the customary law is the most common system of marriage and the most flexible. Often there is no single form of marriage because of significant regional and ethnic differences in marriage rituals and practices. Customary marriages could include such forms as *sororate*, in which a man marries his wife's sister; *widow inheritance*, in which a family member of the deceased remarries the widow but the children born in the remarriage belong to the successor himself; *levirate*, in which the successor of a deceased husband may continue to bear children with the deceased's wife in the name of the deceased; *woman to woman* marriage, in which an infertile woman performs marriage ceremonies for another woman to have children for her; and *ghost marriage*, in which a relative of a deceased young man who did not have a chance to marry and have children marries for the deceased and has children in his name (Fortes, 1950; Gluckman, 1965; Kayongo-Male & Onyango, 1984; Cadigan, 1998; Khapoya, 1998).

2. *Marriage under the Islamic Law.* As expected, Islamic marriage forms entered Africa with the introduction of the Muslim religion and the Arab culture. Guided by the Quran and Shari'a laws, Islamic law marriages derive their legitimacy from religious beliefs that are part of Islamic norms and allow the application of Islamic rules for divorce, child custody, and succession.

3. *Marriage under the Ordinance or Civil Law.* Ordinance and/or civil law marriages have their origins in Euro-Christian traditions. Although members of several African Christian churches have a tendency to marry according to local customs and traditions prior to going to the church and/or civil court to contract the marriage, the contractual status of the ordinance takes precedence over the customary law. Contrary to the customary and Islamic law marriages, which allow husbands to legally marry more than one wife, marriage contracted under the ordinance is supposed to be monogamous by law.

4. *Consensual Unions.* This marriage form, also referred to as cohabitation, may be more common in predominantly urban areas of Africa where traditional rules and norms are not strictly enforced and the role of kinsmen in mate selection has been weakened by the forces of social change (Aryee, 1985; Pool, 1972). Since they do not have the extended family support network and legal recognition, consensual unions are often short-lived. Nevertheless, consensual couples may eventually regularize their relationships one way or the other to receive acceptance and recognition with full rights and obligations.

5. *Polygynous Marriages.* African marriages contracted under customary or Islamic laws have the tendency to be polygynous in nature with levels varying

from anywhere between 20 percent and 50 percent of all marriages (Welch & Glick, 1981; Caldwell et al., 1991; Bledsoe, 1990; Takyi, 1998; Timaeus & Reynar, 1998). First, it has been suggested that having more wives is a status symbol for community leaders. Second, although the evidence is not very conclusive, polygyny may be linked to high fertility. Third, it is argued that the presence of co-wives increases the agricultural workforce. Fourth, the sharing of domestic responsibilities and household chores could help free women from male dominance (Boserup, 1970, 1985; Pool, 1972; Nukunya, 1978; Brabin, 1984; Greenstreet, 1987; Singh & Morey, 1987; Dorjahn, 1988; Khapoya, 1998).

6. *Outside Wifeship*. Legally contracted polygynous marriages may be declining in African societies due to increasing urbanization, industrialization, formal education, and other modernization and westernization influences. But, Karanja (1994) documents that sexual relations with multiple partners have continued with a growing phenomenon called "outside wifeship" or "private polygyny" (p. 211). Under this system, monogamous men and/or married men who contracted their marriages under ordinance or civil laws resort to acquisition of girlfriends, concubines, or mistresses. Women in these private relationships, described as "gold-diggers" by Dinan (1983), often receive their economic support from the married men in their lives. In spite of its lack of legal status, outside wifeship has been used particularly by educated African men as an alternative to divorce and remarriage. This practice thus enables the elite men to put up with the Euro-Christian notion of monogamous marriage, while privately admiring the African traditional idea of polygynous relationships (Morgan, with Ohadike, 1975; Bleek, 1987; Karanja, 1987, 1994; Mann, 1994; Oheneba-Sakyi, 1999).

Childbearing

Africa experienced high growth rates throughout the 20th century due mostly to high fertility coupled with a general decline in mortality. Africa's estimated 1950 population of about 224 million in 1950 reached 868 million by 2003 (United Nations, 2005). African parents have been known to have several children for reasons such as the accumulation of wealth, security in old age, labor force, marriage stability, lineage continuity, companionship, and prestige (Caldwell, 1982; Boserup, 1985; Akuffo, 1987; Lesthaeghe, 1989; Dasgupta, 1994). Although Cohen (1998) reports that a fairly widespread decline in fertility is under way in Africa, the size of the decline is quite small in most cases. Since total fertility rates (TFR) on the continent have remained high and only a few countries have a TFR rate below five children per woman, there is momentum for further growth.

Due in large part to the emphasis on childbearing and pressures for large families, it is no wonder that birthrates have remained relatively high and few people use family planning methods in many parts of Africa to regulate their fertility (Kayongo-Male & Onyango, 1984; Caldwell & Caldwell, 1987; Population Council, 1998; Population Reference Bureau, 1998). Because of the importance of children for the family in traditional African societies, men are allowed to marry more than one woman to guard against the possibility of childlessness. Kayongo-Male and Onyango (1984) note that in Africa a childless marriage is viewed as a troublesome one, since the marriage seems meaningless without children. However, there are variations in the number of children born and desired by African couples by such factors as age at first marriage, rural-urban residence, level of education, occupation, and religious background.

Segregated Gender Roles

African households are for the most part influenced by traditional gender role expectations of division of labor. Both reproductive and productive roles have been performed through membership in lineages and family groups. Although roles may be gender-specific, Oppong and Abu's (1984) study shows that the African plays seven overlapping roles: individual, conjugal, parental, domestic, kin, community, and occupational. Local traditions and customs often proscribe these roles for both men and women with built-in mechanisms for rewards and punishments for nonconformity.

However, men are generally expected to head the household and provide shelter and financial support, while women are expected to be responsible for basic household needs involving cleaning, washing, cooking, and taking care of dependents. And if they work, traditional African women are employed in large numbers in farming, fishing, weaving, pottery, and trading activities either on their own or jointly with husbands or kin (Oppong, 1970; Fiawoo, 1978; Kritz & Gurak, 1989; Lesthaeghe, 1989; Blanc & Lloyd, 1990; Republic of Ghana [ROG] & UNICEF, 1990). The need for women to secure independent sources of income and control of earnings is linked to the "unreliability of financial contributions from husbands," which may come about as a result of death, divorce, illness, or even an unanticipated polygyny (Clark, 1994, p. 338).

While segregated gender roles date back to Africa's own indigenous cultural practices, the colonial experience and conservative religious practices in Islam and Christianity reinforced segregation and unequal access to schooling. The ideologies supported disparity between the sexes in educational attainment that leads to feminized occupations with little money and minimum benefits from the enlarged bureaucracies in the modern economy (Hart, 1973; Date-Bah, 1982; Akuffo, 1990; Mikell, 1997). Following political independence, however, several contemporary African societies have invested heavily in universal primary school education especially for girls (Goliber, 1989; Mazrui, 1994). Similarly, there has been progress in women's employment outside the home and in the nonagricultural sector over the years.

Intergenerational Relationship

Historically, the relationship between the generations in African societies has been developed around the value of the knowledge, respect, and experience that the younger generation receives from the older generation. It is not uncommon throughout Africa to have multiple generations living in the same household. A sizable proportion of the elderly population lives with their children, in-laws, or extended family members. Such arrangements provide the elderly with plenty of opportunities to participate in family life such as assisting young couples in infant/child care and carrying on family traditions. Responsibility to provide support to the elderly and other family members is taken seriously, even among those who have relocated away from their ancestral homes or are not living with their parents (Oppong, 1977).

More than any other institution, the family provides the bulk of social support for old age and retirement throughout Africa. Government-sponsored social security benefits for old age are limited and cover the small number of people who worked for governmental agencies or in the formal sectors of the economy. Family support is especially important for older women, and widows, who in most cases have fewer assets or resources and have a history of work outside a government agency. Intergenerational benefits of family life in Africa are extended to activities surrounding death. Reverence is given to the dead and lavish funeral celebrations are organized (Sai, 1976; ROG & UNICEF, 1990). Not surprisingly, funeral celebrations function as reunions for members of the extended family, the clan, and the lineage and provide occasions for social networking.

In recent decades, however, elderly support, while expected, may be under stress in African societies because of economic difficulties. Brown's (1992) study in Ghana shows that the onus of responsibility for the care of the elderly has shifted from the extended family toward the nuclear family, with children and spouses playing the most important role. He argues that the shift has eroded roles to such a point that the only common thing among the extended family members is, perhaps, the shared responsibility of a decent burial for their members. As the economic means of the family shrink, African governments and other nongovernmental organizations are called on to provide the needed infrastructure and financial assistance to enable family members to care for the elderly in their homes, a notion consistent with African traditional values about caring for the aged.

CHALLENGES FOR CONTEMPORARY AFRICAN FAMILIES

African societies have been resilient over the years and have made great strides in their efforts to improve the lives of their peoples. However, at the dawn of the new century, African families are confronted with a series of developments that are posing serious threats to the traditional family structure.

Some of these changes are internally induced, with some arising out of Africa's contact with the outside world (see, e.g., Mikell, 1984, 1992). What are the major challenges now facing the African family and household? Here we document some of the changes that occurred during the latter part of the last century and those new challenges that are affecting the functioning of the African household and family life.

Modernization, Urbanization, and the Stability of African Families

A major change with significant implications for family studies is that of increased urbanization resulting from rural-urban migration and high rates of natural growth in the cities themselves. Between 1950 and 1985, the urban population in Africa increased from 20 million to 127 million, and by 2005, about 34 percent of Africans lived in cities (Goliber, 1989; Population Reference Bureau, 2005). Indeed, according to Weeks (1999), African cities are consistently growing at more rapid rates than anywhere else in the world, creating unemployment, traffic congestion, poor housing, inadequate sanitation, and health hazards.

While increased urbanization and education have helped to transform the lives of Africans in several positive ways, the whole process of modernization may have led to social disorganization and changes in family dynamics (Lloyd, 1968). For example, the length of postpartum sexual abstinence, which was used for child spacing, has now been shortened. And the duration of breast-feeding for healthy babies has also been reduced in favor of weaning foods and supplements produced by multinational corporations (Oheneba-Sakyi & Takyi, 1991). On a positive note, though, the formal education system has opened up a whole different worldview that encourages young people to question harmful cultural practices in African societies.

Perhaps one of the most disturbing consequences of the processes of modernization and urbanization in Africa has been the increase in marital instability. Although research in this area is limited, scattered reports, especially from the works of ethnographers, suggest that more African marriages are now ending in dissolution (Cohen, 1971; Hagan, 1983; Amoateng & Heaton, 1989; Lesthaeghe, 1989; Dorjahn, 1990; Hutchison, 1990; Mbugua 1992; Lloyd & Gage-Brandon, 1993; Bruce et al., 1995). Indeed, it is believed that by age 50, about half of all African women have experienced a marital dissolution, with divorce accounting for two-thirds of the dissolutions (Mbugua, 1992; Bruce et al., 1995).

What accounts for the growing number of divorces in Africa? In reviewing the limited studies on divorce processes, researchers point to factors such as increased female education, men's declining income, and men's inability/unwillingness to provide adequate resources for the maintenance of the household. Divorce is also caused by structural conditions such as the existence of polygyny, matrilineal kinship system, rural-urban migration, and population dislocation (Takyi, 1998). A consequence of these new developments—increased divorces and dislocations—is the changing household composition in many African societies. Recent studies of socioeconomic trends in Africa have found an increase in the number of households headed or principally maintained by women (see, e.g., Folbre, 1991; Lloyd & Gage-Brandon, 1993). Addressing gender inequity has meant focusing on a number of divisive issues such as universal education for girls, sexual coercion, domestic violence, and child labor that have previously been ignored.

In the last decade, major worldwide conferences—the 1990 UN-sponsored World Conference on Education for All in Jomtien, Thailand; the 1994 UN-sponsored International Conference on Population and Development in Cairo, Egypt; and the 1995 International Women's Conference in Beijing, China—have all brought to the forefront the importance of protecting women and children from economic and sexual exploitation and empowering them so they can live to their fullest potential (UNICEF, 1998; Oheneba-Sakyi, 1999).

It is within the family that many of these issues find their strongest opposition to change. The very meaning of the status of women and children in Africa is bound up in the household as an inherent part of the structure of the family. Since African women bear the major brunt of providing support and daily sustenance for dependent children, their social and legal rights cannot be divorced from many of the activities necessary for children's welfare (Biddlecom, 1999).

During the past two decades, a great deal has been written on the subject of women's empowerment or status and autonomy in the developing world (Cain, 1984; Mason, 1984, 1987; Mason & Taj, 1987; Oheneba-Sakyi, 1999). The findings from these studies increasingly point to the existence of structural and nonstructural barriers that put women at a disadvantage relative to men in accessing power, wealth, and privilege. Among these is the issue of women's right to property. It has been noted in the literature that in many parts of Africa, the death of a husband could be a traumatic life experience. This is precisely the case because women's property rights and claims under the traditional system of inheritance (in the absence of a will) are often less secure or not well defined (Mikell, 1992; Meinzen-Dick et al., 1997). As African societies are continuously changing, it may be time for them to review the laws governing family property rights and to help reduce the hardships that some women face after the death of a spouse.

The HIV/AIDS Crisis and Family Health

Since the mid-1980s, Africa and the HIV/AIDS crisis have become virtually synonymous. Although the first cases of AIDS were not reported in

Africa, seemingly overnight, the continent has come to bear the brunt of the AIDS epidemic. Indeed, African societies are today facing a health crisis of unprecedented proportion and there is no indication that this trend will change soon (Caldwell & Caldwell, 1996; Caldwell et al., 1999). Global AIDS figures from UNAIDS and the World Health Organization (WHO) indicate that sub-Saharan African countries have been affected profoundly by the ravages of HIV/AIDS—perhaps more than any other world region. While the exact numbers of actual HIV/AIDS cases in this region are unknown, due in large part to underreporting, it is estimated that nearly 21 million (i.e., two-thirds) of all the people now living with HIV in the world live in sub-Saharan Africa (UNAIDS & WHO, 1998).

The effects of HIV/AIDS can be seen at both the micro (individual, household, and family) and macro (societal) levels. First, the disease could compromise the African traditional social obligations of sharing, caring, and child fostering. Second, African women's familial role of caring for the sick may in turn expose them to more infection, sickness, and death. Third, because a significant number of those who die are women in their childbearing ages, the HIV/AIDS crisis could influence long-term childbearing trends in Africa. In the short term, though, most societies may not notice the fall in numbers because of previous years of high birthrates.

One of the unintended consequences of HIV/AIDS which needs to be discussed is that it may increase the incidence of sexual and family violence against women. Young and adolescent girls are being infected at a faster rate because some men believe that these girls are virgins and, thus, free of AIDS (Fapohunda & Rutenberg, 1999). Women generally have a higher risk of infection if they are in relationships in which they do not have adequate power to negotiate for the use of condoms or practice safe sex (Schoepf, 1997). The major challenge for African societies is how to deal with the deeply embedded attitudes and beliefs about sexuality and childbearing that impede the use of condoms and other forms of modern contraception which may reduce the spread of the HIV/AIDS infection.

SUMMARY AND CONCLUSIONS

The institution of the family has been at the center of the well-being of African societies over the years. As with all institutions, families in Africa have undergone significant transformations guiding the people through centuries of adversity from slavery, foreign religious infusion, and colonialism to neocolonialism. This chapter examined the historical processes that have shaped the essential elements of African families and reflected on the challenges that confront families on the continent at the beginning of the 21st century. African families have been shaped historically by the interplay of the indigenous African, Arabic/Islamic, and European/Christian cultures. The juxtaposition of these three cultures in the lives of African peoples comprises the "triple heritage" of the continent. Through the triple heritage, we are able to examine the notions of family and the deeper meaning of family in the historical context of the African experience, while at the same time comprehending the roles that the processes of modernization, urbanization, and migration have played and continue to play in the transformations of families across the African continent.

By focusing on the household, we have examined trends in family research in Africa beyond the ideal extended family system. The existence of diverse marriage forms and the concept of the household capture the dynamic nature of the African family and the constantly shifting social forces that influence responsibilities of members. Increasing modernization, rural-urban migration, and economic restructuring have led to the creation of diverse family forms in Africa with challenges for rapid adjustments in structure and function.

With all the diversity that exists in African families, however, most share common themes including emphasis on the extended family, multiple marriage forms, high levels of childbearing, segregated gender roles, and strong intergenerational ties. Although African families have proved quite resilient over the years, they nonetheless face some serious future challenges, including urbanization, migration, marital dissolution, and inadequate economic resources. But perhaps the most serious threat to the African household and communal nature of African families is the HIV/AIDS crisis. What will happen to members of the extended family as AIDS kills a sizable proportion of its members? Who will take care of the elderly, the young, and the vulnerable of society given the absence of well-developed institutional care? Answers to these questions are important because the strength of the traditional family is often dependent on family size, a sense of belonging, generosity, and caring. In general, African societies are as dynamic and as modern as other human societies and not tied to inflexible traditions and cultural practices. It is hoped that the existing strengths of the families in Africa will provide a solid foundation upon which to develop self-help initiatives and public policies that will genuinely promote the interests of contemporary African societies. In the chapters that follow, several authors will critically examine family life and future challenges in specific African countries.

REFERENCES

Akuffo, A. D. (1990). Dimensions of sex discrimination: The Ghanaian working women's experience. *Greenhill Journal of Administration 7(3 & 4)*, 76–107.

Akuffo, F. O. (1987). Teenage pregnancies and school drop-outs: The relevance of family life, education and vocational training to girls' employment opportunities. In Oppong, C. (Ed.), *Sex roles, population and development in West Africa* (pp. 54–164). Portsmouth, NH: Heinemann.

Amoateng, Y., & Heaton, T. (1989). The socio-demographic correlates of the timing of divorce in Ghana. *Journal of Comparative Family Studies 20*, 79–96.

Aryee, F. (1985). Nuptiality patterns in Ghana. In Singh, S., et al., (Eds.), *Demographic patterns in Ghana: Evidence from the Ghana Fertility Survey 1979–80* (pp. 17–48). Voorburg, The Netherlands: International Statistical Institute.

Asante, M. K. (2003). *Afrocentricity: The theory of social change*. Chicago: African American Images.

Assimeng, M. (1981). *The social structure of Ghana*. Tema: Ghana Publishing.

Beckwirth, C., & Fisher, A. (1999). *African ceremonies, Vol 1*. New York: Abrams Publishers.

Biddlecom, A. E. (1999). Preface. In Oheneba-Sakyi, Y., *Female autonomy, family decision making and demographic behavior in Africa* (pp. xvii–xix). Lewiston, NY: Edwin Mellen.

Blanc, A. K., & Lloyd, C. B. (1990, May). *Fertility, women's employment and childrearing over the life cycle in Ghana*. Paper presented at the annual meeting of the Population Association of America, Toronto, Canada.

Bledsoe, C. (1990). Transformations in sub-Saharan African marriage and fertility. *The annals of the American Academy of Political and Social Science 510*, 115–125.

Bleek, W. (1987). Family and family planning in southern Ghana. In Oppong, C. (Ed.), *Sex roles, population and development in West Africa* (pp. 138–153). Portsmouth, NH: Heinemann.

Boahen, A. A. (1989). *African perspectives on colonialism*. Baltimore: Johns Hopkins University Press.

Boserup, E. (1970). *Women's role in economic development*. London: Allen & Unwin.

Boserup, E. (1985). Economic and demographic interrelationships in sub-Saharan Africa. *Population and Development Review 11(3)*, 383–397.

Brabin, L. (1984). Polygyny: An indicator of nutritional stress in African agricultural societies. *Africa 54(1)*, 31–45.

Brown, C. K. (1992). *Aging and family care in Ghana: A study in caring relationships*. Cape Coast: CDS.

Bruce, J., Lloyd, C., & Leonard, A. (1995). *Families in focus: New perspectives on mothers, fathers and children*. New York: Population Council.

Cadigan, R. (1998). Woman-to-woman marriage: Practices and benefits in sub-Saharan Africa. *Journal of Comparative Family Studies 29 (1)*, 89+ Special Issue.

Cain, M. T. (1984). *Women's status and fertility in developing countries: Son preference and economic security*. Working Paper No. 110, Population Council, New York.

Caldwell, J. (1982). *A theory of fertility decline*. Canberra: Australian National University Press.

Caldwell, J., & Caldwell, P. (1987). The cultural context of high fertility in sub-Saharan Africa. *Population and Development Review 13(3)*, 409–438.

Caldwell, J., & Caldwell, P. (1996, March). The African AIDS epidemic. *Scientific America*, 62–68.

Caldwell, J., Caldwell, P., & Quiggin, P. (1989). The social context of AIDS in sub-Saharan Africa. *Population and Development Review 15(2)*, 185–233.

Caldwell, J., Orubuloye, I., & Caldwell, P. (1991). The destabilization of the traditional Yoruba sexual system. *Population and Development Review 17(2)*, 229–262.

Caldwell, J. C., Caldwell, P., Anarfi, J., Awusabo-Asare, K., Ntozi, J. Orubuloye, I. O., Marck, J., Cosford, W., Colombo, R., & Hollings, E. (1999). *Resistances to behavioral change to reduce HIV/AIDS infection in predominantly heterosexual epidemics in Third World countries.* Canberra: Australian National University, Health Transition Center.

Clark, G. (1994). *Onions are my husband: Survival and accumulation by West African market women.* Chicago: University of Chicago Press.

Cohen, R. (1971). Brittle marriage as a stable system: The Kanuri case. In Bohannan, P. (Ed.), *Divorce and after* (pp. 205–239). Garden City, NY: Anchor Books.

Cohen, B. (1998). The emerging fertility transition in sub-Saharan Africa. *World Development 26(8),* 1431–1461.

Dasgupta, P. (1994). The population problem. In Graham-Smith, F., Sir (Ed.), *Population: The Complex Reality* (pp. 151–180). Golden, CO: North American Press.

Date-Bah, E. (1982). *Sex inequalities in an African urban labor market: The case study of Accra-Tema.* Geneva: International Labor Organization.

Dinan, C. (1983). Sugar daddies and gold-diggers: The white-collar single women in Accra. In Oppong, C. (Ed.), *Female and male in West Africa* (pp. 344–366). London: Allen & Unwin.

Diop, C. A. (1960). *L'Afrique noire précoloniale.* Paris: Présence Africaine.

Dorjahn, V. R. (1988). Changes in Temne polygyny. *Ethnology 27,* 367–390.

Dorjahn, V. R. (1990). The marital game, divorce, and divorce frequency among the Temne of Sierra Leone. *Anthropological Quarterly 63,* 169–82.

Du Bois, W. E. B. (2001). *The Negro.* Philadelphia: University of Pennsylvania Press. (Orig. pub. 1915.)

Eze, E. C. (Ed.). (1997). *Race and the enlightenment: A reader.* Cambridge, MA: Blackwell.

Fapohunda, B., & Rutenberg, N. (1999). *Expanding men's participation in reproductive health in Kenya.* Nairobi: African Population Policy Research Center.

Fiawoo, D. K. (1978). Some patterns of foster care in Ghana. In Oppong, C., et al., (Eds.), *Marriage, fertility and parenthood in West Africa* (pp. 278–288). Canberra: Australian National University.

Folbre, N. (1991). *Women on their own: Global pattern of female headship.* Joint working paper, Population Council and International Center for Research on Women, New York.

Fortes, M. (1950). Kinship and marriage among the Ashanti. In Radcliffe-Brown, A. R. & Forde, D. (Eds.), *African systems of kinship and marriage* (pp. 252–284). London: Oxford University Press.

Gage, A. (1998). Sexual activity and contraceptive use: The components of the decision-making process. *Studies in Family Planning 29(2),* 154–66.

Gibbs, J. L. (1965). The Kpelle of Liberia. In Gibbs, J. L. (Ed.), *Peoples of Africa* (pp. 41–79). New York: Holt, Rinehart & Winston.

Gluckman, M. (1965). Kinship and marriage among the Lozi of northern Rhodesia and the Zulu of Natal. In Radcliffe-Brown, A. R. & Forde, D. (Eds.) *African systems of kinship and marriage* (pp. 166–206). New York: Oxford University Press.

Goliber, T. (1989). Africa's expanding population: Old problems, new policies. *Population Bulletin 44,* 1–50.

Goode, W. (1963). *World revolution and family patterns.* New York: Free Press.

Goody, J. (1969). *Comparative studies in kinship.* Stanford, CA: Stanford University Press.

Goody J. (1976). *Production and reproduction: A comparative study of domestic domain.* New York: Cambridge University Press.

Greenstreet, M. (1987). *The Ghanaian woman: Development through education and family planning*. Legon, Accra: University of Ghana, Population Impact Project.

Hagan, G. (1983). Marriage, divorce and polygyny in Winneba. In Oppong, C. (Ed.), *Female and male in West Africa* (pp. 192–203). London: Allen & Unwin.

Hart, K. (1973). Informal income opportunities and urban employment in Ghana. *Journal of Modern African Studies 11*, 61–89.

Hutchison, S. (1990). Rising divorce among the Nuer, 1936–1983. *Man 25*, 393–411.

Karanja, W. W. (1987). "Outside wives" and "inside wives" in Nigeria: A study of changing perceptions of marriage. In Parkin, D. & Nyamwaya, D. (Eds.), *Transformations of African marriage* (pp. 247–261). Manchester, Eng.: Manchester University Press.

Karanja, W. W. (1994). The phenomenon of "outside wives": Some reflections on its possible influence on fertility. In Bledsoe, C. & Pison, G. (Eds.), *Nuptiality in sub-Saharan Africa: Contemporary anthropological and demographic perspectives* (pp. 194–214). Oxford: Clarendon Press.

Kayongo-Male, D., & Onyango, P. (1984). *The sociology of the African family*. London: Longman.

Khapoya, V. B. (1998). *The African experience: An introduction*. Upper Saddle River, NJ: Prentice Hall.

Kritz, M. M., & Gurak, D. T. (1989). *Women's position, education and family formation in sub-Saharan Africa*. Working Paper Series 1.06, Cornell University, Population and Development Program, Ithaca, NY.

Kuenyehia, A. (1978). Women and family law in Ghana. In *Background papers to the Seminar on Ghanaian Women in Development* (pp. 316–337). Accra, Ghana: National Council on Women and Development (NCWD).

Lesthaeghe, R. (1989). Production and reproduction in sub-Saharan Africa: An overview of organizing principles. In Lesthaeghe, R. (Ed.), *Reproduction and social organization in sub-Saharan Africa* (pp. 13–59). Berkeley: University of California Press.

Lloyd, C. (1968). Divorce among the Yoruba. *American Anthropologist 70*, 67–81.

Lloyd, C., & Gage-Brandon, A. (1993). Women's role in maintaining households: Family welfare and sexual inequality in Ghana. *Population Studies 47(1)*, 115–131.

Lockwood, M. (1995). Structure and behavior in the social demography of Africa. *Population and Development Review 21(1)*, 1–32.

Lorimer, F. (1954). *Culture and human fertility*. Paris: UNESCO.

Mann, K. (1994). The historical roots and cultural logic of outside marriage in colonial Lagos. In Bledsoe, C. & Pison, G. (Eds.), *Nuptiality in sub-Saharan Africa: Contemporary anthropological and demographic perspectives* (pp. 167–193). Oxford: Clarendon Press.

Mason, K. O. (1984). *The status of women: A review of its relationships to fertility and mortality*. New York: Rockefeller Foundation Population Science Division.

Mason, K. (1987). The impact of women's social position on fertility in developing countries. *Sociological Forum 2(4)*, 718–745.

Mason, K. O., & Taj, A. M. (1987). Differences between women's and men's reproductive goals in developing countries. *Population and Development Review 13(4)*, 611–638.

Mazrui, A. (1986). Preface. In Mazrui, A. A. & Levine, T. K. (Eds.), *The Africans: A reader* (pp. xv–xviii). New York: Praeger.

Mazrui, A. (1994). Islamic doctrine and the politics of induced fertility change: An African perspective. *Population and Development Review, 20 (Supplement)*, 121–134.

Mazrui, A., & Levine, T. K. (Eds.). (1986). *The Africans: A reader*. New York: Praeger.

Mbugua, W. (1992). The structure and dynamics of family formation in Africa: A review and synthesis of current evidence. In *Structure et dynamique de la formation des familles en Afrique*. Union Pour L'Etude de la Population Africaine.

Meinzen-Dick, R., Brown, L., Feldstein, H., & Quisumbing, A. (1997). Gender and property rights: Overview. *World Development 25(8)*, 1299–1302.

Mikell, G. (1984). Filiation economic crisis, and the status of women in rural Ghana. *Canadian Journal of African Studies 18(1)*, 195–218.

Mikell, G. (1992). *Cocoa and chaos in Ghana*. Washington, DC: Howard University Press.

Mikell, G. (1997). Conclusions: Theorizing and strategizing about African women and state crisis. In Mikell, G. (Ed.), *African feminism: The politics of survival in sub-Saharan Africa* (pp. 333–346). Philadelphia: University of Pennsylvania Press.

Morgan, R. W., with Ohadike, P. O. (1975). Fertility levels and fertility change. In Caldwell, J. C. (Ed.), *Population growth and socio-economic change in West Africa* (pp. 187–235). New York: Columbia University Press.

Nkrumah, K. (1970). *Consciencism: Philosophy and ideology for de-colonization* (rev. ed.). New York: Monthly Review Press.

Nukunya, G. K. (1969). *Kinship and marriage among the Anlo Ewe*. London: Athlone Press.

Nukunya, G. K. (1978). Women and marriage. In *Background papers to the Seminar on Ghanaian Women in Development* (pp. 1–22). Accra, Ghana: National Council on Women and Development (NCWD).

Oheneba-Sakyi, Y. (1999). *Female autonomy, family decision making and demographic behavior in Africa*. Lewiston, NY: Edwin Mellen.

Oheneba-Sakyi, Y., & Takyi, B. K. (1991). Sociodemographic correlates of breastfeeding in Ghana. *Human Biology 63(3)*, 389–402.

Oppong, C. (1970). Conjugal power and resources: An urban African example. *Journal of Marriage and the Family 32*, 676–680.

Oppong, C. (1974). *Marriage among a matrilineal elite: A study of Ghanaian senior civil servants*. London: Cambridge University Press.

Oppong, C. (1977). A note from Ghana on chains of change in family systems and family size. *Journal of Marriage and Family*, 615–621.

Oppong, C. (1981). *Middle-class African marriage*. London: Allen & Unwin.

Oppong, C. (1983). Women's roles, opportunity costs and fertility. In Bulatao, R. A. & Lee, R. D. (Eds.), *Determinants of fertility in developing countries* (pp. 439–473). New York: Academic Press.

Oppong, C., & Abu, K. (1984). *The changing maternal role of Ghanaian women: Impacts of education, migration and employment*. Program Working Paper #143, ILO Population and Labor Policies, Geneva.

Pool, J. (1972). A cross-comparative study of aspects of conjugal behavior among women of three West African countries. *Canadian Journal of African Studies VI(II)*, 233–259.

Population Council. (1998). *Fertility decline in Kenya: Levels, trends and differentials*. Nairobi: African Population Policy Research Center.

Population Reference Bureau. (2005). *World Population Data Sheet*. Washington, DC.

Radcliffe-Brown, A. R., & Forde, D. (Eds.). (1950). *African systems of kinship and marriage*. London: Oxford University Press.

Rattray, R. S. (1923). *Ashanti*. London: Oxford University Press.

Rattray, R. S. (1929). *Ashanti law and constitution*. London: Oxford University Press.

Republic of Ghana, & United Nations Children's Fund. (1990). *Children and women in Ghana: A situation analysis*. Accra, Ghana: ROG & UNICEF.

Robinson, D. (2004). *Muslim societies in African history*. New York: Cambridge University Press.

Sai, F. T. (1976). Rapporteur's Report. In *Family welfare and development in Africa* (pp. 1–32). Proceedings of the IPPF Africa Regional Conference, University of Ibadan, Nigeria, August 29–September 3.

Schoepf, B. C. (1997). AIDS, gender, and sexuality during Africa's economic crisis. In Mikell, G. (Ed.), *African feminism: The politics of survival in sub-Saharan Africa* (pp. 310–332). Philadelphia: University of Pennsylvania Press.

Singh, R. D., & Morey, M. J. (1987). The value of work-at-home and contributions of wives' household service in polygynous families: Evidence from an African LDC. *Economic Development and Cultural Change 35*, 743–765.

Skinner, E. P. (1986). Preface. In Mazrui, A. A. & Levine, T. K., *The Africans: A reader* (pp. 60–81). New York: Praeger.

Takyi, B. (1998). Review essay of polygamous families in contemporary societies. *Journal of Family Relations 47(2)*, 209–210.

Timaeus, I. M., & Reynar, A. (1998). Polygynists and their wives in sub-Saharan Africa: An analysis of five demographic and health surveys. *Population Studies—A Journal of Demography 52(2)*, 145–162.

UNAIDS, & World Health Organization. (1998). *Report on the global HIV/AIDS epidemic and update*. Geneva: Joint United Nations Program on HIV/AIDS & WHO.

UNICEF. (1998). *The status of the world's children*. New York: UNICEF House.

United Nations. (2005). *Demographic yearbook*. New York: UN Department of Economic and Social Affairs.

van de Walle, E. (1993). Recent trends in marriage ages. In *Demographic change in sub-Saharan Africa* (pp. 117–152). Washington, DC: National Academy Press.

Weeks, J. R. (1999). *Population: An introduction to concepts and issues*. New York: Wadsworth.

Weisner, T. S., Bradley, C., & Kilbride, P. L. (Eds.). (1997). *African families and the crisis of social change*. Westport, CT: Bergin & Garvey.

Welch, C., & Glick, P. (1981). The incidence of polygamy in contemporary Africa: A research note. *Journal of Marriage and the Family 43(1)*, 191–193.

Part I
Northern Africa

CHAPTER 2

Continuity or Change: Family Law and Family Structure in Tunisia

Mounira M. Charrad and Allyson B. Goeken

INTRODUCTION

As in other Islamic and Arab countries, key issues with respect to the family in Tunisia concern the interpretation of Islamic family law and the prevalence of extended versus nuclear family systems. A defining feature of Tunisia is the bold family law reform pursued by the state over the last half-century. The reforms have abolished polygyny, given equal rights to divorce to men and to women, increased women's right to custody of children, and to a lesser extent expanded women's inheritance rights. These reforms have to be placed in the context of the family structure that has historically predominated in Tunisia. Lineages organized around patrilineal ties and extended kinship networks occupied a central place in social relationships. Men had power over women not only in their capacity as husbands but also in their roles as kin. Kin-based patriarchy, specifically the primacy of the kin group coupled with the power of male kin over women, has pervaded the history of the Maghrib and many parts of the Islamic world. (*Maghrib* means "west" in Arabic and refers to the western section of the Arab world as constituted by Tunisia, Algeria, and Morocco.) Serious reforms of family law in an Islamic country, such as occurred in Tunisia, in effect redefine concepts of legal personhood. They present a new model of family structure at the same time that they reduce the power of husbands and male kin by giving women greater individual rights (for a fuller discussion of this argument, see Charrad, 2001).

Considering change and continuity, the analysis in this chapter shows how family law and family structure in Tunisia reflect new realities at the same time that they retain distinctive features inherited from the past. The chapter traces the development of family law reforms and the political forces that made them possible. Critical periods considered include colonization and nationalism, the formation of the national state, the consolidation of the postcolonial state, and the concomitant rise of Islamic fundamentalism and feminism with their contradictory demands regarding the family. The chapter then outlines current trends in family structure and critically examines assumptions about the demise of extended kinship.

A few words on the characteristics of Tunisia should help place it in its broader geographical and historical context of Islamic North Africa. A small country of 9.5 million people, Tunisia is a republic (République Tunisienne, 2001). Colonized by France in 1881, it became a sovereign nation-state in 1956. Culturally and linguistically, Tunisia shares much with Algeria and Morocco, which were also colonized by France. Often perceived by Western powers as an island of stability in an unstable region, Tunisia is lodged between Algeria to the west and Libya to the east. Tunisians speak Arabic, most of the educated population also knows French, and Tunisian schools teach both languages. With a relatively insignificant amount of oil, the economy is based on a combination of agricultural products and increasingly successful industrial, manufacturing, and technological development.

FAMILY LAW UNCHANGED UNDER COLONIALISM: THE 1930s–1950s

During colonization, the colonial state and the nationalist party each favored keeping Islamic family law, but they did so for entirely different reasons. While they ruled over Tunisia from 1881 until 1956, the French applied French law to French citizens and left Islamic family law in place for the Tunisian population, in part because they could exert their rule without changing it. Nationalist leaders also wanted to keep Islamic family law, which they took as a symbol of cultural identity to be preserved at all cost in the fight against colonialism (Charrad, 2001, pp. 215–218).

The family law that applied to the Tunisian population in the 1930s was essentially the Shari'a as it had historically evolved in the Maghrib. Despite many shared aspects of Islamic law in the Muslim world, each region also maintains its own distinctiveness, and Orthodox Islam has included four major schools of thought with respect to family law. The school called *Maliki* predominated in Tunisia until the reforms of the 1950s (for a detailed account of the Maliki school of law, see Borrmans, 1977).

In the Maliki legal tradition, there was no minimum age for marriage, except for the stipulation that marriage should take place after puberty. In the actual ceremony that established the marriage contract, it was the father, or in his absence the woman's (male) guardian, not the bride, who uttered consent to the marriage. Over time in the Maghrib, divorce became essentially a private matter in that the husband had a unilateral right to terminate the marriage by repudiating his wife, without court decision. Polygyny was allowed and a man could have as many as four wives.

Islam developed in a Tunisian society in which kin groups functioned as corporate units whose male members usually had control over women. This generated a distinct form of women's subordination. The Shari'a reflects that form. It gives power over women not only to husbands, but also to male members of the kin group. It also sanctions a special bond of community among male members of the extended kin group (Charrad, 1990, 2000). In some instances, as in marriage and inheritance, male kin have considerable prerogative. Strict inheritance rules designate the heirs and specify their shares. One principle holds in all cases: a woman inherits half the share that would go to a man in the same kinship relation to the deceased. For example, a daughter inherits half as much as a son. Inheritance rules also favor distant male kin over close women relatives.

Women in Tunisia, as elsewhere, have found ways around kin-based patriarchy or the combined power of husbands and male kin over women's lives. Women have negotiated power resources in everyday life, even under the stringency to Islamic family law, sometimes with great difficulty and at other times with success (Joseph & Slyomovics, 2001; Joseph, 2000; Bodman & Tohidi, 1998; Bourqia, Charrad, & Gallagher, 1996; Fernea, 1985). Even so, this does not negate the privileges of kin inherent in the law and the legally sanctioned power male kin have over women.

French colonial officials refrained from interference with Islamic family law, even though they changed other laws in Tunisia, including property or contract law. Economic exploitation, which primarily interested the French, made changes in commercial law critical, whereas it did not require similar changes in family law. Furthermore, the particular form of colonization had bearing on the French policy for family law in Tunisia. Other colonies such as Algeria experienced more extensive settlement of individual farmers with small landholdings. Colonization in Algeria resulted in a massive uprooting of the indigenous population, causing profound transformations in family structure. This required French intervention in family law in Algeria. By contrast, large industrial and commercial interests prevailed in the colonization of Tunisia. The French colonial state could protect those interests without immediate concern for the family law and family life of Tunisians.

The French also realized that interference with Islamic family law could provoke a violent response among Tunisians. In Tunisia as in their other colonies, the French wished they could turn everyone into a French man or woman. Sometimes, however, they knew not to try because of the anticipated cost that the attempt could bring. By its very nature, colonial domination threatens culture and cultural identity. To most Tunisians under colonial rule, the definition of being Tunisian included allegiance to Islam. Many saw Islamic family law as the cornerstone of their separate identity from the French. Colonized peoples often experience the family as the last refuge against colonial encroachment. Quite aware of this, French colonial officials avoided confrontation on a point that, in any case, they could accept without undue hardship. Islamic family law in Tunisia was thus left intact and served as a point of differentiation between colonizer and colonized (Borrmans, 1977).

The nationalist movement rallied around the defense of Islamic family law for its own reasons. Organized as a mass party and avoiding ideological divisions during most of the colonial period, the nationalist movement welcomed those committed to lifting the colonial yoke. The nationalist leadership effectively joined a modernizing liberal elite represented by members such as Habib Bourguiba and Tahar Haddad with conservative forces such as Islamic judges and scholars committed to the defense of tradition. An inclusive organization, the nationalist movement brought together several social bases such as the labor union, urban populations, and kin groupings organized in patriarchal communities in rural areas. The nationalist party acted as the only legitimate political organization speaking in the name of Tunisians. Openly striving for state power in a future sovereign Tunisia, it subsumed all questions to the paramount objective of national liberation.

Throughout the colonial period, nationalist leaders took a conservative stand on issues regarding the family. Bourguiba (1903–2000), who later became president of Tunisia (1957–87), voiced the collective position of the leadership in 1929, declaring: "Is it in our interest to hasten the disappearance of our ways of life and customs. . . . that constitute our identity? Given the special circumstances in which we live, my answer is categorical: No" (Bourguiba, 1929, p. 1). He gave his reason: "Tunisians must safeguard their traditions, which are the sign of their distinctiveness, and therefore the last defense of a national identity in danger" (Bourguiba, 1929, p. 1).

The discourse on family law became intertwined with the issue of women's condition and came to the fore of the nationalist debate in Tunisia in the late 1920s and early 1930s. Discussions on the topics were not a separate debate, but part of a broad intellectual confrontation between East and West. A reformist movement, which touched most of the Arab world, raised the question of the family within the context of a general critique of society. Disturbed by the military and technological superiority of Europe in the period, Tunisian thinkers reflected on the reasons for it. Some wanted to find remedies for what they saw as the stagnation of their own society.

Tahar Haddad, a nationalist intellectual, made a loud and clear call for reforms in publishing a polemical book entitled *Women in Law and Society* (1930). In his book, Haddad described the position of women in Tunisian society at the time as a social plague and complained that women were treated no better than dogs. Outlining the negative effects that degrading women had on the women themselves and on the society at large, he called for reforms of marriage and divorce laws in particular. The Islamic religious establishment, which the French had left in place, reacted vehemently against Tahar Haddad. One of its members responded with a devastating critique in a pamphlet with a telling title, *The Shroud of Mourning Thrown on al-Haddad's Woman* (Ben Mrad, n.d.). Joining in the debate, other religious figures condemned Haddad's book as an attack against religion, morality, and law. Tahar Haddad finished his life in public disgrace. The nationalist leadership abstained from defending him, thus siding with the religious establishment de facto.

From the 1930s until the achievement of sovereignty in 1956, the Tunisian nationalists placed national liberation first. They treated all other issues as means to that end. Although the movement included a range of positions on the desirability of social reforms (Chater, 1978), nationalists agreed on two major objectives that shaped their position on the "woman's question." First, they wanted to present a unified front to the colonizer. Second, they strove to retain symbols of Islamic identity and Tunisian separateness from the French. Accordingly, nationalists avoided potentially divisive issues that could have broken the anticolonial consensus holding the movement together. They vehemently defended Islamic family law. Any other position would have meant playing into the hands of the colonial regime. Given the realities of colonial domination, the safeguarding of cultural distinctiveness and political consensus represented the most pressing agenda. In effect, the nationalist leadership treated the family and women's place within it as the embodiment of Tunisian identity for the duration of the colonial period.

THE NATIONAL STATE IN FORMATION AND FAMILY LAW REFORM: THE MID-1950s

The alliance between the leading factions of the nationalist movement ruptured as the French were pushed out of Tunisia in the mid-1950s. An all-out confrontation for control of the nascent sovereign state broke out, with each faction vying for power and seeking to destroy the other. A conflict erupted between the two major nationalist factions, the modernizing and the traditional, on the eve of independence from French colonial rule (Anderson, 1986; Charrad, 2001). The outcome of the conflict goes a long way toward explaining the family law policy of the Tunisian state in the aftermath of independence. The two factions had a different relationship to the Islamic establishment and kin-based corporate communities. They also had different projects for the society as a whole. In 1954–55, in addition to the bloodshed caused by the struggle against the French, the two nationalist factions faced each other in a violent confrontation, with ambushes and physical attacks on members and locales of each faction.

In brief, Bourguiba's faction, which ultimately won, drew its constituency mostly from urban areas and received the strong backing of unions. The competing faction, under Ben Youssef, found greater support among kin-based communities in rural areas and among members of the religious establishment. A lawyer educated partly in French universities, Bourguiba spoke of reason and moderation. An Islamic scholar with connections to Egypt, Ben Youssef made inflammatory speeches in support of Islam. Whatever their ideological preferences at the start of the conflict, the two men sharpened their positions as the conflict intensified. Bourguiba was able to convince the French to help him because, once the end of colonial rule appeared unavoidable, the French preferred a sovereign Tunisia under a leader like Bourguiba rather than Ben Youssef. Helped by French military troops, Bourguiba's forces decimated the foot soldiers and resources of the rival faction. Ben Youssef himself escaped by fleeing Tunisia and taking refuge abroad (Hermassi, 1972).

The victorious faction under Bourguiba moved quickly to weaken the base of the Ben Youssef faction. Fearing that its rivals might rally forces, Bourguiba's government enacted a general policy of state intervention in rural areas by setting up state agencies and programs that intervened in the lives of the previously more autonomous kin-based communities. It also took measures to undermine the religious establishment, which had supported the defeated Ben Youssef faction. It deprived the Islamic establishment of most of its privileges by eliminating religious landholdings and reducing the institutions of religious education to the bone. By 1956, Bourguiba and his faction had successfully annihilated the fighting force of the Ben Youssef faction, silenced its leader, and seriously weakened its social base. Facing no challenger in that period, the modernizing faction promulgated a reform of family law that corresponded to its vision of a future Tunisia, one that was likely to further weaken its now-defeated rival whose power base had been anchored in kin groupings and the Islamic establishment.

In 1956, only a few months after the achievement of national sovereignty, the newly formed government dealt a blow to legally sanctioned kin-based patriarchy. It promulgated the Code of Personal Status or CPS (République Tunisienne, 1991), a unique body of legislation in the Arab-Islamic world. Tunisia has been a pioneer at the forefront of the Arab-Islamic world with respect to reforms of family law. In the 1920s, Turkey, Islamic but not Arab, made reforms similar to those in Tunisia, but did so by rejecting the Islamic legal tradition altogether and adopting an entirely secular law. No Arab country to date has followed the Turkish model of secularization. While staying under the umbrella of Islam, Tunisia made reforms of Islamic family law earlier and more thoroughly than any other country in the Arab world.

The CPS abolished polygyny, eliminated the husband's right to repudiate his wife, allowed women to file for divorce, and increased women's custody rights. The government followed the initial CPS with a series of amendments in the same vein in the late 1950s and early 1960s. Many have seen the action of the Tunisian state in 1956 as revolutionary and others have called it "feminist." However, calling the Tunisian reforms feminist amounts to coloring the motives of the 1950s with present-day attitudes. We must distinguish between the driving force of a policy at the time when it occurred and how the policy appears to us today within the context of current events. The reforms were indeed bold and progressive, but feminist concerns did not prompt them. First, feminism did not enter the political discourse and struggles of the 1950s in Tunisia; neither did a feminist movement exist at that time. Second, a close look at the reforms reveals that their dominant thrust was other than promoting gender equality.

True, the CPS reformulated power relations between men and women by reassigning rights and responsibilities within the family. Regulations on marriage increased women's potential autonomy within the family. The banning of polygyny and repudiation reduced the power of husbands. These and other changes represented immense gains for Tunisian women. At the same time, however, the CPS openly maintained gender inequality in the family. For example, Article 23 stated that the wife should obey her husband (République Tunisienne, 1991, p. 9). The CPS retained the rule by which a woman inherits only half as much as a man. It also gave privileges to fathers over mothers with respect to legal guardianship of children.

The thrust of the CPS was to present a new image of the family. The CPS dropped the vision of the family as an extended kinship group built on strong ties crisscrossing a community of male relatives (Charrad, 2001, pp. 218–232). It replaced it with the vision of a conjugal unit in which ties between spouses and between parents and children occupy a prominent place. For example, the new inheritance laws increased the rights of daughters over those of distant male relatives. By setting the minimum age for marriage at 17 for women and 20 for men, whereas Islamic law had set puberty as the only condition, the CPS made child marriages more problematic. The CPS required that the bride attend the marriage contract and express her consent directly, which could make compulsory marriages difficult. In these ways, the CPS moved away from the model of the family as an extended kin group, instead putting forth a model that emphasized individual rights and obligations anchored in nuclear families. The family law reform of 1956 thus challenged the kin-based patriarchy inherent in the Shari'a with a new, nuclear model.

At independence, the victorious leadership combined considerable power with a specific project for Tunisian society. Calling on all Tunisians to join in a collective effort, in a famous 1960 speech Bourguiba declared, "another form of holy war is the war against underdevelopment..." (Bourguiba, 1978). The CPS was part of "the war against underdevelopment" that included, among other tasks, the elimination of what the government saw as impediments to building a modern state. Kin-based corporate communities and patriarchal arrangements permitted by the Shari'a represented such impediments to be eradicated. The CPS family law reform confronted powerful and cohesive kin groupings with a cultural model that not only was at odds with their practices, but also made them feel excluded from the new social order.

In addition, the reform undermined the influence of the religious establishment, the other potential challenger with a vested interest in keeping the Shari'a unchanged. Individual members of the religious establishment reacted to the CPS by resigning in protest. As a group, however, the religious establishment was powerless. It had lost its collective political voice with the defeat of the Ben Youssef faction that it had supported in the nationalist struggle. It lacked the organizational framework and political capital to challenge the modernizing leadership now in power under Bourguiba.

In sum, the CPS was at once part and by-product of an overall project of state building (Charrad, 2001, pp. 1–13, 201–232). In promulgating the CPS, the government of the mid-1950s was implementing a vision of modern Tunisia in which kin-based communities and the Islamic establishment would be marginalized. In the mid-1950s, the Tunisian state was autonomous from both of these social forces, neither of which was part of its base and both of which had supported the rival contender for state power. The victorious power holders wanted to build a modern state and they were at the height of their power in the mid-1950s. They combined a vision of society with the power to enforce it at a critical time, when a postcolonial national state was taking shape.

From the mid-1950s to the mid-1960s, state officials made a concerted effort to enforce family law reforms and they faced no challenger strong enough to obstruct the effort. People spoke of the police arresting men who practiced polygyny by claiming that they had married one wife according to the new law (which required a marriage certificate) and another wife according to the old law (which did not require a written certificate). Family lawyers commented that, during that period, the government instructed judges to apply the new laws strictly.

Family law reforms continued at a sustained pace, with several amendments clarifying or amplifying the initial text of the CPS (Chamari, 1991; République Tunisienne, 1991). Family law policy appeared to be set on a progressive course. The tide would turn, however, with a change in national politics in the following decades.

THE POSTCOLONIAL STATE—CONSOLIDATION AND CONSERVATISM ON FAMILY ISSUES: THE 1970s

Starting in the 1970s, the interplay of state power, culture, and family took new forms in Tunisia. A new social movement arose to challenge the state modernizing elite in the 1970s. This was a leftist movement rooted among intellectuals and university students and a wing of the trade union movement that had expanded in urban areas when commerce and industry spread after independence. In the 1970s and early 1980s, the left appeared to the existing regime as their most serious cause for concern, with Marxists and socialists operating mostly underground in associations and networks in the context of a single-party system. Although already present in Tunisia, Islamic fundamentalism appeared to be more of a cultural movement in the mid-1970s, rather than a real threat to state power. (It would become such a threat a decade later.) Challenged mainly by political groups on the left and still under the leadership of Bourguiba, the Tunisian state leaned increasingly on Islam as a source of political legitimacy. It tried to create a counterweight to the left and gain popular legitimacy by reaffirming Islamic identity. It established a rapprochement with the much-weakened Islamic establishment.

Accordingly, the government now emphasized policies that reaffirmed Islamic values. For example, the Ministry of Education transformed educational programs such as the teaching of philosophy in secondary schools. Following the French system, Tunisian schools taught philosophy in the last year of secondary education. Not only did the Ministry of Education change the language of instruction in philosophy from French to Arabic, but it also shifted the content of the curriculum from European to Islamic philosophers. Whereas it had sought to undermine the influence of the Islamic establishment in the mid-1950s, in 1970 the government sponsored the creation of the Association for the Safeguard of the Quran (Bessis & Belhassen, 1992, p. 148), in part as an antidote to the Marxist left and as an affirmation of Islamic identity. In another example, in organizing the first Tunisian book fair in 1973, the government helped distribute the writings of the Egyptian-based Muslim Brotherhood, writings that seemed less dangerous than radical socialist literature (Bessis & Belhassen, 1992, p. 148).

As part of its response to the new challengers, the regime gave a backseat to family law policy. The 1970s and 1980s witnessed fewer state actions than earlier periods in this respect. Previous legislation remained in place while the government oscillated between mild reforms and outright retrenchment on family issues. In 1973, a government decree addressed the issue of a marriage between a Muslim woman and a non-Muslim man, a sensitive issue left undiscussed in the CPS. The decree ordered public authorities to refrain from performing and registering such a marriage based on the argument that this would help preserve Tunisian cultural identity by protecting it from Western influences (Chamari, 1991, p. 43). In effect, the marriage of a Tunisian Muslim woman and a non-Muslim man thus could not occur in Tunisia.

In the same vein, the political discourse of the period emphasized that women belonged first of all in the home. For example, in a speech typical of the tone at that time, Bourguiba urged Tunisian women to remember "their family responsibilities as wives, mothers and homemakers." He also reminded them that "their role in public life might sometimes occupy a secondary role" (Bourguiba, 1981, p. 238). The government supported and passed a new law on divorce in 1981 that introduced modifications in alimony and child custody by expanding the rights of mothers (Charrad, 1994). The same government abandoned a project to reform inheritance laws in favor of women, however, for fear that such an action might be read as a rejection of Islam and provoke the opposition of the Islamic establishment and others.

The 1970s and early 1980s thus contrast with the mid-1950s, when the Tunisian state operated in relative autonomy from the Islamic establishment and patriarchally organized kin-based communities. By the 1970s, kin-based communities had lost political leverage and were gradually integrated into the new social and economic order as a result of government intervention in rural areas. Instead of being autonomous from social formations with a vested interest in Islamic law as embodied in the Shari'a, the state of the 1970s and early 1980s formed an alliance with the Islamic establishment and strengthened symbols of Islamic identity. Accordingly, it pursued a relatively conservative family law policy.

FAMILY LAW BETWEEN FEMINISM AND ISLAMIC FUNDAMENTALISM: THE 1990s

The next major turning point in family law occurred in the early 1990s, a period when the state faced the challenge of a militant, political Islamic fundamentalism coupled with the emergence of feminism as a genuine social force. In 1987, Tunisia experienced a change of regime with the peaceful, nonviolent dismissal of Bourguiba, who had been president for three decades. Bourguiba was 87 years old and in poor health. Following an article of the constitution according to which the prime minister takes over if the president is incapacitated, then prime minister Ben Ali formed a new government and became president. Family law remained on the back burner for a while until the government made new reforms in 1992–93. An examination of alliances and conflicts among key political actors in national politics in that period sheds light on the family law reforms of the 1990s.

The intensifying threat of Islamic fundamentalism at home and abroad weighed heavily on the politics of the late 1980s and early 1990s. By then, the voices defending Islam had grown louder and Islamic fundamentalism had changed from a cultural phenomenon to a political threat. It was in this period that Islamic fundamentalists openly coveted state power and that, emerging in earnest, feminism captured political space for women's issues for the first time. After trying a carrot-and-stick strategy for a while, the government attacked the fundamentalists directly in the 1990s at the same time that it invited women to join it in the fight against fundamentalism. In 1991, for example, the National Union of Tunisian Women, which was under government sponsorship, made an appeal to women following the uncovering of a fundamentalist plot against the government, which stated: "We launch an appeal to all citizens, and foremost to Tunisian women, to show vigilance especially at this time . . . and to mobilize themselves even more around our President" (Riza, 1991, p. 4). In making new reforms of family law in 1993, the state not only responded to pressures from women's rights advocates but also solidified its alliance with them. As they both faced the danger of Islamic fundamentalism, the regime in power and feminists formed a partial alliance against a common enemy.

Feminists realized that the CPS could be in jeopardy if Islamic fundamentalism gained strength. They feared that the state might sacrifice family law to appease fundamentalists. For example, a woman active in the labor union said:

Nothing is guaranteed forever and, therefore, the CPS is not protected from all threats. The danger of losing the gains embodied in the CPS exists because the demands of the Islamic fundamentalists can always be raised a notch. We could witness a move backwards with respect to women's rights in Tunisia. (Chater, 1992, p. 267)

Starting in the late 1980s, feminists asked for further legal reforms that would address some of the gender inequalities built into the CPS of 1956. Most Tunisian feminists consider themselves Muslim and locate themselves within the framework of an enlightened Islamic tradition. They speak for a tolerant and open Islam, as opposed to one that is militant and dogmatic.

Given their own agenda with respect to the family, Islamic fundamentalist leaders have called for a return to patriarchy and to a traditional model of the family, an issue that they have placed at the center of their platform. The more conservative leaders want to abolish the CPS and restore a law that they would see as faithful to the Shari'a, even though a more progressive segment accepts the CPS as a reality to be tolerated. Already in 1985, Abdelfattah Mourou, then general secretary of the Islamic Tendency Movement, had proposed a national referendum on the revision of the CPS. He said:

The preface of the CPS of 1956 indicated that its objective was to protect the family. Thirty years later we wonder whether this objective has been met.... I launch an appeal to constitute a national Commission of specialists and ask them to examine the reasons why the cohesion of the Tunisian family leaves much to be desired. (Chater, 1992, p. 38)

Conservative fundamentalists have argued for a restoration of polygyny, a move that would give back to men the privilege of marrying as many as four wives. They also contend that divorce should be the privilege of the husband, in contrast to the CPS, which gives women the right to file for divorce. For example, Cheikh Lakhoua declared in an interview: "It is unavoidable to redo the CPS on the issues of polygamy [polygyny], divorce, and adoption.... The call to total equality between the sexes is a war against Islam" (Chater, 1992, p. 44). Blaming social problems on vaguely defined changes in family life and women's condition, Islamic fundamentalists want to bring back the old social order. They suggest that collective patriarchal organization provides the best kind of family arrangement, one that protects the welfare of individuals and communities.

The Islamic fundamentalist movement in Tunisia acts in part as the political voice of the disillusioned urban poor who often share a nostalgia for a secure past order or, more accurately, for an idealized vision of such an order. In that vision, men have control over women and individuals are never alone in that they can count on extended kin in case of life crisis. Facing hardship and also yearning for the fantasized security of a bygone era, many women find refuge in Islamic fundamentalist networks. For example, a member of a local office of the National Union of Tunisian Women in a poor neighborhood said about Islamic fundamentalists: "They very much help women who have health or divorce problems . . ." (Bessis & Belhassen, 1992, p. 223). When migrating to cities, rural people bring to their new circumstances ideals of a lost society. Longing for the traditional patriarchal family, young male migrants look to Islamic fundamentalism as a way to restore or maintain it.

The Tunisian state in the 1990s thus faced Islamic fundamentalists, some of whom wished to restore kin-based patriarchy, and women's rights advocates, who wanted to reduce it further. Heir to the reformist national state that formed at the end of colonization in the mid-1950s, the Tunisian state of the early 1990s found its base in the modernist segments of Tunisian society, rooted in the middle class and the economic business elite, both of which felt threatened by Islamic fundamentalism. The government affirmed its intent to protect the CPS. Following the change of regime in November 1987, President Ben Ali declared categorically in early 1988: "The Code of Personal Status is a gain to which we attach great importance and which we will continue to uphold. We are truly proud of the CPS, and there will be no going back on Tunisia's progress in the domains of the family and women's rights" (Tunisian External Communication Agency & National Union of Tunisian Women, 1993, p. 21).

The most important state action with respect to the family was a set of amendments to the CPS in July 1993. The revised CPS dropped the clause according to which the wife must obey her husband, a clause that was included in earlier versions. It expanded mothers' prerogatives and reduced fathers' power after divorce with respect to child custody, a point of great concern to women. In the past, the father retained legal guardianship of the child even when the mother had custody. The mother therefore had responsibility for the day-to-day care of the child, but in having guardianship, the father retained control over school enrollment, the issuance of a passport, and financial matters concerning the child. This separation of responsibilities created difficulties for many divorced mothers. After the 1993 reforms, a mother who got custody after divorce could also obtain guardianship if she showed that the father failed to respect the best interest of the child or manipulated guardianship to hurt her as his former wife. A related reform made it possible for a child born to a Tunisian mother and foreign father to be a Tunisian citizen (Charrad, 2000).

The minister of justice accurately described the objectives of his government in making the 1993 reforms. Explaining that the objective was "to strengthen the family, without negating the Arab-Islamic heritage," he stated that the reforms placed Tunisia "at the forefront of the Arab-Islamic world with respect to women's rights" (*La Presse*, 1993, p. 5). Conforming with the stated objective, the 1993 reforms addressed social problems related to family such as the problems of children after divorce and the economic plight of most divorced women. They did not negate the Arab-Islamic heritage, and they kept Tunisia ahead of other Arab countries with respect to family law and women's rights. Continuing to make occasional amendments or additions to the Code of Personal Status, the Tunisian state has remained on a reformist course since then on matters of family law.

SOCIAL CHANGE, FAMILY STRUCTURE, AND FAMILY SIZE

The analysis in this chapter so far has shown how for several decades the Tunisian state promulgated laws that favored a nuclear family system and rejected the model of the extended kinship network. Other structural forces such as urbanization and migration were also at work and combined with legal reforms to shape Tunisian families. Common assumptions about family change are that this set of forces is likely to result in the nuclearization of the family and the disappearance of extended kinship. The next section considers some of the changes that have occurred in family structure in the recent history of Tunisia by focusing on family size and interaction among kin. It shows that, despite some real changes, extended kinship remains a useful concept to understand important aspects of family life in Tunisia.

The traditional Tunisian family followed the model of the patrilineal extended kinship network as reflected in the term *ayla* (plural *'aylāt*). "*Ayla* refers to a group of descendants defined by their common male ancestry" (Ferchiou, 1992, p. 138). In accordance with the emphasis placed on the purity of the patrilineage, marriage between cousins historically was seen as one of the most effective strategies to retain the family bloodline. Much has been written about the preference for marriage with the first paternal cousin in the history of the Arab world. That preference applied to Tunisia where kin endogamy has been documented in several areas (Charrad, 2001, pp. 51–67). Even when cousin endogamy was not practiced, broader kinship ties often governed marriage alliances. Traditionally, the family was viewed as the most important social unit, prevailing over individualism and ideas of self, and requiring each individual to contribute to the stability and collective welfare of the kin group (Barakat, 1985, p. 28).

In analyzing Tunisian family patterns, a number of scholars focus on the shift in household structure and the changing dynamics of the modern family (Ferchiou, 1992; Ben Salem, 1992). In Tunisia as elsewhere, there is a reciprocal relationship between broader social forces and changing family systems. Administrative centralization following the development of sovereign national states and legal reforms such as the Code of Personal Status tend to disrupt the cohesiveness of kin-based communities. In the same vein, industrialization, urbanization, and migration encourage the growth of the nuclear family and the weakening of the extended kin networks, at the same time that these forces are facilitated by the nuclearization of the family. Economic changes contribute to transforming the family structure, especially when both spouses work outside the home, as the employment of women challenges the traditional roles of family members and redefines the responsibilities of women (Barakat, 1985; Ben Salem, 1990).

Migration is a particularly important factor in this respect because families that migrate to urban areas tend to establish nuclear households rather than retain the extended household that was previously more prevalent. Considerable rural to urban migration took place in Tunisia in the 1970s and 1980s. The urban population was at 40 percent in 1966, at 49 percent in 1975 (CREDIF, 1994, p. 43), and at 59 percent in 1990 (République Tunisienne, 2001). By 1999, the urban population had grown modestly to just over 62 percent (République Tunisienne, 2001).

Although urbanization, migration, and family law reform converged to generate pressures toward the nuclearization of the family, one must be cautious in considering the weakening of extended kinship ties. Even if households become more nuclear, this does not imply that individuals abandon interaction with their kin, only that families have to reshape the structure of their households in order to adjust to the urban environment. Extended kin can still continue to interact with each other even when living arrangements have to change. A study by Holmes-Eber (1997, 2003) suggests that we miss a great deal about Tunisian families if we look only at households. In particular we overlook the frequency and intensity of contact with extended kin. Holmes-Eber shows that families which migrate to cities tend to create nuclear households, but that they establish residence near extended family members and continue to visit frequently.

The Holmes-Eber study included 36 randomly selected women from middle-class backgrounds. The women in the sample were married and had children still residing at home. Two-thirds of the women interviewed were first- or second-generation immigrants to Tunis, and an even larger percentage (79 percent) of their husbands were immigrants. With the purpose of analyzing the extent to which women in Tunis continued to interact with their kin, Holmes-Eber assessed the levels of interaction by determining the number of visits women made to their family members' homes. In Tunisia, social interaction takes place in people's homes, and it is expected that relatives and friends will stop by for visits, often unannounced. Taking into account the interaction with all relatives ranging from sisters-in-law to first and second cousins, Holmes-Eber considered the percentage of visits that women made to family members out of the total number of visits they made. She found that, among both immigrant women and women whose families were originally from Tunis, 76 percent of the household visits were to family or kin. The figure was 74 percent for immigrant women and 87 percent for native Tunisian women.

Among the women interviewed, Holmes-Eber discovered that, regardless of level of education and professional status, family dominated women's social networks. Although women working outside the home tended to visit family members somewhat less frequently than women who worked at home, familial interaction dominated the social life of all the women interviewed. The persistence of kin networks in the lives of women who work outside the home is an interesting finding, since these women in principle have more opportunities to make contacts and develop relationships with people outside their kin networks.

The evidence provided by Holmes-Eber illustrates how relationships with family and kin continue to matter, in spite of the fact that many Tunisians have migrated to urban areas. The high levels of interaction among kin remain possible because family members tend to follow each other to urban areas. Once one member has become established in a city, this creates opportunities for other family members to come to the same area. Ties among kin are further reinforced by the moral obligation for many Muslims to take care of children, sick relatives, or elderly parents in need. Holmes-Eber's study shows that kin networks still play a vital role in urban families and that kinship ties continue to remain the most significant network for both emotional and financial support for middle-class urban populations. Studies such as this one, even though they apply to a relatively small sample, should lead us to refrain from broad generalizations about family transformations, and to question the assumption that relationships with kin networks are rapidly deteriorating.

In the same way that the effects of industrialization and migration on familial relations may be overstated, changes in family law with regard to marriage practices do not imply that marriages are no longer based on kin networks. Women do have the legal right to contract their own marriages without the intervention of a matrimonial guardian, ever since the promulgation of the Code of Personal Status in 1956. Marriage nevertheless often remains a strategy for either retaining or increasing the socioeconomic status of the family. Holmes-Eber reports that 50 percent of the women interviewed married a relative, and 23 percent had arranged marriages (Holmes-Eber, 1997). She gives the example of a woman who held a professional-level job with the government and accepted an arranged marriage with her cousin, notwithstanding the fact that her professional status provided her with the ability to meet other potential marriage partners and choose her own husband. This example illustrates the continued importance of kinship ties even for people who could be expected to organize their lives irrespective of such ties.

In the same vein, a study conducted by the National Union of Tunisian Women, cited by Borowiec (1998), supports Holmes-Eber's conclusions about the continued significance of kin networks. The study reported that 51 percent of all marriages and 47 percent of marriages in urban areas were arranged. Even among the women who chose their own spouse, 58 percent reported meeting him through kin acquaintances (Borowiec, 1998, p. 116). This provides further evidence for the survival of extended kinship ties in contemporary Tunisia.

One noticeable shift in the structure of Tunisian families that is not debated is family size. In the past, large families were an indicator of economic and social status. Having several children was not only beneficial to the household economy, because children often began working at a young age, but also a sign of prestige (Barakat, 1985, p. 30). Since the 1950s, however, the fertility rate has drastically decreased in Tunisia, which can be attributed to several developments. One such development is the increase in the average age at marriage, a factor that contributes to lowering the level of childbearing in most countries. The average age at marriage has increased considerably for Tunisian women from 20.4 years in 1970 to 23.9 in 1991, and to 25 years of age by 2000 (CREDIF, 1994, p. 51; Population Reference Bureau, 2000). It is also important to note that the average marriage age tends to be lower in rural areas than in urban areas, just as the fertility levels in rural areas are generally higher.

Another development likely to have had an effect on family size is an active family planning program. The state has repeatedly stated its desire to lower the fertility level (Khalil & Myntti, 1995, p. 201). Khalil and Myntti explain, "Most governments have tied their demographic targets to the time frame of periodic national development plans. Tunisia, for example, since the Fourth Plan for Social and Economic Development (1973–76), has regularly stated its desire to achieve the fertility target of a gross reproduction rate of 1.15 per woman by the year 2001" (Khalil & Myntti, 1995, p. 201). In an essay published in 1995, Youssef Courbage estimated that "fertility projections by educational levels show that replacement level (2.1 children) would be reached" in Tunisia around the year 2000 (Courbage, 1995, pp. 91–94). Courbage's estimate was indeed correct. In 1966, Tunisia's total fertility rate was 7.1 children born per woman (Brand, 1998, p. 209), in 1990 it was 3.38 (République Tunisienne, 2001), and by 2000 it had decreased to 2.1 (World Bank, 2001). The total fertility rate thus made a sharp decrease, from 7.1 to 2.1 in the 34 years from 1966 to 2000.

In 1961, laws were implemented in Tunisia to assist and increase family planning practices (Obermeyer, 1993, p. 361). Importing and selling contraceptives was made legal and the government ceased family allocations for children born beyond the fourth child. Brand notes, "Beginning in 1970 a 'contraception prize' was awarded each year to the governorate that had converted the largest number of women in contraceptive use" (Brand, 1998, p. 209).

Efforts were also made to infuse family planning programs into maternal health care facilities. By 1973, there were only 38 health care facilities with a family planning program, which motivated the government to create the National Office of Family Planning (ONFP) and expand family planning programs. By 1980, the ONFP cooperated with basic health care services and the Ministry of Health. Family planning facilities have been implemented in mobile clinics as well as in other health care institutions in order to provide women residing in rural areas with easier access. By 1982, Tunisia ranked 14th out of 99 countries on a scale measuring family planning efforts (Cochrane & Guilkey, 1995, p. 782).

The percentage of couples using contraception has increased over time, although it is difficult to measure and different sources provide different figures. According to the World Bank, 50 percent of married women aged 15 to 49 were using contraception in 1998 (World Bank, 2001). The ONFP claims that for the same year, 66.8 percent of married women in the same age bracket used contraception and that in 1999 the percentage reached 70.5 (République Tunisienne, 2001). Although the figures provided by the World Bank did not distinguish between modern and traditional methods, it is likely that the figures refer only to modern contraceptive methods, which include birth control pills, condoms, diaphragms, or IUD devices, in contrast to traditional methods such as the rhythm method.

From 1978 to 1988, the prevalence of contraception increased dramatically. Cochrane and Guilkey mention that in 1988, contraceptive use reduced fertility by 35 percent from its natural level, compared to only a 25 percent reduction in 1978 (Cochrane & Guilkey, 1995, p. 781). From 1978 to 1988, the use of modern methods of contraception increased from 25 percent to 40 percent and the use of all methods combined increased from 31 to 50 percent (Cochrane & Guilkey, 1995, p. 781). These figures are fairly close to those made available by ONFP, which indicate the percentage for the same years to be 34.1 percent and 49.8 percent, respectively (République Tunisienne, 2001).

Health care has become more widely available in Tunisia over the past ten years. The World Health Organization estimates that 90 percent of Tunisians have access to health care services and the percentage of the governmental budget spent on health care is increasing as well. Tunisia has not experienced an HIV/AIDS crisis of the kind and magnitude encountered by its African neighbors. This is likely to be due to a combination of factors such as the promotion of contraceptive use, a well-developed health care system, and social norms that prohibit sex outside of marriage.

Although continually on the rise, the number of reported HIV cases remains low. The "Epidemiological Fact Sheet on HIV/AIDS and Sexually Transmitted Infections," published by UNAIDS and the World Health Organization, estimates that by 1999 there were a total of 543 reported HIV/AIDS cases in Tunisia and provides useful information on those cases. Not surprisingly, the rate of infection was significantly higher in urban areas than in rural areas, and the majority of the infected population was between the ages of 25 and 34. Males constituted the vast majority of the infected population, with 429 cases reported in comparison to 112 for women. Among the 429 men, 40.3 percent thought that the use of shared drug needles was responsible for the infection, whereas 28 percent blamed sexual intercourse. Among the 112 women, 54.4 percent reported sexual contact as the cause of infection, whereas only 9.8 percent blamed the use of drug needles. The second leading method of HIV transmission among women is blood transfusion, with 17 percent of the total.

The Tunisian government has been working with the United Nations and the World Health Organization to develop health centers to treat HIV/AIDS patients and to provide counseling for infected patients and their families. The government has been setting up clinics across the country to educate the population about the spread of HIV and methods of prevention. The Red Cross/Red Crescent program has also developed programs to educate Tunisians about HIV/AIDS prevention and to improve home health care for HIV/AIDS patients (International Federation of Red Cross and Red Crescent Societies, 2002).

In sum, several government policies have converged to provide Tunisians with greater access to health care and family planning. The development of contraception in particular has combined with broader economic and political processes to result in smaller family size. Evidence suggests, however, that extended kinship ties remain important in social life despite the general decrease in the size of households.

CONCLUSION

Historically, the institution of the family has been at the center of the social fabric of Tunisian society, as it has been on most of the African continent and in the Arab world. Legal reforms, migration, and urbanization among other factors have brought about transformations to which families had to adapt. Distinctive of Tunisia, relative to other countries of the Maghrib, are the family law reforms that started in the mid-1950s in the aftermath of colonization. The French colonial state present in Tunisia from 1881 to 1956 did not alter Islamic family law and the nationalists waited until the end of colonial rule to implement reforms within a context of national sovereignty. The reforms of the mid-1950s sanctioned a nuclear model of the family in contrast to the extended kinship model that was prevalent in the Islamic legislation that existed in Tunisia before the reforms. The chapter highlighted the main phases in family law reform and traced the development of the Tunisian state that made reform possible in the 1950s and again in the early 1990s.

Other developments, such as migration to urban areas in the 1970s and 1980s, have added to the pressures toward the development of nuclear households. Family size has decreased considerably in the last three decades as a result of several concurrent processes. Legislation was enacted to encourage smaller families at the same time that actions were taken to provide access to contraception in order to reduce fertility. Success in reducing family size can be attributed in part to the government's initiatives to make family planning programs and contraception widely available to women in rural areas as well as in urban centers. This combined with other factors such as increase in age at marriage, educational opportunities, migration, and urbanization.

However, the broader social changes that have occurred in the past half-century of Tunisian history have not eliminated the significance of extended kinship networks in the lives of most Tunisians. Kin groupings, which once were a political force to be counted on, have lost their power as overt agents of collective political action and are no longer relevant in the main struggles of national politics. But extended kinship has not disappeared as a family pattern. The level of interaction with extended kin remains high despite the increasing prevalence of nuclear households. It is the dominant form of social interaction even for women living in urban areas. Despite the changes that they made in response to a changing environment, families in Tunisia have also shown remarkable continuity in their relations with kin. In discussing transformations in family patterns in countries like Tunisia, it is thus important to pay attention not only to new forms but also to the structures that have endured in the face of social change.

REFERENCES

Anderson, L. (1986). *The state and social transformation in Tunisia and Libya, 1830–1980*. Princeton, NJ: Princeton University Press.

Barakat, H. (1985). The Arab family and the challenge of social transformation. In Fernea, E. W. (Ed.), *Women and the family in the Middle East* (pp. 27–48). Austin: University of Texas Press.

Ben Mrad, M. al-Salih. (n.d.). *Al-Hiddad ala Mra'at al-Haddad (The shroud of mourning thrown on al-Haddad's woman)*. Tunis: Imprimerie Tunisienne.

Ben Salem, L. (1990). Structures familiales et changement social en Tunisie. *Revue Tunisienne de Sciences Sociales 27(100)*, 165–79.

Ben Salem, B. (1992). Introduction à l'analyse de la parenté et de l'alliance dans les sociétés Arabo-Musulmanes. In Ferchiou, S. (Ed.), *Hasab wa Nasab: Parenté, Alliance et Patrimoine en Tunisie* (pp. 79–104). Paris: Editions du Centre National de la Recherche Scientifique.

Bessis, S., & Belhassen, S. (1992). *Femmes du Maghreb: L'Enjeu*. Tunis: Ceres Productions.

Bodman, H. L., & Tohidi, N. (Eds.). (1998). *Women in Muslim societies: Diversity within unity*. Boulder, CO: Lynne Rienner.

Borowiec, A. (1998). *Modern Tunisia: A democratic apprenticeship*. Westport, CT: Praeger.

Borrmans, M. (1977). *Statut personnel et famille au Maghreb de 1940 a nos jours*. Paris and The Hague: Mouton.

Bourguiba, H. (1929, January). Le Voile (The Veil). *L'Etendard Tunisien*. Archives of the National Documentation Center, Tunis.

Bourguiba, H. (1978). *Citations*. Tunis: Editions Dar el Amal.

Bourguiba, H. (1981). *Discours. Vol. XXIV, 1974–1981*. Tunis: Publications du Ministère de l'Information.

Bourqia, R., Charrad, M. M., & Gallagher, N. (Eds.). (1996). *Femmes, culture, et societè au Maghreb*. Vols. 1 and 2. Rabat, Morocco: Afrique Orient.

Brand, L. A. (1998). *Women, the state, and political liberalization: Middle Eastern and North African experiences.* New York: Columbia University Press.

Chamari, A. C. (1991). *La femme et la loi en Tunisie.* Casablanca: United Nations University and Editions le Fennec.

Charrad, M. M. (1990). State and gender in the Maghrib. *Middle East Report 20(2)*, 19–24. Updated and reprinted from *Middle East Report*, March-April, 1990, in Joseph, S. & Slyomovics, S. (Eds.), *Women and Power in the Middle East*, Philadelphia: University of Pennsylvania Press, 2001.

Charrad, M. M. (1994). Repudiation versus divorce: Responses to state policy in Tunisia. In Chow, E. N. & Berheide, C. W. (Eds.), *Women, the family and policy: A global perspective* (pp. 51–69). Albany: State University of New York Press.

Charrad, M. M. (1997, Summer). Policy shifts: State, Islam and gender in Tunisia, 1930s–1990s. *Social Politics 4(2)*, 284–319.

Charrad, M. M. (2000). Becoming a citizen: Lineage versus individual in Morocco and Tunisia. In Joseph, S. (Ed.), *Gender and citizenship in the Middle East* (pp. 70–87). Syracuse, NY: Syracuse University Press.

Charrad, M. M. (2001). *States and women's rights: The making of postcolonial Tunisia, Algeria and Morocco.* Berkeley and Los Angeles: University of California Press.

Chater, S. (1978). *La femme Tunisienne: Citoyenne ou sujet.* Tunis: Maison Tunisienne de l'Edition.

Chater, S. (1992). *Les émancipées du harem: Regard sur la femme Tunisienne.* Tunis: Edition La Presse.

Cochrane, S. H., & Guilkey, D. K. (1995, July). The effects of fertility intentions and access to services on contraceptive use in Tunisia. *Economic Development and Social Change 43(4)*, 779–802.

Courbage, Y. (1995). Fertility transitions in the Mashriq and the Maghrib. In Makhlouf Obermeyer, C. (Ed.), *Family, gender, and population in the Middle East* (pp. 80–104). Cairo: American University in Cairo Press.

CREDIF (Centre de Recherche, de Documentation, et d'Information sur la Femme). (1994). *Femmes de Tunisie: Situation et perspectives.* Tunis: Ministère de la Femme et de la Famille, République Tunisienne.

Ferchiou, S. (Ed.). (1992). *Hasab wa Nasab: Parenté, alliance et patrimoine en Tunisie.* Paris: Editions du Centre National de la Recherche Scientifique.

Fernea, E. W. (Ed.) (1985). *Women and the family in the Middle East: New voices of change.* Austin: University of Texas Press.

Haddad, T. (1930). *Imra'atuna fi l-sari'a tua-1-mugtania (Women in law and society).* Tunis: al-Math al Fanniyya.

Hermassi, E. (1972). *Leadership and national development in North Africa.* Berkeley: University of California Press.

Holmes-Eber, P. (1997). Migration, urbanization, and women's kin networks in Tunis. *Journal of Comparative Family Studies 28(2)*, 54–62.

Holmes-Eber, P. (2003). *Daughters of Tunis.* Boulder, CO: Westview.

International Federation of Red Cross and Red Crescent Societies. (2002). http://www.ifrc.org/. Date retrieved: June 15, 2005.

Joseph, S. (Ed.), (2000). *Gender and citizenship in the Middle East.* Syracuse, NY: Syracuse University Press.

Joseph, S., & Slyomovics, S. (Eds.). (2001). *Women and power in the Middle East.* Philadelphia: University of Pennsylvania Press.

Khalil, K., & Myntti, C. (1995). Target setting in family planning programs: Controversies and challenges. In Obermeyer, C. M. (Ed.), *Family, gender, and population in the Middle East* (pp. 199–215). Cairo: American University in Cairo Press.

La Presse (Tunisia). (1993, July 8). Nouveaux Amendements du CSP: L'erEre nouvelle de la femme Tunisienne.

Obermeyer, C. M. (1993, November/December). Culture, maternal health care, and women's status: A comparison of Morocco and Tunisia. *Studies in Family Planning 24(6)*, 354–365.

Population Reference Bureau. (2002). *Women of our world*. http://www.prb.org. Date retrieved: June 15, 2005.

République Tunisienne, Institut National de la Statistique (INS). (1991). *Code du Statut Personnel (Code of Personal Status)*. Tunis: Imprimerie Officielle. First promulgated on August 13, 1956; periodically updated.

République Tunisienne, Institut National de la Statistique (INS). (1998). *Code du Travail*. Tunis: Imprimerie Officielle de la République Tunisienne.

République Tunisienne, Institut National de la Statistique (INS). (2001). *Statistiques economiques et sociales de la Tunisie*. http://www.ins.nat.tn. Date retrieved: June 15, 2005.

Riza, R. (1991). Ensemble pour preserver les acquis de la nation. *Femme* (published by the National Union of Tunisian Women), No. 63.

Tunisian External Communication Agency, & National Union of Tunisian Women. (1993). *Women of Tunisia: Their struggle and their gains*. Tunis.

World Health Organization. (2004). *Epidemiological fact sheet on HIV/AIDS and sexually transmitted infections*. http://www.who.int/hiv/pub/epidemiology/pubfacts/en/. Date retrieved: June 15, 2005.

World Bank. (2001). *Gender profile*. http://www.worldbank.org. Date retrieved: June 15, 2005.

CHAPTER 3

Diversity and Family: Examples from Egypt

Bahira Sherif-Trask

INTRODUCTION

In contemporary Egypt, the family remains a central institution despite class and regional differences. Most people live with or near their natal families, and extended families are in constant contact either through face-to-face meetings, telephone conversations, or among the well-to-do, e-mail. Egypt provides a fascinating case study when examining the relationship between family issues and diversity due to its location in the northeast corner of Africa. Its location at a geographic crossroads, in conjunction with historical events during various periods of colonization, has led to a unique blend of influences from the West, the Arab Middle East, other North African countries, and sub-Saharan Africa. Egypt maintains a unique sense of identity despite a growing fundamentalist Islamist movement that calls for greater identification with the Muslim world. Egyptian roots are in part Arab, Berber, and Islamic as well as Nubian and Coptic. It is this cultural mix that distinguishes Egypt from the other societies in North Africa and the central Middle East. Further complicating the picture are the influences of globalization and Westernization which increasingly affect all Egyptian families as well as families throughout Africa. For example, an increasing number of women are working outside the home in contradiction to fundamentalist voices that advocate a return to more "traditional" roles. Despite such controversies, most Egyptians still feel that family provides for their security in an increasingly unfamiliar world.

Also known as the Arab Republic of Egypt or Jumhuriyat Misr al-Arabiyah, Egypt has an estimated population of 66,050,004, with 36.1 percent of the population under age 15, 60 percent between ages 15 and 65, and 3.7 percent over age 65. Forty-five percent of Egyptians live in cities, many in poverty and slums. Cairo (El-Qahira) has an estimated population of 9,690,000 and Alexandria (El-Iskandriyah), 3,584,000. Ethnically, 99 percent of Egyptians are of Eastern Hamitic stock or Bedouin (Berber). Ninety-four percent of Egyptians are Muslim, mostly Sunni, with the remaining 6 percent Coptic Christian and other religions. The official language is Arabic, although French and English are widely understood by the educated classes. The average life expectancy (2000 estimate) is 60.1 for males and 64.1 for females. The birthrate in 2000 was 27 per 1,000 population; the death rate, 8 per 1,000; and the infant mortality rate, 69 per 1,000, for an annual natural increase of 1.89 percent. The 1995 total fertility rate (TFR) was 3.4 children per fertile woman, giving Egypt a rank of 89 out of 227 nations. Five years of education are compulsory between ages 6 and 13. Literacy in 1995 was estimated at 50 percent. Egypt is a republic with a legal system based on English common law, Islamic law, and Napoleonic codes.

Egypt is located in the northeastern corner of Africa and includes a small Asian peninsula between the Middle East and northern Africa called the Sinai. Almost all of Egypt is arid, desolate and barren, with hills and mountains in the east and along the Nile River. The Nile River and its fertile valley, where most Egyptians live, stretches 550 miles from the eastern Mediterranean Sea south into the Sudan. Three percent of the land is arable and 2 percent is devoted to permanent crops; 2 percent of the land is irrigated. This lack of useable land combined with a burgeoning population puts Egypt at a great risk for economic problems.

HISTORICAL BACKGROUND

Around 5000 BCE, civilization was born in the fertile valleys of the Nile, Indus, and Tigres/Euphrates Rivers. About 3200 BCE, King Menes established the first of many dynasties of Pharaohs that unified the country from the Nile Delta to Upper Egypt, producing a distinctive ancient civilization of great wealth and cultural brilliance, built on an economic base of serfdom, fertile soil, and annual flooding of the Nile Valley.

The decline of ancient imperial power facilitated the conquest of Egypt by Asian invaders, the Hyksos and Assyrians. The last Pharonic dynasty was overthrown by the Persians in 341 BCE. Alexandrian and Ptolemaic Greek dynasties then replaced the Persians, who were in turn replaced by the Roman Empire. Egypt was part of the Byzantine Empire from the 3rd to the 7th centuries of the common era, when it was conquered by Arab invaders who introduced the Muslim religion and Arab language.

Notable in Egyptian history is the Nubian civilization—one of the oldest and greatest civilizations in Africa. The Nubians, who were at one time Christian, stayed in power until approximately the 13th century. They were credited with defeating the Muslims and stopping the spread of Islam beyond Aswan until the conquest of the Sudan in the 1820s by Muhammad Ali. After the collapse of the last Nubian Kingdom in 1900, the Nubians converted to Islam and adopted the Arabic language. Since then Nubian identity in Egypt has been suppressed. However, even today, their dress, traditions, and indigenous language set them apart from non-Nubian Egyptians (http://I-cias.com/e.o./nubians.htm).

For the purpose of this volume it is important to note that the Christian Copts also have a long history in Egypt. Estimated at about 9 million currently, the Copts are fully integrated in contemporary Egyptian society but pride themselves on having maintained a strong religious identity in a primarily Islamic state. The ancient Egyptian language is still used in the Christian Coptic liturgy. For 400 years after the Arab conquest, Egypt remained a Christian Coptic country (www.coptic.net/EncyclopediaCoptica). Around 1250 the Mamelukes, a military caste of Caucasian origin, conquered Egypt, replacing Arab control. However, in 1517, the Turks defeated the Mamelukes and Egypt became part of the Ottoman Empire until 1798. The Mamelukes ruled Egypt in the name of a distant Turkish ruler.

In 1798, Egypt was invaded by the armies of Napoléon which crushed the Mamelukes and occupied Cairo. Napoléon's aim to block British trade routes to India and to establish a Francophone society in Egypt was ultimately unsuccessful. Nevertheless, the Napoleonic invasion of Egypt had profound repercussions for the Arab and Muslim world which continue to influence the region's political and social development. This was the first European conquest of a major Arab country in the history of Islam and it signaled the rapid decline of Islam as a world political power. Some analysts even trace contemporary Muslim fundamentalism to this initial shattering defeat.

The French occupation destabilized Egypt and the defeat and withdrawal of the French left the country vulnerable to an internal political struggle which was won by Muhammed Ali, an Albanian lieutenant in the Ottoman army who set about modernizing the economic and educational structure of Egypt. However, the modernization ultimately put Egypt heavily into debt and the end of the American Civil War, with the resumption of American cotton production, initiated a major recession in Egypt's cotton industry. As a result of the economic crisis the British began to assume greater control over the country.

The Suez Canal, built by a French corporation from 1859 to 1869, was taken over by the British in 1875. After the British Empire expanded into East Africa and the Sudan, the British established de facto rule in Egypt in 1882, although the country remained a nominal part of the Ottoman Empire until 1914. Egypt became a British protectorate in 1914, and a League of Nations mandate in 1922. The autonomy of the Egyptian monarchy was strengthened by the Anglo-Egyptian treaty in 1936, though Great Britain continued its military presence in Egypt and its control of the Sudan.

After the heavy fighting of World War II, a growing nationalist movement led Egypt to abrogate the 1936 treaty in 1951. A military uprising the following year forced King Farouk to abdicate. Farouk was succeeded by Gamal Abdel Nasser who assumed leadership when Egypt declared itself a republic. British troops were withdrawn from the Suez Canal Zone in June 1956 and the following month Egypt nationalized the canal. At the end of October, Israel invaded the Sinai peninsula, and French and British forces came to Israel's aid. United Nations intervention maintained the peace between 1957 and 1967. Egyptian incursions into the Gaza Strip in June 1967 led to a full-scale war that continued through 1970 when Nassar died and was succeeded by Anwar al-Sadat. In October 1973, Egyptian forces crossed the Suez Canal and attacked Israeli positions. Eighteen days later, the Yom Kippur War ended in a cease-fire. Meanwhile, Soviet influence had risen with Russian contributions to the Aswan High Dam, and then waned.

In 1974, Sadat's government became increasingly friendly to the West and American investment and relationships between Egypt and Israel improved. Sadat's economic Open Door Policy encouraged, in particular, the private sector to increase the productive capacity of the economy. However, as the government withdrew its commitment to guarantee employment to all college graduates, unemployment increased. In particular, women were affected by this policy. Though there had been a growing expectation in the 1960s that women would increasingly enter the labor force, the Open Door Policy surprisingly worked against this expectation. The national dialogue about women's work started to shift and the definition of women as primarily playing a role in the domestic arena gained ground. Justifying ideologies based on sexual division of roles began to appear, supported by the newly emerging Islamic fundamentalist groups that advocated that women's place was in the home (el-Baz, 1997, p. 149). Further, a provision was added to Article Eleven of the 1971 constitution which declared the state's commitment to help reconcile women's family obligations and their equality to men in the public sphere. The provision stated, "provided that this did not infringe on the rules of the Islamic Shari'a." The new constitution represented an important divergence from the secular discourse of the 1960s and created opportunities for Islamic groups to oppose women's rights on the grounds that they were in opposition to Islamic principles (Hatem, 1992, p. 241).

Throughout the 1980s, the Open Door Policy became increasingly institutionalized. While this policy has been relatively successful on a macro level, it has had negative consequences for the more vulnerable sectors of society, namely the poor, and specifically poor women and their children (el-Baz, 1997, p. 149). As key resources, such as health care and education, have become more scarce, it is lower-class women and children who are least likely to have access to them. Also affected by the economic restructuring are individuals who would previously have been classified as middle class, namely civil servants and unemployed graduates.

While the pressures and tensions of a rapidly changing world in the last half of the 20th century have affected all the nations and peoples of the world, these tensions have been more obvious in the Islamic nations of North Africa, the Middle East, and Southeast Asia. In particular, the growing Islamic fundamentalist movement symbolizes the tensions and conflicts between Western and indigenous traditions and beliefs. Further, in Egypt, this movement has centered much of its dialogue around the "appropriate" roles for women in society. Gender issues, thus, constitute a principal mechanism for understanding issues of marriage and family. As can be seen from this brief overview of Egyptian history, family life in Egypt is characterized by a pervasive influence of Western, African, and Islamic beliefs. All of these interact in a complex manner that is often oversimplified in representations of family and gender roles as purely "Islamic" or "North African" or "Arab." Furthermore, this representation implies that issues pertaining to family and gender roles are static and that individuals lack the power of agency, and are as such the victims of culture and religion. As will be seen, this representation is far from correct.

Religion, Nationalism, and Gender Issues

Within the context of contemporary postcolonial Egypt, women maintain their role as a crucial symbol of the cultural integrity of dominant ideological beliefs. These beliefs are supported and perpetuated by the dominant voices of religious figures who espouse the importance for women of all classes to be first and foremost wives and mothers. These messages pervade the public media and are found at all levels of society. To earn status all women are supposed to marry and reproduce. Legally, their husbands control their ability to work or travel and hold unilateral rights of divorce. Children belong to the husband's family and may be lost to the mother in the case of divorce. Family honor and reputation or, conversely, shame rest mainly on the public behavior of women, thereby reinforcing a high degree of sex segregation in the society. Nonetheless, in contemporary Egypt, these ideals are often at odds with both women's actual experiences and their aspirations and desires. Through increased access to education, more and more women are receiving the chance to earn their own income and are thus wielding more formalized power in their families. Meanwhile, by retaining their traditional informal access to power through strong same-sex associations, women are also increasingly becoming aware of their legal rights. Their position is thus strengthened both within families and in particular vis-à-vis their husbands.

By embracing both modern and traditional manners, women actively and passively manipulate cultural symbols as forms of resistance to dominant male-privileged discourses. One example can be found in the highly politicized issue of the urban, educated woman's return to veiling in contemporary Cairo. The hijab, the wearing of a head veil and loose-fitting clothing, has come to symbolize distinct gender roles in an "orderly" Islamic society. Thus, in the ideological struggles surrounding the definition of Islam's place in the modern world, the hijab has acquired the status of a modern "cultural symbol." This explains, at least in part, the willingness of many younger and older women to adopt these new forms of Islamic dress, thereby covering themselves both in religiosity and modernity.

Islamic Law versus Personal Status Law

In order to understand the social and legal status of women and children in relation to men it is necessary to include a short discussion of this topic with respect to Islamic law, the Personal Status Law, and cultural conceptualizations of men and women. All of these factors come together in a complex, constantly shifting dynamic.

Differences between men and women are readily apparent in several aspects of Islamic law. Islamic law accords certain rights and capacities to both men and women. A Muslim's legal capacity (*ahliyyat*) begins at birth and ends with death (Schacht, 1964, p. 124). A Muslim male's legal responsibilities are assumed under his legal capacity and are distinguished as a "capacity of execution" and a "capacity of obligations." A free Muslim man who is sane and considered an adult has the highest degree of legal capacity. A Muslim woman, even though she has certain rights, generally has half the legal capacity of a man. This difference only becomes apparent when men and women reach adulthood.

According to the point of view of Islamic law, an adult male is a "legally and morally responsible person, one who has reached physical maturity, is of sound mind, may enter into contracts, dispose of property, and be subject to criminal law. Above all, he is responsible for the religious commands and obligations of Islam" (Lapidus, 1976, p. 93). When a Muslim man reaches maturity, his legal capacity becomes complete; neither his age nor marital status influences his legal rights, responsibilities, or capacity of execution.

A Muslim woman's legal identity also begins at birth, but in contrast to men, her legal capacity and status undergo various changes throughout her life cycle. For a woman, her legal coming of age and her achievement of physical maturity do not necessarily coincide. She is a ward of her father or guardian as a child and, as an adult, is restricted in legal decision making. Her legal persona and social status depend on the state of her sexual status—whether she is a virgin, married, divorced, or widowed. At different times in a woman's life she is treated differently *both* by the law and by the society. Socially and legally, the young woman (*shabba*) is the focus of a great deal of protection, and her freedom of movement is limited. In contrast, an old woman (*'aguza*) is able to move with much greater ease, and may also move in places and participate in situations where the young woman is forbidden even to enter. It is therefore very important to emphasize the fundamental difference between the stability of mature men's status under the law versus the changing nature of women's status (Waines, 1982, pp. 652–653). This legal difference pervades and shapes the lives of women all over the Islamic world.

A discussion of family in Egypt would be incomplete without the mention of the Personal Status Law (PSL), or family law, which is based on and derived from the Shari'a. All aspects of family life, gender relations, and inheritance are governed by the PSL. It is important to point out that attempts to reform the codified family law have become a political issue in the last two decades in all countries, including Egypt, which have retained this part of the Shari'a (Botman, 1999). Egypt follows the Hanafi school of Shari'a law according to which the husband is in charge of financially supporting his wife and children. In return, he is authorized to restrict his wife's movements, confine her activities, and make decisions on her behalf. For her part, the wife must care for her spouse and children and must obey her husband (Botman, 1999, p. 48). An understanding of the PSL is important because the law reflects and defines the patriarchal structure of the society, institutionalizes inequality in the family, and is used by men to validate their domination over women.

Existing side by side, and sometimes in contradiction to the reality of women's daily lives in Egypt, is the societal and religious ideal of complementarity between the sexes. Within this concept, women are not to be considered inherently lesser in value than men or lacking in ability. Instead, men, women, and children are conceptualized as being part of an interrelated community, each contributing equally by properly playing their part. Most Egyptian women and men believe that gender complementarity is part of the message of the Quran and *hadith* and needs to be maintained in order for society to be viable.

CONCEPTUALIZATION OF EGYPTIAN FAMILIES

In contemporary Egypt, family remains the central and most important institution to most people. Few individuals live separately from their immediate family or kin. Single-person households are viewed with great concern and are virtually nonexistent. The importance of family within the community and the nation is a topic of constant discussion in the popular media, among religious figures, and in all sectors of the society. Intergenerational family relations and gender roles provide the basis for many television shows and movies, and are part of a larger more pervasive dialogue about national identity and the effects of globalization and Westernization on Egyptian families. Further, the importance of maintaining "traditional" roles in families is part of a fundamentalist, Islamist dialogue that is increasingly heard in all sectors of the society.

While "family" plays a central role in the lives of Egyptians, it is interesting to note that, linguistically, there is much ambiguity when it comes to defining what a family is. When referring to their families, Egyptians usually use the Arabic word *ahl*, a broad term that encompasses various relationships including immediate family related through blood ties, members of the household, individuals related through marriage, and so on. This concept can refer to anywhere up to 100–200 people. Another word, *a'ila*, is also commonly used, and can refer to either a nuclear or extended group of people, depending on context. The term *a'ila* carries with it the connotation of close relationships and mutual obligation.

The smallest family unit specified by an Egyptian term is *bait*, which means "house." *Bait* is used to denote the actual residence of a family or the group of people who live under the same roof most of the time. While this term primarily refers to the nuclear family, it can also include a spinster aunt, a widowed parent, or any other member of the extended family who is a part of the residential group. This ambiguity in Egyptian family terminology stands in contrast to other North African countries where there are at times strong ties between language and genealogy.

The Egyptian linguistic vagueness about kinship terms allows individuals to manipulate the concept of family to fit in their context and situation. By constantly referring to family and family name, individuals are able to rank one another within the society and to identify important ties and reciprocal obligations. The honor, social standing, and wealth of a family are all interconnected, making the identification with family a primary social marker for every Egyptian. This tie between family and social relationship is very characteristic of many African societies where the link between an individual and his or her family is perceived as the key to identity and social class.

Social Class in Egypt

Social stratification is a crucial aspect of Egyptian society. Egyptians have an incredibly fine-tuned sense of class, and this plays a role in every aspect of people's lives. Most of these divisions are based on family, wealth, education, and experiences and/or education abroad. In addition, regionality, reputation, religious piety, and foreign ancestry (for example, having a foreign-born mother, grandmother, etc.) may raise a family's social status in the eyes of others. The division by class is a distinctive but complex dividing line in the society that is constantly reflected in the written and oral media. Furthermore, there are major distinctions between those individuals who trace their roots to either upper (southern Egypt) or lower Egypt (the Nile Delta region), as well as rural versus urban areas.

Complicating the picture about class is that even though the major cities of Cairo and Alexandria are divided into newer and older as well as richer and poorer sections, it is not customary for Egyptians to move, even if their financial situation improves substantially. As a result, older, well-to-do Egyptians are often found living in sections of the city that, today, are considered middle class or, at times, even lower-middle class. Among these families, it is common for the older generation to buy apartments in their buildings for their children as they marry, thereby keeping their offspring in proximity. In low-income communities, it is not uncommon for all family members to keep living in the same apartment and as the children marry, for their spouses to move in with the extended families. Among this group, individuals rely even more heavily on their families since they have fewer ties to other structures of power in the society. In rural areas, villages often are dominated by just a couple of extended families and migration to an urban area means the exodus of a relatively large group of individuals.

The Role of Family in Individual Lives

In urban and rural areas the importance of family for women and men remains central to their lives. Though upon marriage women become incorporated into the household of their husbands, they remain members of their birth families for life. Women retain their fathers' family names after marriage and, in case of divorce or widowhood, are expected to move back to their natal home. According to both Islamic law and social tradition, men bear the financial responsibility of caring for all single women in their families, even if these women are widowed or divorced. This tradition allows women to feel that their primary kinship ties and their safest source of economic security will be in their relationships to their fathers, brothers, and sons. These relationships with both female and male members of the immediate family remain the strongest links in women's lives. This sense of communal responsibility is a feature of Egyptian society that may have its roots in older sub-Saharan African traditions that stress the role of the group in protecting the individual.

For most Egyptians some version of the extended family still plays a crucial role in their day-to-day existence (Macleod, 1991, p. 37). Contrary to modernization theory with respect to family development, extended families have not lost their appeal or importance. Most people attempt to live near their parents, siblings, cousins, or grandparents, should they still be alive, and maintain an active relationship with many of their relatives. It is important to note that extended family households which are often found in Egypt do not follow the traditional patterns in which genealogically related persons of two generations live together or in which married siblings form one household. Rather, extended families are based on the incorporation of unmarried relatives into a family. Widows, divorcees (especially those with no children), and bachelors do not live separately and would be stigmatized should they make this choice. Further, unmarried sons or daughters live with their parents until marriage, irrespective of age. After divorce or the death of a spouse, both men and women, especially if they do not have children, are expected to return to their parents if they are still alive; otherwise they are supposed to live with a brother, sister, or other relative. Another popular extended family pattern is the one in which a child is "borrowed" by a relative with no children of his or her own. Among lower-class people one tends to find this phenomenon more often among grandparents who need the assistance of a child for housework. Among more well-to-do families, an uncle or aunt will offer to take care of a sibling's children for an extended time period, primarily for sentimental reasons or because the biological parents already have other pressing obligations such as an extended leave abroad.

Another common middle- and lower-class family pattern found in Egypt is the incorporation of nonrelatives, such as apprentices and work assistants, into a particular household. Such individuals have a special position, because even though not all of them sleep in the house of their employer, their food and laundry is part of the household. Upper-middle- and upper-class families are characterized by the presence of domestic servants who may or may not live in the household. Often domestic live-in servants will come from the family's natal village, even if the family has not lived there in several generations.

Migrants, an often ignored group in studies on Egyptian families, exhibit an alternative family pattern: they do not usually bring their families when they first enter the city from the countryside. When migrants arrive in the city, they tend to live in the same neighborhoods as others from their original natal village. Often men will come alone and each will live with other relatives in a local neighborhood until he becomes financially independent and acquires a house of his own. Once firmly established, he will send for wife, his children, and potentially other relatives to join him.

The continuing primacy of extended families can be explained by the fact that for most Egyptians, family provides a sense of emotional, physical, and social security. Egyptians are often puzzled by social relationships in the West, which they see as lonely and self-centered. Household composition may vary over time, but the ideology of the importance of family and what family relationships mean in the life of an individual remain crucial for the resources and sense of identity they continue to provide.

MODERNIZATION, URBANIZATION, AND FAMILY STABILITY

As in most African and developing societies, modernization and urbanization are playing a profound role in the lives of individuals and their families. Urban areas are expanding at a rapid rate, causing overcrowding, transportation issues, and housing problems. Nonetheless, urban areas continue to grow in significance in Egypt. In particular, rural families in Egypt are affected by this phenomenon. The economic draw of large urban areas often encourages men to leave their families and move to cities to find work. A sizeable number of middle-class urban families are currently experiencing a similar phenomenon as men go to other wealthier Middle Eastern countries to find work at higher wages. In both cases, the men then send their earnings back home to their families. Actual contact between spouses is limited to once or twice a year, leaving child rearing to the wives and the larger extended family.

Another significant phenomenon is that increasingly women are working outside of the home in order to supplement the family income. While this has already been discussed, it is important to note that this is happening at all levels of the society, and is not limited to poor or rural areas as in the past.

The HIV/AIDS Crisis and Family Health

Despite worldwide increases in the HIV/AIDS epidemic, so far the disease has not spread significantly in Egypt. Nonetheless, factors that contribute to the spread of HIV/AIDS definitely exist and anecdotal evidence suggests that other sexually transmitted diseases are widespread in the general population. According to UN statistics, North Africa and the Middle East account for less than 1 percent of the total number of people infected worldwide with HIV/AIDS. In this region, 27,000 people have died from HIV-related illnesses compared to 170,000 in Europe and 46 million in sub-Saharan Africa.

The National AIDS Program in Egypt recently published the number of units of blood that have tested positive for HIV/AIDS in each of the last seven years. The prevalence of infection is low and there is no real evidence of an upward trend. For example, in 1990, 136,422 blood units were tested and only 4 were positive for HIV; in 1996, a quarter of million units were tested and only 3 were positive (Lenton, 1997, p. 1005). The data from blood donations is particularly interesting because all blood collected in Egypt's public-health facilities is voluntarily donated by family members of patients. There is no evidence of either voluntary or nonvoluntary donor deferral. Egypt's medical surveillance of blood units is, therefore, a good indicator of the prevalence of HIV/AIDS in the adult population.

However, reliable survey data is not available. Egyptian medical experts claim that the negligible spread of HIV infection and AIDS in the general population is possibly the result of the Islamic moral code that forbids adultery, sex before marriage, and homosexual practices. This indicates that widespread adherence to this code could mean that while HIV infection occurs in small groups practicing sexual behaviors that increase their chance of infection, only rarely do individuals in the general population come into contact with at-risk individuals. Nonetheless, research into patterns of sexuality is needed in order to explain the low prevalence of HIV/AIDS in Egypt. Also, the lack of reliable data makes it difficult to gauge the real situation from the picture presented by official sources.

Family Claims and Property Rights

Due to the predominance of the Personal Status Law, family inheritance is determined by a complex set of rules that fundamentally allow only family members to inherit property. Under the law men inherit twice as much as women. Though this issue is often pointed to in Western literature as an example of patriarchal domination over women, it is important to note that men are legally obligated to take care of the larger extended family while women retain their wealth for themselves.

WHAT DO WE KNOW ABOUT FAMILY RESEARCH IN EGYPT

While it is generally common knowledge that the family plays a vital and fundamental role in structuring social relations within Islamic societies, there is an astonishing lack of scholarship on this institution. Tucker (1993a) expresses this in the following way:

The importance of the family to the daily construction of gender roles and relations is never questioned. We actually know, however, very little about the ongoing evolution of the family in any specific context. There has been a tendency to assume the existence of a "traditional" family, a family defined and regulated by Islamic law, that has remained unchanged throughout the centuries. (p. xv)

Until very recently, studies of the family in North African and Middle Eastern societies have been disadvantaged by the unproven assumption that the family in this part of the world is an institution, which can be termed interchangeably as either the "Arab" family, the "Islamic" family, or the "oriental" family (as most commonly cited from Barakat, 1985). This family is usually characterized in opposition to its Western European counterpart: It is supposed that the institution of family in North Africa and the Middle East has not undergone the significant structural transformations that are associated with the rise of capitalism in the West, nor has it been the object of "modernization" that promoted individualism at the expense of family control (Tucker, 1993b, p. 195). Furthermore, North African families are often subsumed under the study of Islamic or Middle Eastern families with no recognition of the diversity that exists just in this area alone.

The scarcity of studies dealing with North African families stands in direct contrast to recent scholarly interest in the institution of American and European families. While studies of patterns and dynamics of European families are flourishing, the same cannot be said of studies dealing with Islamic families, families in North Africa and the Middle East, or families in the developing world in general. Earlier studies of families emphasized social practice and more contemporary studies have been, until lately, slow to develop. It is important to note that of the North African societies Egypt is probably the most widely studied country with respect to family issues.

The field of North African and Middle Eastern family studies can be roughly divided into two intersecting areas: (1) studies that deal explicitly with the concept of the family in Islam; and (2) ethnographies that concentrate on social practice. Those studies that focus on the supposedly "Islamic" family have become exclusively the focus of Muslim researchers bent on defending their faith against perceived Western imperialistic threats to their social order. These works often do not acknowledge religious variation or interpretation. Instead, they deal with Islam as a unified body of dogma devoid of popular practice. These works have fallen prey to the Orientalist notion that Islam is about texts, rather than people (Said, 1978, p. 305). On the other hand, until very recently, those studies that focused specifically on social practice have tended to ignore the dynamic relationship between individuals, social processes, and ideologies. Even so, the ethnographic evidence in these studies indicates that far from being unvarying institutions, Middle Eastern families change in size, in composition, and according to historical and social circumstances.

More recently there has been a proliferation of work on Egyptian families in particular. The work of Fernea (1985), Hoodfar (1990), Tucker (1993c), Singerman (1995), and Sherif (1999, 2003) has led to a new interest in issues of family. Tucker examines primarily historical concepts of family and gender, while Fernea emphasizes the multiplicity of voices as women struggle to improve not only their situations but that of their societies as a whole. Hoodfar concentrates on informal economic networks and Singerman on informal political networks of lower-class Egyptian families. Sherif has written on middle- and upper-middle-class Egyptian families, a subject that has not been dealt with in the past. These recent studies are characterized by their specific focus on family relations and the importance of gender relations within the family. This research has identified some of the central tenets of Egyptian families.

Gender Roles

Egyptian society is organized on the principle that men and women simply have different natures, talents, and inherent tendencies. This becomes most apparent in the realm of the family in which each gender has a different part to play. Men are thought to have been created for going out in the world and are responsible for providing financially for the family. Women are perceived as most suited for remaining within family boundaries, caring for the home, the children, and the husband. Further, women's inherent sexuality is believed to constantly endanger the social harmony of society (specifically, men) and is, therefore, best controlled through women's modesty and their remaining as much as possible within the private sphere of the family. This belief is reinforced through cultural and religious norms which increasingly advocate that family roles of both women and men are fundamental in maintaining societal structure; dominant gender constructions therefore support keeping women in the home and oppose women working and abandoning their primary roles (Macleod, 1991, p. 85). Nonetheless, contemporary images of women as economic assets and providers are rapidly coming into conflict with what are perceived as divinely inspired roles.

Gender roles in Egypt derive much of their legitimacy from the Quran. In particular, women are often the focus of quotes that supposedly refer to the appropriate roles and behaviors of women. References to the role of women are scattered broadly throughout the Quran. Some passages focus on women's unique nature, some on women's place in society, and some on women's role within the general congregation of believers.

Verses from the Quran, the *hadith*, or theological arguments about their relevance are often used as empirical data for sociological explanations of a gender hierarchy in which women are subordinate to men (Mernissi, 1987). While it is evident that in Egypt Muslim men and women utilize these sources as part of their hegemonic beliefs, contemporary scholarship has shown that rather than determining attitudes about women, parts of the Quran are only used at certain times or occasions in order to legitimate particular acts or sets of conditions that concern women. The Quran is part of the source from which the gender hierarchy and sexuality are negotiated and enforced. It does not provide an explanation of gender roles; instead, it is part of a constant process of gender role negotiation. While central to Islam, the Quran is neither the only nor the most important source of the beliefs and practices that influence the daily life of Muslim women and men. In particular, globalization and its effects are pervading the lives of Egyptian men and women at all levels of society. Furthermore, for the small percentage of individuals who are not Muslim, social rules with respect to gender parallel the behaviors of Muslims. It is, therefore, false to assert that Islam is the pervasive dogmatic cultural law by which everyone lives.

One of the most controversial and significant developments affecting Egyptian family life is the proliferation of women working outside of the home. Although women have officially had the right to work outside of the home for the last 50 years in Egypt, their actual contributions often go unrecognized and are also increasingly the subject of scathing criticism. Current representations of women's labor tend to be inaccurate because they do not account for unpaid work in agriculture, domestic work, and other participation in informal family enterprises. Further, with a shifting economy and increasing fundamentalist pressures, women in the 1990s again became the focus of controversial debates centering on the roles of men and women in society. However, a wider definition of women's economic activities and a more indicative picture of women's employment in Egypt can be found in the Labour Force Sample Survey (LFSS) of 1988 (el-Baz, 1997, p. 152). According to this survey, women's labor force participation is at 35.4 percent, with rural-urban differences at 32.5 percent and 18.8 percent respectively. Women's economic participation in the government is at 29.5 percent, in other parts of the public sector at 13.1 percent, and in the private sector at 39.3 percent. Women's participation in agriculture, estimated at 53 percent, is greater than men's (CAPMAS, 1990, in el-Baz, 1997, p. 152). Furthermore, women also carry out most household chores, especially in rural areas, and are estimated to work up to 16 to 19 hours per day. Despite these figures, women are not recognized as vital participants in the labor force; therefore, they have limited access to government-sponsored training and educational opportunities.

Given the prevalent ideology of men as breadwinners, unemployment is perceived as a male problem even though statistics are estimated at 10 percent for men and 25 percent for women. Women are thus encouraged to retire early, and current legislation offers women half-time employment for half salary. Additionally, recruitment efforts in the private sector focus on men, and women are often perceived as an economic liability due to maternity leave. In the period from 1976 to 1986, the percent of women employed in the private sector sank from 47 percent to 30 percent. By 1993, between 15 and 20 percent of all Egyptian households were primarily dependent on women's incomes (el-Baz, 1997, p. 153). Nonetheless, increasingly conservative social attitudes advocate that a woman's "natural" role is in the home with her children. The conflict between the public discourse about women and the social and economic realities of their lives is reflected in the lack of social services and public policy provided for them.

Mate Selection

Marriage remains at the center of contemporary Egyptian social life. It is the primary focal point in the lives of both women and men, followed only by the birth of a child. The rights and obligations of husband and wife are defined by Islamic law, the sexual division of labor, and Egyptian cultural practice. The selection of marriage partners is, thus, a central concern for all families. Even though, as has been mentioned, Egypt is primarily an Islamic society, mate selection and the cultural traditions surrounding this practice are quite similar for the Coptic segment of the society.

Mate selection in Egypt is a very carefully supervised process that includes a thorough background check of each prospective family as well as the suitability of the bride and groom. Marriage is perceived as the joining of two units, the families, and not just the private actions of two individuals. Even contemporary versions of "love marriages" are based on this principle. Popular culture such as television and movies, as well as religious teachings, continue to promote this idea. Young people are constantly encouraged to interact with "suitable" (defined by class, family background, and education) friends. Dating is virtually nonexistent but meeting your marriage partner at school or work is becoming increasingly common. A relatively high number of marriages are also still arranged by elderly family relatives who will introduce the young person in question to a potential bride or groom. After several supervised meetings, the young people will be asked if they would like to marry the potential individual. An affirmative answer sets the stage for a whole new set of actions.

Egyptian marriages, across class and regional lines, are characterized by a formalized set of negotiations that begin once the suitability of the marriage partners has been determined. The prelude to the marriage contract is the betrothal, which is the request by the man for the hand of a certain woman in marriage. It is at this point that the potential groom will approach her family with the view of describing his status and negotiating with them the marriage contract and their respective demands. In order for the betrothal to be valid, both parties should be aware of the circumstances of the other and should know the potential spouse's character and behavior. This information is obtained through inquiries, investigations, and the direct contact of the couple in the presence of a chaperon. Once the man's offer is accepted by the woman, or by those who are legally entitled to act on her behalf, the betrothal will have taken place. It is usually at the point of betrothal that the man offers his future bride a gift, which in Egypt is referred to as the *shabka*. In some instances, particularly if the man does not know the bride's family through previous contacts, or if he wants to make an extremely favorable impression on the young woman, the man will offer her the *shabka* before the *khutba* (the actual signing of the marriage contract), thereby showing his good will, his good intentions, and, perhaps, his good financial standing. Some kind of gift is common among all classes and will vary in value. It is important to note that betrothal does not constitute a marriage contract: It is merely a mutual promise of marriage between the two parties, and it is not legally binding for either party. In practice, the *khutba* is easily dissolved. However, this period allows the potential bride and groom, as well as their families, to get to know each other before the actual marriage.

A form of this type of marriage negotiation and celebration is practiced across all classes and regions of the country. Most individuals marry only once in their lifetime and generally consider this step the most important one they will undertake in their lifetime. It is rare to divorce, due to extreme social sanctions against divorced individuals, and even rarer to marry again. This makes the marital choice and negotiation a highly significant event.

The Issue of Polygyny

Whereas until recently polygyny was an important part of certain African societies, that has historically not been true in Egypt. Polygyny is allowed by the Quran; however, it is not practiced by the majority of Egyptians, except in remote rural areas or sometimes among the very wealthy. When practiced, polygyny in the Egyptian case varies somewhat from the form of polygyny that was found in many traditional African societies in which men took multiple wives, all of whom lived and worked together. In conjunction with the Quranic ruling that allows a man up to four wives, and advocates that they must be treated fairly and equally, social sanctions are so strong that if practiced at all, polygyny is usually conducted secretly. The wife may not even know that her husband has another woman to whom he is legally married and the concept of multiple wives living and working together is unheard of. In contrast to the stereotypical Western image of Muslim men with multiple wives, Egyptian men bemoan the difficulties of supporting one wife in today's economy, and strong social sanctions work against their even considering polygyny as a viable option.

Male and female reactions must be understood in light of a 1979 ruling, also known as Jihan's law, so named after Anwar al-Sadat's modernist wife, who introduced a decree outlawing polygyny as an option for men. Considerable debate ensued in the media and among secular and religious elites concerning the Personal Status Law and its relationship to the Shari'a (Islamic law). This amendment was eventually partially abrogated on procedural grounds in 1985. However, in June of that year, a similar law (Law No. 100) amending the 1925 and 1929 laws was enacted and is now the law in place (Karam, 1998, p. 145). The new law stipulates that in the case of a polygynous union the first wife retains the right to seek divorce, but it is no longer her automatic right. Instead, she now has to prove that her husband's second marriage is detrimental to her either materially and/or mentally. Further, the first wife now only has the right to sue for divorce in the first year of the new polygynous marriage. However, as mentioned before, polygyny is extremely uncommon.

Levels of Childbearing

Family planning is a complex area even though Egypt has the longest history of contraceptive programming in North Africa and the Middle East. In 1996, the former Ministry of Population and Family Planning was abolished and a new Ministry of Health and Population was created to underscore the renewed importance the government is giving to issues of population growth. Egypt has two significant population problems: rapid rates of population growth related to high fertility and an unbalanced population distribution. The highest fertility level is found in rural Upper Egypt (5.2 births per woman) compared to a lower fertility level in urban Lower Egypt (2.7 births per woman) (Chelala, 1996, p. 1651).

In order to help control population growth, the government has repeatedly, through various programs, advocated the use of family planning methods. However, the quality of family planning services is often poor, contraceptives are not readily available, and poor and rural women in particular are reluctant to use artificial birth control methods, which they have heard rumored to be detrimental to women's health. Many unwanted pregnancies end in self-induced abortions because abortion is prohibited in Egypt except in cases when pregnancy threatens the life of the mother.

The 1995 Egypt Demographic and Health Survey, a nationally representative survey of 14,779 married women aged 14 to 49, shows a leveling off of the contraceptive prevalence rate at around 48 percent from 1991 to 1995. Although contraceptive use in Egypt doubled between 1980 and 1995, from 24 percent to 48 percent, most of the increase happened in the 1980s with no significant change in the overall rate of contraceptive use between 1991 and 1995 (Chelala, 1996). The 1995 survey also revealed significant differences in the level of contraceptive use based on region, with women in Lower Egypt accounting for approximately 53 percent compared to 24 percent in Upper Egypt. This high discrepancy can be attributed, at least in part, to lower socioeconomic conditions and traditional practices and beliefs. Family planning is perceived as primarily a "women's problem." However, to be truly effective family planning should also be targeted at men, who tend to believe that the more sons they have, the better off they will be. It is only by addressing cultural norms that disadvantage women that progress in this area could be made.

Intergenerational Ties

In order to begin to understand the cultural context of intergenerational relations in contemporary Muslim Egyptian society, it is instructive to examine some of the laws and Islamic discourses that are concerned with aspects of the relationship between adult children and elderly parents. According to Islamic law, the relationship between parents and children parallels the rights and obligations that are established through marriage. The Shari'a has developed specialized topics that reflect the highly protective attitude of the Quran toward minor children and aged parents. Specifically, the primary legal relationship between parents and children centers on the question of adequate maintenance of dependent children and needy parents. The economic and social welfare of children is a major responsibility of parents, and it is enforceable under Islamic law. Conversely, it is the legal responsibility of children to take care of their aged parents, both financially and socially. For many Egyptian families, the welfare of both children and old people centers around the economic and social capabilities of the extended family.

Apart from a fear of divine retribution, the values of a majority of Egyptian families strongly support the legal norms of filial duty. As we have seen, both the Quran and Islamic law stipulate that financially capable children must care for their needy parents. Furthermore, according to Egyptian social norms, maintenance means more than just providing the bare necessities. If a child, in particular a son, becomes wealthier than his parents, social norms require that he helps his parents to maintain a lifestyle which is higher than that to which they were accustomed.

Relationships within the extended family, in both a social and an economic sense, play a very important role among the Muslim Egyptians. Nevertheless, while the rights and obligations between children and parents are generally clearly defined, the economic relationship between the individual and his or her extended family is not as obvious, and is usually negotiated on an individual basis. Social norms, intertwined with religious beliefs and personal sentiments, ensure that individual members of families ultimately work together in order to cope with the issues facing elderly relatives. It is this network of family relations that, even today, gives the elderly in Egypt their greatest personal and economic security.

STRENGTHENING EGYPTIAN FAMILIES

The concept of family remains a central feature of Egyptian society at all levels. Religious and cultural ideals promote the importance of family in individuals' lives and it is still highly unusual to find men or women living on their own, not with their families. Even in cases of divorce (which remains rare) or widowhood, the remaining partner will typically move back to his or her natal family. Families are in constant communication with each other—both through visitations and on the telephone. A predominant theme is that in today's changing society, family provides comfort and security in an increasingly dangerous world.

The two major problems facing Egyptian families are similar to those found in most African societies today: socioeconomic issues and rapid population growth. Contemporary Egyptian society is characterized by major class and rural-urban differences that affect all families on some level. Urban centers are overcrowded and make everyday living extremely difficult. Families who live in rural areas are particularly affected by the extreme poverty that pervades most of Egypt and susceptible to even the slightest downward shifts in the economy. Fundamentalist messages that advocate a society based on traditional religious law with static gender roles in the family are making inroads due to the extreme conditions under which many individuals live.

Attempts at strengthening Egyptian families need to focus on rebalancing the enormous economic discrepancies that exist between groups and between families. With respect to gender, educational initiatives need to recognize the prevalence of cultural norms that favor boys over girls when it comes to schooling, access to health care, and training opportunities. Also, within the sphere of the family, women who work outside of the home need social supports that allow them to feel that they are contributing to their families in a significant and equally important manner as their husbands.

Egyptian society is characterized by a unique blend of cultural, historical, and religious diversity. At the crossroads of Africa, the Middle East, and the Mediterranean, Egypt has the potential for setting an example for other developing countries with respect to enhancing the lives of its individuals and their families. Many of the issues described in this chapter are not uniquely Egyptian issues—instead they are issues facing all families in an increasing complex and interrelated world.

REFERENCES

Barakat, H. (1985). The Arab family and the challenge of social transformation. In Fernea, E. W. (Ed.), *Women and the family in the Middle East* (pp. 27–48). Austin: University of Texas Press.

Botman, S. (1999). *Engendering citizenship in Egypt*. New York: Columbia University Press.

CAPMAS. (1990). *Labour Force Sample Survey (LFSS)*, Cairo: Egypt.

Chelala, C. (1996). Egypt faces challenges of population growth. *The Lancet 348(9042)*, 1651.

El-Baz, S. (1997). The impact of social and economic factors on women's group formation in Egypt. In Cahtty, D. & Rabo, A (Eds.), *Organizing women: Formal and informal women's groups in the Middle East*. Oxford: Berg Publishers.

Fernea, E. W. (Ed.). (1985). *Women and the family in the Middle East: New voices of change*. Austin: University of Texas Press.

Hatem, M. (1992). Economic and political liberalization in Egypt and the demise of state feminism. *International Journal of Middle East Studies, 24*.

Hoodfar, H. (1990). Survival strategies in low income households in Cairo. *Journal of South Asian and Middle Eastern Studies 13(4)*, 22–41

Karam, A. (1998). *Women, Islamisms and the state: Contemporary feminisms in Egypt*. New York: St. Martin's.

Lapidus, I. M. (1976). Adulthood in Islam: Religious maturity in the Islamic tradition. *Daedalus 105(2)*, 93–108.

Lenton, C. (1997). Will Egypt escape the AIDS epidemic? *The Lancet 349(9057)*, 1005.

Macleod, A. E. (1991). *Accommodating protest: Working women and the new veiling in Cairo*. New Haven, CT: Yale University Press.

Mernissi, F. (1987). *Beyond the veil—Male-female dynamics in modern Muslim society* (rev. ed.). Bloomington: Indiana University Press.

Said, E. (1978). *Orientalism*. New York: Pantheon.

Schacht, J. (1964). *An introduction to Islamic law*. Oxford: Clarendon.

Sherif, B. (1999). The prayer of a married man is equivalent to seventy prayers of a single man: The significance of marriage to Muslim Egyptians. *Journal of Family Issues 20(5)*, 617–632.

Sherif, B. (2003). Gaining an understanding of non-Western families: Socio-cultural perspectives on Egyptian families. In Ponzetti, J. (Ed.), *International Encyclopedia of Marriage and Family Relationships* (2nd ed., pp. 506–511).

Singerman, D. (1995). Where has all the power gone? Women and politics in popular quarters of Cairo. In Goecek, F. & Balaghi, S. (Eds.), *Reconstructing gender in the Middle East: Tradition, identity, and power* (pp. 174–200). New York: Columbia.

Tucker, J. (1993a). Introduction. In Tucker, J. (Ed.), *Arab women: Old boundaries, new frontiers* (pp. vii–xviii). Bloomington: Indiana University Press.

Tucker, J. (1993b). The Arab family in history: "Otherness" and the study of the family. In Tucker, J. (Ed.), *Arab women: Old boundaries, new frontiers* (pp. 195–207). Bloomington: Indiana University Press.

Tucker, J. (Ed.). (1993c). *Arab women: Old boundaries, new frontiers*. Bloomington: Indiana University Press.

Waines, D. (1982). Through a veil darkly: The study of women in Muslim societies. *Comparative Studies of Society and History 24(4)*, 642–659.

CHAPTER 4

The Sudanese Family: Past Reflections and Contemporary Realities

Carolyn Fluehr-Lobban

INTRODUCTION

As African's largest country, Sudan is a microcosm of the continent. It has also been through the crucible of civil war, ethnic cleansing, and numerous violations of women's and human rights as a result of the chronic warfare and civilian displacement. Nonetheless, the Sudanese family has prevailed and women have been resilient in the face of multiple crises, even though the impact of these events has disproportionately fallen on them and their children. Sudanese history is full of strong women—from the ancient queens of Kush-Meroe to the many women who struggled for their rights and equality in the movement for independence and thereafter. African patriarchy—whether in northern Muslim areas or southern Nolotic regions—remains intact even as women activists set their course for the 21st century.

Demographic and Ecological Profiles

Sudan is Africa's largest nation bordering nine other African countries and encompassing about a million square miles, equal to one-quarter of the size of the United States. The vast regions of Sudan are mainly desert and arid or semiarid in the northern two-thirds of the country, and savanna and rain forest in its southern third. The two Niles—the Blue, originating in Ethiopia, and the White, originating in Uganda—shape the geography and history of the country. Like many other African countries, Sudan is multiethnic, multiracial, and multireligious. Its estimated population in 2005 is about 40 million, with a growth rate of 2.6 percent (U.S. Central Intelligence Agency, 2005). Accurate population statistics are problematical because no official census has been conducted since the end of colonialism and millions of Sudanese have died, been forced into exile, or otherwise been displaced by the chronic civil war especially since 1983.

Although still predominantly agrarian at 80 percent of the labor force, Sudan is a rapidly urbanizing nation and its capital city of Khartoum has swelled to over 4 million, stressing water and electricity resources in the city. The percentage of women working in salaried positions outside of the home may be small in comparison to other African countries, perhaps 10–15 percent of the total workforce, and is negatively affected by both traditional Islamic values of female seclusion and more recent Islamist policies since 1989 of official discouragement of women working in public places. However, as in other African and Third World countries, women's participation in informal economic activities has been increasing due to the increased need for their economic contribution.

With more than 500 languages and ethnic groups, it is not easy to classify such immense variety, especially without using the conventional descriptive terms employed by the colonialist scholars. Sudan is predominantly Sunni Muslim, estimated at about 70 percent, with traditional African religions and Christianity comprising the other 30 percent. In terms that Sudanese might employ, the country comprises the northern Muslim, southern Christian, and traditional African religions. The dividing line between the mostly Muslim north and the traditional African and Christian south has been shaped by centuries of unequal relations. These have been marked by the slave trade, with the northern Muslims and "Arabs" active as slavers against southern ethnic groups. Relations have also been marked by colonial separation of south from north, and chronic postindependence civil war that has raged from 1955 to the present with only a decade of peace, from 1972 to 1983. The difference between north and south is fundamentally about these historical inequities and the lack of political and economic equity. The ramifications of chronic civil war in terms of the toll that it has taken on Sudanese families will be discussed later.

The major northern ethnic groups follow the course of the river Nile north to south and include Fadija- and Mahas-speaking Nubians (historically matrilineal, converting to patriliny after the introduction of Islam), Arabic-speaking Nubians, the Shayqiya and Ja'aliin from whose ranks most of the postindependence elites have been drawn, and other riverine groups referred to as "northerners." Major southern ethnic groups include the Nilotic pastoralists, the Dinka and Nuer, the Shilluk, and central African linguistic groups such as the Azande. The Nilotic societies have been most profoundly affected by the civil war.

Central Sudan, formerly Blue Nile Province, is an area known as al-Jezirah, meaning "island," because it is the fertile region between the two Niles. Cotton growing during the colonial era made this a relatively more economically developed region that began to employ women as informal day laborers in the postindependence period.

Eastern Sudan is geographically marked by the Red Sea littoral and by the hills along the coast, and Sudan's major outlet to the sea, Port Sudan. Pastoral peoples such as the Beja and Hadendowa traditionally occupied these hills. Pastoral societies are patrilineal, marked by a sharp gendered division of labor. The other major eastern city is Kassala at the Ethiopian border, an important contact point between the two countries.

Western Sudan includes Kordofan and Darfur, with the major cities of El Obeid and Fasher. Darfur traditionally connects Sudan with Saharan West Africa, especially from the time of the medieval Islamic African kingdoms. These regions—northern riverine, southern, central, eastern, and western—are geographic mental maps constituting the main indigenous ideas about national identity. These ideas are subject to much discussion and negotiation as a mature, unified national identity has yet to be achieved.

SUDAN'S "TRIPLE HERITAGE"

As in many parts of Africa and the world, women played a more significant role in the histories of their societies than in the colonial and postindependence periods of the modern era. In the ancient civilization of Kush, women held such high positions as queen mother or queen consort, and during the time that Nubians ruled Pharaonic Egypt in the 25th Dynasty (750–675 BCE) a female relative of the king traditionally held the position of God's Wife of Amun at Thebes, the southern capital of Egypt. In Meroë, an exclusively Nubian civilization, during five centuries (between 260 BC and 320 AD) eight queens ruled in their own right, more than during the 3,000 years of Pharaonic rule in Egypt. These regnant queens, known to the classical European world as "Candaces" or "Kendakes" (Amanitore and Amanashkhtete are two examples), ruled alone or were coregents with their brothers, marking this exceptional period of African history (Fluehr-Lobban, 1998). During the Nubian Christian period (6th–9th centuries AD), the queens and queen mothers were active in government affairs and were still referred to by the title "Kandake" (Vantini, 1981, p. 115). Matrilineality was common in pre-Islamic and precolonial Sudan, prevalent in Nubia and in Darfur, among some eastern Beja peoples who display matrilineal remnants into the present, and in the first of the Islamic Sultanates the Funj (Muhammad, 2002). Comparable to West African history, which is replete with women founders of ancient cities in Mali, or Queen Amina of Katsina in northern Nigeria, a woman named Ajuba founded the pre-Islamic city of Soba.

In Darfur, the West African medieval kingship pattern of brother-sister rule prevailed with a long line of sultan corulers. The title of the ruling sister was

"Iya Bassi." After her brother she was above all other male officials and all women. The most famous was sultana Taja or Tajodj who with her brother Ali Dinar resisted the onslaught of British imperialism until 1916, 18 years after the English had conquered the country and given it the colonial Anglo-Egyptian name, Sudan (Muhammad, 2002).

Great Britain rivaled and eventually replaced Ottoman Turkish rule from Egypt south to Sudan, controlling the entire Nile Valley. Resistance to European colonialism was generalized throughout Africa, but Sudan was among the few places where the colonial mission was set back. The Mahdist Islamic movement prevented the English from conquering the Sudan in 1884 and ruled Sudan as an Islamic state from the city of Omdurman. The English returned to besiege the city with gunboats and Gatling guns under the command of Lord Kitchener and established their rule in 1898 at the cost of 10,000 Sudanese lives and a few dozen British soldiers. The English ruled for 58 years under a governor-general, Anglicizing and Westernizing basic institutions of law, education, and commerce, and laying out their colonial city of Khartoum in the shape of the Union Jack. Capitalism and wage labor were introduced as the last vestiges of the slave trade were suppressed. Governance of Islamic institutions was especially sensitive given the Mahdist resistance, so while the religion was not officially suppressed, Islamic law was restricted to family matters and the lineal descendants of the Mahdi were co-opted and kept under close surveillance. Christianity was encouraged in the south, (the stronghold of African Traditional religion) where missionaries from England and Italy were particularly active. The British ruled Sudan until 1956.

Sudan is an excellent example of Ali Mazrui's idea of Africa's triple heritage—many of its hundreds of indigenous languages and cultures retain their unique features and practice of Traditional African religions, resisting both earlier Islamic and later Western Christian-colonial incursions. African-Coptic Christianity lasted a thousand years in Nubia, from the 5th to 16th centuries. Islam then penetrated the Sudan from the northern Nile route and from the western caravan, trade, and Hajj routes passing through Sudan on their way to Mecca from Muslim West Africa. This western route of the entry of Islam proved even more important as the cultural traditions associated with Islamic West Africa are strongly developed in current Sudanese Muslim life.

The colonial institutions of English language, law, and governance had lasting effects until the beginning of the Islamist political movement in the late 1970s and early 1980s. The English sought to eliminate child betrothal, to reduce the power of the male marriage guardian, and to increase the importance of women's consent in marriage. They initiated a process whereby judicial divorce for women became legal on the grounds of abuse, neglect, and desertion. They also attempted to eliminate female circumcision by outlawing it in 1946; however, because this came at the time of the growing influence of the nationalist movement, it was rejected by the masses of northern Sudan as colonialist interference and only served to drive the practice underground.

In the postindependence period, family law developed in a progressive way, combining the indigenous heritage of Islamic and customary law and selectively retaining elements of English law. However, after Shari'a was made state law in 1983, Islamization of civil and family law and basic social and economic institutions became the norm, ignoring the non-Muslim, increasingly Christian orientation of a third of Sudan's population primarily in the south. Islamization sought to restore the authentic Islamic institutions of Shari'a law and establish new ones such as Islamic banks, insurance companies, and other services. In 1989, a military coup led by Omer al-Bashir and backed by the founder of the Muslim Brotherhood, Hasan al-Turabi, seized power and in effect created an Islamic state which has held power ever since. During this time, the Arabic language was instituted as the language of study in the universities and Arabization and Islamization proceeded at an accelerated pace.

So the triple heritage is present throughout Sudanese history and has reshaped Sudan in the contemporary era by official dominance of the Islamic sector and their effort to leave the colonial legacy behind and Islamize the remaining "heathen," that is indigenous parts of the Sudan where traditional African religions are practiced. This official policy fuels the continuing civil war between the north and the south, and has led many southerners who practice traditional African religions to embrace Christianity in an effort to resist what they perceive as imposed Islamization.

Family life has been more resistant to the forces described above and remains one of the stabilizing forces in Sudanese life irrespective of region or rural-urban differences. The majority faith of Islam was not disturbed in major ways by British colonialism, perhaps primarily as a result of the history of anti-imperial resistance associated with Islamic militancy in the 19th-century Mahdist uprising against British and foreign rule. Also, much of popular Islam is Sufi with prominent African religious brotherhoods, such as the Qadiriyya and Tijaniyya orders, maintaining religious traditions without government interest or intervention.

During colonialism the English did seek to outlaw certain "harmful" customs such as female circumcision and child betrothal, and were more successful in the latter than the former. In general, family life has been resistant to external European influence.

CONCEPTUALIZATION OF SUDANESE FAMILIES

Although matriliny was probably more widespread in the past, especially among Nubians and some eastern and western ethnic groups, the coming of Islam, on the one hand, and the traditional pastoralism of many societies on the other, means that patriliny is the predominant type of kinship system found throughout Sudan. Islam modified stricter patrilineal rules that prohibited women from inheriting property from their fathers or any entitlement to the marriage dower. A more pristine, unreformed form of patriliny that excludes women from inheritance is found among the southern Nilotic pastoralists; among northern Sudanese Muslims, in general women inherit half of what their brothers do.

The patrilineal principle means not only that descent and inheritance are traced through men, but also that a core of patrilineally related males known as the *'asaba* in Arabic are the key decision makers of the family. These include the grandfather, father, brothers, and sons who are responsible for family order, marriages, and control over family property and inheritance matters outside of the strict parameters of Islamic law by which certain relatives must inherit. They give family consent in marriage although the informal input of women is critical and consent of the bride must be assured. The dower, which can be a substantial amount of wealth in cash, gold, or property, legally belongs to the wife; however, some fathers may informally claim a part of this considerable wealth negotiated at the time of the marriage contract. This biological core of males is a primary social group as well and women's positions are defined in relation to them. A woman is known as the daughter of her father from whom she has the greatest inheritance rights; she does not take the name of her husband, though her children will.

Southern Nilotic patrilineal families exchange women between clans and lineages through the use of cattle as bride wealth. That marriage property belongs to the father and the patrilineal males, while women maintain usufruct rights over the dairying of cows. Polygyny is unrestricted and a wealthy man or powerful chief may have dozens of wives and hundreds of children. Islamic law limits the number of wives to four, though few men can afford the cost of marriage and maintenance of multiple households, which must be equitably maintained. The civil war has displaced millions of Nilotic peoples, destroyed their cattle-based economy, and thus disrupted family life perhaps to the point of no return.

Essential Features of Sudanese Families

The majority of Muslim marriages are formally arranged by the senior male members of the patrilineage and strongly influenced by the female members of the kin group. Having met at university or a place of employment, some couples select each other in "love marriages," but permission of the male marriage guardian (*al-wali*) is needed so the family "blessing" is sought and the requisite dower is negotiated. The consent of the bride is required by Islamic law and no arranged marriage can be imposed upon her against her will.

Non-Muslim marriage is regulated by customary law based on the necessity of bride wealth exchange in pastoral, patrilineal societies such as the Nilotic groups. Attempts to uphold these customs in the face of the chronic wartime conditions among southerners have been difficult because the essential cattle bride wealth payments are nearly impossible with the cattle and slave raiding, especially along the Bahr al-Ghazal border areas between north and south.

Polygyny is an accepted marital tradition among both northern Muslim and southern traditional and Christian groups, however polygyny is declining in all regions because of the increasing cost of marriage and a more educated population that has come to view polygamy as an old custom.

Infibulation, the most severe form of female genital mutilation (FGM), or female circumcision, is practiced in Sudan among Muslims, but not among the third of the country that is non-Muslim. This makes many in the West associate female circumcision with Islam which is true demographically but not religiously. Feminist writers have preferred the term *FGM* (Toubia, 1993), while the folk classification is female circumcision (Gruenbaum, 2001). It is estimated that over 90 percent of northern Muslim women in Sudan are infibulated.

The movement to ameliorate or eradicate FGM has been both indigenous and global. Female Sudanese doctors have led the way, along with activists from the educational and health care sectors. Although outlawed in 1946, and despite the fact that it is not required by Islam or any other religion, female circumcision remains a widespread practice. International human rights organizations have called for the elimination of the practice on the grounds that it violates the human rights of women and girls (Fluehr-Lobban, 1996). There is evidence that in some of the urban centers of the Muslim north "lighter" forms of circumcision, such as "simple" clitoridectomy are gradually replacing the more severe infibulation in which the clitoris and labia are excised and a small opening for both urine and menses is all that remains of the external female genitalia. This practice is entirely in the hands of women, leaving many Western feminists puzzled as to why women would practice such a drastic and oppressive surgery on their female kin. The reasons for the maintenance of FGM in Sudan are much the same as in other parts of Africa where the practice continues as a long-standing cultural custom: control of female sexuality, marriageability, belief that it is commanded by God, and the idea that it promotes cleanliness and hygiene.

Family health, of course, depends on class and relative access to health care centers and providers in urban areas or more isolated rural locales. Relatively high infant mortality rates combined with low life expectancy rates for males and females are indicative of a poor health care delivery system, consistent with Sudan's standing as one of the world's poorest countries. In spite of the poor health care delivery system, though, Muslim Sudan, like much of Islamic Africa, has been much less affected by the HIV/AIDS epidemic on the continent. Stringent controls on sexual behavior and promiscuity as cultural norms associated with Islam have helped to keep the rates of HIV infection relatively low in Sudan, including in the non-Muslim southern region. Through its police patrols and courts, the country delivers prompt justice for violators of the moral code and sexual offenders.

The Family as a Fluid, Changing Social Force

As with any family in the Third World the economic stresses of daily life can be overwhelming and result in fractures or breakdown. Economic demands have forced many men in rural areas to migrate to the cities; urban husbands and fathers have had to work two or three jobs, one in the formal sector and the others in informal sector jobs such as taxi driving (Ali, 1998). The rising costs of marriage have made it difficult for young men to secure enough money to marry at home and many migrate to the oil-rich states of the Persian Gulf for several years of temporary work until they earn enough to marry. Once married, many return to the Gulf region for years to work so they can support their families at a higher standard than is possible in Sudan, producing the usual effect of matrifocal families at home—extended households of older relatives and children headed by women. An increasing number of judicial divorces initiated by women stem from a migrant husband's failure to support his wife and children. On the other hand, husbands and sons working abroad constitute a huge source of revenue generated for consumption at home. This cash influx in many ways keeps the Sudanese economy from collapse.

With the expansion of supplemental male economic activity women also became active in the formal and informal sectors, expanding their economic contribution outside the domestic realm. Salaried women workers are active in the educational, health care, commercial, communications, and government arenas. Married Muslim women need to obtain the permission of their husbands to work, as do unmarried women from their fathers. Women from regions other than the central urban Sudan are not much involved in the formal sector. Before the current Islamist regime the number of women in the workforce rose to about 15 percent; however, with the rising influence of Islamic values, women are discouraged from working outside of the home unless their economic contribution is vital. The low participation of women in the formal sector does not reflect their economic contributions gained from the informal sector.

The total fertility rate for Sudanese women is 4.6 children. The overall infant mortality rate is 73 per 1,000 live births, and the mortality rate for children under 5 years of age is 115 per 1,000 live births. The relatively high rates of both fertility and infant/child mortality reflect not only the predominately agrarian pattern of large families with poor health care delivery, especially in the rural areas, but also the increasingly impoverished urban areas afflicted by the chronic civil war. The number of displaced or utterly destroyed families in the southern war regions is incalculable, but estimates range as high as 2 million dead or displaced persons and hundreds of thousand of families ruined. The plight of the "lost boys" from southern Sudan who have walked to Kenya or Ethiopia from war-torn regions of the south with their mothers, fathers, and sisters presumably killed or enslaved is by now well-known. Many have been resettled in the United States by American relief agencies.

Under such conditions it is nearly impossible for non-Sudanese to carry out social research and this has been the case since the resumption of civil war in 1983. The major research during the difficult period since 1983, and especially after the Islamist regime seized power in 1989, has been carried out by Ahfad University for Women in Omdurman, which has published the *Ahfad Journal* every year since 1983. Struggling against odds that often pit their research on women and family life against the government, especially critical work on women's conditions in rural areas, they have nonetheless succeeded in keeping a vigorous research agenda alive. Recent articles include contributions about female circumcision, rural development and women, nutrition assessment, and agricultural production. Each issue contains summaries of current research.

During the 1980s, the government conducted the Sudan Demographic and Health Survey (DHS) of 1989/90 (SDHS, 1991), a major research initiative. This survey indicated a higher fertility rate of women at 5.5 children, conforming to the relatively high fertility rates of African women. The average household size was 5.1, reflecting the continuing strength of the extended family. The total percentage of women in the formal labor force was 20 percent; however, estimates of women involved in the informal economic sector would probably double this figure. Life expectancy for Sudanese women was 56 years while it was 55 for men, a figure that has not improved much since independence, reflecting the effects of chronic civil war, static nondevelopment, and a continued low standard of living and health care.

During the 20th century, both during colonialism and after independence, significant change has taken place in the family law as well as in an equal rights clause in the Sudan constitution of 1973. According to feminist critics, the constitutional equality clause for women has had little impact. Feminists assert that women lack full equality in a number of respects, for example, in Islamic areas a woman cannot become head of state, and women do not have equal rights to inheritance. Nonetheless, a number of reforms in Islamic family law were achieved through a combination of feminist agitation, presidential decree, and judicial interpretation. Abolished in 1970 was the Enforced Obedience of Wives Law (*bayt al-ta'a*) whereby wives who fled from their husbands' abuse were forcibly returned to their husbands by court-ordered police action (Fluehr-Lobban, 1987).

As is the usual African colonial pattern female education lagged behind that of male education, but once women gained education they comprised the heart of the women's movement and the nationalist movement. There is one important exception to this rule, and that is the special history of Ahfad University for Women, the only university exclusively for women on the African continent (Kashif-Badri, 1984). Founded in the early 20th century by Sheikh Babiker Badri, it has remained a Badri family institution and has opened its doors to women from all of Sudan, including women displaced by the chronic civil war. Ahfad University developed Sudan's first and only Women's Studies program with a strong emphasis on women-related research and development issues (Ahfad, 2005). Women activists from Ahfad University challenged the fundamentalist al-Bashir regime after 1989 by protesting the imposed Islamic dress code and other restrictions on workplace and public behavior.

THE FUTURE OF THE SUDANESE FAMILY

Peace is the *sine qua non* for basic nation building in Africa's largest country and one of its most diverse. Even as peace accords were signed between the government of Sudan and the southern-based Sudan People's Liberation Movement (SPLM) in March of 2004, war amounting to ethnic cleansing (some have said genocide) has broken out in the western Darfur region. The development of Sudan awaits the long overdue peace, and the strengthening of families throughout the country will only occur in this context. The primacy of family life remains strong in Sudan, although many families have been torn apart by the war and many Sudanese live in exile outside the country in neighboring African countries, Europe, and North America. The revival of child slavery within the context of the civil war and the plight of Sudan's "lost boys" who have been dislocated from their families by war and enslavement are urgent problems. The growing impoverishment of all regions of the nation due to the protracted war and its drain on the Sudanese economy portends a difficult short-term future. But the long-term picture is brighter, with Sudan's abundant physical and human resources. Given a prolonged period of peace with equitable resources distribution and development, women, men, and children throughout the Sudan will rapidly improve their overall status.

Under conditions of peace and stability, long overdue basic ethnographic study of the country's hundreds of different ethnic and linguistic groups will be possible. Exploration of Sudanese antiquity, from the possible origins of agriculture in the Nile Valley through the rise of the state, examining the changes in women's status is highly desirable. An examination of cultural traditions across the Sahel in Sudanic Africa will highlight the role of women in pastoral and farming societies.

Studying the effects of the protracted war on families, especially in the southern regions, will be a priority in the postwar period. Ahfad University researchers are probing ideas about intermarriage between northerners and southerners (El-Obid & Mohamed, 2000) that might be helpful for the country to overcome the conflicts associated with perceived differences of race as well as religion and ethnicity. Studying the effects of rapid urbanization on families, which has accompanied the displacement of millions of Sudanese due to the civil war, will be essential to the provision of services. Although the officially reported HIV/AIDS infection rates are insignificant in Sudan due to its Islamic code and strict enforcement of morality, there is a need to study the impact of the severe disruption and displacement of people stemming from the protracted civil war on the spread of HIV/AIDS and other infectious diseases.

The examination of life in the new multiethnic cities that the war has created will also be a research challenge. This will call for the training of applied social scientists and social workers to meet the many demands that the construction of the new postwar Sudan will require. Throughout all the challenges, the family will remain the bedrock of Sudanese life in the foreseeable future.

REFERENCES

Ahfad. (2005). *Ahfad: Evolving education for women in Sudan*. http://www.ahfad.org/overview/. Retrieved: June 13, 2005.

Ali, N. M. M. (1998). The invisible economy, survival, and empowerment: Five cases from Atbara, Sudan. In Lobban, R. (Ed.), *Women in the informal sector in the Middle East* (pp. 96–112). Gainesville: University Press of Florida.

El-Obid, N. A. M., & Mohamed, N. F. O. (2000). The southern women, as perceived in the mind of the northern man, and the marital relationship between them. *The Ahfad Journal 17(1)*, 46–47.

Fluehr-Lobban, C. (1987). *Islamic law and society in the Sudan*. London: Frank Cass. Arabic translation: *al-Shari'a Islami wa al-mujtema'a fi Sudan*, translated by Mahjoub al-Tigani Mahmoud, Cairo, 2004.

Fluehr-Lobban, C. (1996, June 6). Cultural relativism and universal rights. *Chronicle of Higher Education*, pp. B1, B2.

Fluehr-Lobban, C. (1998). *Nubian queens in Nile Valley and Afro-Asiatic culture history*. Paper presented at the 9th Conference of Nubian Studies, Boston.

Gruenbaum, E. (2001). *The female circumcision controversy: An anthropological perspective*. Philadelphia: University of Pennsylvania Press.

Kashif-Badri, H. (1984). The history, development, organization, and position of Women's Studies in the Sudan. *Social Science Research and Women in the Arab World*. Paris: UNESCO, pp. 94–112.

Muhammad, B. B. (2002). Iya Bassi. In Lobban, R., Kramer, R., & Fluehr-Lobban, C. (Eds.). *Historical dictionary of the Sudan*. Lanham, MD: Scarecrow Press.

Sudan Demographic & Health Survey. (1991). *Sudan Demographic and Health Survey [SDHS], 1989–90*. Columbia, MD: Department of Statistics, Ministry of Economic and National Planning, Khartoum, Sudan, & Institute for Resource Development/Macro International, Inc.

Toubia, N. (1993). *Female genital mutilation: A call for global action*. New York: Women Ink.

U.S. Central Intelligence Agency. (2005). Sudan. *The world factbook*. http://www.cia.gov/cia/publications/factbook/print/su.html. Retrieved: June 13, 2005.

Vantini, G. (1981). *Christianity in Sudan*. Bologna, Italy: Novastampa di Verona.

Part II
Western Africa

CHAPTER 5

Senegalese Families: The Confluence of Ethnicity, History, and Social Change

Loretta E. Bass and Fatou Sow

INTRODUCTION

A confluence of history and modernity, household economics, and cultural influences coalesce to make defining the "typical" Senegalese family a formidable task. Senegalese families take both monogamous and polygynous[1] forms, exhibit a broad array of power arrangements between husband and wife, differ by ethnic group, and present distinctive forms in rural and urban areas. The high urbanization rate provides some indication of the social change that has influenced and continues to shape Senegalese families. When Senegal established its independence from France in 1960, just 23 percent of the population lived in urban areas compared with over 40 percent today. The urbanized areas of Senegal display social patterns such as later ages of marriage, higher rates of divorce, lower rates of polygyny, and lower rates of fertility compared with rural areas and with the national average fertility rate.

The rural or urban residence of Senegalese families affects both economic well-being and social norms. Economically, there are more opportunities for both men and women in urban areas. Families in rural areas are poor, while those who live in urban areas are largely poor but display a wider range of socioeconomic levels. This economic variation between rural and urban areas takes place within the larger context of a generally depressed economy with high unemployment and a large informal sector (Panhuys, Farrell, & Seck, 1989).

Culturally, urban areas exhibit a wider range of acceptable social norms regarding children and family forms. New values are being created in the urban milieu for women and children. As a result, for example, urban women earn more education, enter the labor market, and establish their own households at higher rates than rural women. These changing expectations of acceptable roles, in turn, change the power dynamics in urban Senegalese families and provide urban women with more voice in household decision making compared with their rural counterparts.

Population Growth

Growth in the population is mainly fueled by high fertility in Senegalese families. Women have 5.7 children on average, a rate that is projected to double over the next 25 years (Population Reference Bureau [PRB], 2000). The population of Senegal is roughly 10 million (PRB, 2000) and continues to grow rapidly. The Senegalese population presents a "classic" pyramid age structure characterized by high fertility, high mortality, and a large youth cohort (U.S. Bureau of the Census, 2000). This youthful age structure of the population is the basis for the high level of dependency present in Senegalese families. Children less than 15 years old comprise 45 percent of the total population and are likely to be dependents. In contrast, just 52 percent of the population is of working age, 15 to 64 years old. Thus, there are slightly fewer dependents than working-age persons—a heavy load, especially in Senegal where not everyone of working age is fully employed. Senegalese families are hard-pressed to provide for dependents in the under-15-year-old age group.

Ethnic and Caste Variations

Across ethnic groups, an extended family structure predominates. The four major ethnic groups of Senegal are the Wolof, comprising 43 percent; the Hal Pulaaren,[2] comprising 24 percent; the Sereer, comprising 15 percent; and the Joola, comprising 4 percent of the population respectively (PRB, 2000). The underlying dimensions of ethnicity help explain the differences in women's autonomy and status across Senegalese families. Creevey (1992) found that ethnic background produces differences in Senegalese women's access to education. These differences may then influence women's autonomy and status vis-à-vis their husbands, and may also have implications for differences in the manner of mate selection and the prevalence of polygyny.

The influence of caste distinctions on households across the major ethnic groups has declined since 1960 with changes in the structure of the economy and urbanization. The Wolof, Soninke, and Hal Pulaaren observe seven distinct caste levels from aristocratic to artisan to slave levels, compared with only the blacksmith and slave castes of the Joola. The Hal Pulaaren observe caste more rigidly than other ethnic groups (Sow, 1991; UNICEF, 1995), and their boys generally are expected to learn their father's trade, such as weaving and sculpting, because of caste status (Sène, 1993). However, as the Senegalese economy becomes more diversified and urbanized, these artisan occupations of the Hal Pulaaren are not always considered exclusive future careers for children. These caste-based artisan occupations are still viable and available, but more choices are offered to children with the progress in education.

Ecological Variations

The growing immigrant population is an ongoing ecological concern. Due to the relative poverty of Mali and Mauritania, the deprivation of democratic liberties in Guinée-Conakry, the liberation struggles of Guinée-Bissau and of the Cape Verde Islands, and the political unrest in the 1980s and 1990s in Liberia and Sierra Leone, Senegal has seen many immigrants from these countries seeking either economic and/or political refuge. The shared languages (Wolof, Hal Pulaar, Mandinka) of people from the Gambia, Mali, Mauritania, Guinée, and Sierra Leone facilitate this immigration. This immigration has fueled increases in the population at a time when peanut prices have fallen in Senegal, seriously affecting those who work in agriculture. Additionally, this immigration has occurred at the same time that currency devaluation and other structural adjustment policies have sent shock waves through the economy.

HISTORICAL BACKGROUND AND TRIPLE HERITAGE

The history of the Senegalese family should be viewed first in terms of the early arrival of different ethnic groups prior to the 11th century. The kinship networks of these ethnic groups today show both distinctive and shared characteristics, suggesting that these groups have changed over time with intergroup contact. For example, while dual-lineage patterns and leadership roles for women are characteristic among the Wolof, Lébu, Sereer, and Joola, there is an absence of women's leadership roles among the Hal Pulaaren. The arrival of Islam is another precolonial influence that affected family functioning within each of the ethnic groups. Roughly one-third of the Quran's *akham* or legal injunctions pertain to women and the family (Khurshid, 1974). After Islam, colonial and neocolonial influences have also affected Senegalese family life. Overall, conflict, cohabitation, and convergence all describe the shaping of Senegalese families as they in their local forms have interacted with one another and then with Islamic/Arabic traditions and with Christian/European traditions.

The "triple heritage" concept allows us to consider how the Senegalese family has been shaped by indigenous African culture, Islamic/Arabic culture, and European/Christian culture. The main piece of legislation regulating family functioning, the Senegalese Family Code of 1972 (revised in 1974, 1979, and 1989, Government of Senegal) can be viewed as drawing on this triple heritage. The Family Code specifies rules and obligations of marriage, divorce, and inheritance for Senegalese families. The code requires men to agree to a certain type of family structure at their first marriage, specifying either monogamous, limited polygamous (agreeing to take one or two wives), or polygamous (agreeing to take three or four wives). Women are asked to agree to their spouse's option. If they do not give consent, polygamy becomes the marital agreement. Once chosen, the option of monogamy is irreversible. After a divorce, therefore, men cannot change their option when entering a second marriage.

The code provides two grounds for women to seek divorce: (1) if a husband does not adhere to the specified marital agreement, or (2) if a husband does not provide for his wives. Thus, the part of the code that deals with divorce gives more initiative to women for divorce by requesting a court judgment, showing a colonial/European influence. The code also makes it more difficult for men to divorce women by forcing them to make their claims in formal court, thereby providing an alternative to the Islamic and African customs of divorce that gave women little or no voice in the divorce proceedings.

Overall in West Africa, Muslim women fare better in the area of inheritance and land rights than their Christian or local religion counterparts. Although the laws of inheritance under Islamic teachings are unequal, Islamic law provides rights and advantages to women they did not have in pre-Islamic society. The colonial/Christian influence has not overshadowed the influence of local inheritance customs, although Western education has influenced attitudes toward women's rights and equal treatment, especially among those with secondary or higher education.

The Shaping of Family Life by Africa's Indigenous Culture

Senegalese family life continues to be influenced by African cultures. The extended family structure has African roots. Both extensive horizontal links among those of the same generation and vertical links across generations prevail across Senegalese ethnic groups. Polygyny is also rooted in African culture and remains widespread in Senegal, where nearly 50 percent of all married rural women and just over 40 percent of all married urban women are in polygynous unions (Ndiaye, Sarr, & Ayad, 1988).

Even though polygyny is often associated with Islam, it remains an African custom found even in non-Muslim areas of sub-Saharan Africa. The Senegalese context presents a convergence of African and Islamic forms of polygyny, because Islam's presence has reinforced this African custom while also limiting the number of wives to four. Polygyny was practiced prior to Islam; however, after Islam's arrival it continued to be accepted but by the guidelines outlined in the Quran: a man may take up to four wives, but must be able to provide for each of his wives. In conflict with this Islamic influence, village chiefs or wealthy men may occasionally take more than four wives in some areas in Senegal. This practice is probably a holdover from African custom, which maintains that marriage is compulsory for both genders and that an adult woman must be married and integrated into a family unit. If she is made single by divorce or widowhood, it is her family's obligation to make sure that she remarries in order to maintain her social status.

Again finding roots in local cultures, the importance of kinship relationships is a vital part of current Senegalese family life. Another indication that contemporary Senegalese families draw on African culture is that the four major ethnic groups remain culturally distinctive even though over 90 percent of the population practices Islam (Central Intelligence Agency, 2000). These ethnic groups continue to speak different languages[3] and vary in the practice of rules regulating lineage, kinship, and inheritance (see Callaway & Creevey, 1994; Diop, 1960; Gastellu, 1981). Because Islam did not change all former laws and practices, it was "naturalized" to fit local cultural beliefs and practices.

The Shaping of Family Life by the Arabic/Islamic Culture

The Muslim influence can be viewed as reinforcing traditional African customs like polygyny as discussed above, the marked separation between spouses, and male power in the family. Antoine and Nanitelamio (1996) note that generally in sub-Saharan Africa, "Islam seems to regularize older traditional practices" (p. 132). Likewise, research (Callaway & Creevey, 1994; Sow, 1987) shows that Islam reinforced the patriarchal values of the traditional African societies when it spread to West Africa. For example, at the time of the rise of Islam, both the Sereer and Wolof had a dual system of inheritance that was matrilineal or patrilineal based on caste level. Prior to Islam among Wolof upper castes, family status, land, and slaves were inherited through the female line, while upper-class men were believed to transmit courage and other social values, including honor, power, and authority (Diop, 1985). Among the lower castes, property ownership and caste-based professions were passed from men to male heirs. After Islam's arrival, preexisting patriarchal values became even more pronounced and the patrilineal systems became stronger. These patriarchal ideals have now been written into current Senegalese law through the Family Code (Article 277, Government of Senegal, 1979 [1989]) and stipulate that the father is the head the family. In this way, the Family Code validates the patriarchy already present in African society.

The Shaping of Family Life by the European/Christian Culture

Some protections for women in the Family Code, such as the arbitration of a divorce in formal court or a wife's control of civil status, have roots in European/Christian cultural influence. Prior to the passing of the Family Code in 1972, women did not have grounds for seeking divorce in civil court and mostly men were allowed to initiate a divorce. Prior to the 1989 revisions to the code, a husband had the right to prohibit his wife from working outside the home. Since 1989, revisions to the code have granted wives more control of their civil status, and therefore the right to seek work outside the household (Article 371, Government of Senegal, 1979 [1989]).

Reinwald's (1997) research on the Siin of Senegal from 1890 to 1960 shows that the Senegalese family adapted to the economy and monetarized relations brought about by colonization by entering a transitional stage that accommodates both indigenous and European influences. This stage is characterized by new individual and property rights while maintaining collectively determined age- and gender-ranked systems and behavioral norms. Prior to the European influence wives had more autonomy, lived in separate housing units, and were sanctioned by elders in the village, whereas after the European influence husbands who were more integrated into the new cash economy, became more powerful vis-à-vis their wives and dependents. Husbands expected wives' housework in exchange for bride's wealth, and also began sanctioning their wives within the family unit rather than at the village-elder level. In these instances, a meshing of the two cultures is apparent among the Siin, with women experiencing less authority and autonomy as a consequence of the colonial influence.

In addition, convergence and conflict of the European and Islamic traditions is apparent when examining the different choices families make about their children's education. In the colonial and postcolonial eras, public education takes a French European model. Children who attend public school are taught in French and receive a secular education. While public education takes this French form, many Senegalese Muslim parents choose a private Arabic/Islamic education for their children. A child can enroll in an Arabic school or may study Arabic and the Quran in a less-structured manner with a marabout. Some parents in urban areas resolve the conflict between European and Islamic influences by enrolling their children in Franco-Arab schools or by sending their children to public school and securing additional Quranic lessons for them after school or on weekends. Overall, decisions made at the family level about children's education exemplify the complexity left by the triple heritage.

The colonial/Christian presence has left a larger mark on family functioning and culture among the Joola compared with other ethnic groups in Senegal. Most Senegalese who practice Catholicism are Joola and Sereer and the polygyny rate is strikingly lower among the Joola compared with the Wolof. The tendency of Joola families to send their young girls to school and/or to work as maids in urban areas during the 20th century has been linked to the colonial missionary influence (Enel, Pison, & Lefebvre, 1994). Christian missions first recruited maids in the regions where they worked in the south of Senegal. Even today, the southern region is one of the main sources of maids for Dakar, Banjul, and all the other cities of Senegal and the Gambia.

Heterogeneous and Constantly Changing Senegalese Culture

The triple heritage provides some useful explanations, but more recent history—1960 to the present—should also be considered as impacting Senegalese family life. Through the Westernization of education, urbanization, the change of social values, and the globalization of the entertainment media, namely music, television shows, and film, Senegalese families are being exposed to alternative family forms and family norms. In the Medina area of Dakar, it is common to hear Indian music or to see an Indian romance film playing at the neighborhood movie house. Television shows from France and the United States were increasingly shown on the national Senegalese channel in the 1990s. Western films, television shows, and music that discuss relationships and love clearly have implications for changes in values, family functioning, and social norms which have yet to be analyzed.

In addition, the postcolonial influence of the women's movement cannot be addressed by the triple heritage even though the women's movement has been instrumental in securing protections for women and the family into law. The Ministry of Women and Children was established in 1976, after the International Year of the Woman, and is the main governmental agency working on women's issues. Adding to this momentum, the Senegalese women's movement, composed of feminine and feminist organizations, has taken hold, and women have been organizing and lobbying for social parity with men since the early 1960s.[4] In 1986, a national federation of women's groups was established (Fédération Nationale des Associations Feminine). The organizing of women to enact social change has begun to be felt in Senegalese families, especially in urban areas, where women are demanding more opportunities and rights for themselves and their girls.

Finally, the triple heritage fails to consider the rural-urban divide in explaining differences in family functioning in Senegal. Family stability has been affected by the increased scattering of families between rural and urban areas in Senegal, especially with high rural-urban migration rates since 1960. Currently, 41 percent of the Senegalese population lives in an urban area. Sometimes a father will be a temporary migrant to an urban area, shifting from village to city during months when he is not active in agricultural work.

Sometimes a father may travel to an urban area abroad for work. Even though he may send remittances to the family, this represents a difficult challenge for family stability. Some fathers lose contact with their families and start second ones in the new location. Another stress on family stability is found among children who are increasingly sent to urban areas to work as domestics or in market vending, or to undertake an apprenticeship. Clearly, these children are a sizable part of urbanization and lead to the eventual migration of other siblings or parents. While there are more educational opportunities in the urban areas, these first-generation migrants generally are put to work in menial tasks in order that the family gains a foothold in the urban milieu.

CONCEPTUALIZATION OF SENEGALESE FAMILIES

It is argued that the African household should be defined using two guiding principles: (1) a marital tie between a man and woman, and (2) a shared family name or line of descent (Mafeje, 1991, p. 19). Persons other than parents and their offspring may join the household or the household may be a nuclear family unit. This definition is somewhat conflicting but at the same time accurately characterizes the Senegalese household. In Senegal, there is consanguinity or a shared bloodline among most of the members as well as a family name that identifies household members to outsiders. In addition, kinship ties can be created through marriage and among individuals of shared social experience. In addition to blood-tie kinship bonds, Senegalese kinship ties[5] can be developed by individuals of the same community who share rights of passage, like circumcision or attending the same Quranic or Western school (Sow, 1987). Again de-emphasizing the importance of blood ties, another scholar (Kouassigan, 1978) explains, "Consanguinity is neither sufficient nor even necessary to the existence of kinship ties. Kinship is a community of religious and social life" (p. 45). Thus, individuals who share substantial social obligations have the potential to become members of the same family. The family is defined to outsiders in terms of those individuals who belong to the same household through marriage, consanguinity, or kinship ties, and are associated with the family name.

There is an overlap between the concepts of family and household in Senegal. Families may reside within more than one household, especially in cases of polygyny and first-generation rural-urban migrants. Members of a Wolof household are defined in terms of the *kër* or house, *kër-u Juuf* (house of Juuf), or *kër-u Njaay* (house of Njaay). Thus, an individual not related by blood or marriage may be considered and introduced to others as a part of an extended-family household or even a nonfamily household by living and eating in that household and contributing to its social and economic life. More than one household may therefore claim an individual as a member.

Further, the household can be defined as having members who do not necessarily reside in it but contribute economically and socially to it. Diop's (1985) research on the Wolof found that "there is no longer always concurrence between the residential unit and the socio-economic aspect" (p. 145). This fluid definition of a household sets the context for many created-kinship situations. Specifically, this type of household provides a means for rural-urban migration, especially among rural adolescents or young adults who come to work in urban areas as domestic help or migrant workers, and become anchors for rural family members who seek to migrate to urban areas in the future (Bass, 1997).

Thus, a household is best defined in terms of a certain level of consanguinity where there is parentage or a family name with which members of the household identify and are known by outsiders. However, social ties of marriage and extensive shared social experience may also be sufficient to provide both kin and household membership. Additionally, the household follows an economic strategy to sustain the extended-family unit.

Family Research Areas: Past and Current

To date, the research on Senegalese families falls into three major areas: marriage and family formation, divorce and remarriage, and the defining characteristics of extended family arrangements. The most comprehensive study of the social structure and functioning of the Senegalese family focuses on the Wolof ethnic group. Diop (1985) explains how the Wolof family is structured, the status and power of individuals in it, marriage, and family formation and dissolution patterns. Ndiaye, Thiongane, and Sarr (1991) provide a demographic overview of Senegalese families examining their structure, living arrangements, and patterns of marriage and polygamy.

Getting married and forming a family at an early age is the predominant social norm. Using 1986 Demographic and Health Survey data, Antoine and Nanitelamio (1996) show that marriage is nearly universal in Senegal; women in the 40–44 age group, 91 percent are married, 4 percent are widows, and just 5 percent are divorced. Even though the minimum marriage ages by law are 20 years for males and 16 years for females, many women marry at earlier ages, especially in rural areas. The decision of when and whom to marry typically rests with the parents, and 42 percent of marriages are endogamous or take place with partners in the extended family, typically cousins.

Sow's (1987) analysis of Senegalese law shows that the advances written into the Family Code of 1972 (revised in 1974, 1979, and 1989), even if promising, have not truly protected women's marital and divorce rights. The Family Code can be viewed as subjugating women to men by permitting polygyny on the one hand, but on the other offering certainty to women by requiring the lifetime registration of the type of marriage (monogamous or some form of polygyny) at the time of the groom's first marriage. Many times the certainties provided to women in the law see little legal enforcement, especially in rural areas. For example, even though the Family Code requires women's consent to marriage by making its registration compulsory at the court and by the signing of a contract at the time of first marriage, a national survey of 1,000 women in 1991 found only 21 percent of women had done so. Of those who had signed a marital agreement, 70 percent lived in Dakar (Creevey, 1992, p. 247).

The schisms between protections of the law and practice are abundant. An example of this is when a husband decides to take a second wife even though he originally agreed in the marriage contract to have just one. Even though women can seek a divorce, many do not because they are dependent on men economically and have children to support. Here again the law is weak because if the woman seeks a divorce, there is no enforcement mechanism for men to pay alimony or child support when it is awarded. In this way, the Family Code provides women with an option that is not always economically viable for them and their children, due to the low level of incomes.

The most recent data on remarriage and divorce are dated. Remarriage is frequent in Senegalese society because of social pressures. Mboup (1992) found that 89 percent of divorced women and 95 percent of widows remarry within five years of a marriage's end. Antoine and Nanitelamio (1996) found that urban women are more likely to enter polygynous marriages if they are marrying for a second or third time. Only 24 percent of first-time marriages of their sample of urban women were marrying an already married man, compared with 55 percent of women marrying for a second time and 72 percent of women marrying for a third time. Early marriage and rapid remarriage after divorce or widowhood combine to bring about a high level of polygyny.

Very little is known about divorce in Senegal. It is not widely accepted by society but is tolerated by religion and law. It is more frequent in urban areas. Women who become divorced often live with their parents (if living) or with another member of their family. The number of women living as single-parent households is increasing, though 84 percent of household heads are men (Ndiaye et al., 1991). Most women who report being household heads are urban-based women in polygynous marital arrangements, but more and more, divorced women and widows are among this growing group. Research shows that economic instability, difference in a couple's educational attainment, and polygyny are associated with the increased likelihood of divorce in the urban Senegalese context (Antoine & Nanitelamio, 1996).

The extended-family situation in Senegal often finds more than two generations living under the same roof. The cohabitation of a couple with the parents of the husband is widespread. Ndiaye and colleagues (1991) found that over 45 percent of women reported living with either one of their biological parents or with one of their husband's biological parents. They found that this pattern differs by rural or urban residence; although just 31 percent of adult women in urban areas live with a parent, 52 percent of adult women in rural areas live with a parent.

Vertical solidarity across generations has somewhat diminished in urban areas, but has also been useful for parents as a migration strategy. A close look in many villages will reveal the occasional child in a family who is living in an urban area with an extended-family member of the parents' generation. In many villages you will find mothers, grandparents, and children, with the father working for several months in paid employment in urban areas. If both parents work in an urban area and there is a grandparent to care for in the rural area, the parents may send a child to help this grandparent. A hierarchy between generations affects both social relationships and obligations (Sow, 1987, 1989). Older persons are generally revered, and their children and grandchildren can be tapped to provide economic assistance and companionship. Sometimes, this may be at the expense of a grandchild's education.

Another characteristic of Senegalese families is that the husband does not always live in the same house. On the national level, 20 percent of women who are in their first marital union do not reside with their husband (Ndiaye et al., 1991). In rural areas, migration to work in urban areas for short periods of time is generally the main reason for the separation. In urban areas, polygynous marital relationships require the husband to spend time in more than one household because wives do not generally live in the same compound or household as would be the case in the rural areas.

Rural households generally contain more members than urban households. This is due in part to earlier marriage ages and to higher rates of fertility and polygyny in rural areas. The rate of polygyny is 49 percent in rural areas and 41 percent in urban areas (Antoine & Nanitelamio, 1996). Rural households also have more members because polygynous households are structured differently in rural areas than in urban areas. In rural areas, the wives of a man may reside in the same compound but in different rooms or structures. In statistics tabulated on households, all wives are counted with their shared husband as the household head. In urban areas, women in polygynous marriages often reside in different compounds and as such have smaller household sizes. In some cases, the husband is not considered the household head. Among the Wolof, the smallest household sizes are found in the central area of Dakar, the largest city, and the largest households are in rural areas (Diop, 1985).

Shortcomings of Past and Current Research

What we know about the Senegalese family is predominantly derived from the study of Wolof families. This focus on the Wolof ethnic group leaves much to be documented and explained about the family functioning of other ethnic groups, namely the Joola, Sereer, and Hal Pulaaren. The dated nature of studies of the Senegalese family further limits our understanding (see Diop's 1985 comprehensive study). Senegalese society as a whole continues to undergo considerable social change that affects family power dynamics and functioning. Additionally, more research is needed on divorce in Senegal, and, specifically, the consequences for children and women after divorce. Finally, the fact that men taking additional wives may lead to abandonment or decreased economic support of the first wife and her children is yet another underresearched area of concern, even though it has been the subject of an international best-selling Senegalese novel, Mariama Bâ's (1980) *So Long a Letter*.

ESSENTIAL FEATURES OF SENEGALESE FAMILIES

Mate Selection

The decision of whom to marry is predominantly a family, not an exclusive individual decision in Senegal. In urban areas, young men and women have more voice in the matter, but overall, the decision is still at the family level. Ndiaye and colleagues (1991) found among women in the Demographic and Health Survey of Senegal that the prevalence of endogamous marriages differs by urban or rural setting, by educational attainment of women, and among ethnic groups. Marrying a maternal or paternal cousin is more pronounced in rural areas, 48 percent, compared with 28 percent in urban areas (Ndiaye et al., 1991). These endogamous family unions are more prevalent among those women without any formal schooling, 44 percent, compared with women who have primary or secondary schooling, 26 and 18 percent, respectively. Across ethnic groups, the Hal Pulaaren are most likely to form an endogamous marital union (44 percent) compared with the Wolof (43 percent), the Sereer (40 percent), and the Joola (28 percent). Paternal cousins are preferred over maternal cousins as marriage partners across ethnic groups with the exception of the Sereer, among whom the maternal cousin is preferred. This divergent pattern of maternal cousin preference among the Sereer is best explained by the late conversion of the Sereer to Islam and Christianity in the 20th century. In Sereer society, the matrilineal transmission of values and kinship have persisted next to patrilineal descent patterns even after the spread of Islam and Christianity.

Multiple Marriage Forms (Including Polygyny)

Marriage may take either the monogamous or polygynous form in Senegal. One clear break in distinguishing monogamous and polygynous households is religion. The monogamous marriage is clearly imposed on Catholics by the church, although customary marriage or cohabitation are frequent among them. The remainder of families following African and Islamic religions may consider the polygynous option. Overall, most Senegalese marriages are monogamous (roughly 60 percent). Catholics comprise just 5 percent of Senegal's population, so religion alone cannot explain why the majority of marriages are monogamous.

Evidence provided by Ndiaye, Sarr, and Ayad (1986) shows that across characteristics, older women are more likely than younger women to be in a polygynous marriage. Regardless of age, rural and less educated women are more likely than urban and more educated women to be in a polygynous marriage. Rural women have fewer opportunities outside of marriage, such as education and careers outside the home, to pursue than women living in urban areas. Among ethnic groups, the Sereer have markedly lower rates of polygyny (38 percent) than other ethnic groups (ranging from 44 to 50 percent). The relatively late and tempered influence of Islam among the Sereer in Senegal compared with other ethnic groups may provide some explanation for this pattern.

Generally, polygyny is an accepted part of the African and Muslim cultures in both rural and urban areas. Antoine and Nanitelamio (1996) present extensive demographic data from an urban area to explain why men and women choose to marry polygynously. They found that some men felt that taking more than one wife showed wealth (actual or desired) while others felt that polygyny was a return to traditional cultural practices, especially among urban Muslims. Because the choice of a mate rests at the family level with varying levels of input by the individual bride and groom, there are also some cases in which parents have given a second wife to their son. In rural areas, polygyny appears to be more functional for a family unit than in urban areas, because rural women maintain full-time agricultural work and housework. Rural women who share domestic duties such as cooking, cleaning, and caring for children can use their extra time to engage in income-generating activities such as selling in a local market.

Levels of Childbearing

Senegalese women have 5.7 children on average during their lifetime. Most children are born within marriage, but there is a growing minority of urban women who bear children outside of marriage. High fertility is the result of the cultural desire for large families, the high infant mortality rate, and the low use of modern contraceptive methods. Just 8 percent of married women are using modern contraceptive methods such as the pill, condom, diaphragm, or Depro (PRB, 2000). Women are expected to reproduce in Senegalese society, and women gain social prestige by having many children. This begins in childhood, when male and female children are allowed different opportunities. One clear-cut example of this can be found by analyzing secondary school enrollment data; 61 females are enrolled in secondary school for every 100 males (PRB, 2000). The lack of opportunities, beginning with education and proceeding to the labor market, coalesce to restrict women's identities and self-worth in terms of their reproductive potential.

Even when women wish to obtain modern contraceptive techniques, their efforts are often stifled by patriarchal attitudes and men's desires for larger families. One woman recounts her story, "When I had my seventh child—four are living—I asked the doctor for the pill. He wasn't sure so he called my husband to verify that it was okay with him.... Now I am expecting my eighth child. It is a lot of work for me."[6]

Gender Roles, Female Autonomy, and Family Dynamics

Gender roles are first taught to children by families and then reinforced by societal influences. Boys and girls are taught different parts to play in life. Girls are recruited into household work at an early age and provide a great deal of domestic help by the age of 12; boys help with some household tasks like carrying wood but outgrow these activities by the age of 12. If a decision must be made about whether a child needs to stay home, a girl is generally taken out of school over a boy regardless of age. In youth, less work and more free time are allowed boys, so boys attain more formal education than girls in the same families (Bass, 1997). However, this is changing and girls' education at the primary level is improving.

The different socialization of boys and girls creates the structure by which women and men in Senegal lead separate work and social lives as adults (Callaway & Creevey, 1994). Female autonomy has to be considered in terms of kinship ties and a mother's marital status. A woman's family background and social networks influence the types of opportunities available. One aspect of this is that women retain the profits from their earnings. Another aspect of this is that if a woman comes from a family from which economic opportunities can be secured, this can increase her status. In addition, seniority affects the amount of power women have as co-wives in a polygynous marital relationship in Senegal (see Creevey, 1992). The first wife is supposed to have the ear of her husband and the broader support of the community through respect for elders than second or third wives.

In general, as Senegal has become more urbanized, women have secured more rights. It is in urban areas where the Family Code Legislation of 1972 and its revisions in 1974, 1979, and 1989 have allowed for improvement in women's rights. There remains a gap between rural and urban areas, and between what is the law and what is practiced. Even though women's autonomy and rights have increased in urban areas, Senegalese society is largely patriarchal and cultural norms favoring males still persist. This preference for male over female is even more pronounced in rural areas where parents share their household work and fieldwork with their children, and difficult decisions must be made about whether to send children to school or have them work for the family's economic survival.

There is still a gap between practice and theory when it comes to protecting the rights of women in Senegalese society. For example, even though the Convention Against the Discrimination in Education was signed into law in 1967, boys are much more likely to advance to secondary school and higher education. In this way, the law is ahead of the cultural norms of the time, because parents and teachers have different expectations for boys and girls.

According to the Family Code, men hold social and legal status over women and children in the family. This patriarchy in the letter of the law is further reinforced by patriarchal attitudes in society, where women are required to defer to men. Diop (1985) defines the Senegalese household in terms of hierarchy and communalism. Even though the needs of all household members are taken care of, resources are distributed in accordance with a hierarchy assigning household members a sliding scale of status in terms of age and gender. If the head of the household dies, his younger brother or a close male relative takes over. One counterinfluence to this gender hierarchy that subordinates women to men is that women largely decide how their earnings are spent (Creevey, 1992). Recent research on child labor in urban areas of Senegal has found that women often receive and control the earnings from their children's labor (Bass, 2000). While there is some room for resistance, these gender and age hierarchies overall provide women with less opportunity and power within the household than men, and children with the least opportunity and power. The Senegalese household should be viewed through these inherent systems of stratification.

Inheritance, even after the Family Code legislation, continues to favor men over women. Women may not inherit land or hold firm traditional rights over land. The Quran provides guidelines governing inheritance. In the case of the death of a household head, Muslim daughters are entitled to only half of the estate that their brothers receive, and wives are entitled to a mere one-eighth of their husband's estate. These inequalities run parallel to different levels of kinship such that male cousins are preferred over female cousins. Senegal's newly approved constitution passed in a January 2001 referendum established equal property rights for men and women (Article 12) and guarantees a woman's right to own property and administer her own goods (Article 19, Government of Senegal, 2001). However, few women are in a position to take advantage of this law because African custom and Islamic teachings carry more weight, especially for those in rural areas, than these new protections written into the constitution. In both rural and urban areas, turning theoretical protections into practice is a challenge.

The issue of women's subordination is an ongoing debate among many African scholars and women's associations. Writing on the status of women in precolonial Africa, Pala and Ly (1979) ask, "When did the system of inequality occur?" Assié-Lumumba (2000) asserts the need to contextualize the women's subordination debate because of African cultural specificities regarding gender experiences. There is a negation of historical experiences of African women, even by Western feminists, says Assié-Lumumba. "There is a shift from the so-called primitive African societies where women were perceived by Westerners as beasts of burden in accordance with descriptions by missionaries and anthropologists a century ago, to African experience of the exploitation of women by men" (p. 11). Thus, the dynamic social space—where "parallel autonomy" and complementary functions exist, and where women and men are found as negotiating social actors—is not taken into account (Steady, 1981). Assié-Lumumba asserts the importance of complementary spheres of activity because they reinforce the power of men and women and are constantly being negotiated.

In the same vein, Kañji and Camara (2000) argue against this idea of "universal" subordination of women to men, as a stereotyped vision of African women's status and roles. They state that "this concern of equality between men and women can be found in African languages. Using an example from Wolof: *nit* (meaning *person*) is a term that is neither constructed from *goor* (meaning *man*) nor constructed from *jigéen* (meaning *female*). In no case would *man* signify *humankind* as it does in French, or define the human species (*mankind*) as it does in English (hu-*man*, wo-*man*)"[7] (p. 20).

Religion and the Senegalese Family Code

Islamic religious ideas running counter to the gender advances secured in the Family Code have been cast in a nationalist framework. Because some Muslim leaders view the Family Code as a direct attack on Islam, they portray the protections written into law by the Family Code as Western ideas (Callaway & Creevey, 1994). Muslim leaders and many men's groups hold that increasing the political and social equality of women is another case of the corruption of society by the West and refer to the Family Code as the "Women's Code" (Sow, 1989, p. 9). One Muslim leader accuses Senegalese feminists as being "sometimes disrespectful [to religious leaders] and breaking the bounds of social norms subscribed to by the overwhelming majority of the population" (*Echo*, 1986, pp. 2–3, 9). Muslim groups' ideas, which are based on religious teachings of the Quran, are indeed appealing to Senegalese men, who are dissatisfied with their country's poverty and suspicious of Western interference.

The HIV/AIDS Crisis and Family Health

Currently, less than 2 percent of the adult Senegalese population, ages 15 through 49, is estimated as infected with HIV/AIDS (PRB, 1999). The fact that Senegal is relatively spared from the epidemic can be attributed to several factors. First, sexual contact in Senegal occurs at a relatively high age, 17.5 years on average, among Senegalese women surveyed who are ages 20 to 24 years old (McCauley & Salter, 1995). Also, condom use among prostitutes is promoted and monitored. A 1998 study of condom use found that 99 percent of sex workers reported using a condom with their most recent new client and 97 percent with their most recent regular client. Another 60 percent of sex workers reported using condoms with men who were not clients. In addition, a program has been in place since 1987 to monitor sexually transmitted diseases. This program has been able to organize public conferences where Islamic religious leaders took the floor and encouraged people to learn about HIV/AIDS and how to control it. One measure of the program's effectiveness is the use of condoms, which rose from under 1 percent in the mid-1980s to 68 percent in 1997 (World Health Organization [WHO], 2000).

There is high awareness and understanding of the modes of protection against HIV throughout the country, even in rural areas. The Senegalese government, local nongovernmental organizations, and community organizations have been actively educating the population about the virus and precautions to take to avoid infection. One survey found that over 90 percent of the population was able to list two ways to protect oneself against HIV. By 1995, 200 NGOs and 400 women's associations that included 500,000 members had become involved in efforts to educate and control the spread of HIV/AIDS (WHO, 2000).

CONCLUSION

It is difficult for families to provide basic needs and future opportunities in a depressed economic climate. Poor economic growth, currency devaluations, and decreased peanut production all frame how well families in Senegal can provide for their members. In a more positive vein, some recent changes in the law that advance women's equality vis-à-vis men can be directly related to the widespread formation of women's associations at the local level in both rural and urban areas. With the growth of both women's and men's associations, individuals have come together to collectively lobby for their interests. Such initiatives by individuals to have their voices heard by the state through organizing will likely frame specific issues, such as education and access to public services, affecting the family in the future.

Older individuals are dependent on their families, not the government, to secure their material needs. In lieu of a public social safety net, parents often draw on the kinship ties that they share with others in order to sustain their families. The role of the family as an economic provider speaks to its vitality as a functioning institution in society. Women, who are the keepers of kinship relations in most cultures, are an important part of this in Senegal. For example, women may pool resources, join savings associations, and help support one another in life events such as naming ceremonies, weddings, funerals and so on. The mother's relatives, friends and contacts—her social network or *social capital*—affect opportunities that are available to a household. Like money, social relationships are a valuable resource and have worth that can be called on. Finally, a combination of both blood and nonfilial kinship ties are marshaled to provide for families.

With respect to family formation, future research needs to analyze the increasing voice young women and men have in the choice of their marriage partners, which will likely affect family structure, obligations between generations, and most likely, the rate of polygyny. At present, there is still a need to assess women's contributions of material and financial resources to the family. As women receive more education, it remains to be seen to what extent they will be integrated into full-time paid work outside the home, how they will juggle work and family, and what work positions they will take vis-à-vis men with the same levels of education. If women do become more fully integrated into the paid workforce outside the household, it will be important to monitor whether divorce rates increase as women attain more economic independence, which has been the case in other regions of the world. Future research should analyze how the Senegalese family continues to be affected by urbanization and globalization.

The triple heritage—African, Islamic, and colonial influences—provides a useful prism through which to examine the historical formation of Senegalese families today. More recently, the global nature of the economy and the international spread of films and television also add to our understanding of the contemporary shaping in social relationships. Currently and in the future, household members' social ties, as expressed in opportunities and obligations, will be key to understand the Senegalese family's functioning across ethnic groups in both rural and urban areas, as well as across monogamous, divorced, and polygynous families. Even when families are separated by household structures or the urban-rural migration experience, the vitality of the family remains intact because these persistent social ties that often translate into economic opportunities. We can expect that the Senegalese family will change as women attain higher educational levels and gain rights more equal to those of men. We can also expect the urban Senegalese family to continue to fan the fires of change for Senegalese families.

In Mariama Bâ's (1980) *So Long a Letter*, Ramatoulaye recounts the anguish she felt when her husband took a second wife without consulting her. Though this situation is harmful to her children and has disrupted her family, she honors the institution of the family and remains committed to her children even in the face of rejection and adversity. She draws on her social ties to provide for herself and her children. The future of the Senegalese family will be fraught with social change and adjustments, but like the heroine of Bâ's novel, Ramatoulaye, it will remain resilient if it can continue to draw on the social relationships available with assigned and created kinship ties.

NOTES

1. Polygyny is the pre-Islamic and Islamic practice of a man taking more than one wife.

2. The category Hal Pulaaren is comprised of Peulh and Toucouleur ethnic groups, which share a common language. The Peulh and Toucouleur make up 8 and 13 percent of the national population, respectively. This practice of grouping the two ethnicities is taken from the Senegalese national statistics office.

3. Ethnic groups have remained linguistically distinctive, but Wolof has been a *lingua franca* especially since colonization and urbanization.

4. It started with the women of the Socialist ruling party who required that 25 percent of the parliament seats should be reserved for women.

5. This finding and most of the literature on Senegalese families focus on the Wolof, the dominant ethnic group. However, this same general pattern of defining the household holds true for other ethnic groups.
6. Personal interview by Loretta E. Bass, summer 1996.
7. Translated from Kañji and Camara (2000, p. 20).

REFERENCES

Antoine, P., & Nanitelamio, J. (1996). Can polygyny be avoided in Dakar? In Sheldon, K. (Ed.), *Courtyards, markets, and city streets*. Boulder, CO: Westview.
Assié-Lumumba, N. (2000, October). Gender research in Africa. *Echo, New Serial N° 5*.
Bâ, M. (1980). *So long a letter*. Oxford: Heinemann.
Bass, L. E. (1997). *Working for peanuts: Children's market work in urban areas of Senegal*. Ann Arbor: University of Michigan.
Bass, L. E. (2000). Enlarging the street and negotiating the curb: Public space at the edge of an African market. *International Sociology and Social Policy 20*, 1–2.
Callaway, B., & Creevey, L. (1994). *The heritage of Islam: Women, religion, and politics in West Africa*. Boulder, Co: Lynne Rienner.
Central Intelligence Agency. (2000). *The world factbook*. Washington, DC: Central Intelligence Agency.
Creevey, L. (1992). *The sword and the veil*. Unpublished manuscript. Storrs: University of Connecticut.
Diop, A-B. (1985). *La famille wolof*. Paris: Karthala.
Diop, C. A. (1960). *L'Afrique noire précoloniale*. Paris: Présence Africaine.
Echo. (1986). Publication of Senegalese feminist organization, Yewwu Yewwi. I: 2–3, 9.
Enel, C., Pison, G., & Lefebvre, M. (1994). Migration and marriage change: A case study of Mbomp, a Joola village in southern Senegal. In Bledsoe, C. & Pison, G. (Eds.), *Nuptiality in sub-Saharan Africa* (pp. 92–113). Oxford: Clarendon.
Gastellu, J-M. (1981). *L'égalitarianisme économique des Serers du Sénégal*. Travaux et Documents d'ORSTOM 128. Paris: ORSTOM.
Government of Senegal. (2001). Constitution. In *Journal Officiel*, Dakar.
Government of Senegal. (1979 [1989]). Code de la Famille, in *Journal Officiel* (version révisée, avril 1989), Dakar.
Government of Senegal. (1988). *Recensement général de la population et de l'Habitat (RGPH)*. Dakar: Ministère de l'Economie et des Finances, Direction de la Statistique, Bureau Informatique.
Kañji, S., & Camara, F. (2000). *L'union matrimoniale dans la tradition des peuples noirs*. Paris: L'Harmattan.
Khurshid, A. (1974). *Family life in Islam*. Leicester: Islamic Foundation.
Kouassigan, G. (1978). Droit occidental et conception néegro-africaine de la famille: culture, famille et développement. *Genève-Afrique XVI (2)*, 45–80.
Mafeje, A. (1991). *African households and prospects for agricultural revival in sub-Saharan Africa*. CODESRIA Working Paper, 2/91. Council for the Development of Economic and Social Research in Africa (CODESRIA), Dakar.
Mboup, G. (1992). *Etude des déterminants socio-économiques et culturels de la fécondité au Sénégal à partir de l'enquête démographique et de santé*. Ph.D. diss., Université de Montréal.

Ndiaye, S., Sarr, I., & Ayad, M. (1988). *Enquête démographique et de santé au Sénégal, 1986*. Columbia, MD: Ministère de l'Economie, des Finances et du Plan [Sénégal] et Institute for Resource Development / Westinghouse.

Ndiaye, S., Thiongane, A., & Sarr, I. (1991). *Structures familiales au Sénégal*. Direction de la Prévision et de la Statistique, Sénégal.

Pala, A., & Ly, M. (1979). *La femme africaine dans la société précoloniale*. Paris: UNESCO.

Panhuys, H., Farrell, G., & Seck, O. (1989). *La dynamique de développment extensif du secteur informel Sénégalais dans une économie sous ajustement*. Sénégal: Bureau International du Travail.

Population Reference Bureau. (2000). *World population data sheet*. Washington, DC.

Reinwald, B. (1997). Changing family strategies as a response to colonial challenge: Microanalytic observations on Siin/Senegal 1890–1960. *The History of the Family 2(2)*, pp. 183–195.

Sène, S. (1993). *Le travail des enfants au Sénégal: cas des apprentis*. Dakar: Gouvernement du Sénégal, UNICEF-BIT.

Sow, F. (1987, February). African women, family and laws. Paper presented at colloquium, Negritude, Ethnicity and Afro-Cultures in the Americas, Miami, FL.

Sow, F. (1989, Summer). Senegal: The decade and its consequence. In *Beyond Nairobi: Women's policies and policies in Africa revisited. Issue*, a journal of opinion, African Studies Association, XVII (2), pp. 32–36.

Sow, F. (1991, January). *Le pouvoir économique des femmes dans le département de Podor*. Dakar: IFAN.

Steady, P. (Ed.). (1981). *The black woman cross-culturally*. Cambridge, MA: Schenkman.

UNICEF. (1995). *Analyse de la situation de l'enfant et de la femme au Sénégal*. Dakar: Gouvernement du Sénégal et UNICEF.

U.S. Bureau of the Census. (2000). *International data base, Senegal*. Washington, DC: U.S. Department of Commerce.

World Health Organization. (2000). *Senegal contains the spread of HIV*. Geneva: World Health Organization.

CHAPTER 6

Structural Change and Continuity in the Ivorian Family

N'Dri Thérèse Assié-Lumumba

INTRODUCTION

The family in Côte d'Ivoire, as a social institution within a contemporary African state, has been shaped by socioeconomic, political, and historical factors as well as a cultural heritage shared by other African societies. It is based on the common African ethos that is characterized by a global and encompassing definition of membership in the family that functionally includes the ancestors, the living, and the unborn, who in the invisible world are linked to the ancestors, thus actualizing the circle of life. It includes physical, metaphysical, and spiritual entities and spheres. Given the formation of the contemporary African states that have been framed by artificial colonial borders, precise or unique national traits do not really exist. External influences and various historical factors have shaped the African family. More than any phenomenon related to the nation-state, the indigenous family structures and values have shown resilience and a powerful ability to influence African societies culturally, economically, and politically.

The topics to be examined in this chapter include the concepts of descent, marriage and its related issues of parenthood and legitimacy, the gender factor in family structures, and the evolution of the family. The chapter also deals with the impact of Westernization, urbanization, and the capitalist monetary-driven economy on the structure of the family.

Though the functionalist notion that the family emerged in the historical process to perform specific integrative functions of regulation of sexual behavior, reproduction, and socialization is valid, the advocates of conflict theory who articulate that a dialectical driving force guides family relations in the context of production relations provide an indisputably convincing argument. The physical, metaphysical, and spiritual components of the family have been located in a global African ethos that cuts across contemporary boundaries and that also has a solid common understanding and sharing mechanisms all of which have been labeled as African family values. Indeed, family values are neither neutral nor static. They contribute to the transformation and adaptation of other social institutions.

For instance, the family as a unit of production and consumption affects the nature of economic production, even the colonially introduced capitalist economy in the global context. In turn, the dynamics of the indigenous economic systems and the global capitalist mode of production shape the family. Thus the Ivorian family in the beginning of the 21st century is the result of structural changes and at the same time an institutional agent of change in the socioeconomic organization. It is argued that with or without European influence, the African family organization in Côte d'Ivoire would have influenced, and been influenced by, structural change albeit with a different pace. However, the different degrees of Westernization and urbanization, in addition to existing cultural and historical factors of resistance to change, have led to different levels of acceptance and practical reference to indigenous and/or recently adopted family laws. Thus, there are signs of conflicts, realistic cohabitation, convergence, or concordance between the historically African and newly adopted systems of legal arrangements that govern family life.

It is also significant to note that to the more recent French influence, with secular and religious Christian components, must be added the Islamic factor, which has been present in some areas for centuries, especially in the North. Through the colonial administration and new Europeanized social institutions, the French influence has been asserted in the whole country. However, in the specific case of religion, Christianity has been more widespread in the southern part of the country while Islam is more heavily concentrated in the northern section and in urban areas. The longer an external factor is adopted in a given cultural milieu, the more difficult it becomes to identify precise contours that separate the external from the initial receiving milieu. For instance, reference to "Black Islam" indicates the adaptation and degree of blending between Islam and African cultural aspects, some of which are more compatible (e.g., polygyny) with African family practices than European/Christian cultural elements (e.g., monogamy, celibacy of priests), although regions with early Judeo-Christian influences in Africa have also produced a high level of blending and coexistence between various cultural elements. The impact varies according to how long the Islamic presence has been established in a given social context and the level of concentration or dispersion of the Muslim population.

This chapter addresses some of the major dimensions of structural change. It is divided into five sections. The first section focuses on the historical background and the sociogeographic setting of contemporary family structures in Côte d'Ivoire. The second section deals with the dynamics of the adoption and application of the postcolonial family laws alongside the enduring practices of African family values. The focus of the third section is on gender equity in the contemporary family laws. The fourth section addresses significant dimensions of the migratory movements related to the capitalist economy and their impact on the family. The fifth section is concerned with the new trends and the resistance of the indigenous African system.

HISTORY AND THE SOCIOGEOGRAPHIC SETTING OF CONTEMPORARY FAMILY STRUCTURES

When analyzing the postcolonial period and the family laws that have been adopted since, one can refer to the preexisting social context by using Mazrui's (1986) notion of triple heritage, with a simultaneous presence of the indigenous African culture and the European/Christian and Islamic inputs. All these three elements have secular and religious components, some of which are addressed in this chapter.

The arguments are presented within the methodological framework of the historical-structuralist approach which contends that sociohistorical forces constitute key explanatory factors that shape contemporary processes and influence structures and values of social institutions, in this case, the family. This chapter is also based on studies that have used empirical data collected for different purposes in different contexts. Another source consists of a series of acts that have been adopted by Côte d'Ivoire since its independence. Of particular significance are the acts that were passed in 1964. These acts provide the legal framework for dealing with major aspects of the family, including the following: naming babies, marking of birth and death, marriage, divorce and estrangement, lineage and descent, adoption, inheritance, and gifts and wills. The 1970 act that defines and articulates the age of legal majority is also worth mentioning.

Part of the complexity of the current cultural and legal situation of the family in Côte d'Ivoire can be explained by the ethnic makeup of the country. With a square-like shape, Côte d'Ivoire shares borders with Burkina Faso, Ghana, Guinea, Liberia, and Mali and has a coastal area on the Atlantic Ocean. Like other countries in Africa, its borders were defined by the history of the European conquest of Africa and the subsequent clauses of the Berlin conference (1884–85) that granted the country to France. Côte d'Ivoire as a contemporary state and the evolution of its legal system and social institutions have been profoundly defined for over a hundred years by the French legal system. Formally a colony in 1893, in 1895 it was integrated into the French colonial unit of Afrique Occidentale Française (AOF) that included Benin (then Dahomey), Burkina Faso (then Haute Volta), Guinea, Mali (then French Soudan), Mauritania, Niger, and Senegal.

The ethnic groups that compose Côte d'Ivoire have been classified in six major categories that are themselves made of subgroups with varying degrees of shared and distinctive traits: Akan, Krou, Malinké, Mandé, Lagunaire, and Voltaïque. Côte d'Ivoire illustrates the typical political entity that inherited artificial boundaries which follow the logic of the interests of European colonial powers and reflect their compromises. The Europeans drew boundaries of the new nation-states through indigenous political spaces, ethnic groups, locally defined cultural specificities and social institutions, and family structures. Thus, in terms of the local cultural and institutional structures, various groups can be more closely identified with ethnic groups of a neighboring country than within other Ivorian ethnic groups. For instance, the populations of the Malinké and Voltaïque groups of the northeastern and northwestern parts of the country historically have more specific cultural affinities with similar ethnic groups in the Sahelian countries of Burkina Faso, Mali, and also Guinea, than with the Akan. The Akan groups in Côte d'Ivoire share more common subcultural traditions with the Akan in Ghana. The Mandé and Krou groups have common traditions with indigenous Liberians. However, despite variations and local specificities, the similar African characteristics of the family structure and values in Côte d'Ivoire are common to those of families in other African societies, regardless of the nature and duration of European influence through colonial policies and legacies.

When referring to family structures and the values of subregions and ethnic groups, there should be special mention of the spatial and temporal variation from more cohesive to more heterogeneous cultures. Indeed, as a result of migration, increased urbanization, and mixed ethnic and religious marriages, there has been a trend toward less homogeneous family practices.

Côte d'Ivoire was granted its nominal independence from France in 1960. It played a leading role in the subregion in the resistance movement against French colonial rule, which led to massive repression including executions and deportations, from the time of its entry into AOF until the First World War when the French colonial administration reached its objective of "pacification" by terror. Côte d'Ivoire also constituted a stronghold of the struggle for equality and decolonization as exemplified by its leadership in the initial stage of the formation of popular movements that were transformed into political parties such as the RDA (Rassemblement Démocratique Africain) that was born out of the SAA (Syndicat Agricole Africain) formed by Ivorian landlords. Precisely because of the strong Ivorian position, it became the target of brutal and aggressive French policy that led to the co-optation of the most influential leader of the country and the subregion. By the early 1950s, the future of Côte d'Ivoire as a pro-Western country and an extreme case of neocolonial state formation had been set. Its subsequent alignment with and reproduction of French traditions have been reflected in legal systems and social policies including those that are connected to the family legal code and other related decisions.

There have been conflicts, cohabitation, and possible convergence between at least some elements of the indigenous African family laws and the postcolonial

Western-influenced legal systems and practices of the family. These systems and practices are the results of deeply rooted, old and robust traditions and the emerging ones that are mostly located in the dynamics of structural changes, Westernization, urbanization, and migration. Given the ethos and major sociohistorical reference of each of these three, their constant dynamics reflect conflicts, accommodation, and some indications of the presence of convergent and assimilationist elements. It is thus important to identify and briefly discuss some of the local traditions of family organization as they constitute the reference for stability and change.

What has been labeled as extended family, a fundamental common thread of the African family on the continent and in the diaspora, is the basis of all indigenous family organization in Côte d'Ivoire. Historically, different ethnic groups have had different socio-spatial and political organizations that are linked to the family and explain differences in their dwellings. Their social organizations in general vary in type and complexity. Despite these differences and the ethnic or regional specificities, the populations share a common African conception of the family. This conception is characterized by the notion of multigenerational and horizontally widespread membership in the family unit. This unit includes grandparents, who play both formal and informal roles in the education and socialization of the youth, and various horizontal members including siblings, their spouses and descendents, if any, and intricate layers of parallel and cross cousins. This family transcends the nuclear unit. According to the 1998 census in Côte d'Ivoire, the national average size of households was 6.2 persons. However, such a figure cannot encompass, capture, or translate the complexity of family membership.

The philosophy of line of descent defines the rules of marriage, the criteria for preferential spouses and inheritance, and the basis for transfer of goods, as well as authority vested in specific social positions in the family and the wider society. The criteria for access to social and higher political positions are primarily defined by the laws that govern the line of descent. Côte d'Ivoire is literally divided into two major sections by a descent line than runs North-South. The predominantly matrilineal Akan (e.g., Abouré, Abron, Agni, Baoulé), Voltaïque (e.g., Koulango, Lobi) among whom are the eastern section of the Sénoufo, and also the Eastern section of the Lagunaire (e.g., Attié, Ebrié, Adioukrou) are in the eastern half of the country. The western half of the country is clearly patrilineal and is composed of the Kru (e.g., Bété, Dida, Godié, Guéré), Mandé (e.g., Dan, Gagou, Gouro), and the Malinké who have some pockets of presence in the eastern half. As suggested above, some subgroups among the Lagunaires (e.g., Abidji) and also relatively large sections of the Sénoufo are patrilineal or lean toward patriliny as well.

To these two predominant traditions of descent that follow a North-South line of demarcation, it is important to add that bilateral descent also exists. For instance, as indicated above, the Akan in Côte d'Ivoire, like those in Ghana, are known as matrilineal societies. However, John Mundt (1972) missed an important aspect of the complex and refined conceptions of the family systems in Côte d'Ivoire and most African societies when he stated that not until recently unilineal system of descent was commonly practiced. While matriliny is predominant, and in some spheres of social life constitutes an indisputable norm, metaphysically and in the real world the Akan, for instance, sustain a system of bilateral descent (Etienne, 1972). In the case of the Abouré, Clignet (1970) rightly explained that they "believe that two elements necessarily enter into the development of the human embryo: spirit is provided by the father and the blood by the mother. Thus, certain taboos and certain technical crafts are transmitted along paternal lines. . . . The transmission of assets and status follows the lines of blood, that is, the structure of matrilineal descent group" (p. 73). This case is also applicable to other Akan groups in Côte d'Ivoire. Despite the predominance of matriliny among some ethnic groups, the practice of patrilocal residence has been prevalent. The bilateral tendencies or gradual evolution toward patriliny, at least in some types of inheritance (e.g., land, export crop plantation as opposed to family treasures inherited from the female lines from ancient generations), has been observed among some groups known as matrilineal.

Polygyny is the marriage form that has been historically common to all ethnic groups in Côte d'Ivoire. Though the indigenous family code made polygyny a legal practice, its actual prevalence varies among ethnic groups. According to Clignet (1970, p. 21), the level of political and social stratification as measured in part by economic activities and transmission of resources through inheritance is linked to the incidence of polygyny. Furthermore, within the same society that highly values polygyny, "the function ascribed to plural marriage may also be symbolic and closely related to social differentiation" (Clignet, 1970, p. 34) in the sense that power (economic, social) is largely a determinant of the number of co-wives in a given marriage.

The nature, quantity, and process for the provision and distribution of what is referred to in this chapter as "marriage goods and services," usually known as bride wealth or bride price, varies according to the lineage system. There are several reasons why in this paper the term *marriage goods and services* is preferred to bride price or even the milder and seemingly neutral term bride wealth. First of all, although the system has lost some of its meanings in the capitalist economy especially amidst increasing poverty, it cannot be reduced to a simple material transaction. Second of all, although some among those who criticize the practice claim to argue in the interest of women, they tend to focus on the goods that the bridegroom is required to provide while they ignore the contribution from the bride's side. In this context, there is an unfair and partial assessment of the actual contribution of both sides. Indeed, brides and their families make significant contributions in setting up a new household. There are various forms of goods and services that brides and their family contribute that have not been recognized and analyzed in the literature. In many cases, in the widespread patrilocal practice, the married woman is accompanied, when she moves to her new home, by a young relative who assists her in her activities. Many forms of commodities are also provided during the marriage ceremonies and as she moves to the husband's home.

There is generally a smaller quantity, but not less important in value, of marriage goods and services among matrilineal as compared to patrilineal societies. These goods and services are offered at different stages of the long process of the marriage ceremony, have social and historical significance, and constitute the basis of the legitimacy of the marriage.

This sociohistorical background of contemporary family structures in the country helps locate the processes and dynamics in the adoption and application of the postcolonial family laws amidst the endogenous practices of African family values. The local foundation and external factors of change are addressed in the next section.

POSTCOLONIAL LAWS AND ENDOGENOUS AFRICAN FAMILY VALUES

Levasseur (1976) pointed out that "spontaneous genesis in the field of law is hardly conceivable. In whatever theory of law one supports, a legal rule has its history. Its origin is either in some pre-existing situation which justifies the enactment of such and such law, or in an intellectual process of a few who hope to provoke changes so as to conform to a pre-existing frame" (p. 19).

Thus, the family laws that were adopted in Côte d'Ivoire after independence reflect local sociological realities. However, given the ideology of the leaders of the country at the time of its independence and the postcolonial influence in addition to the colonial legacy, the family laws adopted reflect a lack of political will to consider any elements of the African family system. There is no clearly articulated philosophical framework for the adopted laws. One must interpret them within the context of the political and ideological choices made by the political leaders. Yet there are major differences that have an impact on the law in the case of marriage law, for instance. Meekers (1992) and also Launey (1995) observed that there is a sharp contrast between the African traditions that makes marriage a process instead of a one-time event in Judeo-Christian tradition. This process, in turn, determines the legitimate or illegitimate status of children, the African practice being flexible for negotiation about an offspring's status. As Meekers (1990) argues in another article, the notion of legitimacy is also linked to the line of descent. In a matrilineal society, with or without a father a child always receives a legitimate status because the mother is sufficient guarantor while in patrilineal societies a father is necessary for the legitimacy of a child.

Some of the decisions that were adopted with great fanfare in the postcolonial laws include the abolition of polygyny, bride wealth, and matriliny. In the process of nation building in Africa, the laws adopted by the states have been used as key unifying instruments. Given the diversity of specific local customs and social rites, the laws under colonial rule and in the postcolonial period have affected differently the practices of different ethnic groups. While a new law may coincide and even reinforce an existing practice, it may be in opposition to, or direct conflict with, local norms of another group. Furthermore, a new law may affect differently various categories within the same social group. Thus, the acceptance and appropriation of a new law may vary considerably depending on its convergence toward, or divergence from, the existing laws and the interests of the different subgroups.

Other social institutions can prepare members of the community to initiate and accept change. For instance, formal education has a powerful ability to create the readiness or motivation for promoting the acceptance of one of the new laws. As introduced by the Europeans, it was one of the key instruments that was used to promote the targeted social surgery aimed at transforming the African social fabric and creating new Africans who would accept the new norms and legal dispositions. Through formal education, Africans themselves can continue to reproduce European values as they acquire new standards that are more compatible with ones that prevail in the West or those that were inherited. The process of schooling is one of the most effective means that triggers the process of Westernization. In the case of the French philosophy of colonial administration, the use of assimilation was an additional factor that was planned to make Africans more readily able to adopt French social values. This expectation of the colonial administration was in contradiction to the policy of double citizenship that was based on the Native Law, and did not grant to the majority of Africans even a few "privileges" that were made available to the formally educated.

The change in the family laws that came out of the French legacy in Côte d'Ivoire started during the colonial era. For instance, by a decree dated September 14, 1951, a ceiling was placed on the amount of wedding goods, and if the amount was perceived to be too high, the marriage could legally take place without this requirement. This meant that legitimacy from the local perspective was no longer required. According to the same decree, bridegrooms were given the option to choose, at the time of their marriage, to never be married to more than one wife at a time, meaning that a new marriage could take place only after dissolution of an existing one. As Levasseur (1976, p. 14) explains, these were "timid step[s]" in promoting changes in major aspects of the institution of marriage, including polygyny.

A series of acts comprising the Civil Code of Côte d'Ivoire constitute the legal foundation, framework, and concrete instruments adopted by the newly independent country, with the intention of promoting sweeping changes in all aspects of the institution of the family as hitherto defined and lived by African laws and practices. They include, for instance, several laws adopted in 1964 (i.e., the laws of October 7, 1964) and also August 3, 1970, that were published in the *Journal Officiel Numéro Spécial 27 Octobre 1964* and *Journal Officiel Numéro Spécial 27 Août 1970*, respectively. Some of these acts were amended later. These acts define a new legal framework, without spelling out a new philosophy and rationale, for naming babies, marking of birth and death, marriage, divorce and estrangement, lineage and descent, adoption, inheritance, gifts and wills, minors, and various dispositions regarding specific articles of the laws.

Other major issues in a new nation-state as opposed to the colonial state or preexiting African political entities were addressed, such as membership in the new nation through family ties. For instance, all families were required by law to have patronymic names from the male line. The abolition of matriliny was in conflict with the practice of the Eastern half of the country, mostly the Akan but also the Sénoufo who have a matrilineal tradition. The formally educated segments of the population are more likely to acknowledge (without necessarily practicing) the new law while the majority of the population, especially in rural areas, may not even be aware of it. Thus, they may lean toward preservation of the matrilineal tradition despite some flexibility and trends toward inheritance of land by offspring.

According to Act No. 64-375 of October 7, 1964, which was modified by Act No. 83-800 of August 2, 1983, only marriages that are performed by a registry official are legal. Marriages contracted before the adoption of the law were granted a period to become legalized according to the new law. Otherwise, like other marriages contracted later, they would be considered "common law" marriages and thus would not be recognized by the state law, as the new law prohibited polygyny. Given existing and expected practices, the new law constituted a major source of conflict between individuals and groups, primarily between a man and the women and also the offspring and members of the families of the men and women involved in these unions. The question in this case was who among existing co-wives would be chosen to be the official wife.

These laws were followed by application decrees and circulars over many years. For instance, a circular of the Ministry of Justice dated April 29, 1966, recalled the necessity to "rigorously enforce the law" by punishing those who either requested or received bride wealth with six months to two years imprisonment. The penalty also included the equivalent of twice the value of the required bride wealth or at least 50,000 CFA Francs (approximately $80 U.S.).

In another legal decision, activities related to funeral ceremonies that were considered extravagant were banned. The purpose was to ensure the elimination of funeral ceremonies that might lead to debt and so-called waste of scarce financial resources needed to sustain the well-being of the living. The level of lavishness, the stages and duration of funeral ceremonies, the number of the participants, and so forth, depend on the practices, rules, and regulations of different ethnic groups. As was popularly known, among the first people who broke these laws were the political leaders of the country themselves who, in spite of their level of Westernization, were still rooted in their traditions and were compelled to pay their due.

Funerals exist in all societies. In the African context and among the people of Côte d'Ivoire in general, even when they adopt Islamic and Christian religions with their respective prescriptions of varying rigidity, the African religious foundation maintains supremacy with the strong belief that the funeral ceremonies have multiple functions: to keep the revolving door between life and death functional, to honor the memory of the departed, and to make the spirit happy in ensuring that the living will be showered with blessings. The active members of the family include the living and deceased. They are participants of major family decisions and events. Dignified funerals constitute a gesture to reaffirm that continuity of the lifeline between the visible world and invisible realm, which is an ever-present component of the African cosmos. This is just one example that illustrates the individual and collective reaffirmation of continuity in the African family in Côte d'Ivoire. How can such a practice change by simple promulgation of a law, especially when the sponsors are the first to break it?

The next section deals with the specific case of the gender equity in the new family laws and whether these laws have redressed or created gender-based inequality.

GENDER EQUITY IN FAMILY LAWS

The situation of women in Côte d'Ivoire as defined by the laws and practices are presented in a major work by Kaudjis-Offoumou (1995) in which she analyzes the many facets of de jure and de facto discrimination against women. The grounds for and practices of discrimination against women in the family code are inherent to the conception, design, and implementation of the family code. Kaudjis-Offoumou articulates women's rights in general in Côte d'Ivoire and proposes changes that can help close the gender gap. Given the complexity of the issues involved, what she presented in almost 350 pages can only be briefly referred to in this paper.

The postindependence laws present paradoxical, contradictory, and in many aspects anachronistic positions that tend to diminish the rights of women even though decisions, to ban polygyny for instance, are progressive on the grounds of basic equality. Different legal dispositions regarding children unequivocally establish the rights of children of both genders. Whether they are born inside or outside the marriage, the rights of the children (male and female) to receive protection and equally share their parents' heritage are protected by the law.

Ironically, gender inequality is established in the transition of the status of the woman as an offspring and sibling (with equal rights as her brothers) to her status as spouse (with unequal rights compared to her husband). This paradox, contradiction, and unequal treatment under the law are evidenced by many legal dispositions. The adult and married woman loses status and becomes lower than a dependent minor while the man acquires full rights and a domain (the family) over which his status as a grown and married man gives him full control. Although legal age is 21 years for males and females, the legal marriage age is 18 years for the young woman and 20 years for the young man.

According to article 47 of Law No. 64-374, at the marriage ceremony the husband receives free of charge a family booklet that records the "identity of the spouse, the date and place of the marriage," and later the list of the children born to the couple. The fact that the man receives the documents that contain evidence of the identity of the couple is symbolic of the woman's loss of control over important parts of her life even when she is from a matrilineal group.

The philosophy of naming babies in the African context has ample provision for people to take names that do not follow a linear and patrilineal patronymic frame. Furthermore, the belief in a lineage is clearly established among the families of all ethnic groups but the remembrance of a common line of descent is not necessarily actualized through a patronymic name. Among some ethnic groups the first name of the father becomes the last name of the offspring. In many cases, children bear last names that are different from that of the father and other siblings when he/she lives with them. However, some ethnic groups (e.g., Malinké) have a patronymic tradition.

Even in the predominantly matrilineal systems, children bear the name of the father. In this case, the new law is consistent with the local traditions. However, regardless of the lineage system and of the fact that patrilocal tradition is overwhelmingly practiced, neither the woman nor the man changes her/his name at marriage. Yet, Article 7 of Law No. 64-373 stipulates that "the married woman must use her husband's name," which she loses in case of divorce or estrangement. According to Article 12, the patronymic name can be extinct if "the last male descendant" dies without a male heir bearing the name.

The man and woman must be the only ones who are allowed by law to decide to marry, leaving out family influence and also banning marriage by force (*mariage forcé*) or arranged marriages that ignore the consent of one or both of the future spouses. Although the practice of marriage by force did affect men, it had a greater impact on women. Generally, married women are younger than their husbands. Given the fact that, other things being equal, in African culture seniority carries considerable power and authority, even if the choice is left to the future mates, the woman will be likely to have less leverage than the man.

The practice of marriage by force was real. However, there is considerable variation in the nature and degree of involvement of men, the women, and their respective families in the process of mate selection in different ethnic groups at different stages of the marriage process. There is relatively more freedom for the mates in the selection in matrilineal societies than in patrilineal ethnic groups. Parental/family influence in the selection is more prevalent among the Muslim populations. Meekers (1990) indicates that the Islamic ethnic groups have higher proportions of arranged marriages. However, full participation of the families in the overall process of the marriage is common among all societies in the country.

All ethnic groups value marriage as a means to increase the social prestige and power associated with the size of the extended family. Marriage is also a major factor in legitimizing the status of children. However, there are variations by ethnic groups. For instance, Meekers (1990) found that the matrilineal Baoulé continue to be the most tolerant about having a child with a man who would not be the first husband compared to the Islamic Mandé.

It is important to note that the adoption of the law against the practice of marriage by force emphasized the expression of individual freedom to choose. Yet, while family involvement may infringe on an individual's right to choose, the collective participation in the decision-making process constitutes an important component in the legitimization of the marriage—the couple's and their families' pledge to exercise their right and responsibility to ensure the success of the union. Within this context, families play major roles in the lives of men as well as women, in monogamous as well as in polygynous unions.

While in the new family law there is a general shift from collective to individual participation, in the prescribed monogamous family with no extended-family involvement, the man is granted more power and authority than the woman. With neither the recognized right of the extended family to be involved nor legal provision, the woman becomes a loser on both sides. In contrast, the married man is freed from the collective authority prescribed by the endogenous system and acquires new legal basis for individual exercise of power and authority.

For instance, according to the new law only the husband is allowed to make a decision regarding where the couple's residence shall be. If the woman can provide evidence in court that the residence chosen by the man is not suitable for the well-being of the family, the ruling judge chooses another residence for the woman. Thus, according to the law, the married woman has no say in the choice of her residence. Furthermore, the woman loses her traditional rights to work outside the home, as Article 28 of Law No. 64-375 stipulates that "the woman may have a professional position different from that of the man provided the latter does not object." In this case also, only a judge (Article 41) can overrule the husband's objection to the wife seeking and exercising a profession or working at all outside the home.

Furthermore, Article 34 stipulates that even assets that belong partially to the woman, like the common assets, are managed by the man. Without the woman's consent, the man is allowed by law (Article 35) to sell his, her, or their common assets, whereas the woman must obtain the man's consent (Article 37) to sell even her own assets acquired before or while married, including gifts. The man is the legal head of the family, although for household matters the woman may represent him. Only in the case in which his behavior creates chaos in the family is the woman allowed by a court decision to exercise full authority as head of the family. Only in the case of divorce are the common assets shared equally between the woman and the man. A divorced woman must wait for a period of 300 days before she is allowed to remarry, but the divorced man is not subjected to such a restriction.

There are a few fronts on which the notion of gender equality is recognized. For instance, monogamy and fidelity by both spouses and equal inheritance shares have been adopted by the law. However, practice tends to lag behind the law. For instance, Clignet's (1970) study of matrilineal and patrilineal groups showed that monogamous unions had not become a feature of any social category based on variables such as area of residence (rural versus urban), age, educational status, religion, and occupation. There is no behavioral evidence that trends toward de jure or de facto monogamy are being firmly established.

In addition to the laws that are adopted with the objective of promoting change in habits and practices, other factors can also be analyzed as agents of change for family structures and values. Presented in the next section, migration is one of these factors that help explain why and how changes occur in the family, regardless of the adopted laws.

MIGRATION, CAPITALIST ECONOMY, AND THE FAMILY

Côte d'Ivoire is considered one of the countries in the world with the largest proportion of immigrants, who make up a little more than one-fourth of its population according to the 1998 census. The French population increased at the time of independence and registered a decline only during the severe economic crisis of the 1980s. However, the bulk of immigrants in Côte d'Ivoire originate from other African countries, particularly the neighboring countries, the highest proportions being from Burkina Faso, Mali, Guinea, and also Niger. At some points in the colonial period, Côte d'Ivoire and the then-Upper Volta were run as a two-part unit with large groups of workers for the farms and also public works pulled from Upper Volta to Côte d'Ivoire. The colonial boundaries between the two countries shifted several times.

Several factors have contributed to the movement of population in the contemporary period. While the immigration recorded by the census refers to population from other countries, there is also a great deal of internal migration in Côte d'Ivoire between regions, between rural and urban areas, or between rural areas that interacts with international migration to further complicate impact on families.

Formal education has been one of the most powerful agents that has triggered massive and continued migration, mostly from rural to urban areas. This started during the colonial era when, in the framework of their legendary centralized administrative system, the French created an educational system that was organized on a pyramidal basis whereby children were literally drafted to attend village schools first. Then, through an elitist philosophy even at the primary education level, the highest achievers were selected to attend regional schools from which a few fed urban schools that in turn provided a small number of graduates for federal schools. The latter were created, with specific fields of specialization, for all AOF countries (e.g., a teacher training school in Côte d'Ivoire, a center for agricultural extension in Mali, and a school for medical assistants in Senegal). In this beginning of the 21st century, there are still virtually no secondary schools in rural areas in Côte d'Ivoire (Assié-Lumumba, 1994). Therefore all rural students who pursue their education beyond primary school have to leave their community and immediate family. Because no boarding facilities are made available to all secondary school students, the African extended family system has been essential in housing these seasonal migrants.

Practically and figuratively, attending school means migrating away from a relatively cohesive cultural space to a different or unfamiliar context, often the more culturally heterogeneous urban areas. Students deal with a new system of foster parents called *tuteurs/tutrices*, some with close or distant family ties, others with no initial family relations at all but which become gradually and fully integrated family ties as academic years pass. The flexible and expansive border of the line of membership in the African family has helped solve a major national problem and contributed to reaffirming the vitality of indigenous African structures.

In recent years, the questions of migration and settlement of various population groups in Côte d'Ivoire has been a burning political issue with historical factors affecting discourse and formulation of policy. Citizenship and nationality, political rights acquired through labor as opposed to the family line, and land tenure especially in rural areas are all matters of current discourse and policy consideration that relate to the line of descent and family rights. For the purpose of this chapter, the selected focus is limited to the salient features of the impact of migration on the family structure and process of transformation in different sociogeographic settings. It is impossible here to explore all the important aspects and nuances of migrations in relation to the family. This study deals only with some aspects of the immigration in Côte d'Ivoire and its impact on the family.

A process of change and internal adjustment has been triggered by external factors such as the introduction of a capitalist economy and its impact on the family as unit of production and consumption with traditions of inheritance of assets and goods. To discuss some of these aspects of the family, this section draws on a study that was conducted between 1988 and 1990 by two scholars including this author (Assié-Lumumba & Lumumba-Kasongo, 1991). This research aimed at showing that, although many studies on migration in Africa tend to focus on rural-urban movements of the migrant population, intrarural migration of farmers from Côte d'Ivoire or neighboring countries in search of land for cash crop cultivation is considerable and yet had garnered little attention. For the purpose of this chapter only one aspect of the findings of this study is presented.

The migrant farmers were Ivorians from the old Cocoa Belt and the savanna as well as citizens from the neighboring countries of Burkina Faso, Mali, and Guinea. The first group (Ivorians) moved to the central-western part of the country and then, as they noticed signs of exhaustion or scarcity of land several years later, moved to the southwest. Seasonal migrants who offer their labor for a wage include men and women who return home after every harvest and receipt of their wage. However, migrants in search of land to establish cash crop plantations are usually men. The authors indicated that one striking fact in the lives of these migrant farmers, even those who established plantations, is the strict continued relation that they maintain with their initial homes. For them, migration is never a decision about cutting family ties to home.

Given the centrality of the nuclear family in the European/Western traditions, it is quite common for a family to make a final move to leave their home, with their belongings, history, and memories. But in the African context it is practically impossible for all the members of the same family to migrate. For instance, in the process of migration of polygynous farmers, the husband and one spouse and a few children leave first, leaving behind the other woman/women and children. Even when the latter join them, the migrant farmers' own parents, often old, and other children remain in the native village. The migrants continue to take an active part in the economic and social life of their original home. They return frequently to visit and for specific events such as funerals and other major social ceremonies. They return home after they sell their commodities (cocoa and coffee). One constant fact observed was that when migrant farmers secure enough financial resources, the first and by far most important action they take is to build a new house in their original village. Any building constructed in their new location is considered temporary. When they want to invest, for example in real estate in an urban area, they tend to invest in the town or city that is the nearest to their village.

The national migrants in the sample of this study were Akan, more specifically Baoulé from the savannah region around Bouaké. Most were from the former Cocoa Belt forest area. In their tradition, the temporary home is not allowed to have a cemetery. Very precise criteria and lengthy and special ceremonies are required to make it possible to bury the dead in a hitherto temporary home constructed for the purpose of facilitating access to land and work in the farms. When there is a death in a temporary home near their plantations, they are required by their tradition to carry the corpse home for burial. In very rare cases, a deceased man may be buried near a temporary settlement. But a deceased woman's body must always be carried home for burial. If out of extreme necessity the body is buried, special rituals are performed to invite the spirit of the deceased person to return to the original home. Guiding the spirit of the deceased person home constitutes an eloquent statement about the permanence of the attachment to the family.

However, as these farmers and those from neighboring countries spend time in their new home they tend to organize a de facto dual household arrangement. Once the first small unit becomes stable, other members of the family join. They may work for them until they acquire their own plantations. In the case of migrants who want to return home permanently, they usually hand the plantation over to another member of the family.

One of the major findings of this study is that the African family in rural areas is solidly grounded in an African ethos, even when it is deeply affected by the global capitalist economy of cash crop production that triggers migration. The family has responded to the new demands but has made the new economic realities reckon with the not-yet-negotiable essence of expanded membership and unconditional reciprocal solidarity that defy geographic distance.

In a study on migration in Côte d'Ivoire, Lambert (1994) argued that migration is in fact a family and a collective "risk-sharing" decision. In this area, Ivorian men and women who have migrated around the world, some as part of what has been labeled the "brain drain," defy geographic distance to fulfill their family obligations. They continue to visit and participate in major events, and become foster parents of nieces and nephews (in many African languages referred to as daughters and sons) by sponsoring their education from a distance or by bringing them where they live, in other African countries, Europe, or the Americas. Within Côte d'Ivoire, it is even more common for formally educated individuals and couples to de facto adopt family members especially to give them a chance to have access to better educational facilities so that they can in turn help other members of the family. Ainsworth (1996) found that children aged 7–14, even though they were not orphans, were nonetheless living away from either of their natural parents. In fact, Sombo et al. (1994) report that the percentage of children who were not living with their biological parents increased from infancy to adolescent years, from 2 percent among children who are less than 2 years of age up to 30 percent among those who were at least 12 years. Harrison (1995) and Antoine and Guillaume (1984) also found that extended families tended to share the cost of the children's formal education. This is a modern expression of an old tradition of collective responsibility for the education of the youth. Thus, while the means and forms change, the value and meaning of collective obligation and reciprocity remain.

Despite these indications of continuity, there are new challenges, tests of endurance, and emerging trends and patterns that deserve careful analysis.

CHALLENGES, ENDURANCE, AND EMERGING PATTERNS

With or without colonization and the laws that have subsequently been adopted by the state, the various dimensions of the family would have undergone some form of change—as there is no static society—although probably at a slower pace. The change may be in the means used to fulfill old functions, but the novelty of the means may also alter some aspects of the family. Several studies have noted that some of the most salient aspects of these changes that vary according to the local realities and their receptivity to the new global context and specific laws.

In a study of villages and rural communities from two regions and ethnic groups in Côte d'Ivoire, it was found that urbanization, migration, a monetary economy, the emergence of a wage-earning class, Western cultural impact, and some effects of the new family laws have started to constitute constraints on the family structure (Vimard, 1987a, 1988). According to the author, the small class of educated and Westernized elite has accepted more easily the new family code. However, the presence in the household of relatives other than members of the nuclear family suggests an enduring effect of African family structure and value although the proportion decreases from rural to semiurban and urban households. Vimard (1987b) also found the emergence of single-parent households, relatively larger proportions of singles in the urban areas compared to the rural areas, and an increasing number of female-headed households with most of the women widows. This suggests that life in the city, away from the social context and influence of the extended families in the past and/or rural communities, may offer new choices or present difficulties in complying with the practice of widows' remarriage in the deceased husbands' families. Another interesting finding is the relatively large proportion of female household heads (41 percent compared to 31 percent of women in the general population) who are married in polygynous families. This suggests that, unlike in the past when co-wives tended to live in the same compound with their common husband, men in this contemporary and urban context may be involved in several households. Thus, the women become the de facto heads of their respective space, regardless of the law of monogamy and a single home (that of the man) for the married couple.

The divorce rates in this study do not show a significant difference between urban (9 percent) and the rural (8 percent) areas. In fact, in his study comparing Côte d'Ivoire and Cameroon, Clignet (1977) found that one of the consequences of urbanization on polygynous households is the creation of plural residences, and as co-wives no longer interact, their roles are redefined. In a study that included Côte d'Ivoire and other countries, Frank (1988) argued that African wives and mothers in general have a status and structural dependence that is similar to women of other developing regions. However, she adds that African wives and mothers are more economically independent and have greater residential autonomy than other women do. Thus, it appears that in the case of Côte d'Ivoire, in spite of some postindependence laws that tend to reduce married women to dependent minors, the reality and negotiation at the family level in the African cultural context challenge and ignore these laws.

Women are in charge of economic activities and household life beyond what the laws permit. These laws do not take into consideration the reality of economic contribution and residential arrangements that value all the members of the family. Even the men whom such laws are expected to favor may not benefit from them if they are indeed applied. It is doubtful that most Ivorian men, in rural and urban areas, the nonformally educated and even those who are highly educated and closer to the origin and spirit of these laws, are prepared to become the sole "breadwinners" of families. Indeed, even nuclear families are expected to express solidarity with the less fortunate members of the extended family on both the husband's and wife's sides. With the global economic crisis and the erosion of the economic power of even the "middle class," women's work is a sheer necessity, needed to sustain the family. Furthermore, working outside the home is not a simple economic exercise. It is a cultural factor located in an African world vision that does not confine women in the private sphere while men alone can work outside for wages.

There is an additional factor that must be considered when assessing the relevance of some laws. Immediately after independence all African countries made formal education the main instrument that would help them achieve socioeconomic development. The skills acquired by men and women are supposed to be inputs for such development. Even the state-planned economy was adopted with effort to match the human resource need of the economy with adequate training, especially at the higher education level. By making married women's chances to work outside the home conditional on their husband's approval, the state is renouncing its rights and contradicting its proclaimed needs to use its human capital to promote socioeconomic development, unless its conception of human capital is reduced to male capital. In this case, it will have to give a different official meaning to the education of the female population.

Sometimes, more recently imported ideas, especially those related to colonial policy and legacy, are not taken seriously because they have not been fully accepted or rooted in the culture. For instance, while Christianity, especially the Roman Catholic Church, does not favor or even accept divorce, Brandon (1990) found that Christian families in Côte d'Ivoire experience higher rates of divorce than Muslim families.

Marriage and having children still constitute high social norms. Some new trends are emerging which suggest that more individual choices impacted by individual and structural changes are being made. For instance, in a study that compared Côte d'Ivoire, Senegal, and Congo-Brazzaville, it was found that in the three countries the age at first marriage has been increasing and the proportion of women who remain unmarried is also increasing due mainly to higher level of formal education and also the impact of urbanization. However, another study (Westoff, 1992) cites Côte d'Ivoire among the African countries where there appears to be no evidence that there is an established trend of later marriage and birth of the first child.

According to the findings of a comparative study on Abidjan, Dakar, and Yaoundé, poverty is a major determinant of the process of nuclearization of the family. However, even among the poor there is a strong preference for maintaining the extended family system. In another study (Antoine & Herry, 1983) it was found that among urban residents, the nuclear family structure is more frequent among the recent and poorer dwellers while the extended family is more extensive and more frequently observed among wealthier and long-term residents. This suggests that the constraints of the urban life (space, resources to support a large family) impact the decision of family size. However, it is not the urban life per se but rather the economic constraints that impact the family size. There has not been yet an urban experience, across generations, in which the power of the African family value of mutual support and solidarity has been significantly eroded. As a matter of fact, as the same study suggests, when urban families secure some financial means, they respect their family obligation to bring other members along, if indeed they are in a location and position that gives access to services (e.g., school) to other family members. The migration rationale and stages in the process of migration of the extended family members are in essence similar to those of farmers in rural areas.

Given some of these factors mentioned above, it is worth mentioning some major and new trends of a structural nature that are likely to impact the family. For instance, since the 1980s, there has been a severe economic crisis worsened by the prescribed "solutions" of structural adjustments programs (SAPs) that increased hardship with none of the promised improvements in sight. Indicators such as increased infant and child mortality (Barrere & Poukouta, 1995) show the severity of poverty.

In a comparative study that used monographic data on Côte d'Ivoire and Togo, Vimard (1993) analyzed some of the changes that have taken place in the family as a result of socioeconomic and demographic changes as well as urbanization and migration during the colonial era and particularly after independence. The author was particularly interested in finding out whether autonomy of domestic groups and new forms of family arrangements have been gradually replacing the traditional family lineage organizations. The findings indicate that there is a trend toward smaller family organization as a unit of production, which is less important than has been established by the lineage mode of production with redefinition of individual relationship within the family unit, affecting relations between spouses and between them and their offspring. Marriage for instance, this author argues, is no longer the instrument for establishing alliances between two extended families but is rather more focused on the individuals involved. According to the author, individual factors such as educational attainment, occupation, and marital status have become more important determinants of social roles than membership in extended family structures. According to the author, this leads to a more vulnerable position for the woman. This assertion can be explained by the fact that even in African patrilineal and/or patrilocal tradition, married women still remain full members of their original families who provide them protection. The lineage of the husband's family, not the husband alone, is held accountable for the well-being of the married women. It is significant that Vimard (1993) indicates that the tradition of foster-parenting within the extended family still persists.

With regard to marriage, it is important to note that the new family code prohibits polygyny. The sanctions for breaking the law include from six months up to three years in jail and a fine of 50,000 ($80 U.S.) to 500,000 CFA francs ($800 U.S.). However, there are no indications of the enforcement of the law. Fierce debates that began in 1996 regarding the possibility of legalizing polygyny have not been concluded.

It is interesting to note that there has been a trend toward an increased number of informal unions (Gage-Brandon, 1993). There are variations among ethnic and religious groups, areas of residence, and also by age cohorts. For instance, Christian women are 2.7 more likely to live in formal unions than Muslim women. Younger women and women living in urban areas are 32 percent and 37 percent respectively more likely to engage in informal unions than older women and rural dwellers. Also Akan women, and more generally women in matrilineal groups, are twice as likely than Voltaïque groups who are, in turn, twice as likely as the Mandé and other patrilineal groups to contract informal unions.

Indeed, one of the main purposes of formal matrimonial unions is to establish legitimacy of the offspring. As mentioned before, among the matrilineal groups child legitimacy, though it may not be complete without a father, is more determined by the mother whose marital status is not relevant in conferring legitimacy to her child. A child born in an informal union of patrilineal groups may not be fully connected. Level of education, which also has a positive correlation with economic ability, is another ground of differentiation. Women with no formal education are two times more likely to be involved in informal unions than those who have some formal education. Either type of marriage (indigenous or recently adopted systems) requires financial ability. As a matter of fact, the practice of providing wedding goods persists, in spite of its prohibition by law. Similarly, the "modern" marriage model set by the wealthier Westernized elite is also associated with lavish and costly ceremonies even if it is a one-time event, often with secular and religious components. Therefore, a stable economic situation is often what prompts the couple to move from an informal union to its formalization. The formalization of up to 49.3 percent of unions, compared to 34.1 percent that end up in dissolution (Gage-Brandon, 1993), indicates that the unions indeed tend to be temporary arrangements. In the many cases in which people marry according to their respective customs without the state-required public rituals, it is worth asking what reference is used for the classification of the informal or formal status unions.

Another dimension of the process of formalization of unions is related to the major phenomenon of moving from the formal polygynous marriage to the practice of having concubines. This practice seems to be more prevalent among the formally educated men who are aware that the law does not permit polygyny and yet want to have more than one woman with whom they are involved on a regular and/or long-term basis. In some cases, the official wife is married according to the requirement of the new law that prescribes monogamy and the concubine according to the requirement of the African and/or Islamic family codes that permit polygyny. It is significant that this practice is well entrenched in French culture and cuts across all social classes including the top political elite, although there is no ground to assume that the practice in Côte d'Ivoire is a simple reproduction of a French social phenomenon. In this case, the conflict between preexisting practices and the requirements of the new laws may be the primary source of the emergence of this practice that is found in other African countries.

The issue of the legalized or de facto practice of polygyny is the source of a controversy and an ongoing debate, with regard to the problems and perceived merits associated with it. Even among women, including some with high levels of formal education, there is no consensus. However, in the context of the spread of sexually transmittable diseases, especially HIV/AIDS, new arguments are being formulated against the practice of polygyny or any forms of multiple sexual partnerships, which in this case includes women.

In terms of the process and patterns of change in the family, Vimard and N'Cho (1993) show that there are emerging varieties of household arrangements, which may or may not be related to the enforcement of any marriage code. Their analysis was based on 44,622 households and 269,623 persons grouped into seven socioprofessional categories. They found two dominant households: the nuclear family (29 percent) and the nuclear family and other relatives (26 percent). The following categories were also identified: the single-person household (14 percent), the household with other relatives (9 percent), the one-parent family (6 percent), the one-parent family with other relatives (also 6 percent), the couple only (5 percent), the couple with other relative (3 percent), and the head and unrelated individuals (2 percent).

It was also found that the nuclear family is the most prevalent form among farmers, salaried laborers, and salaried employees (60 percent), each of the disaggregated occupational categories. Executives and professionals (54 percent) and traders (43 percent) also had large proportions of nuclear families, although they had 17 percent and 16 percent of single-person households and 12 percent and 15 percent household heads and other relatives, respectively. Households that included other relatives represented 45 percent of the total sample.

While some of these figures appear insignificant, they may provide an early indication of future trends in the dynamics of structural change. Indeed, the main message may be that emerging varieties of households of different occupational categories are appearing or they may also indicate signs of resilience in the African family structure and organization.

On the whole, the most significant finding in this study is that people's economic means and capacity constitute a key determinant of their household types. However, the household type at some stages in people's economic power does not affect the value attached to the extended family. Indeed, a nuclear family household does not imply nuclear family obligations. The presence of the extended family cannot be reduced to spatial terms. That is to say that the extended family and the obligations that accompany it can be assumed even when family members are physically apart. Whenever the financial means permit, family members may be brought into the common living space of migrants and/or urban dwellers. Thus, the essence of the extended African family that defines rules of responsibility and obligations of sharing still lives on.

CONCLUSION

Despite national laws and the new practices that have occurred as a result of structural changes, there is evidence that indigenous African family systems and values are resisting the trial of time. Furthermore, there is ample evidence which supports the argument that practices specific to regions and ethnic groups continue to exist side by side with the new postindependence laws.

There appears to be a call for changes in the laws to reflect the needs for rooted policies in alignment with the policy of development of the entire society. Adjustment is needed, for instance, to the positive aspects of the gendered foundation of the African family. Ivorian women, like other African women, have been a major economic force and will not be reduced to socially dependent minors. It is in the interests of families—men, women, offspring, other members of the extended family—and also societies at large to rewrite the family laws with women as members of the committee or the group in charge.

More generally, there is need for a critical assessment of the legal framework adopted immediately after independence, when there were fewer Ivorians, especially women, whose educational attainment and professional experience could have permitted them to conceptualize, design, and propose for adoption the laws that are today the major state legal reference. There is a need to bring in the insight of qualified professionals and experienced experts who can critically examine the dynamism of society and the relevant laws in order to make proposals, not just for a few amendments as is usually the case, but for new laws with a philosophical framework. The urgent need is to conceive family laws that can read the sociological reality and constitute a major component of a comprehensive state program for social progress. The fact that, while economic constraints may temporarily force family composition to be minimal, inclusion of additional members resumes when economic means permit is an indication of the resilience of the collective and extended foundation of the African family.

Despite recent conflicts with some segments of the migrants from some neighboring countries, it is safe to state that Côte d'Ivoire will continue to be a major recipient country in the migratory movements in the West African subregion. Given the large number of these migrants (one-quarter of the total population) in the urban and rural areas, it will be important to study the impact of the short- and long-term migrants on the sociological landscape of the family in Côte d'Ivoire. In addition to the classical rural-urban migration, it will be also important to study the impact of massive intrarural and urban-urban movements, especially between Abidjan and other urban areas. New laws are being discussed regarding a new policy of administrative and economic decentralization. How will such policies impact population movements and families? There has also been a renewed stated policy of making education a priority for promoting development. What will be the impact of a larger formally educated and Westernized segment of the population on the application of the postcolonial and indigenous family laws and practices? Since 2000, in addition to the Ministry of Health, a new unit has been created with the mission of dealing specifically with the HIV/AIDS epidemic. What will be the behavioral responses with regard to some family values and practices, if and when the full impact of HIV/AIDS is uncovered, and new programs of information and prevention that are set up appear to be in conflict with some of these values and practices?

These are a few guiding questions and areas of possible research to capture the new trends, adaptation, and continuity in the African family within the national, subregional, and global contexts. To identify and better analyze emerging aspects, persistence of the common core foundation, and ethnic/regional specificities, it is crucial to undertake longitudinal studies that can provide the data and interpretations of the contemporary trends and patterns of the family in Côte d'Ivoire.

Following the December 1999 military coup d'état, a failed coup attempt in September 2002 was transformed into a rebellion that led to the de facto division of the country into a northern half controlled by the rebels and the southern half by governmental troops. Bloody battles led to massive movement of the population, mainly from the occupied zone into neighboring countries. The internally displaced population was equally massive. For instance, within two to three months after the beginning of the 2002 armed conflicts, according to the UN Office for the Coordination of Humanitarian Affairs (2003), "The scale of displacement in Côte d'Ivoire [was] massive and increasing rapidly. Out of a population of 16 million, an estimated 600,000 were displaced internally by the end of November.... Fighting in the west has since forced the displacement of perhaps an additional 500,000. The total number of IDPs topped 1.1 million by the beginning of January."

On July 30, 2003, the Accra III Agreement was signed with the purpose of moving forward with the implementation of the peace process that started with the January 24, 2003, Linas-Marcoussis Agreement. With the adoption of Resolution 1464 (2003), the United Nations Security Council authorized the deployment of the forces of the Economic Community of West African States (ECOWAS) and France for the implementation. However, the disarmament process has been stalled, with the country's de facto division making it impossible for people to return to their original or adopted homes in the occupied areas. In this unprecedented crisis in the history of the country, African family values have been put to the test. The massive population movement from the occupied zone toward the government-controlled zone included farmers from the central region who migrated to the west in search of arable land for cash-crop plantation. Those among them whose villages and homeland were not occupied returned home, fleeing their earlier migration destinations and their adopted, second homes related to their plantations. The bulk of the internally displaced people moved in with family members. The urban areas, especially Abidjan, are cosmopolitan spaces where all ethnic groups and people from various parts of the country converge. People from every part of the country have close or extended family members in Abidjan and perhaps other urban areas. Some of the refugees—the displaced people who crossed national borders—also joined family members.

Without having conducted a scientific study, but based on simple observation around Abidjan, it is safe to state that the family members in government-controlled locations have gone beyond their objective capacity to accommodate displaced family members. Visits and informal discussions lead to the conclusion that many households have at least doubled in size as a result of the influx of family members seeking refuge. Many families are crumbling under the weight of this sudden load of exceptional magnitude.

This suggests that international relief and humanitarian agencies should take seriously the plight of the suffering populations. It is beyond the scope of this article to make recommendations about ways in which the assets of the social fabric can be used to develop a more effective approach to relieve the suffering of the displaced and receiving populations. The point of this chapter is that the Ivorian family under duress has been drawing from its roots and from the African family ethos, showing that indeed the African family system is alive and well in the best and also worst experiences of life.

REFERENCES

Ainsworth, M. (1996). Economic aspects of child fostering in Côte d'Ivoire. *Research in Population Economics 8*, 25–62.

Antoine, P., & Herry, C. (1983). Urbanisation et dimension du ménage: le cas d'Abidjan. *Cahiers ORSTOM: Série Sciences Humaines 19(3)*, 295–310.

Antoine, P., & Guillaume, A. (1984). Une expression de la solidarité familiale à Abidjan: Enfants du couple et enfants confiés. In *Les familles d'aujourd'hui: démographie et évolution récente des comportements familiaux: Colloque de Genève (17–20 Septembre 1984)* (pp. 289–297) Paris: Association Internationale des Démographes de Langue Française.

Assié-Lumumba, N. (1994). Rural students in urban settings in Africa: The experience of female students in secondary school. In Stromquist, N. P. (Ed.), *Education in urban areas: Cross-national dimensions* (pp. 199–218). Westport, CT: Praeger.

Assié-Lumumba, N. T., & Lumumba-Kasongo, T. (1991). *Les migrations inter-rurales liées à l'économie de plantation et leur impact sur la scolarisation primaire en Côte d'Ivoire: Le cas de la bocule du cacao.* Rapport soumis au programme des petites subventions. Dakar: CODESRIA.

Barrere, M., & Poukouta, P. (1995). Mortalité des enfants. In Sombo, N., Kouassi, L., Koffi, A. K., Schoemaker, J., Barrere, M., Barrere, B., & Poukouta, P. (Eds.), *Enquête démographique et de santé, Côte d'Ivoire, 1994: Rapport de synthèse.* Abidjan: Institut National de la Statistique.

Clignet, R. (1970). *Many wives, many powers: Authority and power in polygynous families.* Evanston: Northwestern University Press.

Clignet, R. (1977). Social change and sexual differentiation in the Cameroun and the Ivory Coast. *Women and national development: The complexities of change.* Chicago: University of Chicago Press.

Etienne, P. (1972). *Les interdictions de mariage chez les Baoulé*. Abidjan: Centre ORSTOM Petit-Bassam.

Frank, O. (1988). *The childbearing family in sub-Saharan Africa: Structure, fertility, and the future*. Unpublished paper.

Gage-Brandon, A. J. (1993). The formation and stability of informal unions in Côte d'Ivoire. *Journal of Comparative Family Studies 24(2)*, 219–233.

Harrison, S. M. (1995). Education. Game of numbers? *West Africa (4065)*, 1401–1402.

Kaudjis-Offoumou, F. (1995). *Les droits de la famme en Côte d'Ivoire*. Abidjan: Editions KOF.

Lambert, S. (1994). La migration comme instrument de la diversification intrafamiliale des risques. Application au cas de la Côte d'Ivoire. *Revue d'Economie du Développement (2)*, 3–38.

Launay, R. (1995). The power of names: Illegitimacy in a Muslim community in Côte d'Ivoire. In S. Greenhalgh (Ed.), *Situating fertility: Anthropology and demographic inquiry* (pp. 108–129). New York: Cambridge University Press.

Levasseur, A. A. (1976). *The civil code of the Ivory Coast*. Charlottesville, VA: Miche Law Publishers.

Mazrui, A. A. (1986). *The Africans, a triple heritage.* Program 2, *A legacy of lifestyles* [videorecording] / a coproduction of WETA-TV and BBC-TV; produced by David Harrison; a commentary written and presented by Ali A. Mazrui. Santa Barbara, CA: Distributor, Intellimation.

Meekers, D. (1990, May). *Consequences of premarital childbearing in Côte d'Ivoire*. Paper presented at the Annual Meeting of the Population Association of America, Toronto, Canada.

Meekers, D. (1992). The process of marriage in African societies: A multiple indicator approach. *Population and Development Review 18(1)*, 61–78.

Mundt, R. J. (1972). *Family structure, polity, and law: The implementation of the civil code in the Ivory Coast*. Unpublished Ph.D. thesis, Stanford University.

Sombo, N., Kouassi, L., Koffi, A. K., Schoemaker, J., Barrere, M., Barrere, B., & Poukouta, P. (1994). *Enquête démographique et de santé, Côte d'Ivoire, 1994: rapport de synthèse*. Abidjan: Institut National de la Statistique.

Vimard, P. (1987a). *Structures des ménages en pays Baoulé. Compositions et typologies familiales à Brobo (Département de Bouaké)*. Etudes et Recherches No. 14, Ecole Nationale Supérieure de Statistiques et d'Economie Appliquée, Abidjan.

Vimard, P. (1987b). *Diversité des structures familiales en Côte d'Ivoire: Une approche à partir d'études de cas en milieu rural Akan*. Abidjan: Institut Français de Recherche Scientifique pour le Développement en Coopération, Centre ORSTOM de Petit Bassam.

Vimard, P. (1993). Modernité et pluralité familiales en Afrique de l'Ouest. *Revue Tiers Monde 34(133)*, 89–115.

Vimard, P., & N'Cho, S. (1993). *Conséquences sociales de la structures des ménages selon les groupes socio-économiques en Côte d'Ivoire: Premiers éléments d'analyse*. Unpublished paper presented at International Population Conference, Montreal, Canada.

Wakam, J., Rwenge, M., & Kuepi, M. (1998). Pauvreté et structures familiales dans trois métropoles africaines: Yaoundé, Abidjan et Dakar. *Universités francophones, actualités scientificques*, 167–182.

Westoff, C. F. (1992). *Age at marriage, age at first birth, and fertility in Africa*. Washington, DC: World Bank.

CHAPTER 7

The Family in Ghana: Past and Present Perspectives

Elizabeth Ardayfio-Schandorf

INTRODUCTION

As in the case of other African countries, the family in Ghana has undergone dramatic changes during the past several decades. For example, these changes are visible in attitudes toward childbearing, mate selection, and property devolution. Some of the changes can be explained in terms of spatial processes (e.g., increased urbanization), intercultural processes, and political and economic transformations. Even though the Ghanaian family has undergone significant transformations since the colonial period, several aspects of the traditional family can still be identified alongside other "emerging" family forms. In this chapter, I examine the changing Ghanaian family, focusing on how Islamic and European influences have affected family processes in postcolonial Ghana. Before that, I provide a brief demographic and historical review against the backdrop of the changing family.

DEMOGRAPHIC, ECOLOGICAL, AND HISTORICAL PROFILES

Ghana, formerly known as the Gold Coast, had a population of barely 6 million at independence in March 1957. During the first postindependence population census in 1960, its population was 6.7 million with an intercensal growth rate of 4.2 percent between 1948 and 1960 (Government of Ghana, 1994). This rose to 8.6 million with an annual growth rate of 3.4 percent in

1970, and 12.3 million in 1984 with an intercensal growth rate of 2.6 percent. The 2000 population of Ghana is 18,412,247, showing a doubling of the 1970 population in less than 30 years. Ghana's population may be described as relatively young because 42 percent are younger than 15 years of age (Ghana Statistical Service [GSS], 1998), giving a high dependency ratio. Total fertility rates are still high. This may be accounted for by the fact that the death rate in the country is declining while life expectancy is rising, from 45 years in 1960 to 57 years in 1998 (Government of Ghana, 1984; GSS, 1998). The urban population is also increasing, from 23 percent in 1960 to 34 percent in 1998. Seventeen major ethnic groups have been identified, based on language and cultural ties (Government of Ghana, 1964). Similarly there is religious diversity in Ghana, even though Christians represent the single largest religious grouping in the country, accounting for over half of the population (GSS, 1998). The remainder identify themselves as Muslims, followers of traditional African religions, or not affiliated with any religion.

Covering a total land area of 238,537 square kilometers (92,075 square miles), Ghana is centrally located in the West African subregion. The country is bounded on three sides by French-speaking countries. On the west is Côte d'Ivoire, on the north Burkina Faso, on the east the Republic of Togo, and on the south the coastline of the Atlantic Ocean. Ghana tends to be tropical, but rainfall and temperatures vary. There is one rainy season in the north and two rainy seasons in the south, with an average annual temperature of 79° Fahrenheit. Differences in the amount and duration of rainfall have been largely responsible for the country's three vegetational zones and three ecological zones: the coastal savanna, the forest belt, and the northern dry savanna.

Ghana was originally named the Gold Coast by Europeans, and changed its name to Ghana upon receiving independence in 1957. It became a republic in the British Commonwealth of Nations on July 1, 1960. In the past four decades there have been four military coups; however, today Ghana is a multiparty democracy with a parliamentary system of government. This system is based on a three-tier local government structure, with ten administrative regions and 110 administrative districts.

Brief Precolonial History

The precolonial period in Ghana started about the 1st century AD, well before the indigenous people came into contact with the Arabs and the Europeans. Oral traditions and the limited existing documentary evidence have it that the Mole Dagbani states of Mamprussi, Dagomba, and Gonja and the Mossi states of Yatenga and Wagadugu were among the earliest of the kingdoms to emerge in modern Ghana. Northern Ghana and the Upper Volta (Burkina Faso) area were occupied by the Vagala, Sisala, Dagarti, and Tampolensi. The Guan occupied the territory west of the White Volta River. Apart from the

Guan, the people belonged to the same linguistic group, the Gur, and the same culture and civilization (Boahen, 1966).

Most of these people were acephalous in the sense that they developed neither states nor governments; each family head was a chief in his own right. The people had similar religious beliefs and systems of land ownership. Lands occupied by the Gur people were divided into well-defined areas called Tengani. Each Tengani was headed by a Tengdana who was usually the head of the kinship group of the area. He acted as the political leader, the chief priest, and spiritual mediator between the earth and the people.

Boahen (1966) reported that the regions occupied by these people lay across the trade routes leading to the Asante (land of gold and kola), the Ivory Coast (Côte d'Ivoire), and ancient Ghana, Mali, Songhai, and the Hausa Empires. They therefore developed to become key to the economic life of not only the forest regions but also the western Sudan. The trade was dominated by the Mande Dyula or the Wangara (as they were known by the Akan). By the end of the 14th century, the Wangara had founded the commercial centers of Ua, Buna, and Bole along the western trade route and Begho. The Wangara had been influenced by the Soninke of Ghana and had converted to Islam. Thus they brought into modern Ghana trading commodities as well as Islam.

The first real states to emerge in this region appear to be those of Mossi, Mamprussi, Dagomba, and Gonja. With the exception of the Gonja, the rulers of all the states came from the same parent stock. The Gonjas, however, maintained that they originated from a band of Mande warriors who had invaded northern Ghana from the region of the Songhai Empire. They had managed to impose themselves on the peoples already living there and to establish the kingdom of Gonja with Yagbum as their capital. The states mentioned, though not Mossi states, were organized broadly on Mossi lines. By and large, their rulers left the social and religious institutions of the conquered peoples under them intact, as were the land divisions. Meanwhile, the conquered continued to occupy the important posts of Tengdana and to play political roles.

As a result of the interaction process, the Mamprussi, Gonja, and Dagomba now exhibit strong Islamic features superimposed on the traditional system. This can be seen in the use of the Muslim calendar, in the universal observance of the major Islamic festivals and the adoption of Islamic fashions, and in naming and burial ceremonies. In all the above states, the imams and the mallams played important roles in the installation of new kings. By the second half of the 18th century, the Mossi had also come under the ambit of Islam.

Family Life under Indigenous Culture

The indigenous cultural milieu into which a person is born has a strong influence on his or her future relations as the family occupies a unique place in indigenous society. Traditionally, the concept of the "family" in Ghana transcends the definition of two parents married to each other and their biological children. It involves kinship and filial relations well beyond the immediate father-mother-children relationships.

The physical setting within which the functions of the family (nuclear and/or extended) are performed are varied and complex and are based on kinship ties. The way people went about their daily activities were all functions of culture and religion. Within the indigenous culture, families lived together, worked together, owned property jointly, and took responsibility for the upbringing and the enculturation of the young together. There was a high premium on childbearing, and polygyny was allowed and even encouraged under certain circumstances. The communities in which people lived were smaller, and communality reigned. Thus, apart from procreation, economic cooperation and production within the family, socialization, and caregiving to family members as well as the enculturation of the young were tasks usually performed not only by the biological parents but also the extended family.

Control of economic power and other power relations favored males, who were usually heads of both the nuclear and the extended families. Family obligations and contacts were realized whether or not relatives lived together. Even when the extended family existed as a single residential unit, family obligations were never limited to those within the residential group (Addai-Sundiata, 1995).

Family Life under Arabic/Islamic Culture

One of the dominant factors that shaped indigenous family life in Ghana was Islam. The spread of Islam came about as a result of the Trans-Saharan Trade, and followed three specific paths. The first was through contact between Arabian traders and the people of the east African coast including the neighboring islands (Mazrui, 1986). The second began around AD 900 and continued until the 19th century. This process was enhanced by the Trans-Saharan Trade routes (Poh, Tosh, Waller, & Tidy, 1982). Toward the end of that century, Islam as a religion was diffused through holy wars and jihads by Fulani zealots, preachers, and warriors in search of grazing lands. These wars were to influence the political and social organization of the societies in the western Sudan. The third path was through trade between Egypt and Arabia and within the Horn of Africa. In this latter area the processes of Islamization and Arabization was so strong that by the 14th century, Islam had become well entrenched in this part of Africa (Olaniyan, 1982). In addition to the earlier diffusion waves, more recent migrations have resulted in the spread of Islam to several urban centers like Accra and Kumasi in Ghana, which originally were not within the Islam belt but now provide a home for large and influential Muslim communities (Olaniyan, 1982).

Through such a strong diffusion process, Islam has influenced Ghanaian indigenous culture in many ways. It helped form political states and influenced the development of a trade language. It established the basis of an Arabic educational system and impacted food choices and dress codes. Adherents to the religion in various parts of Africa have had the opportunity to adapt the religion to their specific local milieu (Mazrui, 1986; Skinner, 1986).

Family Life under European Culture

Europeans from Portugal were the first to make contact with Ghana in the early 15th century. The Europeans came with both economic and political motives. Only after the abolition of the slave trade did many Europeans begin serious attempts to spread their culture and Christianity in West Africa (Khapoya, 1994). Christianity became firmly planted along the coast, with missionaries setting up primary and secondary schools as well as training colleges. In the process almost all aspects of the life of Ghanaians were touched and influenced by Christianity. One of the main outcomes of this encounter has been the emergence of a new type of African, an educated Christian with European taste in food, drink, dressing, and music; an African exposed to the ideas and influences of Europe, who still maintains Ghanaian tradition and carries out his or her responsibilities to the extended family and traditional authority (Boahen, 1966). This introduced contradictions and confusion into basic indigenous Ghanaian institutions. The missionaries tended to look down on anything African and Ghanaian, including African art, music, dancing, and systems of marriage, naming, and festivals, all of which Ghanaian converts had to renounce. Compared with western European influence, the impact of Islam on sub-Saharan Africa was not as disruptive.

It is clear that colonialism has resulted in major political dilemmas and upheavals for modern African states like Ghana. To ensure efficient extraction of resources from the hinterland to the coast, the colonial administration set up administrative structures to ensure law and order in the colonial territory. The colonial powers relied on the system of indirect rule using traditional political institutions as buffers between them and the local Ghanaian people (Davidson, 1994). The political impact was authoritarian with all power vested in colonial administrators.

The prime objective behind Europe's colonization had been the extraction of agricultural and mineral resources to boost burgeoning industries back in Europe. The economy of Ghana, like others in Africa, was therefore linked to the world economy in a peripheral and subordinate manner. The net effect of this policy was the creation of dual and dependent economic structures. Many scholars have noted that to ensure the relegation of Africans to mines, agricultural plantations, and small farms, a combination of forced labor laws and poll and household taxes were enacted (Mazrui, 1986; Davidson, 1994). The effect on the traditional sector was detrimental because land and labor were siphoned off to the modern sector, while efficient food production for local consumption in the traditional sector declined. Consequently, economic dependency was reinforced by cultural dependency.

Colonialism of this nature turned out to be an important factor that profoundly influenced Ghanaian development socially, economically, politically, and culturally. In place of local languages, English became the official language. The leading religion became Christianity. While the Ghanaian culture emphasized cooperation and community, the European culture emphasized competition and individuality. Again, the Ghanaian culture emphasized sharing but the European focused on accumulation and hoarding. Whereas in Ghanaian culture land belonged to the lineage—that is, the living, the dead, and the yet to be born—European culture considered land as capital to be traded and commoditized to accumulate more capital and wealth (O'Connor, 1992).

Postcolonial Period and Beyond

Urbanization and modernization, which emerged with and after colonialism, are rapidly changing useful traditional values. For instance, Ghanaian society used to view the aged members of the family with dignity and respect because they are considered wiser and worthy of honor. Therefore, the extended family played a central role in providing and caring for the elderly in an integrated system in which the elderly provided child care services and helped with various activities in addition to having specific functions in the family. Modernization is now putting the elderly at risk of isolation. A young family member who works in an urban center gets detached from the family home and returns less often to the village. The elderly, therefore, tend to be neglected without adequate means of subsistence by the young members of the family (see United Nations, 1985).

Mazrui (1986) pointed out that another stressful cultural conflict is in the area of kinship obligations. Ghanaian culture requires the privileged to assist less-privileged members of the family. In the modern state, such a practice is not feasible as it is the most qualified who deserves to be hired at the formal workplace and not necessarily the closest relative. Many political leaders in Ghana and elsewhere in Africa are torn between the European value of individual merit and the collective solidarity of indigenous culture (Mazrui, 1986). The same cultural confusion has been at play in the debate surrounding the European and the Ghanaian conceptions of marriage (Vellenga, 1983).

The cumulative outcome of the past cultural influences—the triple heritage—on the Ghanaian family was that some of the aspects of Islamic religion and culture converged with some of what pertained in the Ghanaian traditional cultural domain and, therefore, found easy acceptance in some sections of society. The European/Christian culture, however, totally revolutionized the way of doing things. It introduced the money economy and European education, which were in conflict with polygynous tendencies. It reorganized production and influenced other significant social systems (Nukunya, 1992). Whereas Islam reinforced polygyny, child fostering, and communal living, Christianity encouraged monogamy in which the socialization function of the family fell squarely on the shoulders of the parents alone. As a result, combinations of these experiences have worked against the functions of indigenous families especially those who are exposed to modernization. With growing emphasis now on nuclear families most grandparents are living less and less often with grandchildren, breaking intergenerational ties with dire consequences for the traditional Ghanaian culture and family life.

CONCEPTUALIZATION OF GHANAIAN FAMILIES

The family is the bedrock of Ghanaian society. It is one of the principal institutions by which the critical tasks of living are organized, directed, and executed. The family serves a variety of functions for the society. It regulates sexual conduct and ensures the replacement of the members of society through reproduction. It is the basic unit of production and consumption. It socializes the young. It serves as the center of political power, and enforces norms and laws. It transmits cultural heritage and serves as the first line of social security. In spite of the lack of precision in defining what constitutes a family, a family can be said to be a group of persons linked by kinship connections in which the older ones take care of the younger ones (Giddens, 1989).

At this stage, it is important to distinguish between the nuclear and the extended family. In the Ghanaian context, family may refer to all persons related by blood, marriage, fostering, or adoption. Though members of a family usually live in the same residential unit, the reverse is also true—family members also live apart. Every person is a member of two families, a nuclear family and an extended family. The latter could be the customary family of either parent depending on the kinship group to which the parent belongs.

There are also two basic family types: the patrilineal family that inherits from the male line and the matrilineal family that inherits from the female line of descent. The composition differs for each line of descent (Ollenu, 1960). Thus, a patrilineal family is made up of a man's children (male and female), the children of his paternal brothers and sisters, his paternal grandfather, the paternal brothers and sisters of his grandfather, and the descendants of his paternal uncle in the direct male line. Therefore, a male parent belongs to the same family as his children; this also means that all of the man's children belong to the same family.

On the other hand, the matrilineal family is made up of a woman's children (male and female), her maternal brothers and sisters, the children of her maternal sisters, her maternal grandmother, the maternal brothers and sisters of her grandmother, and the descendants of the aunts in the direct female line. Every Ghanaian is a member of one of these families. However, some people may be members of both patrilineal and matrilineal families. A person whose father is from a patrilineal family and whose mother is from a matrilineal one is recognized as a member of both families with concomitant benefits and responsibilities.

Legal Definitions of Marriages and Family Life over Time

As stated earlier, the indigenous family consists of all lineal descendants of a common ancestor both for the purpose of ownership of property and for social life (Ollenu, 1966). Membership in families is guided by certain legal rights and entails specific duties. The most important of these include common ownership of property by all members of the family, common liability of all members to contribute toward the payment of family debts, and common right to sit in or be represented in the family council. Thus, by custom every Ghanaian and the property he or she owns belong to the family. If a person is of sound mind and is of age at maturity, he or she has control over the property and is at liberty to deal with it the way he/she sees fit. In case of death intestate the self-acquired property becomes family property devolving to members of the immediate family (Kludze, 1983; Ollenu & Woodman, 1985). Every Ghanaian is a member of the group into which he or she is born. The group may be bound by common blood and flesh acquired through the mother (*mogya*) or a common controlling spirit (*ntoro*) derived from the father (Ollenu, 1966; Antubam, 1963). In this connection, one can succeed through either the patriclan or the matriclan or in some special cases both clans (Ollenu, 1966; Goody, 1973).

Marriage is the foremost institution by which family is established, and it is contracted primarily through customary law. Apart from the customary marriage, there are Islamic and ordinance/church and common marriages. More than 80 percent of all Ghanaian marriages are contracted under the customary law. Such marriages comprise a series of elaborate ceremonies including, in certain cases, payments to establish the legality of the union. The payments and the elaborateness of the ceremony vary depending on factors such as ethnic background and educational level attained (Oppong, 1982). Polygyny is allowed under customary law and the extended family is the channel for the transfer of self-acquired intestate property. Another essential aspect of a valid customary marriage is the consent of the families of the couple because marriage normally unites not only two individuals but also entire families.

Islamic marriages are celebrated under the marriage of the Mohammedans Ordinance. As in the case of customary marriage, Islamic law allow polygyny and men are permitted to marry a maximum of four wives (Charmie, 1986). The transfer of property in this type of marriage is through the relevant Quranic laws. With regard to ordinance/church or European marriages, the marriage is monogamous. If a man dies intestate, his self-acquired property is transferred only to the wife and children of the ordinance marriage.

The marked departure of ordinance unions from traditional marriages led to serious conflict between the European and the customary conceptions of marriage mentioned previously. Due to the socioeconomic problems created by this, the first marriage law in Ghana (the Gold Coast), the Marriage of the

Ordinance Law, was passed in 1884 by the British colonial administration. This law created alternate forms of customary marriage. It also legalized all existing marriages solemnized by the Christian churches. Furthermore, it made provisions for the devolution of the self-acquired estates of the deceased, resting one-third in the surviving spouse and two-thirds in the children in equal shares. It also made monogamy the only form of legal marriage. There was such a hue and cry against this that the ordinance was modified in 1909 to provide that one-third of the man's estate would go to his lineage and two-thirds to the widow and children. Polygyny was also accepted as another form of legal marriage (Ollenu, 1966).

The first postindependence government tried in vain to change certain aspects of customary marriage and intestate succession law. The Marriage, Divorce, and Inheritance Bill of 1961 proposed to make monogamy the only form of legal marriage. It was defeated in parliament, even after repeated revisions (Vellenga, 1971). In 1963, the Administration of Estate Act Bill was passed by parliament, then in 1965 the Maintenance of Children Act. The Administration of Estate Act was further amended in 1971 and 1977.

In 1985, the Provincial National Defence Council (PNDC) government promulgated the Intestate Succession Law (PNDC 111) in order to confront specific problems that women faced in marriage and intestate succession (Ray, 1986). Sections 48 and 10 of the Marriage Ordinance and the Marriage of the Mohammedans Ordinance respectively introduced changes in the customary law of succession by laying down special rules of succession for persons marrying under the two ordinances. These statutes have been repealed by PNDC Law 111, which is applicable to all marriages contracted in the country (Awusabo-Asare, 1990). This makes it possible for communities where children did not have a specific share in the estate of their deceased parents to now do so.

There is a basic recognition that the traditional family relations and the legal rules no longer appear to be tenable. Thus, whereas in the past the nuclear family was subordinate to the extended family, this is no longer the case in the real lives of a large section of the Ghanaian population (Mensa-Bonsu, 1994). An emerging sense of individualism, coupled with other factors such as urbanization and migration, has disrupted the notion of communality of property holdings, which is one of the pillars of the extended family system. The Intestate Succession Law of 1985 tends to emphasize the nuclear family rather than the extended family. However, it should not be overlooked that the customary family serves some purpose during the lifetime of its members.

It is clear from the legal policies that have been made over the years that emphasis has been put on the nuclear family system, though some provisions are made for the extended family, especially in the area of inheritance when a family member dies intestate. The 1992 constitution of Ghana takes into consideration the welfare of the family and, therefore, enjoins every father to look after his children even if he divorces the mother of his children or does not marry her at all.

ESSENTIAL FEATURES OF GHANAIAN FAMILIES

Fortes (1950) draws together concepts of marriage with related concepts such as divorce, separation, and widowhood in the African censuses. He indicates that the Ghanaian concepts are beset with some conceptual and definitional problems. Whereas in contemporary Western culture marriage is a clearly defined legal state with recognized corresponding rights, obligations, and duties, marriage in Ghana is a developmental process rather than a definite act. Aryee's (1985) contribution, on the other hand, is on nuptial patterns in Ghana. He points out that there are some ethnic variations with regard to certain marriage practices, which have an important effect on nuptial patterns among various subgroups of the population.

The process of mate selection has evolved in Ghana over time. In Ghana, marriage is not only a union between two people but also one between two families. When a couple is joined in marriage, their respective lineages and families automatically become affine relatives and the children of the marriage are kin to all those mentioned above (Rattray, 1923). In traditionally selecting and appointing a potential spouse, certain qualities and conditions have to be met (Nukunya, 1992). The relatives of each party make sure that their potential affine does not have serious diseases; is not a noted criminal or witch; is not given to quarrelling; and that the prospective spouse is hardworking and respectful. It is only when the families are satisfied on these points that the proposal is made or acceptance given.

In contemporary terms, however, social change has led to the diminishing role of parents and the family in the selection of spousal partners. The school environment, migration, and the generally flexible contemporary atmosphere, coupled with increased mobility, have made it easier for boys and girls to associate more freely in an atmosphere that promotes individualistic tendencies when it comes to mate selection (Takyi, 2003). Hence, the more education one acquires, the lower the chances of parents interfering in one's selection of a marriage partner. The initiative on the part of the parents to select spouses for their children, and to insist that the latter accept the parents' choices, is disappearing. Though paternal initiative is uncommon, parental agreement and support for the choices are still necessary.

In selecting a mate, whether by oneself or on one's behalf by parents or relations, certain rules apply in many ethnic groups. Traditional law and belief require that certain categories of kin may not marry each other because their relationship is too close (see Rattray, 1923, 1929). In essence, there may be prescribed marriages or preferred/preferential marriages depending on the circumstances. Complications deriving from marriages chosen by young adults are less likely to enjoy sympathy and support from the family. This may lead to problems of coping in stressful situations and may lead to eventual divorce and separation.

Female-Headed Households

As leaders of Ghana attempt to improve the living conditions of the people by adopting various strategies of economic development, few of the basic social institutions are likely to remain the same, including the institution of family. One changing trend common in African families in recent times has been an increasing incidence of female-headed households. Studies carried out in Ghana before 1960 show that when men move to the cities, mining areas, or cocoa plantations, they tend to leave their wives behind in the rural areas, at least, in the early stages of migration, thus creating de facto female-headed households (Murray, 1981; Lloyd & Gage-Brandon, 1993). Changing family structures and living arrangements are pressuring women into assuming greater responsibilities for household organization. Women have increasingly taken responsibility for their own and their children's welfare with or without the support of a husband. In Ghana, female-headed households are on the increase and are closely linked to poverty (Lloyd & Gage-Brandon, 1993; Ardayfio-Schandorf, 1994).

Levels of Childbearing

Children are of special value to both men and women in Ghanaian society. As a pronatalist country, it is believed that children confer respect and status on their parents and they ensure the continuity of lineage in both matrilineal and patrilineal societies. It is believed that a man must have children to ensure that the names of his forebears survive into the future. Otherwise, he will either marry other women who hopefully will bear him sons, or if he is married according to the ordinance law or Christian marriage, he may try to have a son outside his marriage. In certain cases, women may even be divorced for not being able to bear children and sons in particular. Above all, children are considered as the insurance that parents have against poverty in their old age.

Despite family pressure on young couples to have many children and the high premium on children and male children, most urban households and families are being compelled by the rising cost in living and maintenance to reduce family size. In Ghana, the number of children born to a woman in the course of her productive years has averaged well over six or even seven (Friedlander, 1966; Gaisie, 1966; Ghana Statistical Service & Micro International, 1994), though total fertility rate is declining. Currently, the overall fertility rate of women is about five. This indicates a significant demographic trend in fertility, which has been long awaited by the government who wanted the overall fertility rate to drop.

Gender Roles, Female Autonomy, and Family Dynamics

It has been argued generally that women's status improves with economic development. Arguments like this frequently fail to take into consideration the common structures of patriarchy, which hold women in subordinate positions. Many social structures in Ghana, including kinship systems, customary practices, and the gender division of labor among others, work to the detriment of women. Patriarchy and other ideological structures influence the position of women in Ghana irrespective of their socioeconomic attainment. For this reason, it is often stated that the emancipation of women within the family is a nebulous concept.

In Ghanaian society, even higher education does not guarantee women that their status within the marital union will improve. Husband-wife relations are important in this regard. A husband's views concerning authority, respect, and gender roles do not seem to change regardless of his wife's level of education. Thus, there are other important determinants of women's status. The respect that society in general accords women is still more associated with their being wives and mothers than to the new roles that they perform. Education may not necessarily lead to a marked improvement in the Ghanaian women's status within conjugal unions unless it is accompanied by change in cultural values relating to appropriate roles for men and women. Women's productive work or formal employment outside the home is considered by some men to be subordinate to household activities, which are expected to be performed by women regardless of whether they are preoccupied with formal or productive work.

Issues of patriarchy have worked against women in their ability to own and inherit property. The matrilineal system in Ghana has tended to deny women access to, and continued control over land (Mikell, 1975). In patrilineal societies, as in the case of the Anlo of southern Ghana, women may own property (including land) through direct purchase or through inheritance (Nukunya, 1972), but women are generally restricted in their access to essential and strategic resources. Certain social structures prevent them from having equal access to land, labor, credit, education, and extension services compared with men in Ghana. These structures most often have roots in traditional Ghanaian society (Bukh, 1979; Benneh, 1992). Such restriction has clearly undermined the type and extent of women's participation in economic production, especially in farming and other enterprise development (Ardayfio-Schandorf, 1991).

The majority of Ghanaian women are self-employed or unpaid family workers. They engage in a variety of productive activities inside and outside the home like farming, processing, marketing agricultural produce, and trading in local and imported commodities. Their right to work is supported under Ghanaian customary law, which recognizes their exclusive right to separate property. It is within the informal sector that women work and attempt to meet their obligations to the household. The informal sector provides the needed linkages between various sectors of the economy. Most women carry out more than one trade at a time. Many find it relatively convenient within the informal system to care for their children, perform household activities, and also engage in numerous economic activities. The informal system is considered the key sector for the survival of a large proportion of the Ghanaian population, especially women.

The proportion of women working in the formal sector is low, reflecting the limited participation of females at tertiary levels of education. Though women can now be found in most of the formal professions, such as engineering, medicine, and civil service, their influence on decision making is not felt because they are in the minority.

Intergenerational Ties

The relationship existing between family members who belong to different generations has been undergoing change for some time now. Of particular interest are changing residential arrangements, changing roles and responsibilities of generational groups within the family, and the effects and problems emanating from these changes. Traditionally, families lived together in the same extended residential unit. In this arrangement, grandparents, parents, and children live in the same compound or nearby, sharing good times and bad times and generally working together to bring up the young. With the new focus on the nuclear family and the diminishing attention on the extended family, newer generations do not have the opportunity to live with their biological parents, grandparents, great grandparents, uncles, and aunts all in the same household.

The traditional living arrangements had some advantages not only for the older generation (who enjoy family support) but also for the parents who had greater latitude to travel or pursue careers without worrying about child care. Children were handled and socialized by the grandparents and other family members. Such family arrangements served as a bastion of social, economic, and psychological security in troubled times. In the traditional extended family system, the various divisions of labor by sex and age often allowed an interchange of roles as the young grew into adults and as adults grew into old age (Brown, 1992). It was this interdependence that provided the strength of the family support system.

With increasing social change, this family interdependence that provided a support system has been eroded by the separation of the generations through migration, death of key family members, and the lack of surviving siblings of elderly persons. The onus of the responsibility for the care of the elderly has shifted from the extended family system to the nuclear family, and the special role performed by one's own children is crucial. In this respect, the important filial obligations, which siblings have toward their parents, provide emotional support and encouragement. On the other hand, young people usually find it difficult to care as much as they would wish for the aged due to their own financial constraints (Apt, 1981).

In the traditional setup, there was little if any pooling of resources between spouses or a pooled conjugal budget. Husbands and wives invariably maintained separate incomes and expenditures in cash or kind. This flexibility for financial income generation and investment allowed family members who had a strong economic base and means to meet perceived obligations to provide for the needs of their elderly relatives and nieces and nephews. This obligation was so strong that it cut across rural-urban and international boundaries. Such obligations among Ghanaians have led to the development of special financial arrangements to facilitate the transfer of funds usually by children who live abroad to their parents and other elderly. The program, which started with the Agricultural Development Bank, is diffused to other parts of the country and is being operated by such major banks as the Ghana Commercial Bank and Ecobank.

The African family is based on communality and sharing. In this spirit the fostering of children is traditionally a common occurrence within the Ghanaian family system. The transfer of a child from his or her biological home to a new home due to economic constraints has a long history dating back to traditional times (Ardayfio-Schandorf, 1995). For instance, when a family had many closely spaced births, a woman was likely to foster at least one of her children to her own parents to reduce the financial burden of her family. Similarly, a well-off relative might be willing to relieve a family of the number of mouths to feed. This practice enabled members of the extended family to assist in bringing up and maintaining the next generation of children in the family at large. It has, however, been argued by demographers and development agents that fostering tends to encourage high fertility rates among poor people. The effectiveness of the traditional family depends on the demographic and the life cycle evolution of the family unit and its members. A close intergenerational tie in an acceptable form that may enhance the quality of life not only of the elderly but also of the young and the entire society.

Urban and Rural Families—Household Types

Though blood and social relations are important in determining various forms of family, place and location are also influential. In Ghana, families who dwell in settlements with more than 5,000 persons are considered "urban families," while those living in settlements with fewer than 5,000 persons are considered "rural families." It must be noted, however, that there is no single criterion by which the "rurality" or "urbanity" of a place may be determined. Population size and density are not alone sufficient to constitute urban phenomenon. Heterogeneity and complexity of the population, as well as the presence of certain essential services such as piped water, electricity, police stations, post offices, hospitals, shops, schools, and churches, among others, may be very important and may be used to determine whether a particular place is rural or urban in character. By extension, these may assist in determining, to some extent, the nature of families living in these communities.

Another distinguishing feature is the living arrangement of families in the locality. Generally, whereas most rural families tend to live in a traditional family house with other relations, many families in urban areas live in their own houses, whether owned or rented, albeit with a few live-in relatives in some cases. In a typical rural communal setting, families normally interact almost on a daily basis with other extended family members. This kind of interaction space is considerably diminished in an urban cosmopolitan setting, where limited opportunities exist for such communal interaction.

In the rural areas or the indigenous areas of an inner city as in Accra, a family residence may either be patrilocal or matrilocal, duolocal (among the Ga, men and women have separate lineage residences), or avunculocal (among the Akan, husbands and wives do not necessarily coreside after marriage). If any, there are only a few neolocal residences. On the other hand, there is a preponderance of neolocal residences of the family in the urban areas, even though some level of the other residence types can be found. The determining factors, however, include proximity to one's natal home, the presence or lack of accommodation opportunities, the ability of a couple to afford a new and separate home, and also the culture of the family.

Although polygynous households do occur in urban centers in Ghana, they are more prevalent in rural areas. According to Caldwell (1967), "The physical family does in fact encounter many problems in town, especially, physical and economic problems. Accommodation costs can be ruinously expensive, especially if the wives are housed separately. The same is true of food. The fact that the wives are willing to enter into polygamous marriage shows that they are not educated enough to earn the kind of wages as paid in town for professional or skilled work" (p. 178). Polygyny is markedly less common in Ghanaian towns and the average number of children born per woman at every age is lower than in the villages (Tetteh, 1967). A compound house, exclusive for members of the lineage, is usually the residential type for the extended family. It is not uncommon to find three or four nuclear families embedded in the extended or joint family complex. This may occur irrespective of the economic or social status of the domestic unit (Republic of Ghana & United Nations Children Fund, 1990).

In the urban areas of Ghana, church marriage or marriage by ordinance is more common than in the rural areas. Even though such marriage is supposedly expected to support monogamy for women and men, there is a continued presence of private polygyny. A pattern has emerged whereby elite monogamously married men seem to adopt a more informal type of polygyny outside formal marriage in an institutionalized system of girlfriend relationships (Dinan, 1983). Some scholars, therefore, appear cynical about the potential for genuine monogamy in Ghana. This practice raises a public debate over the impossibility of a "common budget" between husbands and wives. Some of the churches prescribe pooling of income by married couple, but the demands of other women, girlfriends, and kin undermine the practicality of this practice. Several cases in the courts underscore the conflict that arises when a relationship breaks down.

In view of the persistence of private polygyny, it has been argued that monogamous marriages in urban areas seem to be more of an economic adaptation to conditions in the cities rather than an ideological one (Omari, 1960; Oppong, 1982). In recent times, private polygyny has been found to have important implications for the diffusion of HIV/AIDS in Ghana, where the disease was first detected in 1986. In many cases, spousal and emotional links are so weak in marriages that there is little discussion about sex between spouses and between the generations. A large number of Ghanaian women know that the greatest danger presented to them comes from their husbands. Some studies indicate that it is probable that the many female AIDS victims have been infected by their husbands (Anarfi, 1993; Carael, 1994). Women generally have limited control over marital sexuality in Ghana. Studies have shown that although most women say they have the right to refuse sex to a husband who is promiscuous, very few actually do so for economic reasons. Finally, the possibility that wives also infect their husbands cannot be ruled out (Carael, 1994).

CHALLENGES FOR CONTEMPORARY GHANAIAN FAMILIES

Urbanization

The growth of Ghanaian towns, associated with increased population and modernization, has brought with it many alterations in social life as well as social problems not hitherto associated with the traditional social organization in rural areas. Slums, overcrowding, organized crime, juvenile delinquency, and other problems have come to be associated with Ghanaian life and adversely affect family stability.

The size, density, permanence, and heterogeneity of the urban population give rise to certain lifestyles of which impersonal behavior, anonymity, and secularism stand out together with a diminution of kinship ties. These characteristics are clearly the opposite of those associated with traditional, rural, and small-scale settlements. With change, the family tends to lose or relinquish many of its former functions. Both in terms of structure and functions, under the impetus of industrialization and urbanization the family is comparatively smaller and is headed toward relative isolation. Despite the seriousness Ghanaians attach to marriage, not all families are able to achieve marital stability. Occupational and geographical mobility and desertion are leading to broken marriages. The pressures from urban life engender additional stresses that affect or militate against marital stability. These have contributed to a rise in the incidence of female-headed households and single parenthood in contemporary times.

The Social and Legal Status of Women and Children

The status of the child is acquired in various ways. A child may be the natural offspring of a person or deemed to be such by reason of adoption, which can either be statutory as under the Adoption Act or through customary law. Certain rights and responsibilities follow from a child's status as a natural offspring of a person. The child has specific rights such as care, maintenance, and succession. Some of these rights are customary in origin and some have been granted by statute (Mensa-Bonsu, 1994). There are also duties inherent in the enforcement of these rights. Some of the areas of concern that need attention with regard to children include child labor, slavery, and child abuse in various forms and degrees.

The state as an institution has a responsibility toward all citizens of its territory as well as a special responsibility for children. It is for this reason that Ghana signed and ratified the International Convention on the Rights of the Child in 1990. The role of the state is as the ultimate protector or ultimate parent of every child. The state is also involved in ensuring the moral welfare of children, preventing sexual offences against children, and providing assistance to families with respect to the health of mothers and children. All these provisions and others are enshrined in the 1992 constitution, including paid maternity leave for mothers and tax relief for overburdened families.

In the past, property of individual members of the family was held communally. This concept is changing fast and being reinforced by an emerging sense of individualism. In matrilineal societies it is often the case that when the man dies intestate, his widow(s) and children are dispossessed of his property and sent packing. Even in patrilineal societies the autonomy of the nuclear family is not being readily accepted. The problem is more acute in matrilineal societies, where the principal beneficiaries in the traditional system are those outside the nuclear family of the deceased. It is in this light that the PNDC Law 111 (1985), which vests the property of the deceased mainly in the spouse and the children, is seen as a victory for the nuclear family in Ghana. While recognizing this law as a breakthrough in the fight against the system, which virtually excluded children and their mothers from the inheritance system, by itself the law may not achieve much except in enlightened circles because of social pressures that are likely to impede implementation. This law has also negative implications for some women. It tends to favor men and all his children regardless of the marital status of the children's mother(s). To some, it also favors polygyny to the detriment of women who are married monogamously, are without children, and have high investment in the nuclear family property.

The fight for independence and consequent feelings of solidarity with this cause is an important feature in many African countries. However, the processes that culminate in this feeling of nationalism, especially in Ghana, and events following thereafter have some influences on strengthening or suppressing of gender biases in the sociopolitical system. As a patriarchal society, there is an inherent gender bias in favor of men in all spheres of economic, political, and social life. It is not surprising that long after women became doctors, professors, and the like, many people still address them with masculine titles. In recent years, the government has adopted mechanisms for promoting gender equality in Ghana. Among these are the establishment of the National Council on Women and Development in the 1970s, the Ministry of Women and Children Affairs, and the Ministry of Girl Child Education in 2000. In the area of the family, the recent establishment of the Women and the Juvenile Unit of the Ghana Police Service, which has witnessed rising reported cases of domestic violence perpetuated against women, gives a voice to abused women. To these efforts should be added those of nongovernmental organizations and women's groups that promote the interest of women in the family in the face of rising crises like the HIV/AIDS menace.

HIV/AIDS Crisis and Family Health

HIV/AIDS was first reported in Ghana in 1986. Out of the 42 cases reported, 85 percent were female (Konotey-Ahulu, 1989). By 1993, the cumulative proportion of all HIV/AIDS cases that were female dropped; however, female HIV/AIDS cases still outnumbered male cases. Most of the initial victims were single, divorced, or unattached. They worked mostly in the informal sector of the economy and had limited or no formal education. Studies also show that they were commercial sex workers who indulged in the activity for economic survival (Anarfi, 1993).

The female ratio of HIV/AIDS patients rose from 1:8 in 1986 to 1:3 in 1990. However, the proportion of victims with a history of staying abroad dropped from 89 percent in 1986 to 56 percent in 1990. Thus, HIV/AIDS is being diffused within the country from the original core areas. Studies on HIV/AIDS in Ghana have shown that over 70 percent of male and female patients are between the ages of 20 and 39 years. Thus, a number of children being born are HIV positive with 1 percent of all HIV/AIDS patients now under 5 years of age. Many children are also being orphaned at an early age because of the concentration of the disease among the reproductive age group of the population (Anarfi, 1989; Crock et al., 1991). The care of AIDS patients is putting an increasing financial and emotional burden on affected families.

Programs such as the Adolescent Sexual Reproductive Health (ASRH), Community Sexual and Reproductive Health Programs, and the National AIDS Commission attempt to address HIV/AIDS-related issues, complementing the educational campaigns of both national and nongovernmental organizations. They try to improve and safeguard the health needs of family members, especially those with HIV/AIDS cases.

Street Children

In the urban areas of Ghana, a growing number of school-age children roam the streets during school hours. Most of them are from broken homes or immigrant families whose parents are poorly employed (GNCC, 1990). These children drop out of school and take to the streets to do odd jobs for survival. They are undernourished and lack adequate health care and development (Apt, Blavo, & Opoku, 1992). Some are children of petty traders in the market areas who have to sell in order to supplement the meager income of their mother or guardian for the maintenance of the household.

Street children have various motives for working in the street. Some children engage in economic activities because they need the money for various school expenses, while others engage in trading to supplement the household budget. Among the street girls in Accra, most have migrated to work as porters, popularly called "kayayee," for money; as many as 88 percent are there for this reason (see Apt & Grieco, 1995). Others are there to escape forced marriages or dysfunctional families. The work of the street children seems to be dominated by unskilled categories like hawking petty commodities, carrying heavy loads of goods, running errands for shopkeepers, and doing many other odd jobs to get money. Survival on the streets requires strength and fortitude, and a reasonable level of good health management.

The activities of these street children may have both positive and negative consequences. Apart from earning some income, it has destructive effects on the performance of the girls in school (Apt et al., 1992; Korboe, 1997). It leads not only to dropping out but is also the root cause of truancy and delinquency and children falling into illicit drug activities. In the case of girls, they may become victims of unwanted teenage pregnancy when they drop out or take to the streets.

Trokosi

The practice of *trokosi* is a complex and multifaceted ancient institution with environmental, ecological, sociocultural, and religious dimensions. It has been described as enslavement of female virgins in Ghana. There are various versions of how the practice originated. One of the versions has it that the practice was started centuries ago by the ancestors in the ethnic areas where it is practiced. Usually when mysterious deaths occur in a family, the family members consult a soothsayer who happens to be connected with a shrine. A female virgin between 6 and 22 years of age is then sent to the shrine to atone for the sins supposedly committed by the family member. Whenever a vestal virgin dies at the shrine, her family must replace her with another virgin from the family (Pappoe & Ardayfio-Schandorf, 1988).

Another version substantiated by other ethnic groups indicates that the practice came into existence through their forefathers. It was originally meant to eradicate evils in the society. Formerly animals like sheep and goats were used, but were later replaced with female virgins. On rare occasions males may be used. According to the third version, the actual name of the *trokosi* is *troxovi*, meaning "a divinity which adopts children" (African Renaissance Mission cited in Pappoe & Ardayfio-Schandorf, 1998). In its application, it is regarded as a divinity of justice, morality, public security, education, and social welfare. The *troxovi* shrine belongs to the communities, not individuals. This implies that apart from the community shrines there are others that have been set up by individuals like the one-man established churches. *Trokosi* shrines can be found among some sections of the Ewe (Volta region) and the Ada (Greater Accra region).

The vestal virgins are granted their liberty only after the deities are pacified by the families. They are allowed to marry only within a clan that worships the deity since they are considered wives of the deity and mothers of the clan. They live and serve the shrine. If liberty is not granted and the vestal virgin has a child with a priest, the child stays at the shrine. Previously, the virgins were isolated without exposure to formal education. As a response to repeated campaigns, the children are now given some formal education, and the women are introduced to income-generating activities. The Commission on Human Rights and Administrative Justice and other NGOs are fighting for the abolition of this practice, which dehumanizes virgins in families.

Witch Camps

Witchcraft is an African traditional belief. It is mostly women who are accused of witchcraft. Generally, a witch camp is a place where witches, or women who claim to have some magical powers, assemble and undertake their operations. In the case of the Gambaga camp, the women do not operate as witches; rather they seek refuge against the hostile communities from which they have been rejected. The camp was established to end the plight of poor women who were accused of witchcraft and subjected to strenuous and inhuman treatment by their families (Pappoe & Ardayfio-Schandorf, 1998). The camp was set up by the grandfather of the reigning chief of Gambaga, who has the antidote to rid any accused witches of their magical powers. The chief priest carries out the purification or de-witching sacrifices of accused witches. The family or relations of the witches are allowed to take them back after the cleansing if they so wish. However, many of these women are not taken back and they remain refugees of the camp until they grow old and die. Most of the women in the camps are old, some over 90 years old.

Female Genital Mutilation

Female genital mutilation (FGM) is a precondition of marriage for women in certain ethnic groups in the northern sector of the country. In those societies where FGM is practiced, girls tend to imbibe the culture to the extent that by the time they grow up, they think of the operation as being good for them, and believe that without it they would not be accepted as women in their own society (Pappoe & Ardayfio-Schandorf, 1998). The rites are supposed to confer social acceptability on the initiates, so parents will ensure that their children participate in it for fear that they will be ostracized. FGM is now being practiced at an earlier age. Many communities advocate the abolishment of FGM because of its health and sociocultural effects. These include the fact that it is cruel and wicked, and may lead to barrenness, bleeding to death, and many gynecological problems.

CONCLUSION

The changing dynamics of the family in Ghana have raised several issues concerning the quality of life of the Ghanaian people, the plight of women, and the strengthening of the family and intergenerational family ties. The family in Ghana has been in a state of flux since the indigenous state came into contact with varied cultures, mainly from the north and south of the country. The spatial relations and the resultant interactions transformed the indigenous family institution over time. Some of the changes may be traced to Islamization from about AD 700.

The major and most far-reaching influence, however, was Christianity starting in the 15th century. Christianity revolutionized Ghanaian society and influenced all aspects of the family. Unlike Islam, Christianity introduced dualism into Ghanaian society. It reorganized production and affected forms of marriage, socialization and maintenance of children, kinship obligations, inheritance, and property distribution. In certain areas there have been conflicts and confusion because Christianity reinforced individualism as opposed to the communal living and sharing practiced in the Ghanaian indigenous family. Thus, the family has undergone redefinition from prehistoric through Islamic penetration, colonial to postcolonial times. One clear legacy that has emerged is the Traditional-Islamic-Christian heritage. In Ghana there are three recognized marriages, the customary, Islamic, and the ordinance/church. In practice, customary marriage is common preceding the Islamic, ordinance, or church marriage.

Western colonialism introduced the money economy and European education, both of which were in conflict with polygynous tendencies. This influence encouraged monogamy and challenged kinship obligations. With growing emphasis on the nuclear family, family members and most grandparents are living less frequently with children and grandchildren, thus breaking the intergenerational ties with serious consequences for the cohesion, care, and maintenance functions of the indigenous family. The emerging family structure questions and seeks solutions for the oppression of women in the patriarchal indigenous family. At the same time, the new system is putting pressure on women as female-headed households become more common in both urban and rural areas dwindling resources in the midst of rising social responsibilities. The situation is worsened as more family care and maintenance responsibilities fall on women. While it is important to make deliberate efforts to maintain cohesion in the family and strengthen intergenerational ties, the role of the state is equally crucial. The state should promote togetherness, cooperation, and conflict resolution to strengthen the family. Government policies such as the Maintenance of

Children Decree and the Intestate Succession Law (PNDCL 111) have been promulgated to promote effective and fair family relationships, but there are many challenges to their implementation and their impact needs to be periodically reviewed.

It is of utmost importance that changing trends in family structure are systematically studied and documented to aid fuller comprehension of family dynamics and stabilization of families in Ghana. There is also a need to fill gaps in research on the family by conducting studies of Islamic and non-African families, which are less covered in Ghana. New family frontiers also need to be explored in the wake of HIV/AIDS diseases and globalization. Innovative research methodologies should be developed to demonstrate how these factors change households and how women and children are faring under the circumstances.

REFERENCES

Addai-Sundiata, H. (1995). *Family dynamics and residential arrangements in Ghana*. Family and Development Program [FADEP] Technical Series, University of Ghana, Legon.

Anarfi, J. (1993). Sexuality, migration and AIDS in Ghana. In Caldwell, J. C. et al. (Eds.), *Sexual Networking and HIV/AIDS in West Africa* (pp. 45–68). Supplement to Vol. 3, *Health and Transition Review*. Canberra: Australian National University.

Antubam, K. (1963). Ghana's heritage of culture. Leipzig: Koehler & Amelang.

Apt, N. A. (1981). *Ageing in Ghana*. Legon: University of Ghana.

Apt, N. A., Blavo, E. Q., & Opoku, S. K. (1992). *Street children in Accra*. Accra: Save the Children's Fund.

Apt, N. A. & Grieco, M. (1995). *Listening to girls on the street tell their own story*. Legon: Social Administration Unit, University of Ghana.

Ardayfio-Schandorf, E. (1991). *Enhancing opportunities for women in development*. (PAMSCAD Women in Development Project, a Baseline Survey Report, and Western Region). Accra: WID Secretariat, Ministry of Local Government.

Ardayfio-Schandorf, E. (1994). *Family and development in Ghana*. Accra: Ghana Universities Press.

Ardayfio-Schandorf, E. (1995). *The changing family in Ghana*. Accra: Ghana Universities Press.

Aryee, F. (1985). Nuptiality patterns in Ghana. In Singh, S., Owusu, J., & Iqbal, H. S. (Eds.), *Demographic patterns in Ghana: Evidence from Ghana Fertility Survey 1970–80*. Voorburg, Netherlands: International Statistical Institute.

Awusabo-Asare, K. (1990). Matriliny and the new intestate succession in Ghana. *Canadian Journal of African Studies 24*, 1–16.

Benneh, G. (1992). Family and development: An overview. In Ardayfio-Schandorf, E. (Ed.), *Family and development in Ghana*. Accra: Ghana Universities Press.

Boahen, A. (1966). *Topics in West African history*. London: Longman.

Brown, C. K. (1984). *Improving the social protection of the ageing population in Ghana*. ISSER Technical Publication Series. Legon: University of Ghana.

Brown, C. K. (1992). *Aging and family care in Ghana: A study in caring relationships*. Cape Coast: CDS.

Buah, F. K. (1980). *A history of Ghana*. London & Basingstoke: Macmillan.
Bukh, J. (1979). *The village woman in Ghana*. Uppsala: Scandinavian Institute of African Studies.
Caldwell, J. C. (1967). *Migration and urbanization. A study of contemporary Ghana. Some Aspects of Social Structure*. Canberra: ANU Press.
Carael, M. (1994). The impact of marriage change on the risks of exposure to sexually transmitted diseases in Africa. In Bledsoe, C. & Pison, G. (Eds.), *Nuptiality in sub-Saharan Africa: Contemporary anthropological and demographic perspectives* (pp. 255–273). Oxford: Clarendon.
Charmie, J. (1986). Polygyny among the Arabs. *Population Studies 1*, 55–66.
Davidson, B. (1994). *Modern Africa: A social and political history*. London: Longman.
Dinan, C. (1983). Sugar daddies and gold diggers: The white-collar single women in Accra. In Oppong, C. (Ed.), *Female and male in West Africa* (pp. 344–366). London: Allen & Unwin.
Fortes, M. (1950). Kinship and marriage among the Ashanti. In Radcliffe-Brown, A. R. & Forde, D. (Eds.), *African systems of marriage* (pp. 252–284). London: Oxford University Press.
Friedlander, D. (1966). *Measuring fertility in Ghana*. Paper presented to the 1st African Population Conference, Ibadan, Nigeria.
Gaisie, S. K. (1966). *Some aspects of fertility studies in Ghana*. Paper presented to the 1st African Population Conference, Ibadan, Nigeria.
Ghana Statistical Service & Micro International, Inc. (1994). *Ghana demographic and health survey 1993*. Accra & Calverton, MD: 6SS & MI.
Ghana Statistical Service. (1998). *Third Ghana living standards survey (GLSS-3)*. Accra: Ghana Statistical Service.
Giddens, A. (1989). *Sociology*. London: Polity Press.
Goody, J. (1973). Polygyny, economy and the role of women. In Goody, J. (Ed.), *Character of Kinship* (pp. 175–190). New York, Cambridge University Press.
Government of Ghana. (1984). *Ghana demographic and health survey*. Calverton, MD: Ghana Statistical Services and Macro International Inc.
Government of Ghana. (1994). Census report, 1948. In *Demographic and health survey*. Accra: Ghana Statistical Service.
Khapoya, V. (1994). *The African experience: An introduction*. Upper Saddle River, NJ: Prentice Hall.
Kludze, A. K. P. (1983). Property law and rural development in Ghana. *Rural Africana 17*, 57–67.
Konotey-Ahulu, F. (1989). *What is AIDS?* Worcester, MA: Tetteh-A'Domeno.
Korboe, D. (1997). *A profile of street children in Kumasi*. Legon: Centre for Social Policy, University of Ghana.
Lloyd, C. B., & Gage-Brandon, A. J. (1993). Women's role in maintaining households: Family welfare and sexual inequality in Ghana. *Population Studies 47(1)*, 115–131.
Mazrui, A. A. (1986). *The Africans: A triple heritage*. Boston: Little, Brown.
Mensa-Bonsu, H. (1994). The maintenance of children decree: Some implications for child welfare and development. In Ardayfio-Schandorf, E. Family and development in Ghana, pp. 111–122. Ghana Universities Press.
Mikell, G. (1975). *Cocoa and social change in Ghana. A study of development in the Sunyani district*. Unpublished doctoral dissertation, Columbia University, New York.

Nukunya, G. K. (1972). Land tenure and inheritance in Angola. Technical publication series (University of Ghana. Institute of Statistical, Social, and Economic Research); No. 30. Legon: University of Ghana.

Nukunya, G. K. (1992). *Tradition and social change in Ghana: An introduction to sociology.* Accra: Ghana Universities Press.

O'Connor, A. (1992). The changing geography of Eastern Africa. In Chapman, G. P. & Baker, K. M. (Eds.), *The changing geography of Africa and the Middle East.* New York: Routledge.

Olaniyan, R. (1982). Islamic penetration in Africa. In Olaniyan, R. (Ed.), *African history and culture.* Ikeja, Lagos: Longman, Nigeria.

Ollenu, N. A. (1960). *The law of succession in Ghana.* Accra: Presby Book Depot.

Ollenu, N. A. (1966). *Law of testate and intestate succession.* London: Sweet & Maxwell.

Ollenu, N. A., & Woodman, G. R. (1985). *Principles of customary land law in Ghana.* Birmingham: CAL Press.

Omari, P. T. (1960). Changing attitudes of students in West African society towards marriage and family relationships. British Journal of Sociology, 11: 197–210.

Opoku, C. (1982). The world view of Akan. *Tarikh 7(2).*

Oppong, C. (1982). *Middle-class African marriage.* London: Allen & Unwin.

Pappoe, M., & Ardayfio-Schandorf, E. (1998). *The dimension and consequences of violence against women. A study report.* Legon: University of Ghana.

Piel, M. (1977). *Consensus and conflict in African societies: An introduction to sociology.* London: Longman.

Poh, K., Tosh, J., Waller, R., & Tidy, M. (1982). *African history in maps.* Harlow, Eng.: Longman.

Rattray, R. S. (1923). *Ashanti.* London: Oxford University Press.

Rattray, R. S. (1929). *Ashanti law and constitution.* London: Oxford University Press.

Ray, D. (1986). *Ghana: Politics, economics and society.* London: Pinter.

Republic of Ghana & United Nations Children's Fund. (1990). *Children and women in Ghana: A situation analysis.* Accra: UNICEF.

Skinner, E. P. (1986). The triple heritage of lifestyles. In Mazrui, A. & Levine, T. K. (Eds.), *The Africans: A reader.* New York: Praeger.

Takyi, B. K. (2003). Tradition and change in family processes: Selecting a marital partner in modern Ghana. In Hamon, R. R. & Ingoldsby, B. B. (Eds.), *Mate selection across cultures* (pp. 79–94). Thousand Oaks, CA: Sage.

Tetteh, P. A. (1967). Marriage, family and household. In Birmingham, W., et al. (Eds.), *A study of contemporary Ghana.* Vol. 11. London: Allen & Unwin.

United Nations. (1985). *The world aging situation: Strategies and policies.* Department of International and Social Affairs. New York.

Vellenga, D. D. (1971). Attempts to change the marriage laws in Ghana and Ivory Coast. In Foster P. & Zolberg, A. R. (Eds.), *Ghana and Ivory Coast: Perspectives on Modernization.* Chicago: University of Chicago Press.

Vellenga, D. D. (1983). Who is a wife? Legal expressions of heterosexual conflicts in Ghana. In Oppong, C. (Ed.), *Female and male in West Africa* (pp. 144–155). London: Allen & Unwin.

Yeboah, I. E. A. (1997). Historical background of sub-Saharan Africa: Opportunities and constraints. In Aryeetey-Attoh, S. (Ed.), *Geography of sub-Saharan Africa.* Upper Saddle River, NJ: Prentice Hall.

CHAPTER 8

The Nigerian Family: Contrast, Convergence, Continuity, and Discontinuity

Obioma Nnaemeka

BACKGROUND

Nigeria, a West African country about twice the size of California, was a British colony until 1960 when it gained political independence. With an estimated population of 137 million as of June 2004, it is the most populous country in Africa.[1] The name of the country derives from the intersection of two defining features—geography and colonial history—that contribute to shaping certain fundamental aspects of the country. Prominently marked by two rivers that converge to divide the country into three unequal parts inhabited by the three major ethnic groups—Hausa-Fulani (29 percent) in the north, the Yoruba (20 percent) in the southwest, and the Igbo (17 percent) in the southeast—Nigeria took its name from one of the rivers, the Niger. But Flora Shaw, an Englishwoman who later became the wife of the British colonial administrator of Nigeria, Frederick Lugard, provided the word *Nigeria*.

Prior to 1960, Nigeria's economy was dependent on food and cash crop production. To a large extent, Nigeria was able to provide for the nutritional needs of its citizens. Since then, the country has transitioned into an economy that is almost entirely dependent on oil. The country's overdependence on the oil sector and the government's inability to diversify the economy decimated the subsistence agricultural sector, pushed rural population to the urban areas in search of employment, and saddled the cities with the problems of high population density and urban blight. Nigeria is currently faced with a high death rate

(13.99 deaths/1,000, a high infant mortality rate (70 deaths/1,000), and a low life expectancy (50.49 years) that is exacerbated by increasing incidence of HIV/AIDS. The adult prevalence rate of HIV/AIDS is 5.4 percent, with 3.6 million people living with HIV/AIDS and annual HIV/AIDS deaths of 310,000.

Since 1960, Nigeria's political landscape has been marked by many years of military rule/misrule and political instability, In fact, Nigeria was under military rule for 28 out of the 45 years since independence. The Gowon administration introduced the state structure; the creation of more states by subsequent administrations has brought the number of states currently to 36. Decades of misrule, particularly under the military, have impoverished the resource-rich nation and thrown the majority of its teeming population into abject poverty and despair. Questions about distribution of and access to resources exacerbate ethnic politics, fuel disaffection and alienation, and flare protests and insurgencies. About three decades ago, these divisions plunged the country into a civil war (1967–70) that cost millions of lives. The current democratically elected government is under the leadership of President Olusegun Obasanjo (a former army general) who came into power in 1999 and is serving a second term expected to end in 2007.

INTRODUCTION

> The family is the primary social unit that maintains other institutions and reinforces existing patterns of domination. At the same time, however, family networks provide support systems that can reduce the indignities and/or challenge the inequities produced by various systems of inequality in society.
> —Shaw and Lee (2004, p. 287)

A family means different things in different places and time periods. As an institution, the family is both social and affective. As a social institution, it has complex relationships with other institutions and systems—religion, law, economy, politics, health, education, and so on. A family is also "a place where individuals experience intimate relationships" (Shaw & Lee, 2004, p. 287). The familial space has many contradictions. It responds to the material, spiritual, and emotional needs of its members. But it also replicates many forms of inequalities, hierarchies, and privileges that breed domination, conflicts, and violence.

The family is culturally and historically constructed with the result that its configurations and meanings shift across and within cultures. For example, these shifts and configurations have occurred in the United States in different places and historical moments—nuclear, multigenerational, blended, polygynous, extended, gay and lesbian, and single-parent families. The state's refusal to recognize and legalize certain configurations of the family remains a contested issue in the United States. Furthermore, the understanding of family is anchored in a major conflict between myth and reality. Often, the family is wrapped in a mythology of normalcy. In the United States, normalcy is enshrined in a two-parent, heterosexual family. In Nigeria, as in many parts of Africa, the mythology is anchored in nostalgia—the normalcy of the good old days (the past) and the aberrant fragmentation and abnormality of nowadays (the present).

The rich, complex, and sometimes conflictual texture of Nigeria derives from the country's extraordinary diversity of cultures and ethnicities. It is estimated that Nigeria has over 250 ethnic groups that are distributed as follows: Hausa-Fulani (29 percent); Yoruba (20 percent); Igbo (17 percent); Tiv and Plateau groups (9 percent); Ibibio, Efik, and related groups (6 percent); Kanuri (5 percent); Edo (3 percent); Idoma, Igala, and Igbirra (2.5 percent); Ijo (2 percent); and others (7 percent) (Neher, 1999, p. 32). Given this immense diversity and heterogeneity, it would be problematic to argue on the basis of a totalizing concept such as "the Nigerian family" that appears in the title of this chapter. It is as difficult to speak of "the Nigerian culture" as it is to speak of "the Nigerian family."

Rather than grounding its arguments in an imagined homogenized construct, this chapter will examine the notion of family and how it has constructed different realities culturally, geographically, and historically within the Nigerian context. The chapter will also investigate how the family has been shaped and reshaped by encounters in the past and present—particularly colonialism, modernity, and globalization. The chapter will focus on the three major ethnic groups in Nigeria—Hausa-Fulani, Yoruba, and Igbo. It will tease out the differences and delineate the commonalities, revisit the question of the (re)conceptualization of the family in a time of change, and reassess the tradition-modernity binary. Given the crucial role gender relations play in understanding family dynamics, the chapter will probe the issues of marriage and divorce. Finally, the chapter will evaluate the impact of internal and external migration and dislocations on the Nigerian family.

ETHNICITY AND LOCATIONS OF DIFFERENCE

> Usually, ethnicity refers to a complex of cultural practices, including language, kinship organization, economic activities, location, types of dwellings, and religious practices.
> —William Neher (1999, p. 8)

The three ethnic groups that are the focus of this chapter have shared histories but are also marked by differences engendered by different geographies and varying impacts of foreign contacts and influences. It is estimated that of the 38 million Hausa-speaking people in West Africa, 32 million live in northern Nigeria and majority of the remaining live in the Republic of Niger. There are Hausa communities in other African countries such as Cameroon, Sudan,

Ghana, Mali, Gambia, Senegal, and Sierra Leone. Islamic influences are the strongest in northern Nigeria where the Islamic religion had its beginnings in the 14th century. The Jihad Movement in Hausaland in the 19th century contributed to collapsing traditional Hausa culture and Islamic culture. The majority of non-Western-educated Hausa women interviewed in Knipp's (1987) study echo the view expressed by one of the interviewees: "Islam is a great influence on what I say and do, what my relation is supposed to be with my husband, my family, and my children" (p. 407). Most Hausas are Sunnis and follow the Maliki school of law. The formal education provided by Quranic schools offers less access to females and more to males. The Hausa society is class-conscious and stratified:

The Hausa are divided among several social classes. At the top of the hierarchy were the ruling class, made up of the "chiefs" or *Sarakuna* (singular, *Sarki*) and courtiers. The Muslim *ulama* (scholars, judges, teachers) and wealthy merchants were politically and socially prominent. Then there were the urban populations of the towns and cities, both free and slave, and the people of the countryside who were both free peasants and agricultural slaves. On the margins of the Hausa society were the pastoral nomads living in Fulani cattle encampments. (Neher, 1999, p. 34)

Each family unit lives in a compound (*gida*) that is under the authority of the family head (*mai gida*) who is usually the oldest male member. The family in this agricultural society in which mechanized agriculture is virtually nonexistent is heavily dependent on its members for labor and response to social and economic needs. Culturally, the Hausa frown on the selling and purchase of labor (Shenton, 1986). Sex, age, and class determine the distribution of responsibilities, privileges, and authority. Solivetti's study of the Hausa community in the Niger valley of Sokoto State underscores the link among gender, religion, and work. The Hausa-Fulani acceptance of the Islamic practice of female exclusion (*purda*) accounts for women's restricted engagement in work outside the home. Adult males are mainly responsible for farmwork and providing for the family's nutritional needs. Because the women are generally in seclusion, they are exempt from farmwork and restricted to home duties such as threshing and grinding cereals, cooking, cleaning, and child care. However, women who are not in seclusion can venture outside the *gida* in search of firewood and water.

Child marriage is more prevalent in northern Nigeria where "marriage is nearly universal and virtually obligatory . . . [and] pressure is exerted on women, particularly, to marry quite young and to stay married throughout their fertile years. Over half the women are married by age 14 and nearly 100 percent are married by age 19" (Neher, 1999, p. 34). Because single women are perceived as prostitutes and marginalized, divorcees and widows strive to remarry. There have been instances when authorities in some northern states handed down ultimatums to single women to get married or leave town.

Child marriage also accounts for the higher prevalence of vesico-vaginal fistula (VVF) and recto-vaginal fistula (RVF) in northern Nigeria. A 1997 study by Stolz and Faure (cited in Adamu, 1998) shows that 70 percent of the 200,000 Nigerian females suffering from VVF are from the north. Because the child brides are not physically mature for the burdens of pregnancy and childbirth, they are more prone to having protracted and obstructed labor that are the major causes of VVF and RVF. Adamu (1998) notes that the situation is exacerbated by the Hausa custom of expecting women to endure labor pains (*kunya*). Local and international organizations are joining forces to campaign against child marriage and repair the damage caused by VVF and RVF. In 2003, the United Nations Population Fund (UNFPA) launched a global Campaign to End Fistula. From February 21 through March 6, 2005, UNFPA joined forces with Nigerian federal and state governments, the Nigerian Red Cross, Volunteer Service Overseas, Virgin Unite, Nigerian nongovernmental organizations, and health professionals from Nigeria, United Kingdom, and the United States to organize a "Fistula Fortnight" during which more than 500 sufferers of fistula were treated (Agence France Presse, 2005).

The second major ethnic group in Nigeria is the Yoruba. There are 17 million Yorubas living in southwestern Nigeria in addition to a sizable number of Yoruba families residing in the Republic of Benin. The Yoruba are city and town dwellers who depend largely on the agricultural sector. Many farmers are also craftsmen and traders. The diet and food produced (mostly root crops) are different from that of the north where cereals are staple. Like the Hausa-Fulani, the Yoruba also had slaves who worked in the households or farms. The composition and living arrangements of families in Yorubaland differ from the configuration in the north:

Traditionally, the Yoruba were town or city dwellers, with smaller farming communities associated with each town or city. The towns were made up of a combination of large family compounds (each compound housing as many as 1,000 people). The compounds were organized around and based upon lineages. These lineages held the farm land in common in areas beyond the boundaries of the town itself. This feature of living in a town some distance from one's farm is distinctive of the Yoruba. Each town at its center had an "Afin" or a dwelling place for the town's oba or chief who is seen as the townspeople's priest and protector. (Neher, 1999, p. 37)

The patrilineal descent group structure among the Yoruba excluded women from being family and lineage group heads. The marginalization does not, however, exclude women from active participation in politics and the economy (Okonjo, 1976; Awe, 1977, 1979; Mba, 1982; Aina, 1993; Sofola, 1998). Yoruba women play an active role in internal and regional trade and also participate in food production, processing, and distribution (Adeyokunnu, 1984).

The Igbo are the third major ethnic group in Nigeria mostly occupying the southeastern part of the country. They are generally farmers who live in villages. The family structure and participatory model in village affairs provide a more democratic and less hierarchical structure for intergroup and intragroup interactions. The extended family unit is generally the norm. Several households (extended families) make up a compound and several compounds make up a village. Given the patrilineal nature of the lineage groups, compound heads are male. Women play a crucial role in the political and economic life of the Igbo. They engage in tedious tasks such as bush clearing, planting, weeding, harvesting, and marketing. However, the cultural structuring of a hierarchy of females (daughters of the clan over wives of the clan) creates tension and the potential for woman-on-woman abuse and violence.

THE TIES THAT BIND

> The diversity—the vast number of subcultures [in Africa]—is undeniable. But there is a foundation of shared values, attitudes, and institutions that binds together the nations south of the Sahara, and in many respects those of the north as well.
> —Etounga-Manguelle (2000)

The ethnic group consists of a collection of clans and lineages that share the same culture, customs, language, history, and practices. Despite regional variations and ethnic diversity in Nigeria, there are shared values and beliefs among different ethnic groups that can be used as organizing principles in discussions about the family in Nigeria. The Hausa-Fulani, Yoruba, and Igbo live in patrilineal, agrarian societies in which male authority is dominant. The family unit produces the labor necessary for its economic and nutritional needs. Women participate in farming although the intensity of their involvement is dictated by cultural, regional, and socioeconomic differences.

Among the Hausa-Fulani, Yoruba, and Igbo, kinship is a determining factor in identity formation and allocation of privileges, duties, and responsibilities. Two common features of the kinship organization are the unilineal (patrilineal) descent grouping and the practice of polygyny (acceptable in Islam and traditional Nigerian cultures). Most Nigerians are rural dwellers and households configure as multigenerational extended families consisting of a man, his wife/wives, children, uncles, aunts, grandparents, and servants (or in the past clients such as slaves). Individual identity is defined by layers of complex relationships and affinities with different constituencies such as family, lineage, age group, clan, and ethnic group. Nigerians exercise full citizenship in a double gesture of belonging—*belonging in* and *belonging to* the group (Neher, 1999). Individuals exercise citizenship rights, obligations, and freedoms within the context of the group in which and to which they belong.[2]

As a basic social unit, the Nigerian family fulfills cultural (imparting beliefs and cultural literacy), economic (providing for nutritional and material needs), and reproductive (ensuring the survival of the lineage) functions. At the center of these functions and considerations is the child. Children are extremely valued; they occupy a central place in family and community life for many reasons—they ensure the availability of labor; they are vehicles through which cultural values are perpetuated; they ensure the survival and continuity of the lineage; they are insurance for elderly parents; and they serve as links between families and between the family and the community. Male children are very much desired, not out of sexism or dislike for girls but because of the nature and exigencies of the patrilineage where descent is through the male. Marriage is exogamous and requires that females leave their natal clans to join their husbands' clans. Males stay in their natal clans to ensure lineage survival and continuity. The three ethnic groups under study require bride wealth to officially seal the marriage contract between families or other kinship groups.

The dependency ratio in the Nigerian family is usually high. The complex, multilayered bonds and relationships between the individual and the family or other lineage groups are sustained by shared obligations and responsibilities. Family members who are employed and have the resources assume responsibility for the welfare of resource-challenged members, especially the young, the elderly, and the disabled. The implication of the high dependency ratio is captured in a Yoruba proverb which states that a family of one rich member and nine poor members ends up as a family of ten poor members.

(RE)CONCEPTUALIZING THE FAMILY IN CHANGING TIMES AND REASSESSING THE TRADITION-MODERNITY DICHOTOMY

In conceptualizing the family in changing times, it will be necessary to revisit the two units of analysis that are sometimes used interchangeably—household and family. Although the two overlap, they are distinguishable in many respects. Bradley and Weisner (1997) aptly note that "households and families are constituted differently and would call for different methods. In western Kenya, for example, a household is easily defined as 'those who share a cooking pot.' ... 'Household' and 'family' would then overlap but remain analytically distinct as units for analysis and conceptualization" (p. xxv). This observation about western Kenya is equally applicable to the Nigerian situation in which the household is a coresidential unit whose members could be multigenerational with biological or nonbiological children. Family, as it is used in this chapter, covers a wider terrain that includes family members who have moved away due to internal or external migration.

In popular culture and the academy, Africa is often pathologized as crisis, chaos, and dilemma (Ayittey, 1998). It is often argued that Africa's encounters with external forces and realities (colonization, modernization, globalization, etc.) have been disruptive and deleterious to "traditional" institutions such as the family that is increasingly becoming more atomized and less stable, and losing grip of cultural beliefs and values. Thus, the notion of the African family in crisis is gaining ground although there are different perspectives on the nature and unfolding of the crisis. What is certain is that shifts are occurring in the African family in general and the Nigerian family in particular.

Scholars such as Popenoe (1988) see the shift as a mark of family decline and disintegration resulting in weakening of ties between members and loss of cultural values. But in their studies of African families and communities in western Kenya and eastern Uganda, Bradley, Weisner, and their colleagues argue that the African family is not as deinstitutionalized as Popenoe argues. Bradley and Weisner (1997) see the shift not as a breakdown or a meltdown but as a crisis-laden continuity that harbors the salience of institutional structures:

The African family circumstances described in our study suggest that the institutional structures of Kenyan families are becoming more diverse but are still highly salient; that some functions (support and care for children, care of the elderly, control of property, health care, nutritional status) are as strong as ever, although changing in form and perhaps not as homogeneous or as reliable; that the state affects the economy and polity differently than it directly impinges on the domestic world; and that family life has become more unstable more because of migration and fertility change than a change in the values of familism per se. (p. xxii–xxiii)

Arguing along the same line, the Nigerian historian Ade Ajayi insists that colonialism is one of many episodes in African history and despite the changes it brought in its wake, it did not obliterate the relevance and salience of precolonial institutions: Rather than a history only of changes, it is also one of continuity (Ajayi, 2000). It will be, therefore, misleading to study and analyze the Nigerian family in the context of a clearly defined tradition and modernity dichotomy. Modernity has its contradictions; in asserting its newness, it lays claim to a past (the old). Or as Rey Chow (1993) elegantly puts it, "Modernity is ambivalent in its very origin.... In trying to become 'new' and 'novel'—a kind of primary moment—it must incessantly deal with its connection with what precedes it—what was primary to it—in the form of a destruction" (p. 41).

A meaningful understanding of the Nigerian family in a time of change must move away from the nostalgia of a reified "tradition" (past) and focus instead on what Ake calls the "indigenous" that is dynamic and evolutionary:

We cannot significantly advance the development of Africa unless we take African societies seriously as they are, not as they ought to be or even as they might be; that sustainable development cannot occur unless we build on the indigenous. Now, what is the indigenous and how might we build on it? The indigenous is not the traditional, there is no fossilized existence of the African past available for us to fall back on, only new totalities however hybrid which change with each passing day. The indigenous refers to whatever the people consider important to their lives, whatever they regard as an authentic expression of themselves. We build on the indigenous by making it determine the form and content of development strategy, by ensuring that developmental change accommodates itself to these things, be they values, interests, aspirations and or social institutions which are important in the life of the people. (Ake, 1988, p. 19)

The distinction Ake makes between the traditional and the indigenous is an important one because it interrogates the reified notion of culture as it is evoked by "tradition" and argues instead for the functioning of the now and then, and the here and there—a dynamic, evolving hybrid of different histories and geographies. This chapter will keep in view Ake's use of the "indigenous" in the exploration of gender relations, marriage, and divorce both in the so-called traditional Nigerian society and the shifts in family configuration in a rapidly changing world.

MARRIAGE AND DIVORCE

Several types of marriages are contracted in Nigeria and they are all binding, although they derive their legitimacy from different contexts. Consequently, when marriages break down, divorce settlements differ from one marriage type to the other. Culture, Westernization (colonialism), and religion (Christianity and Islam) are factors that shape marriage type. Traditional or customary marriage is anchored in native law and custom; statutory marriage is grounded in English law inherited during the colonial period. There are Christian marriages and some others are contracted under Muslim law. Some marriages evolve as a combination of two systems—for example, before wedding in the church Igbo couples usually perform the traditional marriage ceremony. Polygyny and woman-to-woman marriage are legal.

In Nigerian cultures, marriage is not viewed as a union between two individuals exclusively. Rather the union of the couple is seen as a symbol of a larger union between families: "Nigerians believe that families marry families. This in no way suggests that traditional marriages are arranged" (Achebe, 2003, p. 321). It is misleading to see conjugally based Nigerian families through the lens of "nuclear" family. As Sudarkasa (1986) aptly notes, conjugally based families are subgroups of extended families and not the primary unit around which extended families are constructed.

Early and arranged marriages are more prevalent in Islamic northern Nigeria than among the Igbo of the southeast. Igbo traditional marriages are usually preceded by a protracted period of *iju ase* (asking questions) during which each family checks out the other to ensure that there is no disturbing information (e.g., madness, violence, infidelity, spousal abuse, etc.) lurking in the family history. The bride wealth that is paid before the marriage is consummated "is a token that is paid to the bride's family in order that the future husband be granted rights over his future children and that they bear his name. If the bride wealth were not paid, then any children born out of the marital union belong to their mother's lineage and bear her name" (Achebe, 2003, p. 321).

Because marriage is a union of families, the words *wife* and *husband* acquire new meanings that are not necessarily determined by sex: "The position of 'wife' refers not only to the conjugal relationship to a husband, but also to the affinal (or in-law) relationship to all members—female and male—of the husband's compound and lineage" (Sudarkasa, 1986, p. 27). Thus, among the Igbo and Yoruba, a woman married into a family is the wife of her in-laws, and all the members (male and female) of her husband's family are her "husbands."

The interrogation of notions of sex and gender also resonates in the practice of woman-to-woman marriage in which jural relations, but no sexual relationship, exist between the "female husband" and her spouse. Children produced in a woman-to-woman marriage belong to the "female husband," her male spouse or other males in her lineage. Marriage confers authority on a husband regardless of gender. Thus a female husband appropriates the same authority over a wife that accrues to a male husband. These practices that interrogate rigid notions of gender sustain and promote the gender complementarity that is the hallmark of traditional Nigerian cultures (Uchendu, 1965; Okonjo, 1976; Amadiume, 1987; Sofola, 1998; Nnaemeka, 2005).

Nigerian traditional cultures as well as Islamic culture permit polygyny. Under Islamic law, a man can marry up to four wives if he can afford to do so. In both instances, the emphasis is on male responsibility and care of women and their children. A Population Council survey shows a decline in the number of polygynous families in the 1990s (cited in Achebe, 2003, p. 320).

Equally noteworthy are the new configurations of polygynous families that are emerging in Nigerian cities. Typically, traditional and Islamic polygynous families are coresidential in the sense that the man, his wives, and children live in the same location. But what is emerging in Nigerian urban areas is an arrangement whereby the man rents or purchases homes in different parts of the city, each home is occupied by one of his wives and her children, and the man navigates from one home to the other. This urban variant of polygyny is prevalent in other African cities (Bâ, 1981). Two factors contribute to the flourishing of this variant of polygyny—affluence and flexibility of urban living arrangements. A majority of these "vagrant polygynists" are affluent urbanites who have the economic resources to maintain such an expensive lifestyle. Furthermore, it is difficult or even impossible for this type of polygyny to function in the traditional and rural settings where living patterns mandate coresidential households.

In Islamic northern Nigeria, "marriage is arranged by agreement between the "elders (of both sexes) of the two families, but in particular between the fathers or guardians (*wali*) of the future couple" (Solivetti, 1994, pp. 256–257). Indeed, the micromanaging of marriages by family is inevitable in instances in which early marriage ensures that the bride is a jural minor and as such dependent on parents or guardians for marital decisions. Furthermore, Hausa culture invests in the father the authority to choose his daughter's first husband regardless of her age. Usually, brides do not resist forced marriages but those who do have three options: "desert her husband soon after the wedding to live independently outside marriage as a prostitute or courtesan; get a divorce from her husband; or commit suicide (threaten to do so, at the least)"

(Solivetti, 1994, p. 256). Runaway brides/wives can sometimes face severe and tragic consequences. In February 1987, Nigerians were horrified to learn that a young girl in northern Nigeria, Hauwa Abubakar, had her limbs chopped off by the old man she was forced to marry because of her persistent attempts to run away. Hauwa later died of her wounds.

Premarital affairs and adultery are strongly condemned in Islamic Hausaland and the sanctions, particularly for female transgressors, are severe. The husband provides for the material needs of his wife and in return expects obedience, loyalty, fidelity, and the "exclusive right to sex.... The demand for wives to be faithful is the reason for the practice of seclusion (*purdah*). Consequently, a married Hausa girl of age ten is put in seclusion, but an unmarried adult of whatever age and family background is not" (Adamu, 1998, p. 9). The community frowns on adultery not as betrayal or breach of trust but as a severe antisocial behavior. In the past few years, the institutionalization and strict enforcement of Shari'a law in some northern states have led to stiff sentencing (death by stoning) for women accused of adultery. Fortunately, no death sentence has been carried out so far (Kalu, 2003).

In principle, divorce is regulated by the system under which the marriage was contracted—customary law, statutory law, Islamic law, and so on. Divorce from civil marriages is settled under the aegis of the Matrimonial Causes Act of 1970. Unfortunately, there are instances in which inheritance laws and practices (based on customary law) that are unfavorable to women are enforced even for Christian marriages. Solivetti notes that surprisingly divorce rates are extremely high in Muslim Hausaland, although one can surmise that the remarriage rates are also high given the society's insistence that females marry early and remain married throughout their reproductive years. The formality of divorce procedures in Hausa society attests to the importance of divorce. A female initiating a divorce follows procedures that are different from those stipulated for a man seeking divorce:

A man seeking divorce makes the fact known to his wife through a written statement; there is no need for him to reach an agreement with her or to get an authorization from the court. However, the wife is expected to register her husband's statement with the court, thus making the divorce formally a common knowledge. When the wife is seeking divorce, the procedure is more complicated. The wife has first to go to court to show reason for her petition and the reasons must be the acceptable valid reasons for divorce—such as severe physical abuse, refusal of companionship, deliberate sexual desertion, prolonged absence, failure to maintain wife, irreligiousity, leprosy, impotence, or madness. (Solivetti, 1994, p. 263)

The intergender, intragender, and interhousehold negotiations in which Nigerian women engage and the cultural and socioeconomic contexts in which the negotiations are made have serious health implications for the women in particular and the entire population in general. The vulnerabilities of females in the face of increasing incidence of sexually transmitted diseases

(STDs) and HIV/AIDS function in the context of gender inequities that are socioeconomically induced and culturally sanctioned. Krieger and Margo (1994, back cover) aptly note that "AIDS is far more than its microbiological and virological aspects. It is just as much a disease of society as it is a disease of the human body. Not merely does it exploit the weakness of society to spread to new persons, but these same weaknesses of society make it hard to marshal the ideas and resources we need to defend ourselves against the virus." Adamu (1998) locates some of these social weaknesses in the household and the negotiations females are compelled to make in it. In Hausa society, Islamic culture and Hausa customs combine to determine intergender relations and intrahousehold dynamics in terms of expectations, rights, and responsibilities. Some customs that relate to marriage, such as polygyny and levirate, create the possibilities for multiple sexual partners and the spread of STDs and HIV/AIDS.

(DIS)LOCATIONS

> As localized communities that are disequilibrated by the so-called forces of globalization strive to maintain affirming systems of meaning and continuity, some cultivate counterpolitics of identity defined by distinctive cultural and religious categories that they deploy to renegotiate globalized spaces.
> —Obiora (2005, p. 197)

Culture, as a dynamic arena of political and ideological struggle, derives its meanings, evolution, and reformulation from people's encounters with and negotiations with regard to the culture in the context of historical imperatives. Nigerian cultures, similar to other cultures, are evolving, embracing new terrains with old memories. Many have decried the deleterious impact of modern strains on African families that reach the breaking point under the combined weight of modernization and urbanization, producing social pathologies that range from alcoholism and drugs to corruption and HIV/AIDS.

These pathologies are described by Ocholla-Ayayo (2000):

Unwanted children, orphans, criminals, delinquents and prisoners, all of whom need special social care, present problems beyond the family's abilities to cope. In the traditional set-up, some of these problems would have been dealt with through kinship networks, but today such networks are disintegrating.... Marriage and family instability have increased considerably under modern strains, giving rise to higher rates of divorce and separation than in traditional life. (pp. 98–99)

The dislocation, instability, and atomization may be present in Nigerian families, but it is not clear that the institution of the family is so dysfunctional and so irretrievably broken that it is purged of the solidarity, affection, humanity, and sense of community that are the glue that held it together. Continuity and hope exist in the residues of cultural values that endure even among migrant families and despite crises and dislocations.

The past decade or so has seen a sharp increase in the number of Nigerian families who have emigrated overseas, especially to Europe and North America. Patterns of migration and family configuration vary. The majority of Nigerian families who emigrate do so in search of employment, better educational opportunities, or freedom from persecution. Irked by the collapsing educational system in Nigeria, many parents who have the financial resources are opting to send their children to schools overseas while maintaining homes on both sides of the Atlantic. Parents who are well established in Nigeria are usually not keen on emigrating. If the children are grown, both parents may decide to live in Nigeria and visit the children but if the children are minors, one of the parents (usually the mother) will live with the children and transatlantic visits and vacations are arranged. However, with the rapid growth of excellent boarding schools in Nigeria in the past few years, a new trend is emerging. Many Nigerian immigrant families residing in North America and Europe are sending their teenage children back to Nigeria to attend school and be grounded in the culture.

Traditional cultural values of community and solidarity with extended family are the driving force behind Nigerian immigrant families' remittances to and investments in Nigeria. Nigerian immigrants contributed significantly to the $80 billion of remittances to developing countries in the past decade. Indeed, immigrants' remittances are so huge that they currently rank as the largest source of external inflows to developing countries after foreign direct investment (Osili, n.d.). Osili concludes from her U.S.-Nigeria Migration Study of a matched sample of Nigerian immigrants in Chicago that transfer of funds to the origin family is motivated by altruistic reasons. Osili also notes that Nigerian immigrant families' desire to maintain economic and social ties with their ancestral home communities makes them more inclined to acquire assets—land, real estate, businesses, and financial investments. Osili's (2004) explanations for the Nigerian immigrant families' decisions to invest in their origin communities are indeed revealing:

First, there may be family-related motives for migrants' housing investments. In the family investment model, migrants' housing investments may provide direct benefits to their home families through housing services, as well as indirect benefits.... Second, migrants' investment decisions may be motivated by the need to secure and strengthen membership rights in the community of origin for the event of a return. The third motivation for housing investments, which I term the "community-investment model" centers on altruism. Migrants care about the communities they left behind and invest in order to contribute directly to the development of the housing stock in their hometowns. (pp. 821–822)

CONCLUSION

Plus ça change plus c'est la même chose. (The more things change the more they stay the same.)

Internal exigencies, external pressures, and increased mobility impel Nigerian families to respond to various types of shifts and develop mechanisms and strategies to adapt to change. There are universal problems facing families—from raising children and maintaining healthy relationships to education and financial security in rural and urban setting as well as inside and outside Nigeria. A majority of Nigerians still live in rural areas and maintain an agrarian lifestyle. Families continue to depend on members for labor needed for subsistence farming and cash cropping. However, poor fiscal policies, political instability, insecurity, and all sorts of state-sponsored violence have severely depressed the rural areas, forced younger family members to migrate, and severely tested family relationships and stability.

Concocting a reified past that can be evoked nostalgically in an attempt to explain and reject the present sidesteps a meaningful and genuine engagement with the present. Meaningful adaptive tools and strategies can only be developed when families see change in terms of continuity and not as a rupture with the past, imagined or real. According to Bradley and Weisner (1997) the continuity "derives in part from the importance of locally situated family practices that still encode (in symbols, practices, beliefs, and institutions) useful ways to deal with some of the universal adaptive problems facing families" (p. xxix).

NOTES

1. Nigeria has not had a reliable census for decades and as such the population figures are suspect.
2. In Igboland, a popular name for boys is Nwora (child of the community) and a popular name for girls is Adaora (daughter of the community).

REFERENCES

Achebe, N. (2003). Nigeria. In Tripp, A. M. (Ed.), *Women's issues worldwide: Sub-Saharan Africa* (pp. 311–337). Westport, CT: Greenwood.

Adamu, F. (1998). *Household relations and women's health in Hausa Muslim society of northern Nigeria*. Paper presented at the international conference on Women in Africa and the African Diaspora (WAAD), Indianapolis, IN.

Adeyokunnu, T. O. (1984). Women and rural development in Africa. In *Women on the Move* (pp. 45–57). Paris: UNESCO.

Agence France Presse. (2005). 545 women operated on during "Fistula Fortnight" in Nigeria. http://naijanet.com/news/source/2005/mar/8/1003.html. Retrieved: May 17, 2005.

Aina, O. I. (1993). Mobilizing Nigerian women for national development: The role of the female elites. *African Economic History 21*, 1–20.

Ajayi, A. J. (2000). *Tradition and change in Africa: The essays of J. F. Ade Ajayi*. Trenton, NJ: Africa World Press.

Ake, C. (1988). Building on the indigenous. In Frühling, P. (Ed.), *Recovery in Africa: A challenge for development cooperation in the 1990s* (pp. 19–22). Stockholm: Swedish Ministry of Foreign Affairs.

Ayittey, G. B. N. (1998). *Africa in chaos*. New York: St. Martin's.

Amadiume, I. (1987). *Male daughters, female husbands: Gender and sex in an African society*. London: Zed.

Awe, B. (1977). The Iyalode in the traditional Yoruba political system. In Schlegel, A. (Ed.), *Sexual stratification: A cross-cultural view*. New York: St. Martin's.

Awe, B. (1979, October). The Yoruba women in traditional society. *Gangan: A Magazine of Oyo State of Nigeria 8*, 12–16.

Bâ, M. (1981). *So Long a Letter*. London: Heinemann.

Bradley, C., & Weisner, T. S. (1997). Introduction: Crisis in the African family. In Weisner, T. S., Bradley, C., & Kilbride, P. L. (Eds.), *African families and the crisis of social change* (pp. xix–xxxii). Westport, CT: Bergin & Garvey.

Chow, R. (1993). *Writing Diaspora: Tactics of intervention in contemporary cultural studies*. Bloomington: Indiana University Press.

Etounga-Manguelle, D. (2000). Does Africa need a cultural adjustment program? In Harrison, L. E. & Huntington, S. P. (Eds.), *Culture matters: How values shape human progress* (pp. 65–77). New York: Basic Books.

Kalu, O. (2003). Safiyyatu and Adamah: Punishing adultery with Shari'a stones in twenty-first-century Nigeria. *African Affairs 102*, 389–408.

Knipp, M. (1987). *Women, western education and change: A case study of the Hausa-Fulani of northern Nigeria*. Ph.D. dissertation, Northwestern University, Evanston, IL.

Krieger, N., & Margo, G. (Eds.). (1994). *AIDS: The politics of survival*. Amityville, NY: Baywood.

Mba, N. (1982). *Nigerian women mobilised*. Berkeley: Institute of International Studies, University of California.

Neher, W. (1999). *Nigeria: Change and tradition in an African state* (3rd ed.). Acton, MA: Copley.

Nnaemeka, O. (2005). Mapping African feminisms. In Cornwall, A. (Ed.), *Readings in gender in Africa* (pp. 31–41). Bloomington: Indiana University Press/Oxford: James Currey.

Obiora, A. L. (2005). The anti-female circumcision campaign deficit. In Nnaemeka, O. (Ed.), *Female circumcision and the politics of knowledge: African women in imperialist discourses* (pp. 183–207). Westport, CT: Praeger.

Ocholla-Ayayo, A. B. C. (2000). The African family in development crisis in the second millennium. *The African Anthropologist 7(1)*, 85–113.

Okonjo, K. (1976). The dual-sex political system in operation: Igbo women and community politics in midwestern Nigeria. In Hafkin, N. J. & Bay, E. G. (Eds.), *Women in Africa: Studies in social and economic change* (pp. 45–58). Stanford, CA: Stanford University Press.

Osili, U. O. (2004). Migrant and housing investments: Theory and evidence from Nigeria. *Economic Development and Cultural Change 52(4)*, 821–849.

Osili, U. O. (n.d.). Remittances from international migration: Theory and evidence from Nigeria. Unpublished paper.

Popenoe, D. (1988). *Disturbing the nest: Family change and decline in modern societies*. New York: Aldine de Gruyter.

Shaw, S. M., & Lee, J. (Eds). (2004). Family systems, family lives. In *Women's voices, feminist visions* (2nd ed.; pp. 287–300). Boston: McGraw Hill.

Shenton, R. W. (1986). *The development of capitalism in northern Nigeria*. Toronto: University of Toronto Press.

Sofola, Z. (1998). Feminism and African womanhood. In Nnaemeka, O. (Ed.), *Sisterhood, feminisms, and power: From Africa to the Diaspora* (pp. 51–64). Trenton, NJ: Africa World Press.

Solivetti, L. M. (1994). Family, marriage and divorce in a Hausa community: A sociological model. *Africa, 64(2)*, 252–271.

Sudarkasa, N. (1986). The "status of women" in indigenous African societies. In *The strength of our mothers: African and African American women and families: Essays and speeches* (pp. 165–180). Trenton, NJ: Africa World Press.

Uchendu, V. (1965). *The Igbo of southeastern Nigeria*. New York: Holt, Rinehart, & Winston.

Part III
Central Africa

CHAPTER 9

Reflections on the Changing Family System in Cameroon

Chuks J. Mba and Martin W. Bangha

INTRODUCTION

Families and households constitute an important unit of analysis for the study of the socioeconomic, cultural, and demographic processes in the African setting. The extended family, consisting of the nuclear family and some other relatives (parents, brothers, sisters, etc.), is most common in Cameroon and most African societies and constitutes the raison d'être of all social cooperations and responsibility, and acts as a social security for the members of the family. This is because individuals usually live in domestic groups that have shared characteristics which range from the financial resources they can draw on, through the authority they acknowledge for decision making, to the reciprocal influence of members on each other's behavior.

An assessment of the influence of modernization on the Cameroonian family is important in several respects. For example, in the absence of any functional social security system, the welfare of the elderly in this country and in most parts of Africa is primarily a family responsibility (Dixon, 1987). However, modernization is impacting adversely on this traditional African system (Apt, 1996; Mba, 2001; Mbamaonyeukwu, 2001a). Most theories on the challenges that confront the family in some parts of the developing world emphasize the effects of modernization and cultural norms, and focus on the effects of technological advancement, industrialization, and the spread of modern education (Goode, 1963; Cowgill, 1986; Treas & Logue, 1986; Berquo & Xenos, 1992).

The history of the independent African countries will be incomplete without reference to the colonial past. In a rapidly changing world, it is imperative to trace the changes the family in Cameroon has been subjected to before, during, and subsequent to independence. As Africa has been described as a continent of geographic and climatic, cultural and linguistic, economic and social diversity (Alexandre, 1973; Ayisi, 1979; Ben-Jochannan, 1989; Goheen, 1996), this chapter attempts to highlight this condition in the Cameroonian context, with particular reference to the socioeconomic, cultural, and demographic evolution the country has gone through as a result of the traditional and colonial past and the impact of contemporary global changes. In this attempt, the main reference data sources will be nationally representative sample surveys like the Demographic and Health Surveys (DHS) conducted in 1991 and 1998 and the World Fertility Survey (WFS) conducted in 1978. Reference will also be made to the 1976 and 1987 postindependence censuses of Cameroon, as well as a few other sources, notably, the United Nations and the World Bank publications and reports.

DEMOGRAPHIC AND ECOLOGICAL PROFILES

Population Data

Efforts aimed at assessing the population characteristics of Cameroon began during the German colonial administration, and were continued by the British and French administrators (République Unie du Cameroun, 1983). Their approach was basically ethnological, anthropological, and sociological, and therefore provided rough and incomplete estimates of the population and major characteristics. Demographic sample surveys and an administrative head count were conducted after independence in 1960–65 and in 1967–68. These were essentially limited to particular areas of the country and at varying periods of time. However, it was in April 1976 that the first national census was carried out (République Unie du Cameroun, 1976). The 1976 Population and Housing Census estimated that the population was 7.7 million, with an average density of 16.5 persons per square kilometer. The corresponding values for the 1987 census stood at 10.5 million and 22.6 persons per square kilometer, respectively (Direction National du 2éme RGPH Cameroun, 1992). The population has been unevenly distributed over the current ten provinces of Adamawa (4.7 percent), Central (15.7 percent), East (4.9 percent), Far North (17.7 percent), Littoral (12.9 percent), North (7.9 percent), West (12.8 percent), and South (3.6 percent) for the francophone population; and North West (11.8 percent) and South West (8.0 percent) for the Anglophone population.

Cameroon's capital is Yaounde in the Central Province, while Douala in the Littoral Province is the commercial nerve center of the country. The country's land area is 465,400 square kilometers, with an estimated current population of about 15.4 million, 44 percent of whom are younger than 15 (Population Reference Bureau [PRB], 1999; United Nations, 2001a). The current population growth rate is 2.1 percent per annum (for the 2000–05 period), while a significant proportion of the people reside in the southern part of the country (United Nations, 2001a).

The drift toward the adoption of the modern European cultural value system gained currency with the expansion in education and health services. At present, about 51.8 percent of the male population has primary education and another 25.9 percent have secondary/higher education (Fotso et al., 1999). The corresponding values for females are 45.2 percent and 18.6 percent, respectively. The magnitude of social change, social mobility, and improvements in the status of women that have occurred over the decades have direct influence on the family setup. However, it should be noted that the economic downturn currently plaguing the country has resulted in, among other things, salary slashes, making it impossible for parents to meet the educational needs of their children and wards.

The consistent reduction in overall mortality and infant mortality especially, as well as gains in life expectancy over the years, suggests some improvements in nutrition and health services in Cameroon. Also, the United Nations (2001a, 2003) projections show that life expectancy in Cameroon will rise to 70.7 years (69.5 years for males and 71.9 years for females) during the 2045–50 period, which is comparable to the developed world at the present time. However, there are concerns as to whether this is really achievable under the current conditions in which there are still signs of malnutrition in the country, and improvements in life expectancy are minimal when compared with other African countries (Bangha, 1995; Fotso et al., 1999). A review of the mortality situation shows that Cameroon remains a country with very poor health for adults, as mostly children have benefited from the reduction in overall mortality to a "moderate" level (Bangha, 1995). For example, life expectancy for the 2000–05 period is 50.0 years in Cameroon, while in Libya and Egypt, the corresponding values for the same period are 70.9 years and 68.3 years, respectively (United Nations, 2001a).

Ethnic/Ecological Variations

Cameroon is populated by people of diverse origins who seemed to arrive at the country at various periods of time from different corners of the globe, resulting in pronounced ethnic, linguistic, socioeconomic, and cultural disparity (Bahoken & Atangana, 1976; Todd, 1982; DeLancey, 1989; Burnham, 1996; Delancey & DeLancey, 1999). Presently, there are about 500 ethnic groups of various sizes in the country.[1] Paramount among the many ethnic groups in Cameroon are the Bantu, Bantoid, and Semi-Bantu groups in the south, and the Sudanese, Paleonegritic, and Hamito-Semitic groups in the north. The Bantu and Bantoid groups are made up of the Bassa, Boulou, Ewondo, Douala, Bakweri, Eton, Fang, Bakossi, Maka, and Babinga; the Semi-Bantu group consists of the Bamileke and other Tikar groups such as the Nso, Bali, Bafut, Kom, Bamoun, and other smaller groups in the West and North West Provinces. The northern groups include the Sudanese who comprise the settled Foulbe (Yillaga), and the Bororo (Vollarbe) who are mainly nomadic stockbreeders. The Paleonegritic group is made up of the Kirdi, the early inhabitants of the area (Burnham, 1996). In terms of numerical strength, some of these ethnic groups have always been comparatively small even by African standards.

In terms of linguistic profile, Cameroon appears to approximate a cross-section of the African continent (LeVine, 1971; Hedinger, 1987). This is because the country is estimated to have over 225 different languages and an even larger number of dialects distributed among three of the four major language families of Africa (Greenberg, 1966), alongside two borrowed official languages—English and French. These are (1) the Niger-Congo to the South and Southwest, represented by the Bantu languages and the West Atlantic subgroup (Fulfude); (2) the Nilo-Saharan, represented by Kanuri; and (3) the Afro-Asiatic, represented by Arabic, which is firmly rooted in the Quranic schools of the north. As a consequence of this ethnic diversity, experts have called Cameroon a melting point in which the dark-skinned people of the Guinea Coast, the light-skinned Fulani, the Arabs of Western Sahara, and the Bantu-speakers who have occupied most of Central, Eastern, and Southern Africa have intermingled (Hedinger, 1987; Kaberry Research Center, 1993; Chiabi, 1997; DeLancey and DeLancey, 1999).

Lying approximately between latitude 2° and 13° north (more than 1,300 km) and longitudes 9° and 16° east (about 800 km), Cameroon is situated in the middle of Africa. The country shares borders with Nigeria in the west, with Lake Chad in the north, with Chad and Central African Republics in the east, with the Republics of Congo, Gabon, and Equatorial Guinea in the south, and the Atlantic Ocean in the southwest. Thus, Cameroon particularly enjoys a strategic geographical location as it lies at the junction of the West and Central African subregions.

HISTORICAL BACKGROUND

Brief Precolonial History

Cameroon was originally inhabited by small migrant Bantu groups from the Congo basin in the south and by Hamito-Semitic groups from Sudan and other parts of North Africa in the north. Although the territory was first spotted by the Carthaginians in around 5 BCE, it only came into modern history when the Portuguese landed on its coasts in 1472 (Fernão do Pó was the first European to view the Cameroon coast) and gave it the name "Cameroes" after the prawns they found in abundance at the shores of the Wouri River (LeVine, 1971; Britannica, 2000). In July 1884, the Germans acquired Cameroon as a colony and began the conquest of the hinterland during which they founded

Yaounde in 1887 as their starting station for expedition further inland. In 1901, a decree was promulgated naming the capital of the country Douala and the country, Kamerun.

The 32 years of the German administration (1884–1916) laid the foundation of a modern state in terms of the economy, transport, and education (Johnson, 1970; Chiabi, 1997; Njoh, 2001). This is evidenced in the establishment of the road and railway system, a series of agricultural plantations, and several administrative buildings and forts that are still in use today. During World War I, the British and French forces attacked Cameroon and drove out the Germans in 1916, splitting the country into British and French protectorates at the end of the war. In December 1958, the French-administered region was granted self-government as the Republic of Cameroon. Full independence and United Nations membership were gained in 1960. In 1961, British Southern Cameroon was federated with the Republic of Cameroon, while British Northern Cameroon joined Nigeria.

Among the factors that have induced considerable social and cultural change in Cameroon is the exposure to Western influences that began during colonial rule when European administrators attempted to establish a European model of development. This led to the establishment of schools, and in the process of time, a shift toward the promotion of foreign trade and internal commerce via the improvement of the transportation system. Over a long period of time, this gradually led to the shift from a subsistence economy to a market economy in most of the urban communities. Vast amounts of foreign capital were invested in the banks, insurance companies, commercial enterprises, and the industrial and agricultural sectors.

Political Economy

The first constitution of the independent Federal Republic of Cameroon stipulated that the official languages of the country would be French and English. This bilingual policy placed Cameroon in a unique position in Africa by having two foreign languages as official languages, in contrast to other African countries where only one of the colonial languages (French, English, Spanish, and Portuguese) was adopted as the official language at independence. Instead of being a powerful force, this has affected the progress and possible successful marriage of the Anglophone and Francophone Cameroon with little intercourse between the two. Cameroon currently is supposed to be a constitutional republic. The president and bicameral legislature are supposed to be popularly elected, with ministers appointed by the president and precluded from legislative office. Cameroon still seems to enjoy relative political stability, unlike many countries in the turbulent African region. However, as Nyamnjoh (1999) argues, this relative stability has been fostered by the common ethnic or regional ambition to preserve various differences under the delusion of maximizing opportunities.

The country's official currency since independence is the CFA Franc, and the economy is mainly agricultural (World Bank, 2000). The principal commercial crops are cocoa, coffee, tobacco, cotton, and bananas. Petroleum products make up more than half of all exports. Timber is also a major export. In the early 1980s, Cameroon was one of Africa's economic success stories. However, underlying economic and policy weaknesses were exposed in 1985 when sharp declines in coffee, cocoa, and oil prices led to a 60 percent degeneration in the external terms of trade. There are claims (particularly among the government hierarchy) that macroeconomic performance has been satisfactory since 1996 with growth rates rising to almost 5 percent during 1996–2000, and that encouraging progress has been made as indicated by the government's commitment to revamping the economy and to creating a more conducive basis for sustained growth. However, there is little evidence that such economic progress (if any) has so far brought any tangible benefits to the poor as poverty reduction continues to be a daunting challenge with dilapidated physical infrastructure and poor public delivery of basic social services. In addition, the political crisis of the early 1990s, the devaluation of the CFA Franc in 1994, and the two successive salary slashes for civil servants have contributed to the impoverishment of the citizenry.

Cameroon's "Triple Heritage"

Cameroon is the only African country that happens to have been colonized by three different colonial (European) powers. With a multitude of ethnic groups and over 200 distinct languages, it also occupies a unique position as a country that has adopted two official languages. Using 1987 census figures, the 2005 population was projected at 16.6 million (United Nations, 2001a, 2003), of which about 63 percent are Christian, followed by Islam and traditional African religions, with a combined 35 percent of the population (Fotso et al., 1999). Christianity was introduced systematically through the southern coastal area during the 19th century, the pioneer having been Reverand Alfred Saker who founded the first Baptist mission in Douala-Victoria (now Limbe) in 1842. The Catholics, through German missionaries, began their work in 1890 along the coast. Thus, the first Christian missionaries to Cameroon were Protestants and Catholics. The origin and denomination of the missions (see Britannica, 2000, for more details) changed frequently, but the Presbyterians, Baptists, and Roman Catholics have always been the most important. Besides their main religious function of getting more converts and spreading the holy word through the proliferation of churches, these different missions are well established and often compete among themselves as well as with the government in the educational and health sector. Religious-related schools (ranging from primary to high school and university of late, technical and vocational training institutions) and health care facilities (dispensaries, health centers, maternity clinics, and hospitals) are scattered all over the national territory. However, these facilities tend to be more concentrated in the southern part of the country partly because this naturally coincides with the point of introduction of Christianity and also because this area was seemingly more receptive to Christianity. Due to their influence through the schools, Cameroon has become progressively more Christianized.

Islam, on the other hand, penetrated Cameroon through Mandara in the north as early as 1715 and became an influential force in the northern and central portions of the country through immigration and the spread of commerce from north and northwestern Africa. The most significant bearers of this faith, the Fulani, entered northern Cameroon beginning in the 18th century. The Fulani expansion reached its southernmost point with the conquest of Bamoum, a kingdom founded in the 17th century, which was one of the largest of numerous kingdoms that emerged in the grassland areas of Cameroon at least 300 years ago. Though there have been recent waves of migration into the major cities over time, coupled with improvement in education, rapid urbanization, and so on, probably and partly because of the Fulanis' nomadic nature their initial conquest was rather brief and did not result in much Islamization of Cameroon. Besides, as history suggests (Britannica, 2000), the Fulani became frustrated under non-Muslim rule and the majority were eventually incorporated into the Sokoto empire in northern Nigeria. Consequently, Islam has not had as powerful an influence on the systems of law and education as it did in neighboring Nigeria. Unlike in the case of Christianity and the Christian missions, Islam is not so well entrenched into the Cameroon culture. There are very few Quranic or Arabic schools and these are not so well structured. Muslims are more concentrated in the northern part of the country where the populations are largely nomadic cattle grazers. The populations there have always been more backward and less modernized than those in the south which has experienced more intense prolonged exposure to modern educational, public, industrial, and social facilities. Besides the religious factor, it was partly for this reason that the northerners expressed great hostilities toward the southerners, considering them to be overprivileged and the northerners neglected. Over the years, the government's educational policy has been focused on raising the educational level among the northern populations by opening up more formal educational facilities and sending teachers, as well as offering attractive employment positions to those highly educated from the area.

Traditional African religion, though it may appear to be in rapid decline as a result of modernization and Westernization, is still entrenched in Cameroon to the extent that many Christians continue to observe various traditional African rituals. It should be noted that the arrival of the Christian missions and the initial introduction of Christianity met with heavy resistance and conflicts with the traditional religion/beliefs of the indigenous populations. With time they have managed to accommodate each other and cohabit to an extent that can be seen or characterized as the eventual "Africanization" of the European Christian churches. For instance, contrary to the initial attempts by the

European Christian missionaries to enforce monogamy as one the basic tenets and religious obligations of their adherents, a substantial portion of the present-day Christians are polygynists. The recent DHS data show that close to one of every four Christian women and one in five Christian men are polygynously married. In addition, church ceremonies are performed alongside certain traditional rituals. Churches make good use of the different cultures to spread and explain their message. This practice was further encouraged by Pope John Paul II. During one of his visits to Cameroon (September 1995) he jointly addressed representatives of the different Christian communities, of Islam, and of the African traditional religion, calling for dialogue among the Christians and the believers of the different religions. In fact, a recent television documentary[2] recorded in the three provinces of Cameroon (Central, North, and West Provinces) seems to confirm this compatibility of Christianity and traditionalism in Cameroon in particular and Africa in general.

Cultural change may be viewed as the process by which the existing order of a society is altered from one type into another. This process is a permanent factor of human development as it goes on everywhere and at all times, and may be induced by conditions arising within a particular society (independent evolution) or it may be the result of contact with different cultures (diffusion). Having gone through colonization, most countries in Africa and other parts of the developing world experience the latter aspect of cultural change. They are left to grapple with the problem of grafting a colonial cultural legacy onto a more or less heterogeneous traditional cultural heritage. This dilemma has particularly confronted Cameroon. In fact, the synthesis of cultures in Cameroon is rather unique in that it involves an additional dimension of complexity: the fusion of two foreign (British and French) cultures over the background of indigenous and, to some extent, German cultures, because the three European countries colonized it.

As indicated previously, the Portuguese Fernão do Pó is said to be the first European to have viewed the Cameroon coast. He was followed by traders, many of whom were involved in the Trans-Atlantic slave trade, which all along the African coast and in Cameroon in particular was a highly specialized business. With its proximity to the coast, Cameroon became a significant location, with slaves sold and traded at Bimbia, Akwa (now Douala), and other ports. For instance, it is reported that one of the many European captains traded for slaves only from Cameroon coastal locations; of his 15 voyages from Liverpool all were to Old Calabar and Cameroon (Eltis, 2001). Routes were eventually developed to link the ports far inland where the Bamileke, Bamoum, and other major kingdoms provided the needed supply of healthy slaves.

The suppression of the slave trade in the early part of the 19th century (Todd, 1982) and the increase in demand for the mineral and agricultural products of the African continent contributed not only to the rise of a number of important trading towns but also to the scramble for territorial possessions. Accordingly, during this period trading posts on the Cameroonian coasts, such as Bimbia,

Douala, Big Batanga, Kribi, and Campo, were converted and expanded into communities based on European models (Johnson, 1970; Chiabi, 1997). The acculturative processes by which Western influences began to change, and eventually to transform, the traditional societies in Cameroon began with the creation of the trading communities on the coast. In the early 1800s, the slave trade declined and attention turned to "legitimate" trade in rubber, palm oil, and other items. Earlier Portuguese and Dutch influences were largely replaced by the British and the Germans. With establishment of plantations, forced labor was also acquired from the same interior populations or ethnic groups that had provided the slaves. These groups eventually came to dominate the agriculture export sector of the country as well as the local labor market, resulting in ethnic tensions between the immigrant populations or settlers and the indigenous groups in the areas where the plantations are located.

CONCEPTUALIZATION OF CAMEROONIAN FAMILIES

One of the most common household typologies designed to aid family studies is that suggested by Hammel and Laslett (1974). The typology has six basic categories: solitary household (or one-person household); simple (or nuclear) household; extended household (a simple family plus other kin); multiple household (household having two or more simple families); no family household (two or more persons who do not share a simple family); and other household. Since variations of this scheme are commonly employed, and in the light of the sociocultural makeup of the Cameroonian society, "extended family household" is used to refer to a combination of extended and multiple households. The extended family—most often composed of the conjugal couple and their kin—is more widespread as in most African societies (Johnson, 1970; Ben-Jochannan, 1989; Kaberry Research Center, 1993; Gohen, 1996). In the Cameroonian context (and indeed in many African families), there seems to be a continuum of various family types with varying memberships. While there is some degree of "nuclearization" of the family with modernity and adoption of Western culture, for the most part even a nuclear family household in Africa and Cameroon in particular does not necessarily imply "nuclear family" obligations exclusively in the Western sense.

The extended family has mainly furnished the support systems with respect to the well-being of the elderly and other members of the family (Mba, 2001; Mbamaonyeukwu, 2001a). The traditional family system in Cameroon, and indeed in other parts of Africa, has been providing a viable and enviable alternative to the universal social security system that prevails in much of the developed world (Weekes-Vagliani, 1976; Berquo & Xenos, 1992; Apt, 1996). This is because the economic cost of raising children in the traditional extended family does not impinge solely on the biological parents. This scenario is partly responsible for the low age at first marriage, unlike in the developed countries (Kumari & Ubaidullah, 1997). At the same time, the young wife is motivated to have offspring as early and as frequently as possible in order to receive recognition in an extended family.

However, the extended family is currently at the receiving end of unbridled and consistent social and economic changes that weaken it and threaten its continued existence. Researchers such as Lorimer (1954), Davis (1955), Martin (1990), Chen (1996), Palloni (2000), and Kinsella & Velkoff (2001) have employed living arrangements and behavioral patterns to describe family structure. Living arrangement or coresidence refers to relatives living in the same household, whereas behavioral pattern means regular interaction among a network of kin such as visiting, financial exchanges, and so on. Studies using these dimensions reach the common conclusion that modernization has been adversely affecting the traditional family system in the developing world (United Nations, 1991, 1994; Mbugua, 1997).

It should be stated from the outset that family research is not well documented in Cameroon and other parts of Africa. As a result, researchers have had to rely on sources such as diaries, letters, legal documents, and financial and parish records, all of which must be used with caution (Doenges, 1991). The little that is known is essentially based on fragmentary evidence from a few focused studies and what may be extrapolated from national surveys that collect information on a wide range of topics. By their very nature, these surveys exclude detailed information on the characteristics and dynamics of the family.

It can be argued that modernization and urbanization have been altering the traditional family system not only in Cameroon but also in other parts of Africa and the developing world. Various scholars have viewed modernization from different perspectives, often within the confines of their disciplines (Goode, 1963; Levy, 1966; Easterline, 1983; Ansari, 1998; Dreyer, 2000; Mol, 2001). Broadly, modernization is that form of societal change encompassing changes in the economic, political, social, and psychological aspects of human society that began in Europe around 1800. Briefly, these changes include significant increases in economic production, advances in technology and science, a realignment of family structures, and a change in kinship relations.

Thus, modernization brings about environmental changes, as well as changes in attitudes and values, and the process allows modern individuals to live in traditional environments and vice versa, as well as enable traditional people to work in modern environments. Despite the fact that many societies move from traditional to modern stages, the pattern and process of modernization show variations over time and space. It has been noted that the situation in the developing world today has few parallels in the urbanization process historically experienced by the developed countries (Robirosa, 1971; Roberts & Hite, 2000). This is because in the latter urbanization was accompanied by industrial revolution with a dramatic increase in the demand for urban labor, which gradually absorbed most of the available labor force, thus consistently reducing unemployment.

In contrast, contemporary developing nations are contending with massive technological advancement unprecedented in human history with its extreme labor-saving forms that prevent the full utilization of labor. Moreover, industries tend to be capital- rather than labor-intensive, even though cheap labor is supposed to be the main attraction for foreign investment (International Labor Organization, 1972). As a result, unemployment is widespread. Only 35.1 percent of the female population in Cameroon was currently working at the time of the 1998 DHS, with about 86.1 of them in self-employment (Fotso et al., 1999). As for men, 21.2 percent of them were not employed at the time of the survey, while only 38.4 percent of those currently employed were in the white-collar, nonagricultural jobs.

FEATURES OF CAMEROONIAN FAMILIES

Mate Selection

As empirically demonstrated, the ultimate goal of mate selection, whether contracted via traditional or civil procedure, was and still is procreation (Balepa et al., 1992; Bangha, 1996, 2003; Fotso et al., 1999). Marriage in Cameroon is considered more than just the union of two individuals because it involves several people or families. In many cases, the families of both parties handle the arrangements, sometimes to the exclusion of the parties concerned. Both families investigate each other's past very carefully to ensure that nothing in their backgrounds will tarnish the alliance. Once both families are satisfied, the bride's family will ask for and receive a marriage bride wealth. Bride wealth in the Cameroonian context is not a payment for purchasing a wife, and does not make the bride the property of the bridegroom. On the contrary, it is considered a token or symbolic gift in compensation for the supposed good upbringing that also guarantees the stability of the marriage by ensuring that both parties will meet their contractual obligations. It is in light of this approach of mate selection that the husband is expected to help his in-laws in clearing and cultivating their farmlands, as well as in harvesting their crops and regularly providing fuelwood. Thus, marriage creates a relationship of reciprocal rights and duties among the parties concerned, as the husband compensates the wife's family by rendering some services she would have rendered if she were unmarried and living with her family. Meanwhile, it also acts as a counterforce to marital stability as the wife's family members are bound in some cases to refund the bride wealth in case of divorce.

At the other end of the spectrum, however, it is not uncommon to find some parents or ethnic groups who view their girl children as "commodities," subject to maximum bargaining deals. This is also a factor associated with modernization as such parents or groups tend to consider the education or general upbringing of the girls as an investment that should be reimbursed by the girls' eventual husbands.

Generally in Cameroon, the man in principle does the selection of his conjugal partner(s) and pays the bride wealth. In practice, the final decision involves several members of both families, allowing the man and his mate(s) to have few options. However, as a society modernizes, one notices significant changes in the dynamics of the traditional family system. These changes include new ideas of intimacy and privacy for the couple, as well as a growing emphasis on love, personal attraction, and compatibility as the basis for mate selection. It is not uncommon these days in Cameroon to find young persons choosing their own mates, even resorting to pregnancy before marriage if necessary. Such behavior ensures that they eventually marry the persons they choose rather than persons imposed on them by extended family members. Other relatives are increasingly becoming peripheral, while bonds among nuclear family members are growing more intense and emotional, in line with what happens in the developed world (Dizard & Gadlin, 1990).

Childbearing and Marriage Forms

Marriage represents the very beginning of family life and is vital in the family formation process. It is an important institution for both the individual in particular and the society at large. Marriage unites several persons of different families and constitutes the creation of a production and consumption unit, as well as one for the exchange of goods and services. In family research, the study of nuptiality has acquired prominence due, among other things, to its strong bearing on the incidence of procreation.

To an average Cameroonian woman, marriage is an important landmark in her life because it means that she will start having children (Bangha, 1996, 2003). As the socioeconomic status of women is generally poor in the country, marriage and the concomitant childbearing enhances the image of the married woman. This close link between socioeconomic status and marriage makes it most desirable and almost imperative for women to enter into some sort of marital relationship. The results of the WFS and DHS surveys have consistently confirmed that marriage is almost universal in Cameroon. However, there seems to be a decline in the proportion of married women precipitated by uptake in formal education which invariably delays entry into marital relationships. About 85.3 percent of women in 1978, 81.4 percent of women in 1991, and 76.6 percent of women in 1998 within the reproductive age group of 15–49 years had been married (Balepa et al., 1992; Fotso et al., 1999). Furthermore, analysis of the data suggest that by the time a cohort of rural Cameroonian women survives through the peak age of childbearing (25–29), about 97 percent of them will have entered a marital union (Bangha, 2003). This implies that almost all rural women eventually get married before they are midway into the reproductive age span. As a result, fertility has remained high in Cameroon.

The total fertility rate, which measures the number of children a woman will have during her reproductive years (15–49) at prevailing age-specific fertility schedules, is 3.9 per woman in the urban areas and 5.8 per woman in the rural areas (Fotso et al., 1999). This disparity is expected since people who live in urban areas are more likely to be exposed to Western lifestyles, including use of contraception to limit or space out births.

It should be noted, however, that although Cameroon's fertility rate is still high, it has been consistently declining as a result of modernization (Bongaarts & Potter, 1983). This is because the singulate mean age at marriage (SMAM)[3] has been increasing, particularly in the rural areas where fertility is very high, from 17.4 years in 1978 to 18.2 years in 1991 (Bangha, 1996, 2003).

The practice of polygyny, in which the man is permitted to marry more than one wife, seems quite appreciable in most parts of Africa. In Cameroon, the 1978 CFS results indicate that 38.8 percent of women were in polygynous unions, and the Demographic and Health Survey findings continue to show the prevalence of polygyny—38.6 percent in 1991 and 32.7 percent in 1998 (Balepa et al., 1992; Fotso et al., 1999). In fact, evidence from rural Cameroonian women reveals that about 42.6 percent of currently married women are in polygynous marriages, thereby confirming the fact that polygyny is not only a socially accepted form of marriage but is also widely practiced and has been maintained at a significant level for quite some time (Bangha, 1996). Researchers argue that this form of marriage has proven more resistant in Tropical Africa than was generally anticipated (Pison, 1987; Romaniuc, 1988; Timaeus & Graham, 1989). This form of marriage offers more women a chance to enjoy the benefits of marriage. Consequently, polygyny may not be the by-product of sexual insatiability, rather it may be the result of strong religious, sociocultural, and economic considerations.

In Cameroon, and indeed other parts of Africa, the historical motive behind the prevalence of polygyny has reference to the traditional need for agricultural labor and subsistence farming as a significant proportion of the population was and still is living in the rural areas (United Nations, 2001b). According to Caldwell and Caldwell (1990), polygyny as a family form is well suited to a shifting agricultural system using abundant low-yielding communal land farmed by labor-intensive technologies. Hence, a man with several wives is considered wealthy because he can summon their help and further his productivity, as well as foster a larger progeny for old-age support (Timaeus & Graham, 1989; Bangha, 1996).

Young urban wives now prefer living away from their husbands' extended families because they no longer are willing to play the subservient role in the family, such as running errands, fetching water, and cooking (Eloundou-Enyegue, 1992; Kaberry Research Center, 1993). In fact, modernization, which has resulted in urbanization, educational advancement, and adherence to Christianity (with monogamy as its marriage tenet), has given women in Cameroon some measure of freedom from the control of the extended family (Weekes-Vagliani, 1976; DeLancey & DeLancey, 1999). This is especially true for those with higher education and urban dwellers (Kumari & Ubaidullah, 1997). But traces of the traditional mate selection procedure are still found in certain parts of the country, particularly in the rural areas (Kaberry Research Center, 1993).

The incidence of marital disruption appears to be relatively low in Cameroon. The 1987 census results suggest that the proportions of women who are widows and divorced/separated are respectively 6.6 percent and 2.6 percent (Direction National du 2éme RGPH Cameroun, 1992). According to the 1991 and 1998 DHS findings, the proportions of women who experienced widowhood and divorce/separation in 1991 was 2.5 percent and 4.8 percent, respectively; the corresponding figures for 1998 was 3.2 percent and 6.6 percent, respectively (Balepa et al., 1992; Fotso et al., 1999). Remarriage rates tend to be high and frequent such that at any time and indeed over time the proportion of women never in a union has remained virtually constant and relatively low (Bangha, 1996, 2003). Seen in this light, the prevalence of polygyny enhances the chances that most women remain continuously in marriage for the greater part of their marriageable life.

However, in the African context monogamy does not necessarily preclude multiple sexual partners, particularly for those inclined to move toward "modernization." This appears to be the "civilized" or modern form of polygyny. In Cameroon particularly and across most of Francophone Africa including Côte d'Ivoire and Congo (DRC) where polygyny is outlawed, this has come to be popularly known as the acquisition of outside wives (concubinage, mistresses, girlfriends)—a phenomenon of the "deuxième bureau" or "private polygyny" in contemporary Africa (Lacombe, 1987; Karanja, 1987, 1994).

While polygyny is frequently practiced by African men, there are indications that some women are involved with multiple sexual partners as well. In the face of current economic downturns and the associated hardships of life in Cameroon, it is now common for women to have several older and wealthy partners as they try to maximize the financial benefits of their relationships. Hence, a new terminology has emerged—the *three v's (voiture, villa, virement)*—that characterizes the men frequently sought by these women as those with cars, a villa or house, and money. There is also the recent evidence of individuals who live in stable relationships but outside legal or formally recognized marital unions in what has been termed informal or consensual unions. This new trend is particularly common in the urban areas.

MODERNIZATION AND THE FUTURE OF CAMEROONIAN FAMILIES

Since the Cameroonian family system is traditionally of the extended family type, the typical family spans about four generations, which includes children, parents, grandparents, great-grandparents, brothers, sisters, cousins, in-laws, and so on. The individual is not only part of the family but also part of a community or ethnic group, hence the dependence of a person on his/her fellow kinsmen. This state of affairs has generally kept the family size in the country consistently high (Balepa et al., 1992; Bangha, 1996; Fotso et al., 1999). The belief in the extended family is so strong that the members of the family see it as a duty to help each other. Even when they are geographically separated from one another, the belief in family ties is generally sustained emotionally to the extent that financial assistance is given from time to time as an evidence of this commitment. As Eloundou-Enyegue (1992) indicates, remittances from the well-to-do members of the family usually help to support the underprivileged ones.

However, modernization has brought in its wake a number of social problems, including the erosion of such family solidarity as individuals tend to focus more on the close family, resulting in a reduction of the level of remittance. It should be noted that an important characteristic of the traditional Cameroonian family system is the respect and honor accorded to elderly members. The younger members of the family, their age and economic position notwithstanding, must give due respect to the elder ones and this is reflected in speech patterns, manners, and behavior. Elderly persons are regarded as the bastion and repository of wisdom from the ancestors and, as a result, occupy a high and enviable position in the family. Consequently, they are supported with food, shelter, and financial and physical care within the context of the extended family network.

Modernization has produced conflicts between present values and those upheld by the traditional Cameroonian society. With increasing social changes, the interdependence that gave the extended family support system its strength is being eroded. In fact, it is increasingly being documented that the extended family system worldwide is in rapid decline (Martin, 1990; Berquo & Xenos, 1992; De Vos, 1995; Mbamaonyeukwu, 2001a).

In Cameroon, modernization, with its concomitant urbanization, has contributed to the dispersion of family members who once lived and ate under the same roof. Young adults have the tendency to migrate to the two major cities, Douala and Yaounde, in search of better occupational opportunities and independence. This process has received profound impetus from Western education and the growth of the youth culture. In addition, the economic depression, resulting in the devaluation of the currency and salary slashes for public servants, has heightened the difficulties of urban life. These changes have also resulted in a remarkable shift in the role of the elderly persons within the family, especially in the urban areas. This is because with limited home space, income, and time, the young family now tends to withdraw from the care of the older folk and other kin, and instead concentrate on the nuclear family, which by its very nature promotes individualism and personal freedom (Warnes, 1986; Wolf, 1994). The inevitable fallout of this scenario is that the present elderly population in Cameroon and much of Africa will more likely have less help and security from fewer children than in the previous generations.

Cameroon is generally a patrilineal society in which men exercise authority both within the household and in public, although matrilineal cultures are also found in rural areas. But available evidence suggests that a significant proportion of women are no longer confined to the home and household chores (Beneria,

1981; Cooksey, 1982). Long before the 1980s, the government created the Ministry of Women Affairs to improve the status of women and coordinate all national activities related to their welfare. In fact, Cameroonian women have advanced faster in education than in any other sector of national life, especially in primary education which, in the past, was inaccessible to most of them. In towns and cities such as Yaounde, Obala, Eseka, and Mbalmayo, more girls than boys attend primary school (Cooksey, 1982). At other levels of education, women continue to make significant inroads, albeit at a much slower pace. Women are being given ministerial and other administrative positions in the government and play major roles in party politics. Also, in the cities they often participate in social activities with their husbands, and are no longer confined to joining the circle of other women, as is the case in the rural areas.

Notwithstanding this visible progress, however, women in Cameroon still face seemingly insurmountable obstacles. The extent of their representation in national institutions, agencies, and politics is still disproportionately small considering that they are the majority in terms of number (Fotso et al., 1999; World Bank, 2000; United Nations, 2001). Furthermore, as males continue to migrate to the cities in search of better opportunities, and children attend school and are trained to perform skilled work, the burden of sustaining the family continues to fall on women's shoulders, particularly in the rural areas, though the men in most cases continue to provide resources.

Another important point is that every society has certain rules that regulate sexual practices. Traditional Cameroonian society, and indeed much of African tradition, regards sex as the most important factor in marriage and therefore a high premium is placed on premarital chastity and virginity (Ayisi, 1979). Upon marriage, girls are expected to be virgins and they and their parents are rewarded accordingly with gifts. However, such cases are rare today as a result of the diffusion and spread of Western values. Latest empirical evidence indicates that whereas the median age at first marriage for women in Cameroon is 17.4 years, the median age at first sexual intercourse is 15.9 years (Fotso et al., 1999).

Another challenge to the modern African family is the prevalence of HIV/AIDS. This is especially true when we consider that a majority of the population is living in abject poverty and barely able to keep body and soul together and families are barely managing to survive (World Bank, 1992; Bangha, 1998). With particular reference to Cameroon, the evidence suggests that the current adult HIV/AIDS prevalence rate is 7.7 percent among persons aged 15–49 years, while the estimated number of children who have lost a mother or both parents to AIDS by 1999 was 181,344. Although the prevalence level of HIV/AIDS in Cameroon is relatively low compared to the high prevalence countries such as Botswana (35.8 percent), Kenya (14.0 percent), Malawi (16.0 percent), South Africa (19.9 percent), and Zimbabwe (25.1 percent), it is obvious that the disease poses a formidable threat to the Cameroonian family. The promise of better conditions in the cities has led to a considerable influx into the urban areas/cities by rural people. In the absence of any accompanying improvement in facilities to respond to this rapid urbanization, the immigrants have been forced into risky lifestyles leading to the potential spread of HIV/AIDS among young people in the prime of life.

CONCLUSION

The variety of cultural, social, and technological changes that are occurring in contemporary Cameroon, which were triggered by the European penetration, occupation, and administration, are presenting enormous challenges to the traditional family system in the country. The acquisition of modern education leads to changes in values and intellectual development across generations as younger people place greater emphasis on self-fulfillment as individuals rather than on their responsibilities toward their relatives. Thus, modernization renders living in extended family households in Cameroon less essential and economically less viable and therefore facilitates the transition to conjugal or nuclear family living arrangements. The preservation and continuity of the support and respect accorded the elderly in traditional societies should be of paramount importance as Treas and Logue (1986) have warned that the older population may be viewed as victims of modernization efforts if their status declines with development.

Since there is no universal social security system in Cameroon and those currently employed are not sure of retirement benefits, the evolution of a strong and effective social security for the country is long overdue. It is important that the scope of the current system, which covers only a handful of people in formal employment, should be extended to reach the unemployed individuals of working age. The government should make it mandatory for every employer to contribute toward that scheme on behalf of the employees. This will ensure some minimum financial security for people as the modernization process is seriously threatening the traditional family system that hitherto has assumed that role. It is very important that the national social insurance fund be revamped so as to avoid the current situation in which workers are left at the mercy of their poor family members after having contributed all their working years. In particular, the elderly are the most vulnerable, and the proposed scheme is likely to reduce the poverty and destitution currently being experienced by a significant proportion of the people (World Bank, 2000; UNFPA, 2004).

On the other hand, Cameroon is feeling the impact of a global economic recession that has hit Africa the hardest (World Bank, 2000; UNFPA, 2004). Consequently, the country is undergoing many deleterious economic and social changes that impact the quality of living standards of families and households. For example, access to potable water and electricity is still a major problem in the country, particularly in the countryside and the northern area that experiences little rainfall. The health consequences for families, especially the most vulnerable segments of the family (women and their children), should be of special concern to the government. In fact, the women's position within a class-stratified structure of ethnic affiliation, polygyny, and labor force participation places many of them in even more vulnerable positions.

It can be argued that economic and social development is not just a matter of producing needed skills, but of producing the opportunities to use those skills as well. The lack of absorptive capacity in Cameroon's economy has led to a situation in which graduates of university and other tertiary institutions are unemployed. Those professionals and skilled persons who are fortunate to obtain employment are frequently dissatisfied with the working conditions and salaries they receive. This has precipitated massive emigration not only from Cameroon but also from other parts of Africa and the developing world to other countries as people seek better economic prospects. In fact, the brain drain that has bedeviled most developing countries for a long time has now been documented for Cameroon (United Nations Institute for Training and Research, 1971). This state of affairs is detrimental to the welfare of the family, to say the least. An unemployed person cannot fend for his family. Some of those who emigrate find themselves in even worse economic conditions and have little or nothing to remit to members of their families languishing in abject poverty at home. It is recommended that the government institute broad administrative reforms as well as effective and workable manpower and employment policies that will not only create jobs for those completing school or dropping out but also make working in Cameroon attractive.

The authorities in Cameroon are faced with a number of stumbling blocks in dealing with the HIV/AIDS epidemic. The most notable problem lies with the highest risk group—young adults. Although government health and social welfare departments and NGOs have started major campaigns, distributing free condoms at schools and universities and to the public, statistics continue to show an increase in infections, underscoring the ineffectiveness of such campaigns. The fact remains that unbridled and promiscuous sexual behavior among the young contributes to the rapid spread of the virus. Among the adult family members in both Cameroon and elsewhere, the largest proportion of persons with HIV/AIDS have contracted the disease through multiple heterosexual partners (Mbamaonyeukwu, 2000, 2001b). Therefore, the disease will be partly contained if a determined effort targets the youth with an abstinence approach and discourages adults from having multiple sexual partners.

It is strongly advocated that sex educators in institutions of learning now stress abstinence as the best way to avoid HIV/AIDS and unwanted pregnancy, both of which contribute to the misery of the impoverished family. However, the spread of HIV/AIDS in the country is further exacerbated by the ever-increasing poverty that limits people's abilities to escape HIV/AIDS (IMF/World Bank, 2004). The weak economic conditions and further misallocation of scarce resources have rendered the majority of the population incapable of sustaining themselves and their families, resulting in risk-taking lifestyles just for survival (Bangha, 1998). It will therefore be more effective and meaningful to include in the prevention packages strategies to provide the vulnerable masses with some income-generating jobs for minimal economic independence.

Since modernization touches on all major aspects of the economy, a large number of variables are thought to be concomitants of the modernization process. Lack of data and space constraints preclude exhaustive treatment of these with respect to the family system of Cameroon. However, it is hoped that this chapter's contribution represents a modest attempt aimed at expanding knowledge about modernization and the changing traditional African family system.

NOTES

1. An ethnic group is a relatively large number of people who speak the same language, share the same culture and history, and live in a recognizable territory sanctioned by tradition. It should be stated that the ethnic profile of Cameroon is unique in that it is official policy not to collect any empirical information on the basis of ethnicity because it is seen as divisive (Bahoken & Atangana, 1976; Nyamnjoh, 1999). As a result, both censuses and surveys are silent on ethnicity. Much of what we know is based on best guesses from the preponderance of linguistic affiliation.

2. This documentary was part of a series on five African realities titled *Voix d'Afrique* (*Voice of Africa*) that was aired on the French public television channel France 2 in February–March 2002. The other four parts covered Religious Peace in Senegal (a country close to 90 percent Muslim); Reconciliation Process in South Africa; the War in Sudan; and HIV/AIDS in Uganda.

3. The SMAM is the average number of years lived in a single (unmarried) state by those who eventually marry before age 50 (United Nations, 1983).

REFERENCES

Alexandre, P. (Ed.). (1973). *French perspectives in African Studies.* London: Oxford University Press.

Ansari, S. J. (1998). *Political modernization in the Gulf.* New Delhi, India: Northern Book Center.

Apt, N. A. (1996). *Coping with old age in a changing Africa: Social change and the elderly Ghanaian.* Brookfield, Eng.: Avebury Aldeshot.

Ayisi, E. (1979). *An introduction to the study of African culture.* 2nd ed. London: Heinemann Educational Books, Inc.

Bahoken, J., & Atangana, E. (1976). *Cultural policy in the United Republic of Cameroon.* Paris: UNESCO Press.

Balepa, M., Fotso, M., & Barrère, B. (1992). *Enquête démographiques et de santé Cameroun 1991.* Columbia, MD: Direction Nationale du 2éme RGPH [Cameroon] and Macro International Inc.

Bangha, M. W. (1995). The mortality situation in Cameroon. *African Population Studies 10(1),* 103–122.

Bangha, M. W. (1996). The fertility performance of polygynous marriages in Cameroon. *African Anthropology: Journal of the Pan African Anthropological Association 3(1)*, 45–64.

Bangha, M. W. (1998). The poverty implications of HIV/AIDS for sub-Sahara African nations. *African Population Studies 13(2)*, 121–138.

Bangha, M. W. (2003). How early is the timing of family formation in rural Cameroon? *African Population Studies 18(1)*, 1–18.

Ben-Jochannan, Y. (1989). *Black man of the Nile and his family*. Baltimore: Black Classic Press.

Beneria, L. (1981). Conceptualizing the labor force: The understanding of women's economic activities. *Journal of Developmental Studies 17*, 39–45.

Berquo, E., & Xenos, P. (Eds.). (1992). *Family systems and cultural change*. New York: Oxford University Press.

Bongaarts, J., & Potter, R. G. (1983). *Fertility, biology, and behavior: An analysis of the proximate determinants*. New York: Academic.

Britannica. (2000). The history of Cameroon. *Encyclopedia Britannica*.

Burnham, P. C. (1996). *The politics of cultural difference in Northern Cameroon*. Washington, DC: Smithsonian Institution Press.

Caldwell, J., & Caldwell, P. (1990). High fertility in sub-Saharan Africa. *Scientific American 262(5)*, 118–125.

Cameroun, République Unie du. (1976). *Recensement Générale de la Population et de l'Habitat d'Avril 1976: Vol. II Tome 2 Analyse*. Etat Matrimonial Nuptialité. BCR, DSCN, Ministère de l'Economie et du Plan.

Cameroun, République Unie du. (1983). *Enquête Nationale sur la Fécondité du Cameroun 1978*. Rapport principal Vol. I. DSCN, Ministère de l'Economie et du Plan.

Chen, C. (1996). Living arrangements and economic support for the elderly in Taiwan. *Journal of Population Studies 17*, 59–81.

Chiabi, E. (1997). *The making of modern Cameroon: A history of substate nationalism and disparate union, 1914–1961*. Lanham, MD: University Press of America.

Cooksey, B. 1982. Education and sexual inequality in Cameroon. *The Journal of Modern African Studies 20*, 15–23.

Cowgill, D. O. (1986). *Aging around the world*. Belmont, CA: Wadsworth.

Davis, K. (1955). Institutional patterns favoring high fertility in under-developed areas. *Eugenics Quarterly 2*, 33–39.

DeLancey, M. W. (1989). *Cameroon: Dependence and independence*. Boulder, CO: Westview.

DeLancey, M. W., & DeLancey, M. D. (1999). *Cameroon*. Santa Barbara, CA: Clio.

De Vos, S. M. (1995). Household composition in Latin America. The Plenum Series on Demographic Methods and Population Analysis. New York: Plenum Press.

Direction National du 2éme RGPH Cameroun. (1992). Démo 87: Résultats Bruts, République du Cameroun. Vol. II Tome 1 et Démo 87: Analyse Préliminaire, Synthèse des Rapports Préliminaires. Vol. III Tome 9.

Dixon, J. (Ed.). (1987). *Social welfare in Africa*. London: Croom Helm.

Dizard, J., & Gadlin, H. (1990). *The minimal family*. Amherst, MA: University of Amherst Press.

Doenges, C. E. (1991). Patterns of domestic life in colonial Mexico: Views from the household. *Latin American Population History Bulletin 19*, 14–21.

Dreyer, J. T. (2000). *China's political system: Modernization and tradition*. New York: Longman (3rd ed.).

Easterline, R. A. (1983). Modernization and fertility: A critical essay. In Bulatao, R. A. & Lee, R. D. (Eds.), *Determinants of fertility in developing countries, Vol. 2.* (pp. 562–586). New York: Academic Press.

Eltis, D. (2001). The volume and structure of the Transatlantic Slave Trade: A reassessment. *History Cooperative, 58(1).*

Eloundou-Enyegue, P. M. (1992). *Solidarite dans la crise ou crise des solidarites familiales au Cameroun? Evolutions recentes des echanges entre villes et campagnes.* Les Dossiers du CEPED, No. 22. CEPED, Paris, France.

Fotso, M., Ndonou, R., Libite, P. R. Tsafack, M., Wakou, R., Ghapoutsa, A., Kamga, S., Kemgo, P., Fankam, M. K., Kamdoum, A., & Barrère, B. (1999). *Enquête Démographiques et de Santé, Cameroun 1998.* Calverton, MD: Bureau Central des Recensements et des Etudes de Population and Macro International, Inc.

Goheen, M. (1996). *Men own the fields, women own the crops: Gender and power in the Cameroon grassfields.* Madison: University of Wisconsin Press.

Goode, W. J. (1963). *World revolution and family patterns.* New York: Free Press.

Greenberg, J. (1966). *Languages of Africa.* Bloomington: Indiana University.

Hammel, E., & Laslett, P. (1974). Comparing household structure over time and between cultures. *Comparative Studies in Society and History 16,* 73–109.

Hedinger, R. (1987). *The Manenguba languages (Bantu A. 15, Mbo cluster) of Cameroon.* London: School of Oriental and African Studies, University of London.

IMF/World Bank. (2004). *Poverty reduction strategy papers.* Washington, DC: IMF. http://www.imf.org/external/np/prsp/prsp.asp.

International Labor Organization. (1972). *Employment, incomes and equality: A strategy for increasing productive employment in Kenya.* Geneva: ILO.

Johnson, W. (1970). *The Cameroon federation: Political integration in a fragmentary society.* Princeton: NJ: Princeton University Press.

Kaberry Research Center. (1993). *Rites of passage and incorporation in the western grassfields of Cameroon, Vol. I.* Bamenda, Cameroon: KRC.

Karanja, W. W. (1987). Outside wives and inside wives in Nigeria: A study of changing perceptions of marriage. In Parkin, D. and Nyamwaya, D. (Eds.), *Transformations of African Marriage* (pp. 247–261). Manchester, Eng.: Manchester University Press.

Karanja, W. W. (1994). The phenomenon of "outside wives": Some reflections on its possible influence on fertility. In Bledsoe C. & Pison, G. (Eds.), *Nuptiality in sub-Saharan Africa: Contemporary anthropological and demographic perspectives* (pp. 194–214). Oxford: Clarendon.

Kinsella, K., & Velkoff, V. (2001). *An aging world: 2001.* U.S. Census Bureau, Series P95/01-1. Washington, DC: U.S. Government Printing Office.

Kumari, V., & Ubaidullah, M. (1997). *Explaining cross-cultural variations: Women and the age at marriage.* New Delhi, India: M.D. Publications.

Lacombe, B. (1987). Les unions informelles en Afrique au sud du Sahara: Le cas du deuxième bureau congolais. *Genus 43(1–2),* 151–63.

LeVine, V. (1971). *The Cameroon federal republic.* Ithaca, NY: Cornell University Press.

Levy, M. B. (1966). *Modernization and structure of societies.* Princeton, NJ: Princeton University Press.

Lorimer, F. (1954). *Culture and human fertility.* Westport, CT: Greenwood.

Martin, L. (1990). Changing intergenerational family relations in East Asia. *The Annals 510,* 102–114.

Mba, C. J. (2001). Nigeria's aging population: A call for attention. *BOLD Quarterly Journal of the International Institute on Aging, 12(1)*, 15–24.

Mbamaonyeukwu, J. C. (2000, December 2). AIDS: A threat to humanity. *The Spectator*, 3.

Mbamaonyeukwu, J. C. (2001a). Africa's aging populations. *BOLD Quarterly Journal of the International Institute on Aging, 11(4)*, 2–7.

Mbamaonyeukwu, J. C. (2001b, March 24). The battle against HIV/AIDS: The winds are contrary. *The Spectator*, 3.

Mbugua, W. (1997). The African family and the status of women's health. In Adepoju, A. (Ed.), *Family, population and development in Africa* (pp. 139–57). London: Zed Books.

Mol, A. P. (2001). *Globalization and environmental reform: The ecological modernization of the global economy.* Cambridge, MA: MIT Press.

Njoh, A. J. (2001). *Planning rules in post-colonial states: The political economy of urban and regional planning in Cameroon.* Huntington, NY: Nova Science Publishers.

Nyamnjoh, F. B. (1999). Cameroon: A country united by ethnic ambition and difference. *African Affairs 98(390)*, 101–118.

Palloni, A. (2000). Living arrangements of older persons. In *United Nations Technical Meeting on Population Ageing and Living Arrangements of Older Persons: Critical Issues and Policy Responses*, February 8–10, ESA/P/ WP.157/Rev.1. New York: United Nations.

Pison, G. (1987). Polygyny, fertility and kinship in a region of sub-Saharan Africa. In *The Cultural Roots of Africa's Fertility Regimes* (pp. 16–27). Proceedings of the Ife Conference, Ile-Ife, Nigeria.

Population Reference Bureau. (1999). *World population data sheet.* Washington, DC: PRB.

Roberts, T., & Hite, A. (Eds.). (2000). *From modernization to globalization: Perspectives on development and social change.* Malden, MA: Blackwell.

Robirosa, M. C. (1971). Internal migration, human resources and employment within the context of urbanization. *International Review of Community Development*, vol.1, 49–65.

Romaniuc, A. (1988). *La polygamie et la parente en Afrique tropicale: Le point de vue d'un demographe.* Congres Africain de Population, Dakar, IUSSP: 5.1.45–5.1.60.

Timaeus, I., & Graham, W. (1989). Labor circulation, marriage and fertility in Southern Africa. In Lesthaeghe, R. (Ed.), *Reproduction and social organization in sub-Saharan Africa* (pp. 365–400). Berkeley: University of California Press.

Todd, L. (1982). *Varieties of English around the world.* T1: Cameroon, Heidelberg, Julius Groos.

Treas, J., & Logue, B. (1986). Economic development and the older population. *Population and Development Review 12(4)*, 645–673.

UNFPA. (2004). *State of world population 2004. The Cairo consensus at ten: Population, reproductive health and the global effort to end poverty.* New York: Information, Executive Board and Resource Mobilization Division, UNFPA.

United Nations. (1991). *Aging and urbanization.* New York: Department of International Economic and Social Affairs, ST/ESA/SER.R/109.

United Nations. (1994). *Aging and the family.* New York: Department for Economic and Social Information and Policy Analysis, ST/ESA/SER.R/124.

United Nations. (2001a). *World population prospects, The 2000 revision Vol. I: Comprehensive tables*. New York: Department of Economic and Social Affairs, Population Division, ST/ESA/SER.A/198.
United Nations. (2001b). *World urbanization prospects: The 1999 Revision*. New York: Department of Economic and Social Affairs, Population Division, ST/ESA/SER.A/194.
United Nations. (2001c). *World population prospects, The 2000 revision: Highlights*. New York: Department of Economic and Social Affairs, Population Division, ESA/P/WP.165.
United Nations. (2003). *World population prospects, The 2002 revision Vol. I: Comprehensive tables*. New York: Department of Economic and Social Affairs, Population Division, ST/ESA/SER.A/222.
United Nations Institute for Training and Research. (1971). *The brain drain from five developing countries (Cameroon, Colombia, Lebanon, The Philippines, and Trinidad and Tobago)*. UNITAR Research Reports No. 5, New York.
UNAIDS. (2000). *Report on the global HIV/AIDS epidemic, June 2000*. Geneva: Joint United Nations Program on HIV/AIDS.
Warnes, A. M. (1986). The elderly in less developed countries. *Aging and society 6*, 373–380.
Weekes-Vagliani, W. (1976). Family life and structure in southern Cameroon. Technical Papers. Organization for Economic Co-operation and Development (OECD). Washington DC: OECD Publications Center.
Wolf, D. A. (1994). The elderly and their kin: Patterns of availability and access. In Martin, L. G. & Preston, S. H. (Eds.), *Demography of aging* (pp. 146–194). National Research Council. Washington, DC: National Academy Press.
World Bank. (1992). *Tanzania: AIDS assessment and planning study*. A World Bank country study. Washington, DC: World Bank.
World Bank. (2000). *World development indicators database, July 2000*. World Bank Group. Washington, DC: World Bank.

Part IV
Eastern Africa

CHAPTER 10

Kenyan Families

Miroslava Prazak

> The hooks of extended family cut into the hearts and pocketbooks of almost every African ... family loyalty operates on a smaller, more intimate stage—one populated exclusively by blood relatives. With its labyrinthine web of rights and duties, the extended family is a day-care, social security, and welfare system. It babysits the children of working parents and keeps the elderly from feeling useless. It feeds the unemployed and gives refuge to the disabled and mentally ill. It pays for all this by redistributing resources between haves and have nots.
> —Harden (1990, pp. 62–63)

INTRODUCTION

Written by Blaine Harden, the *Washington Post* bureau chief in sub-Saharan Africa in the late 1980s, the above description of the centrality of family in African societies continues to be true at the beginning of the new millennium. The strength of the African family is surprising, given that the dissolution of the African family has been authoritatively prophesied for over 40 years. In the words of eminent anthropologist Colin Turnbull, "[t]he family cannot survive under a Western economic and political system, and if the family cannot survive neither can the values [of African] morality and spiritual pride and strength" (cited in Harden, 1990, p. 67).

This chapter is an exploration of the ongoing importance of the family as a fundamental social and economic institution in Kenyan society. That it persists in this role as linchpin in the social relations of life—increasingly pulled apart by the country's steady economic decay, decades of economic restructuring, and the undermining forces of globalization—testifies to its strength. But the ideal family of Kenyan society, the extended, multigenerational domestic group, is under stress. Responding to decades of Western education, urban migration, and increased incorporation into global capitalism, family members exist in different worlds from each other. The rural old and the urban young are separated by vast distances, geographic and ideological. In only a decade, Kenya's urban population has more than doubled, from 4.2 million in 1989 to 9.1 million in 1999. Though only 32 percent of Kenya's population lives in towns and cities, that statistic is up from 18 percent a decade ago (Republic of Kenya, 2001, p. xxvii; Republic of Kenya, 1999, p. 3). But it is not only the urban exodus that is pushing more and more Kenyans into the wage economy, requiring their children to attend Western-type schools, and isolating the elderly back in villages. Even in the rural areas, production for the market is a necessary ingredient in subsistence strategies. There is a growing chasm between the rural old and the rural young, each filled with ideas and expectations produced in distinct eras. Young people, having attended school and secured jobs, find less and less value in the authority, knowledge, and skills of their elders.

Family loyalty can hobble the careers and limit the achievements of individual Africans. Jealous relatives often harm each other. Gossip, curses, land disputes, homicide, and witchcraft are aimed at successful relatives whose remittances to the family fail to meet expectations (Harden, 1990, p. 69). But in the absence of social and welfare services, the sense of mutual obligation will continue for a long time to sustain kinship ties as the dominant concern of everyday life (Harden, 1990, p. 70).

DEMOGRAPHIC AND ECOLOGICAL PROFILES

Population Data

According to the 1999 population census, there were more than 28.5 million Kenyans, representing an increase of 34 percent over the 1989 enumerated figure (Republic of Kenya, 2001, Vol. 1, p. xxvi). Forty-four percent of Kenyans were younger than 15, a decline from 49 percent in 1989. The decline is attributed to the overall national fertility decline experienced during the 1989–99 intercensal period, itself the subject of a vast literature (see, e.g., Cross, Obungu, & Kizito, 1991; Robinson, 1992; Brass & Jolly, 1993; Dow, Archer, Khasiani, & Kekevole, 1994; Republic of Kenya, 1994).

Kenya's population increased from 5.4 million in 1948 to 16.2 million in 1979 to 23.2 million in 1989. According to the 1989 census, the intercensal population growth rate was 3.4 percent per annum. The 1999 census data indicate this rate had declined to 2.9 percent in 1999 (Republic of Kenya, 2001, Vol. 1, p. xxx), driven by declining fertility and increasing mortality rates, particularly due to the HIV/AIDS epidemic (Republic of Kenya, 1999, p. 2).

Most Kenyan people live in rural areas. According to World Almanac Education Group (2002, p. 819), 32 percent of the population was urban and the ratio of urban to rural population has increased significantly in the last decade (Republic of Kenya, 1999, p. 3). Rural to urban migration continues, and is largely responsible for the growing provincial shares of the total population for Nairobi and the Rift Valley, as well as for the Coast Province (Republic of Kenya, 2001, Vol. 1, p. xxvii).

Ethnic/Racial/Class/Religious Variations

The fossil record leads us to believe that human history traces some of its beginnings to what is now Kenya, where early hominid ancestors evolved. Today, the country is home to many ethnic groups and races, most of African descent, woven together by culture and history. Descendants of Asians and Europeans constitute a minor segment of the population numerically.

The country is home to a tremendous diversity of people. Members of 43 ethnolinguistic groups are classified into three linguistic groups: Bantu, Nilotic, and Cushitic. The Bantu language speakers are concentrated in three main geographical regions—Western Kenya and Lake Victoria (Luhya, Kisii, Kuria), east of the Rift Valley (Kikuyu, Embu, Meru, Kamba), and the coastal belt (Mijikenda). Nilotic language speakers are represented by the Luo, Kalenjin, Maasai, and related groups. The Luos are concentrated in the Lake Victoria Basin, while the Kalenjin linguistic group is concentrated in the area north to south and west of the central highlands. The Maasai live in the Rift Valley. The Cushitic language group includes Somali-speaking peoples occupying eastern portions of the arid and semiarid northeastern Kenya. Rendille and Orma-speaking groups occupy the northwestern part.

The two most recent censuses have been heavily contested by various groups, and the figures are not reliable. There is general agreement that the Kikuyus, who live primarily in Central Province, make up about 22 percent of Kenya's population and are the largest ethnic group. The Luhya in Western Province make up 14 percent of the country's population; the Luos who inhabit the western and northern parts of Nyanza Province 13 percent; the Kalenjins in Rift Valley Province 12 percent; and Kambas in the southern part of Eastern Province 11 percent. The Merus and Embus in the southern part of Eastern Province account for 6 percent of the population, as do the Kisiis in the eastern part of Nyanza province (Republic of Kenya, 1999, p. 1; World Almanac Education Group, 2002, p. 819). Other small African groups comprise 15 percent of the population, and people of non-African (Asian, European, and Arab) descent account for 1 percent (U.S. Central Intelligence Agency [CIA] website). The distribution of population between various ethnic groups is a highly politicized issue, and counts vary from source to source. For example, "Kenya Profile" by Newafrica.com has the following distribution: Luhya, 24 percent; Kikuyu, 21 percent; Luo, 20 percent; Kalenjin, 17 percent; Kamba and Meru at 10 percent each; Kisii, 6 percent; and non-African 2 percent (Newafrica.com). Apart from juggling the standings, this profile doesn't account for the numerous smaller groups.

Christianity and Islam are the major religions (Republic of Kenya, 1999, p. 1). About 38 percent of the population is Protestant, 28 percent is Roman Catholic, and 26 percent of Kenyans practice/hold indigenous beliefs (World Almanac Education Group, 2002, p. 819). The remaining 8 percent are mostly Muslim, though Hinduism is also practiced among the Asian minority (CIA, p. 3).

Ecological/Geographical Variations

Bordered on the east by the Indian Ocean, Kenya lies across the equator, between 3° north and 5° south latitude, and between 34° and 41° east longitude. The country covers an area of 582,650 square kilometers, and borders Ethiopia in the north, Sudan in the northwest, Uganda in the west, Tanzania in the south, and Somalia in the east. It is a land of fascinating topographical and climatic contrasts. These range from scenic palm-fringed coastal humidity to expansive dry savanna plains; from the crisp alpine scenes of the highlands to the semidesert stretches to the north; and from the spectacular formations of the Rift Valley to the tropical equatorial climate of Nyanza (Gatabaki, 1983, p. 12). Climate is closely associated with altitude, which plays an important role in Kenya's weather and rain patterns, patterns of human settlement, and agricultural activities.

Approximately 80 percent of the land area of Kenya is arid or semiarid and only 20 percent is arable. A large proportion of the arid and semiarid land has been set aside for wildlife conservation. Agriculture is the mainstay of Kenya's economy, accounting for 26 percent of the gross domestic product, whereas manufacturing accounts for about 14 percent. Tea, tourism, coffee, and horticulture are the main foreign-exchange earners (Republic of Kenya, 1999, p. 1).

HISTORICAL BACKGROUND AND HERITAGE

Brief History

Historians agree that throughout the length of the Iron Age—a period of almost 2,000 years before the present—numerous Bantu and Nilotic population movements took place. Most often migrations were slow and gradual, involving peaceful penetration and settlement. As populations increased and more land was required expansion and migration proceeded, and new territory was cleared from the wild for homesteads and fields. This was true of the pastoralist Nilotes and the agriculturalist Bantu, though the possibility that some of the more pastoral Nilotic migrants may have moved across the northern plains and grasslands as conquering waves or as desperate splinter groups in search of land or refuge has not been completely ruled out. The older populations of hunter-gatherers probably entered into relationships with the newcomers and exchanged products. Many were absorbed into the expanding food-producing ethnic groups (Sutton, 1974, p. 91). The most extensive processes of assimilation by Bantu and Nilotes are believed to have taken place in the highland regions of Kenya and northern Tanzania, which were already occupied by the southern Cushitic-speaking food producers. Long processes of intermingling have left a deep mark on the customs, beliefs, economies, and social and political organizations of the Bantu and Nilotes who now inhabit the highlands (Sutton, 1974, p. 92).

The geographic expansion of the early Bantus was associated with the introduction of agriculture and of more efficient iron tools, which facilitated the opening up of the thick forest and more extensive cultivation of the land than had been possible previously. Because the Bantu were basically cultivators by occupation, they tended to prefer the more fertile and well-watered land in the region (Were, 1974, p. 170). Unlike the more nomadic hunters and gatherers and pastoralists, the Bantu built more permanent homesteads and formed settled communities (Were, 1974, p. 171).

From the 6th to the 19th centuries, the peoples inhabiting the territory of Kenya were loosely controlled by the Arabic rulers of Oman (Turner, 2002, p. 980). Arab colonies exported spices and slaves from the Kenyan coast as early as the 8th century (World Almanac Education Group, 2002, p. 820). In 1886, a Muslim community made up of Arabs from the Middle East and Indians from the Indian subcontinent had settled on the Kenyan coast. These traders converted some Africans to Islam. In 1896, when Britain decided to build a railway across the whole country, people from India were hired as the laborers, and many remained after the completion of the task (Kuria, 1987, pp. 288–289).

Kenya was born in 1886 when Britain and Germany divided between themselves the territory that today makes up Kenya and Tanzania respectively. The British share, or "sphere of influence," became Kenya and was until 1895 administered for Britain by the Imperial British East Africa company. The company failed commercially and Britain declared Kenya a protectorate in 1895. Most of the inhabitants then were Africans who belonged to different ethnic groups, which had their own economic and political organizations. Some, like the Maasai, Samburu, Turkana, and Rendille, were pastoralist. Others, like the Dorobo, lived by hunting. Most of the other groups practiced mixed farming at a subsistence level (Kuria, 1987, pp. 287–288). Life centered around the domestic group, often regulated by ideas of descent, and land, the primary resource, was communally held. Mutual assistance and cooperation were necessary elements of life on the local level.

In 1920, the East Africa Protectorate became known as the Colony of Kenya. The influx of European settlers picked up pace, and Africans resented the immigrants because they appropriated land and had exclusive political representation in the colonial Legislative Council (Turner, 2002, p. 980). A state of emergency existed between October 1952 and January 1960 during the period of the Mau Mau uprising, during which over 13,000 Africans and

100 Europeans were killed. The Kenya African Union was banned and its president, Jomo Kenyatta, imprisoned. Full internal self-government was achieved in 1962 and in December 1963, Kenya became an independent republic and a member of the Commonwealth. In 1978, Daniel arap Moi succeeded Jomo Kenyatta as president. In 1982, Kenya became a one-party state but in 1992, due to pressure by donor governments and agencies, multi-party politics were reintroduced. In December 2002, Mwai Kibaki was elected as the third president of the republic.

Kenya's Triple Heritage

Although traditional beliefs and practices vary in detail among Kenya's ethnic groups, they share many general characteristics. The four most significant ones include a concept of god, belief in spirits, importance of ancestors, and belief in sorcery and witchcraft. Religious beliefs and practices form an aspect of everyday life, and imbue daily activity with meaning and structure. For many of the ethnic groups, such as the Kuria, the performance of rituals, particularly rites of passage, provides a defining characteristic of their ethnicity (Ruel, 1965).

The God of traditional beliefs is an eternal, omnipotent creator envisaged as remote from men. Called *Ngai* by the Kikuyu, Maasai, and the Wakamba, the divinity cannot be seen, but is manifested in the sun, moon, thunder and lightning, stars, rain, the rainbow, and in the great fig trees that serve as places of worship and sacrifice (Kenyatta, 1965, p. 225). Called *Irioba* or *Nyanokwe* by the Kuria, the divinity is said to have created and ordered the world and all that it contains (Ruel, 1965, p. 295). Further, many indigenous religions also recognize spiritual forces at work in the world that are close to the living and more involved in their daily affairs. If men and women please the spirits, success is ensured; if they incur the spirits' anger, illness or evil may occur (Kenyatta, 1965, p. 256). For many indigenous believers, ghosts form a distinct category of ancestral spirits that are thought to return to seek revenge on the living. Sorcery and witchcraft play important roles in many indigenous belief systems and often persist after conversion to Christianity or Islam even when other elements of traditional religion have faded (African Studies Center website). Twenty-six percent of Kenyans adhere to and practice indigenous beliefs (CIA).

Christian missionary activity began at the end of the 19th century in Kenya's interior when it was opened to rail travel between Mombasa and Uganda. Churches were founded in the 1920s and 1930s, especially in areas where the Kikuyu, Luo, and Luhya predominated. Some sought to combine Christian and indigenous beliefs. Since colonial authorities maintained a policy of allocating a mission to a particular territory, most churches tended to be ethnically homogeneous. There are now several independent Christian churches that have broken ties with missionary-introduced Christian denominations. The number of Kenyan clergy has grown in past years, and most of the Roman Catholic and Church Province of Kenya hierarchies are Kenyan (African

Studies Center). Currently, approximately 66 percent of Kenyans are Christians, of which 38 percent are Protestant and 28 percent are Catholic (CIA).

African belief systems and customs (termed "Africanity" by Skinner, 1986, p. 60) place a great deal of importance on rites of passage, which include birth, circumcision or other physical alteration at the threshold to adulthood, marriage, and childbirth. Descent, kinship, and other social relationships are central values. Also characteristic of Africanity is the transfer of valuables or services from the family of the bridegroom to that of the bride. The bride wealth legitimizes marriages and the children born to them (Skinner, 1986).

Dating back to the 14th century, the Galla-speaking peoples and the Swahili-speaking community on the Kenyan coast had contact with Muslims from the Arabian peninsula (Kurian, 1992, pp. 970–971, cited by African Studies Center). Today, about 7 percent of Kenyans are Muslim, over half of whom are of Somali origins (CIA).

In Skinner's assessment, African Islam has always been associated with urban life and those concomitants of urban life (crafts, industry, and commerce) that are the attributes of a complex civilization. In East Africa, Muslim ivory and slave traders functioned as Islamic missionaries (Skinner, 1986, p. 66). African Muslims have largely accepted Islamic marriage practices. The Shari'a's conception of marriage as a voluntary contract between individual spouses has been incorporated into the African practice of arranged marriages between two families. Only wealthy African Muslims can take advantage of the permission to marry four wives. The payment of the marriage settlement gives men full rights to spouses as sexual and domestic partners and to all children born of the union (Skinner, 1986, p. 67). Perhaps because the overwhelming majority of Kenyan population is not Muslim, the literature on Muslim families in Kenya is rather sparse.

Christianity entered East Africa linked to imperialism (Skinner, 1986, p. 69). The adoption of European notions of monogamy and family structure were a part of the dogma urged on converts, though polygyny continues to be a significant family form into the 21st century. But Western-educated persons, whether Christian or not, were encouraged by colonial governments to take only one lawful wife by ordinance. Such persons were able to take additional wives by customary marriage, but these marriages were not accepted by church or state. In contrast, some independent African churches argue that monogamy is more European than Christian and that polygyny should be fully accepted by Christianity in Africa.

According to Skinner (1986), most Christian and educated Africans consider the nuclear family to be the ideal domestic unit. A rather rigid gender-based division persists, whereby men and women work, socialize, and worship separately. Traditional practices, such as postpartum sexual taboos, are abandoned when conditions necessitate a change. Strong ties with extended families continue, as does the tendency of married couples to become closer to parents later in life in order to serve the needs of the family (Skinner, 1986, p. 72).

FAMILY RESEARCH IN KENYA

In the introduction to the 1997 collection of essays titled *African Families and the Crisis of Social Change,* Bradley and Weisner name a number of areas that draw the focus of recent writings, both academic and popular, on the crisis in the African family. These include "the disintegration of the multigenerational family, the breakdown of morals, the loss of economic viability, the dispersion of family members, and the loss of values, language, and cultural traditions in the wake of colonialism, modernization, and marginalization" (Weisner, Bradley, & Kilbride, 1997, p. xix). The authors focus on health, gender, children, the elderly, and population in western Kenya, especially among the Abaluhya, Kalenjin, Luo, and Gusii peoples.

The family circumstances described suggest several generalizations: that the institutional structures of Kenyan families are becoming more diverse but are still highly salient; that some functions, such as support and care for children, care of the elderly, control of property, health care, and nutritional status are strong as ever, although changing in form and perhaps not as homogeneous or as reliable as previously; that the state affects the economy and polity differently than when it directly impinges on the domestic world; and that family life has become more unstable as a result of migration and fertility change rather than as a result of change in the values of familism per se.

The important contribution of this book is its description of what family change means to Kenyans themselves, the different manifestations of change, and the shape of future resilience and continuity in the Kenyan family. The book offers a view that we are seeing selective crises that arise when, for a variety of reasons, family members can no longer effectively engage in the shared adaptive project—tied to customary, defended cultural models of family life experienced in the past and partially reinforced in the present—that is the heart of family life (Weisner, Bradley, & Kilbride, 1997, p. xxiv).

The literature on family in Kenya is often less positive than the previously cited collected volume. Recent coverage of the Abaluya people in Western Kenya serves as a good example of two divergent interpretations of a situation. In their 1990 monograph *Changing Family Life in East Africa: Women and Children at Risk,* the Kilbrides argue that political economy and values have interacted over time so that the "modernization of tradition" has meant loss of power for women and children in East Africa. Children are increasingly at risk because political-economic and value-cultural conditions are unfavorable to women and extended family life (Kilbride & Kilbride, 1990, p. 241).

In Kilbride and Kilbride's (1990) interpretation, the spread of capitalism in Kenya involved the introduction of only certain of the characteristic features, and was not completely established as a localized, total social system (p. 241). In the precapitalist society, kinship was the essential idiom of social relations embedded in a subsistence mode of production. Today, both kinship and the capitalistic element of monetary relations are salient, but often contradictory, idioms of social interaction. Being as highly valued as formerly, children are still cared and provided for, but nowadays they are costly in terms of clothing and schooling while their labor, although important, is less significant than in the past. The Kilbrides argue that one of the consequences of such a contradiction, itself resulting from delocalization in a peripheral capitalist economy, is child abuse and neglect (Kilbride & Kilbride, 1990, p. 242).

Abwunza (1997), on the other hand, sees the patriarchal system as persisting despite modernization and the accompanying changes in values and political economy. The author documents the ways in which increasing capitalism and commodification simultaneously empower and disempower women. Though many women posture an adherence to patriarchy, they realize the disproportionate burden it places on them. For their economic survival, the Avalogoli depend on women's work as well as on their decision making. And women, through their "back-door" decisions, have significant power to influence local as well as national events. Adherence to patriarchy is necessary, because it allows women to gain access to resources.

Much of the literature on family still focuses on the contrast between traditional (localized, enduring) and modern, delocalized systems in flux. This bipolar framework obscures the continuities between systems, which can be clarified with more long-term, longitudinal data. Very little research has been done on urban Kenyan families and households, with the exception of a focus on women's survival strategies for themselves and their children, including work in the sex industry (Nelson, 1987; White, 1990) and the illicit brewing and trading of alcohol.

The work of Kilbride and Kilbride is a good example of the poles of the dichotomy. Indigenous ideas were, on the whole, quite favorable to the status of children, adults, and both genders. They depict extended family and polygyny as essentially "positive" institutions that, regrettably, are showing signs of becoming delocalized in history and cultural meaning (Kilbride & Kilbride, 1990, p. 151). Contemporary life consists of "delocalized modernity." Forces such as industrialism, nationalism, missionary activity, formal education, and monetized economy have influenced marriage and family life, largely negatively. Economic delocalization is the assumed primary antecedent for the related processes of cultural and moral delocalization. Gender relations reflect the growing power disparity between men and women as modernization has proceeded. "Men and women are both, of course, comparatively 'powerless' in a delocalized economy compared to previous times, but the modern situation has become particularly acute for women" (Kilbride & Kilbride, 1990, p. 151).

CONCEPTUALIZATION OF KENYAN FAMILIES

One common feature of Kenyan family structure is polygyny, a structure that is reflected in the terms used to refer to other family members. The distinction between siblings is not necessarily based on a gender distinction, but terms indicate whether the sibling is a child of your mother or of your father by a different wife. Likewise, a child often has a term for mother and another term to indicate the 'little mother' or mother's co-wife (McCall, 1995, p. 177).

The family is more than a bond between people for the purpose of sexual union and child rearing. It is an institution for the organization of labor. The unit is often called a household, to designate a group of people who live together and recognize a common head of household. The household consists of a man, his wife or wives, and their children; but it can also include any number of their relations. A man with a large household has a sizeable labor force to mobilize. Because of his wealth in people he may be able to gain high status within his community. In more industrialized areas, alternatives to the agricultural life are becoming more available. As both men and women seek work in commerce, civil service, and education, the logic of polygyny appears less viable, particularly from the women's perspective. In urban areas, monogamous families are becoming more common, and in some cities women are actively advocating the reform of polygynous marriage practices (McCall, 1995, p. 178). Also evident is delocalized polygyny (Parkin, 1978) in which a man has one wife and children in the rural area, and one in the city.

Through the practice of polygyny the family extends to include multiple wives and their children. It likewise extends across generations to include elders. Children, particularly sons, are expected to take care of their parents when they become elderly. People strive to have many children and to assist them to become successful and wealthy, because these children are their legacy who will care for them in old age, give them a burial when they die, and keep their memory alive long after they have passed on. Children have considerable reason to honor these wishes, because it is through their parents that they secure rights to property and status in the community (McCall, 1995, p. 80).

The Gikuyu family has been envisioned as circular. Each new generation "replaces" their grandparents, who are then free to become ancestors (Davison, 1989, p. 19). The northern Gikuyu live in homesteads, located adjacent to their fields. Each homestead is enclosed by a hedge or log fence with a single entrance. Ideally, it contains the paternal head of family, his wife or wives, their unmarried children, often his married sons, and sometimes single male or female relatives. The Gikuyu are traditionally polygynous, but with the influence of Christianity and Western education, the trend has been toward monogamy. A polygynist is expected to provide bride wealth and a separate house for each wife within the homestead (Davison, 1989, p. 19).

Social ties are also significant in defining the family, especially ties created through the payment of bride wealth. Thus, for example, among the Kuria, a widow is expected to continue bearing children after the death of her spouse—children who are recognized as offspring of the deceased husband and belong to his lineage by virtue of the fact that he paid the bride wealth. They are not recognized as offspring of the genitor. A similar practice is found among the Nandi (Oboler, 1980).

Marriage is a key institution in the formation of the family, and is widely seen as a requisite step in the life course of any individual.

For African peoples, marriage is the focus of existence. It is the point where all members of a given community meet: the departed, the living and those yet to be born. All dimensions of time meet here, and the whole drama of history is repeated, rewarded and revitalised. Marriage is a drama in which everyone becomes an actor or actress and not just a spectator. Therefore, marriage is a duty, a requirement from the corporate society, a rhythm of life in which everyone must participate. Otherwise, he who does not participate in it is a curse to the community, he is a rebel and law breaker, he is not only abnormal but "under human." Failure to get married under normal circumstances means that the person concerned has rejected society and society rejects him in return. (Mbiti, 1969, p. 133, cited in Kuria, 1987, p. 288)

One of the great strivings continues to be to attain personal immortality, which is achieved through having children within the framework of a marriage.

Unless a person has close relatives to remember him, when he has physically died, then he is nobody and simply vanishes out of human existence like a flame when it is extinguished. Therefore it is a duty, religious and ontological for everyone to get married, and if a man has no children or only daughters, he finds another wife so that through her, children (or sons) may be born who would survive him and keep him (with other living dead of the family) in personal immortality. Procreation is the absolute way of insuring that a person is not cut off from personal immortality. (Mbiti, 1969, p. 26, cited in Kuria, 1987, p. 288)

After 1895, when Britain started developing Kenya as a settler colony, the English type of family law was introduced to govern the colonists and, throughout colonial rule, was changed to reflect the changes that took place in England. Legislation was enacted to enable the conversion of African marriage into the monogamous English type of marriage. After conversion, the family law of the colonists governed. Colonial administrators made no provision for conversion of a monogamous marriage into the customary potentially polygynous one "because it was unthinkable that anyone might wish to do that" (Kuria, 1987, p. 289).

In 1897, Britain established a legal system for Kenya through an order-in-council. That order-in-council envisaged that the four systems of family law—namely, customary, Islamic, English, and Hindu—had to be put in force in Kenya. At independence, it was decided that they should be put on a par and remain in force until a common way of life emerged when one family law would replace them. Each of them gives effect to the respective philosophy of life of the community to which it applies. Anyone in Kenya can opt for any of these four systems of family law (Kuria, 1987, p. 289).

African, or customary, marriage in Kenya takes many forms. The common type or the ideal comes into existence between a man and woman who have capacity to marry and comply with the formalities laid down by customary law. It may be monogamous, but the man can marry as many additional wives as he wishes. Customary law, like English law, permits a marriage to come into existence through exceptional circumstances, when formalities are not complied with. Marriage by elopement is an example (Kuria, 1987, p. 291).

Other forms of marriage are enacted to meet special needs. The leviratic union allows a brother to take over in all respects a man's obligations to the widow. The latter is not regarded by customary law as the wife of the levir. Widow inheritance allows a brother to inherit the widow of his brother and she is recognized as his wife. Woman-to-woman marriage allows a mother-in-law to pay bride wealth in order to gain a daughter-in-law who is married to a fictitious or deceased son and bears grandchildren for the mother-in-law. In a sororate union, on the death of a wife her sister replaces her as wife. In "forcible marriages" a man who only has daughters may prevent the youngest daughter from marrying so that she remains at home and has sons by a man or men of her choice. Finally, "child betrothals" allow parents to make arrangements for their daughter to marry a man of their choice when she becomes an adult. Today, woman-to-woman, forcible, and child betrothal marriages are unconstitutional, as enforcement of them would entail holding a party to them in servitude. By law, the leviratic union, widow inheritance, and sororate union may take place only with the consent of the woman concerned (Kuria, 1987, p. 291).

The relationships created by marriage, especially that between a husband and his wife, are basically social in nature. In the Kenyan context, they are paralleled, if not surpassed, in importance, by relationships based on descent or on biological ties, such as between parents and offspring.

The traditional African family is best understood as resulting from a principle of "consanguinity" or blood descent whereby social groups beyond the nuclear family are social units for economic cooperation. The children are links in a generational family ideology, and spouses are linked to each other by their reproduction of children for specific consanguineal groups of relatives. The significant family unit in Africanity is not the two-parent household but the extended family in some form. Moreover, African polygyny results in an emphasis within the household where wives and their husband, or wives together, or mother and children, in addition to the husband-and-wife unit, are economically functional family relationships. (Kilbride & Kilbride, 1990, p. 242)

The family requires cultural definition, spilling over as it does in African contexts to the community (Abwunza, 1997, p. 185). But certain elements are widely shared by the various ethnic groups in Kenya. Chief among these are bride wealth and polygyny (Parkin & Nyamwaya, 1987, pp. 10–11). Bride wealth continues to be an institution of central significance, in spite of the many changes it is undergoing. Most commonly, as for the Iteso in western Kenya, these include a change in the mode of transfer, from full payment before or within a relatively short period after commencement of cohabitation to prolonged and piecemeal payments over many years, and the introduction of cash as a part of the bride wealth in addition to the traditional component of cattle and goats (Nagashima, 1987, pp. 183–84).

As the practice of bride wealth is changing with time, so is the practice of polygyny. Though highly valued in traditional conceptions, the Demographic and Health Survey tells us that the actual practice of polygyny continues to decline in Kenya. "Sixteen percent of currently married women are in a polygynous union (i.e., their husband has at least one other wife), compared with 19 percent of the women in the 1993 KDHS, 23 percent in the 1989 KDHS, and 30 percent in the 1977/78 KFS" (Republic of Kenya, 1998, p. xvii).

From the point of view of youth a different perspective emerges.[1] In 1988, 54 percent of the girls surveyed had polygynous fathers, and 46 percent of the boys. In 1993, 50 percent of the girls and 30 percent of the boys had fathers with more than one wife. At neither point in time did any of the girls want to have a husband with more than one wife. At both points in time, 10 percent of the boys wanted to have more than one wife when they grew up, showing a quite remarkable consistency over time in the ideas of the youth.

Mate Selection

In Kenya, mate selection is generally up to the young people, though often the timing is not. A young man may be told the time has come for him to find a wife because bride wealth is available, usually following the marriage of a sister. Or a young woman may be told by her father that a suitor is offering bride wealth in order to marry her, and that he (and her mother) would like her to consider the suitor. In the opinion poll, 53 percent of the girls and 63 percent of the boys in 1993 thought their father would tell them when they should marry. In 1988, 62 percent of the girls and 60 percent of the boys thought so.

A young man will set out to identify eligible girls, and to examine them for the characteristics he considers important in a wife. For boys, the most important characteristic for a wife is to be obedient, in 1993 for 55 percent of the boys and in 1988 for 76 percent of the boys. For girls, the most important characteristic for a husband is to be hardworking (in 1993, 71 percent) and to be from a good family (in 1988, 38 percent).

Couples might decide to marry as a result of prior meetings, in which they have had the opportunity to examine one another, to see each other's behavior, temperament, and social skills. Or a boy, seeking a wife, might discuss with a friend or a brother that he is looking for a wife. The friend might help him identify eligible women, and sometimes even act as a go-between in arranging a meeting. Both these practices are common among the Kuria people, for whom the marriage process for a young man is often initiated by the receipt of bride wealth cattle by his father from the marriage of a daughter. Anxious lest they be lost through raiding, the father urges his son to find a wife, soon.

In many parts of Kenya, the first step to marriage is bride wealth discussion. The exchange of bride wealth—a gift of goods (especially cattle) and money from the husband to his new wife's family—usually accompanies marriage, and continues to be seen as a significant aspect of marriage, and the beginning of affinal reciprocity (Abwunza, 1997, p. 103). Bride wealth is seen as a way of repaying a girl's natal family for the care with which she was brought up, and the amount given often reflects the level of education the girl has attained. It is also, quite significantly, the means by which lineage affiliation of offspring is secured, and their rights to a share in land and livestock assured. Bride wealth in cattle is advantageous to women in two main ways: first by providing a direct economic asset, and second as a means of generating kinship categories or units, which are a basic source of security for women and their children (Ngubane, 1987, p. 173).

Due to the difficulties in bride wealth discussions and payment, couples often elope, as Abwunza describes for the Maragoli. Bride wealth presents a paradox.

[A]ll women were adamant that *uvukwi* [bride wealth] should be paid, and men agreed. Most people recognize that adherence to the institution of uvukwi is difficult given the lack of finances. . . . Uvukwi is an impossibility for most ordinary people. Many men and most women in rural areas do not have access to wage labor, and even if they do, wages do not allow for this kind of expenditure. (Abwunza, 1997, p. 108)

Women acknowledge that bride wealth payments provide reason for the continuance of reciprocity, of the gift giving and receiving that allows some institutions to continue to function smoothly. Abwunza cites women from Friend's Church as saying,

It is the reward for parents and the young man feels very proud for having given *uvukwi*. It is another system of saying, "this is my wife." If not, the wife can say, these are not your children. In death, the parents would demand the body and children, even if there were ten children. Even if one cow is given, it makes the difference. (Abwunza, 1997, p. 108)

Bride wealth is seen as assisting family at the parental home the bride is leaving. It also gives strength to the married girl because she is seen as someone with power, not just someone picked from the market (Abwunza, 1997, p. 108). In fact, girls take pride in the number of cattle that are given to their fathers as bride wealth. The youth agree that the tradition of marriage dowry should continue as it is practiced. In 1993, 71 percent of the girls and 60 percent of the boys thought so, a response quite similar to that given in 1988, when 77 percent of the girls and 57 percent of the boys thought that the paying of bride wealth should continue. Bride wealth also binds the woman to her husband's family. In case of marital disharmony, it prevents her from being able to leave with her children, which is possible only if her natal family returns the bride wealth cattle, which have, of course, been used by her brothers to secure wives for themselves.

Multiple Marriage Forms

In Kenya, a woman can be married under the four systems of family law identified earlier. Each marriage system imbues values that are peculiar to the particular community they are meant to serve. But they all share some common features. In almost all the communities in Kenya, custom bestows a husband with rights over his wife's reproductive and productive capacity as well as the custody and control of children from the union (Gituto & Kabira, 1998, p. 36). Because of this, she has no control over the allocation of family income, which limits her ability and opportunity to partake her role in the marital union as an equal. Further, she is prevented from engaging in the larger, extrafamilial society on an equal basis with men. Therefore, according to these authors, "customary marriage shields the woman from enjoying other basic protections under the bill of rights and section 82[3]" (Gituto & Kabira, 1998, p. 37). They maintain that many women experience a customary domestic regime that provides "a most inhuman environment for the woman.... In consequence the home is the most dangerous environment for the Kenyan woman" (Gituto & Kabira, 1998, p. 37).

Nagashima (1987) maintained that changes in bride wealth payments mean that many couples cohabit before any payment is made to the bride's family. Gituto and Kabira blame the marriage law system for the fact that nearly half of all couples in Kenya's urban centers are cohabiting without being married (Gituto & Kabira, 1998, pp. 37–38). They argue one of the main reasons for cohabitation is financial insecurity for the female. In cases of extreme poverty, such as in the urban slums, a woman may cohabit with several men simultaneously. Each of these men will provide for specific needs, such as rent, food, clothing, and so on. In some cases, a woman will lie to a man that he has fathered one of her children in order to maintain the security of her relationship with him. Women in such unions will tolerate great cruelty in order to maintain the relationship on which their livelihood depends. To support their sense of the prevalence of this situation, the authors claim 80 percent of the urban population in Nairobi live in extreme poverty, with 70 percent of the estimated 3 million inhabitants living in the slums (Gituto & Kabira, 1998, p. 38).

In the ideal scenario, marriage ought to be organized and overseen by parents, and by all elder relatives. The importance of the lineage and extended family context within which individual marriages take place is central to the argument Kilbride and Kilbride (1990, p. 60) make. They see the cultural ideology of kin-based support groups as retained from premodern times, and currently being challenged by the values introduced from delocalized capitalism. In their study of Abaluhya family structure in sisal estates, 63 percent consisted of extended families, of which the most frequent type was the stem family, consisting of a female-headed household (husband absent) with her affines (relatives by marriage) and her consanguines (blood relatives), especially grandchildren (Kilbride & Kilbride, 1990, p. 62). Extended families serve as a support network in time of crisis such as sickness, death, and food shortage (Kilbride & Kilbride, 1990, p. 62; Abwunza, 1997, p. 99).

Childbearing, Patriarchy, and Intergenerational Ties

Kenya had the highest natural increase in population ever recorded in the world for a single country. Measured at 3.8 percent annually in 1980–88 and 4 percent in the mid-1990s (Abwunza, 1997, p. 134), it is at present estimated at 2.9 percent per annum (Republic of Kenya, 2001, Vol. 1, p. xxx.). Despite the great emphasis placed on family planning, and the fertility transition that has already taken place, the population of the country continues to increase. Fertility levels remain high, though Kenyan women have experienced a steady decline in total fertility level, from 8.1 in 1977–78 to 6.7 in 1989 (Abwunza, 1997, p. 136), and 4.7 in 1998 (Republic of Kenya, 1999, p. xvii).

Agrarian societies value large families. The system in place is promoted and sustained by labor needs in rural areas and ties to a subsistence mode of production that depends on large families. Men migrate to urban areas to seek work (Abwunza, 1997, p. 137), or fail to help with women's work. Agriculture and home work (women's work) are labor-intensive, and women thus need children to help them. Patronage relationships based on ethnicity and kinship are vital to gaining access to resources, jobs, schooling, or money. Children are valuable assets even in urban areas, especially because people face economic risk (Abwunza, 1997, p. 138).

The Kenyan government continues to promote measures to curb the rate of population increase. Yet the effectiveness of campaigns varies by area and socioeconomic status. In some areas, high fertility preferences remain among farmers where the requirements for human labor are significant and rates of infant mortality also threaten. In other areas, the cost of children is being recognized as outstripping the abilities of the families to provide for them. The difference is clearly demonstrated in terms of total fertility rate. In 1998, rural women could expect to bear 2 children more than urban women (5.2 as compared to 3.1 children, respectively), and educated women 2.3 children fewer than uneducated women (3.5 as compared to 5.8 children, respectively) (Republic of Kenya, 1999, p. xvii).

Patriarchal values continue to prevail in most of Kenyan society. Gender roles are clearly defined, and activities of the sexes take place within different and distinct spheres. This is especially true in rural areas, where everyday life for men and women occurs largely in the performance of work defined according to a gender-based division of labor. However, as Seppala (1993) argues for the Bukusu, "[i]t is a simplification to speak of sexual division of labour. One could also speak of gendered division of consumption, ownership, spatial order, etc." (p. 77). She goes on to argue that behind the flexibility of actual behavior there is a strict division according to the spheres of responsibility which are often hierarchically organized. As these rigid delineations are increasingly undermined by the demands of producing for and within the global economy, gender relations continue to be politicized by patriarchal values that both men and women posture. Writing about Maragoli, Abwunza (1997) explains that women posture an acceptance of patriarchy for men's benefit as well as their own because it provides them with the ideological basis for structuring their own reputations. "Good Logoli wives" adhere to patriarchal ideology. Gaining a reputation as "good wives" permits their access to the collectivity necessary for survival in today's stressful economic situation (Abwunza, 1997, p. 184).

Abwunza (1997) describes how women in Maragoli move between collective and capitalist modes using the same cultural avenues for accessing resources and amassing power. Their cultural posture of submission in fact denotes a recognition of the avenues of their power. When analyzed in research findings, this posture has led to women's power being identified as informal, a mere strategy, or second order of power. But as she points out, not recognizing that women posture an acceptance of patriarchy as an astute social action may have provided the mistaken contexts in which some research has portrayed African women as "oppressed, "under valued," or as a "dependent class" (Abwunza, 1997, p. 184).

In today's Maragoli, women are conscious that their best interests may no longer be served by assuming a posture of ideological and institutional acceptance of patriarchy. A reduction of value in men's labor and a recognition of its ineffectiveness reveal that men are impotent rulers who do not act in the best interests of those they rule. The assumptions of patriarchal sentiment are symbolic statements for the way things used to be for both women and men. Participation in the cultural expression of patriarchy still provides women with some benefits, but also with increased gender inequality. Thus, women may change the way they relate to the structures of patriarchy. The increase of back-door decisions points to an increase in the degree to which men are unable to maintain patriarchal control. Men's increased violence on the home front speaks directly to the demise of patriarchy. (Abwunza, 1997, p. 184)

Writing in 1980, Obbo recognized the gender struggle taking place among urban Luo. She described how religious movements were used by men as a mechanism for controlling women, by inducing them to confess their financial sources of income or holdings.

This was obviously an attempt to deal with the threat to male dominance that resulted from women acquiring independent incomes. Like women from other ethnic groups, Luo women not only wanted an independent income, but were willing to seek it through employment or by misappropriating the housekeeping money. (Obbo, 1980, p. 119)

As participants in the economic sphere, women's opportunities and options are determined by the positions they occupy within the family structure. For this reason, descent systems and residential rules governing married people greatly affect the strategies and options available to women (Obbo, 1980, p. 33). For most Kenyan ethnic groups, descent is traced through the male line. Marital residential patterns tend to be virilocal, the wife living with her husband and his people, or neolocal, where the married couple establish themselves, independent of relatives (usually in a move to an urban area).

Bride wealth and polygyny are key to the dynamics of the descent system. Bride wealth in the form of cattle and money is given to the bride's people, and in exchange the woman's sexual and reproductive powers are surrendered to the man and his lineage. The children belong to the husband irrespective of who has begotten them. The social father (*pater*) in his role as husband counts for much more than the adulterous genitor. For the Nilotic peoples, in the case of illegitimate children, the woman's male relatives claimed custody of the women's children and the biological father's rights to custody and filiation were only transferred upon the payment of compensation (Obbo, 1980, p. 34).

Divorce is rare but separations are common. The latter do not bother men because women are not allowed to take their children. The elders usually work hard to reconcile the separated couple and to discourage divorce, which is very complicated. The wife is expected to labor in the growing and preparing of food, reproduction of children and their rearing and socializing, and sexual partnership, as services to her husband.

Upon marriage, the wife lives and identifies closely with her husband's lineage group and her links with the group into which she was born weaken. Among the Nilotic peoples, widows were inherited by a brother or son of another wife of the deceased husband. In most of the ethnic groups, women owned no property, having only right of usage over land for purposes of providing food for the family. Since women were outsiders to the descent system, they were excluded from ownership because land had to circulate within the family (Obbo, 1980, p. 34).

Most women have some access to cash, whether through the sale of their labor, or the crops they produce, or from trade. They do not automatically hand cash gained through exchange to their husbands, although the demand is usually made. More commonly, they avoid these demands by spending available cash purchasing commodities like tea, sugar, and kerosene, paying for school fees or buying uniforms.

There is an assumption among Maragoli people that women "always" have cash, but that women choose when to give money. Some husbands ask, demand, search and beat for the money they are sure wives have hidden away.... Women's self-image and community reputation is enhanced as their cash and commodity flow circulates the network of reciprocal relations. Their ability to provide an advantage to their children is also increased. Money for school fees comes from both mothers and fathers, and is given to both daughters and sons.... In return, they [daughters and sons] will contribute to the exchange network that which has been offered to them, and sometimes even more. (Abwunza, 1997, p. 101)

Polygyny afforded some women leverage within a male-dominated descent system. Women, as mothers, were necessary for the formation of the lineage descent lines since there could be no recruitment of men by descent without the nuclear families headed by wives as mothers, who were themselves recruited by marriage. Jealousy between co-wives who form the segments of a polygynous family is generally expected, and some societies, such as the Luo, institutionalize it (Obbo, 1980, p. 34). Each woman with her children forms a matrifocal residential unit (referred to as a "matrisegment" by Seppala, 1993, p. 81) that competes with the other residential units within the family for resources and the husband's patronage. The matrisegment is the basic unit for production and consumption, and for the devolution of marriage cattle, but importantly, not of land (Sepalla, 1993, p. 81). The relationship between matrisegments has been described as one of complementary opposition between segments of the lineage (headed by wives) that are coordinated to form minor lineages headed by the father/husband (Obbo, 1980, p. 34).

In Kenyan families men are the decision makers. The dominant ideology supports the authority and power of men over women, the rights of men to treat women as they wish (including physical abuse), and to benefit from their labor, support, and incomes. Central to this sentiment is the right of men to make decisions and the obligation of women to obey (Abwunza, 1997, p. 87).

Husbands are generally more educated than their wives and, due to migrant work and contacts, have knowledge on many practical issues and traits of the wider world. Their male friends are persons to share these issues. Males represent the ethics of the wider world and its consumption patterns, and an alternative for the domestic group as a culture group of reference. A wife does not generally have such a strong alternative reference group (Seppala, 1993, p. 77). Children carry responsibilities toward their parents, especially when they grow up. "Your child is the supporting stick of your back" (Abwunza, 1997, p. 99). Additionally, children are responsible for making "[their parents] name go up, in that children should 'buy this for me' or 'build this for me.'"

The respect for and the importance of the old has been a paramount element of customary ideas, and is a significant aspect of Africanity. In the largely acephalous ethnic groups of Kenya, power and authority were traditionally vested in the elders of the community (especially males), and this continues, despite the posited possibility for weakening intergenerational interdependence among family members in the market-oriented, postcolonial society of today. The beginnings of pressure from modernization and Westernization to undermine the relatively comfortable position the elderly enjoyed in traditional society because of the disintegration of the extended family and the system of mutual obligations was seen already in the 1980s (Khasiani, 1987, p. 118). Current research, especially that spanning significant periods of time (e.g., Sangree, 1997) shows a much more positive picture, confirming the continued important status of elders. "Tiriki elders enjoy perhaps a higher overall status today than they did . . . in 1954–56" (Sangree, 1997, p. 204). Their management of the extended-family homestead farm and the care of resident grandchildren allow the elders to manifest their authority and affirm their continuing high status in the local community. It also allows their children to pursue the wage earning off-farm endeavors. In Kenya, where there is no alternative to family support, Cattell (1997) shows that extended families, though overstretched and often with inadequate resources, continue to be the primary support system for vulnerable members, including children and the elderly.

CHALLENGES FOR CONTEMPORARY KENYAN FAMILIES

Modernization, Urbanization, and Family Stability

The general trend is to see modernization and urbanization as undermining family stability. Kilbride and Kilbride (1990) argue that normative (and positive) interrelated patterns of child care remain to some extent in East Africa today, as do a reliance on the extended family for support, a subsistence economy with women and men as agriculturalists, and a moral system with elders as moral leaders. But a systematic breakdown in this social pattern is becoming apparent with the advent of a monetary economy through "delocalization." One consequence of this is that child abuse and neglect are becoming more prevalent throughout Kenya. Many males have less power than in the past, due, as in the case of women, to changing social, educational, and economic circumstances associated with delocalization. For this reason, some men are avoiding the burdens of expensive child care responsibilities. The modern condition is particularly stressful for women, given that the gender imbalance in power is far more threatening than in the past, when social control was less individualistic and more in the hands of the collectivity.

This premise is held not only with regard to Kenya, but with respect to most African nations. In the 2001 collection of essays on women and children in southern and eastern Africa edited by Rwomire, the essays unfold against the backdrop of growing poverty, disease, exploitation, and oppression in various spheres of their lives. The focus on women and children as victims places the men in a very awkward and uncomfortable spot, and renders the family asunder.

There is no doubt that the penetration of the world economic system poses great challenges, and the strains and conflicts generated by this intrusive change have themselves generated further changes (Siegel, 1996, p. 238). The family is threatened, for children are less dependent on parents and less mindful of filial obligations; the social importance of producing children has diminished; husbands are not so dependent on their wives; and the family is less intimately connected with other social groupings (Schapera, cited in Siegel, 1996, p. 239). Migrant labor or cash cropping presumes a monetized economy, and this entails economic individualism and commoditization of social relations (Siegel, 1996, p. 239). However,

> Reports concerning the death of the extended family are ... both exaggerated and premature. It is often claimed, for example, that the extended family system is an obstacle to economic development and that the obligatory diversion of scarce resources to assist less fortunate relatives is not only wasteful but discourages entrepreneurship and capital accumulation. (Siegel, 1996, p. 239)

The strain of extended family obligations is felt most strongly by the urban and educated African elite, since they often constitute the first and most important resource—both for food and lodging and personal contacts for relatives who graduate from school or have to leave school to seek work in town. Such hospitality is a financial and emotional drain, and it tends to wear thin over time (Siegel, 1996, p. 239; Harden, 1990, Chap. 2). But the strength of family ties and obligations varies between groups. The Luo rely on their urban relatives for assistance, and are famous for the strong patrilineal organization that links urban and rural kin (Parkin, 1978).

African elites are generally tied to their rural kin. Most send some money home—at least to the parents or other kin who reared them. The elite may entrust their children to their parents' care back home (Sangree, 1997; Cattell, 1997). Others provide school fees and lodging for their own or for classificatory siblings, and provide accommodations for relatives visiting the hospital or market. The gifts of food these visitors bring are a welcome supplement to the household diet. Elite wives maintain extended family ties to recruit relatives for household and child care assistance when they are away at work. Elite men maintain their family ties so they can retire among their relatives at home, or to claim a share of land (Oppong, 1981, cited in Siegel, 1996, p. 242).

Extended family ties often place a real emotional strain on African elite marriages, particularly between the wife and her in-laws. The partners in such marriages are often from different ethnic groups, and the husband's kin may, if they disapprove of the wife's background, do everything to sabotage the marriage (Schuster, 1979, cited in Siegel, 1996, p. 242). In turn, the wife may object when her lower-class in-laws insist on their customary rights to coresidence, property and financial maintenance. Paring down extended family obligations in an attempt to realize the Euro-American model of the closed and cooperative nuclear family is an elusive goal for the first-generation African elite who have little previous experience with geographical and social mobility, but is far easier for the rare second- and third-generation members of the African elite (Siegel, 1996, p. 242). The legal case involving S. M. Otieno, discussed below, stands as a case in point.

In 1986 and 1987, a major family and legal feud surrounded the death of a prominent Kenyan lawyer, S. M. Otieno. The case, which brought forth special editions of newspapers for the months that it raged, has been covered to a corresponding extent in academic literature (see, e.g., Stamp, 1991; Cohen & Odhiambo, 1992; Gordon, 1995).[2] Much of the discourse centers on issues of family, lineage, marriage, and gender. The themes drawn out deal with the dynamic nature of "custom" and "tradition," the relations between the governing regime and the politically powerful elements of society, and struggles over "tradition" and women's place (Stamp, 1991). According to Harden (1990), "[t]he case cut to a fundamental fault line in the African psyche: the rub between tribal tradition and modern, mostly Western, values" (p. 100). At stake in the case was the burial of Otieno, a deceased lawyer, who had lived his life in Nairobi, married a wife from a different ethnic group, and was fully separate from the people of his lineage. He raised his many children to see "tradition" as negative, and embraced modernity as a way of life for himself and his nuclear family. After his death, the lineage came forth to fight the wife's insistence that Otieno be buried in his chosen site, rather than on lineage land. The case took over 150 days to settle, involved reams of testimony from scores of witnesses, and pitted modern ideas versus tradition. In this case, tradition won. The wishes of the lawyer, his wife, and children were not honored. The lineage and its interpretation of tradition prevailed.

Tradition is also invoked to justify abuse. Abwunza argues that given the effects of the capitalist market and the disadvantage this introduces for men, women's influence is actually growing in Maragoli, where the power from the front door (yielded by men) is being increasingly questioned by women as the power from the back door (yielded by women) expands. Men often respond to these changes by retaliating. For some men, women's independence has gone too far. When interviewed on the subject of conjugal abuse, 43 percent of the women in Abwunza's study said they were physically abused by their husbands. Another 52 percent said that although physical abuse was infrequently experienced, incidents of abuse were increasing. Men provided an economic rationale for this by saying that women "harass" men for support while they "only laze around" (Abwunza, 1997, p. 119).

Conflicts within families spill over into the collectivity. Consanguines and affines debate about who should provide resources and how the resources should be distributed. Wives complain of husbands not sharing resources they receive from relatives and affines. Husbands complain that wives are hiding gifts, or that their provision of food to relatives and affines leaves the home yard without food. Women and men both complain that children do not provide them with support or argue about how much each should receive if support is given, accusing each other of hiding the "real" amount provided. Children in contexts such as these accuse parents of having "big pockets that never get filled" (Abwunza, 1997, p. 121).

Notwithstanding the difficulties that patriarchal ideology and capitalist systems impose, women are increasingly taking a central role in production. The expectation that women should provide sustenance for their own families continues to permeate the kinship network, and women are using the cultural rules to empower themselves, in Maragoli, gaining in the process considerable economic and political power in relationships with men (Abwunza, 1997, p. 121). "Women keep kinship networks working for them, fulfill their 'home work' responsibilities, and engage in 'outside' work. Their ability to access avenues of reciprocity provides the economic basis for the survival of Avalogoli society. This represents a power for women that men fully recognize. Women are vigilant caretakers of patriarchal ideology to the extent that this sentiment is productive in their everyday lives. Today, women are beginning to speak of the unfairness contained in this sentiment" (Abwunza, 1997, p. 122).

The HIV/AIDS Crisis and Family Health

One of the most serious contemporary challenges to the Kenyan family is the spread of HIV/AIDS. According to the government (Republic of Kenya, 1999, p. 127), 1 in 11 adults is infected with HIV. In June 1997, it was estimated that over 240,000 people in Kenya had already developed AIDS since 1984, when the first AIDS case was reported, although officially only 80,000 cases of AIDS had been reported to the Ministry of Health. Currently, it is estimated that about 1,325,000 adults and 90,000 children are HIV infected (Republic of Kenya, 1999, p. 127). According to data broadcast by the Kenya Broadcasting Corporation, 1.5 million people had died by the end of 2001. One in eight adults in rural Kenya are HIV infected, and one in five adults in the urban area are infected. In the same broadcast, Diana Baruch of USAID said that 2,000,000 Kenyans live with HIV, and 200,000 have AIDS (Kenya Broadcasting Corporation, English Broadcast, "Special Feature," January 9, 2002).[3]

In Kenya, the principal mode of HIV transmission is through heterosexual contact, which accounts for 75 percent of all HIV infections in Kenya. This is followed in importance by perinatal transmission, whereby the mother passes the HIV virus to the child during pregnancy or around the time of birth. Approximately 30 percent of babies born to HIV-positive mothers are infected with the HIV virus in Kenya; the remainder (70 percent) may not become infected with HIV but are at risk of becoming orphans once one or both parents die from AIDS. In 1998, over 70 percent of men and women reported that they knew someone with AIDS or who had died from AIDS, up from 40 percent in 1993 (Republic of Kenya, 1999, p. 142). Also, 14 percent of women and 17 percent of men reported that they had already been tested for HIV/AIDS (Republic of Kenya, 1999, p. 156). KDHS respondents who had heard of AIDS were asked whether they had changed their sexual behavior since they learned about the disease in order to avoid getting AIDS; 23 percent of women and 10 percent of men said that they had not changed their sexual behavior. The most common way for those who changed was to limit sex to one partner, or to fewer partners for men. Broken down further, respondents with a low educational level and respondents living in rural areas were more likely not to have changed their sexual behavior than their urban counterparts. In rural areas, 23 percent of women and 11 percent of men had not changed their behavior, compared with 16 percent and 7 percent, respectively, in urban areas (Republic of Kenya, 1999, p. 148).

The conclusions that Ocholla-Ayayo draws (1997, p. 121) from his long-term study of the problem is that Kenyans' view of premarital and extramarital sexual relations has changed, so that relationships that were unacceptable in the past are now widely practiced in the modern setting, an artifact of modernization and Westernization. Although AIDS awareness is high, indiscriminate sexual activity has not declined. The long-term implications of heightened mortality of the most productive segment of the population, the problems associated with growing numbers of orphans, and the strain on family resources and structures that is beginning to entail are areas not yet fully studied in the Kenyan context.

Kielmann (1997) critiques the "authoritative Western medical paradigm of 'African AIDS' [that] crystallized the identities of 'prostitutes in Africa,' without reference to indigenous notions of identity, behavior, risk and health, and identified women as the locus of infection." Imposed on lay populations for whom these categories fluctuate with the social context and subjective content of individual lives and perceptions, the efficacy of prevention programs is limited (Kielmann, 1997, p. 377).

CONCLUSION

The demographic transition theory holds that large African households will gradually diminish in size due to the changing demands, structures, and opportunities in modernizing societies. Further, the growing acceptance of Western economic and social directives is seen as leading to a rationalization of the family that will transform from the large, extended, polygynous unit to the small, nuclear variety found in the developed world. Though the Demographic and Health Surveys show that statistically this is the trend in Kenya, some scholars rightly observe that this has not happened uniformly (Moloo, 1996; Wortham, 1999; Weinreb, 2001). Even where modernizing influences are redirecting the energy and efforts of family members, family size and composition often remain unchanged (Prazak, 2000). Development in Kenya is not following the same track as European countries took in their transformation to capitalism. There is no reason to expect that the role and importance of family should go through the same processes of nucleation as took place in Western Europe. Despite these predictions, the African family continue to be one of the strongest institutions on the continent (Harden, 1990), and Kenyan families are no exception to that.

First, conditions leading to nucleation of the family unit in Europe involved a series of transformative processes, including enclosure of lands and migration for work in manufacturing, that have no broad parallel in Kenya. As we have seen, the pattern of migration for work and opportunity is well established in Kenya. Yet for the migrant, the tie to ancestral lands remains strong and unconstrained. Second, while the demand for labor and the scarcity of employment in rural areas stimulate migration, migration does not presently erode the underpinning sociocultural structure of extended family, community, and ethnic culture.

The diversity of sociocultural systems and communities in Kenya creates a national context that validates the extended family and its importance as a central and fundamental part of successful economic and social functioning. Kenyan families respond to the socioeconomic and political contexts within which they operate. But these demands on the family so far have not changed or weakened the customary roles and functions of families. The family continues to be the locus of social direction, including norms and behaviors, and it integrates external socioeconomic changes with locally generated customs and beliefs. It projects values, opportunities, concerns, and future direction for mainstreamed as well as marginalized members of society. As such, family in Kenya is both the signpost and the shaping influence of social change.

The extended family structure in Kenya faces pressures from education and salaried work, migration, globalized capitalism, and cultural devaluation. However, the fundamental benefits of extended family—as a source of wealth, productivity, and distribution of goods and opportunities; as a sociocultural bulwark and integrator of change; and as a regulator of childbearing and interpersonal relationships—have not been replaced by any other institutions.

NOTES

1. These data were gathered by the author in opinion polls conducted in a day in October 1993 and November 1988 of Standard 8 students attending school on that day. In 1993, 62 girls and 134 boys participated. In 1988, 26 girls and 106 boys answered the poll. The respondents were in all the schools in the administrative locations inhabited by the Abairege clan of the Kuria people in Nyanza province in southwestern Kenya.

2. There are over 10,000 entries in reference to this case at the Library of Congress.

3. These data deserve to be treated cautiously, as the most common single source of knowledge about AIDS is the radio (Republic of Kenya, 1999, p. 136).

REFERENCES

Abwunza, J. M. (1997) *Women's voices, women's power: Dialogues of resistance from East Africa*. Ontario: Broadview.

Brass, W., & Jolly, C. (Eds.). (1993). *Population dynamics of Kenya*. Washington, DC: National Academy Press.

Cattell, M. (1997). The discourse of neglect: Family support for the elderly in Samia. In Weisner, T. S., Bradley, C., & Kilbride, P. L. (Eds.), *African families and the crisis of social change* (pp. 157–183). Westport, CT: Bergin & Garvey.

Cohen, D. W., & Odhiambo, A. E. S. (1992). *Burying SM: The politics of knowledge of the sociology of power in Africa*. London: Currey.

Cross, A. R., Obungu, W., & Kizito, P. (1991). Evidence of a transition to lower fertility in Kenya. *International Family Planning Perspectives 17(1)*, 4–7.

Davison, J. (1989). *Voices from Mutira: Lives of rural Gikuyu women*. Boulder, CO: Lynne Rienner.

Dow, T. E., Archer, L., Khasiani, S., & Kekevole, J. (1994). Wealth flow and fertility decline in rural Kenya, 1981–92. *Population and Development Review 20(2)*, 343–364.

Gatabaki, N. (1983). *Twenty great years of independence: 1963–1983*. Nairobi: Productions and Communications.

Gituto, B. M., & Kabira, W. M. (1998). *Affirmative action: The promise of a new dawn*. Nairobi: Collaborative Centre for Gender and Development.

Gordon, A. (1995). Gender, ethnicity, and class in Kenya: "Burying Otieno" revisited. *Signs 20*, 883–912.

Harden, B. (1990). *Africa: Dispatches from a fragile continent*. Boston: Houghton Mifflin.

Kenyatta, J. (1965). *Facing Mt. Kenya: The tribal life of the Gikuyu*. New York: Vintage Books.

Khasiani, S. A. (1987). The role of the family in meeting the social and economic needs of the aging population in Kenya. *Genus 43(3–4)*, 103–120.

Kielmann, K. (1997). "Prostitution," "risk," and "responsibility": Paradigms of AIDS prevention and women's identities in Thika, Kenya. In *The anthropology of infectious disease: International health perspectives*. Amsterdam: Gordon and Breach.

Kilbride, P. L., & Kilbride, J. C. (1990). *Changing family life in East Africa: Women and children at risk*. University Park & London: Pennsylvania State University Press.

Kuria, G. K. (1987). The African or customary marriage in Kenyan law today. In Parkin, D. & Nyamwaya, D. (Eds.), *Transformations of African marriage* (pp. 283–306). Manchester, Eng.: Manchester University Press.

Kurian, G. T. (1992). *Encyclopedia of the Third World* (4th ed.), Vol. 3. New York: Facts on File. Cited at http://www.sas.upenn.edu/African_Studies/NEH/k-relig.html.

Mbithi, J. (1969). *African religions and philosophy*. Nairobi: Heinemann.

McCall, J. C. (1995). Social organization in Africa. In Martin, P. M. & O'Meara, P. (Eds.), *Africa* (3rd ed., pp. 175–189). Bloomington: Indiana University Press.

Moloo, P. W. (1996). Women's position and fertility: The case of Asians in Kenya. In *Shifting Circles of Support: Contextualizing gender and kinship in South Asia and sub-Saharan Africa*. Walnut Creek, CA: Altamira.

Nagashima, N. (1987). Aspects of change in bridewealth among the Iteso of Kenya. In Parkin, D. & Nyamwaya, D. (Eds.), *Transformations of African marriage* (pp. 183–198). Manchester, Eng.: Manchester University Press.

Nelson, N. (1987). "Selling Her Kiosk": Kikuyu notions of sexuality and sex for sale in Mathare valley, Kenya. In Caplan, P. (Ed.), *The cultural construction of sexuality* (pp. 217–239). London: Tavistock.

Ngubane, H. (1987). The consequences for women of marriage payments in a society with patrilineal descent. In Parkin, D. & Nyamwaya, D. (Eds.), *Transformations of African marriage* (pp. 173–182). Manchester, Eng.: Manchester University Press.

Obbo, C. (1980). *African women: Their struggle for economic independence*. London: Zed Books.

Oboler, R. S. (1980). Is the female husband a man? Woman/woman marriage among the Nandi of Kenya. *Ethnology 19*, 69–88.

Ocholla-Ayayo, A. B. C. (1997). HIV/AIDS risk factors and changing sexual practices in Kenya. In Weisner, T. S., Bradley, C., & Kilbride, P. L. (Eds.), *African families and the crisis of social change* (pp. 109–124). Westport, CT: Bergin & Garvey.

Oppong, C. (1981). *Middle-class African marriage: A family study of Ghanaian senior civil servants*. London: Allen & Unwin.

Parkin, D. (1978). *The cultural definition of political response: Lineal destiny among the Luo*. London: Academic.

Parkin, D., & Nyamwaya, D. (1987). *Transformations of African marriage*. Manchester, Eng.: Manchester University Press.

Prazak, M. (2000). Seeds of continuity, lines of change: Families and work in rural Kenya. *Anthropology of Work Review XXI(4)*, 21–30.

Republic of Kenya, Central Bureau of Statistics, Ministry of Finance and Planning. (2001). *1999 population and housing census: Counting our people for development*. Volumes I & II. Nairobi, Kenya: Government Printer.

Republic of Kenya, National Council for Population and Development, Central Bureau of Statistics (Office of the Vice President & Ministry of Planning & National Development), & Macro International Inc. (1994). *Kenya demographic and health survey 1993*. Calverton, MD: NCPD, CBS, & MI.

Republic of Kenya, National Council for Population and Development, Central Bureau of Statistics (Office of the Vice President & Ministry of Planning & National Development), & Macro International Inc. (1999). *Kenya demographic and health survey 1998*. Calverton, MD: NCPD, CBS, & MI.

Robinson, W. C. (1992) Kenya enters the fertility transition. *Population Studies 46*, 445–457.

Ruel, M. J. (1965). Religion and society among the Kuria of East Africa. *Africa 35(3)*, 295–306.

Rwomire, A., ed. (2001). African women and children; Crisis and response. Westport, CT and London: Praeger.

Sangree, W. H. (1997). Pronatalism and the elderly in Tiriki, Kenya. In Weisner, T. S., Bradley, C., & Kilbride, P. L. (Eds.), *African families and the crisis of social change* (pp. 184–207). Westport, CT: Bergin & Garvey.

Schapera, I. (1940). *Married life in an African tribe*. Harmondsworth, Eng.: Penguin Books, 1971.

Schuster, I. (1979). *New women of Lusaka*. Palo Alto, CA: Mayfield.

Seppala, P. (1993). *The changing generations: The devolution of land among the Bakusu in western Kenya*. Transaction No. 35, Finnish Anthropological Society, Helsinki.

Siegel, B. (1996). Family and kinship. In Gordon, A. & Gordon, D. (Eds.), *Understanding contemporary Africa* (2nd ed., pp. 221–247). Boulder, CO: Lynne Rienner.

Skinner, E. P. (1986). The triple heritage of lifestyles. In Mazrui, A. & Levine, T. (Eds.), *The Africans: A reader* (pp. 60–74). New York: Praeger.

Stamp, P. (1991). Burying Otieno: The politics of gender and ethnicity in Kenya. *Signs: Journal of Women in Culture and Society 16(4)*, 808–845.

Sutton, J. E. G. (1974). The settlement of East Africa. In Ogot, B. A. (Ed.), *Zamani: A survey of East African history* (pp. 70–97). Nairobi: East African Publishing & Longman.

Turner, B. (Ed.). (2002). *The statesman's yearbook: The politics, cultures and economies of the world*. New York: Palgrave.

Weinreb, A. (2001). First politics, then culture: Accounting for ethnic differences in demographic behavior in Kenya. *Population and Development Review 27(3)*, 437–467.

Weisner, T. S., Bradley, C., & Kilbride, P. L. (Eds.). *African families and the crisis of social change* (pp. 184–207). Westport, CT: Bergin & Garvey.

Were, G. S. (1974). The western Bantu peoples from: A.D. 1300 to 1800. In Ogot, B. A. (Ed.), *Zamani: A survey of East African history* (pp. 170–194). Nairobi: East African Publishing & Longman.

White, L. (1990). *The comforts of home: Prostitution in colonial Nairobi*. Chicago: University of Chicago Press.

World Almanac Education Group. (2002). *The world almanac and book of facts 2002*. New York: World Almanac Books.

Wortham, R. (1999). The geography of fertility reduction in Kenya. *The Social Science Journal 36(1)*, 3–84.

Internet Sources (in order of appearance in the text):

NewAfrica.com—http://www.newafrica.com/profiles/profile.asp?CountryID=25

U.S. Central Intelligence Agency (CIA)—http://www.odci.gov/cia/publications/factbook/geos/ke.html

African Studies Center, University of Pennsyvania—http://africa.upenn.edu/Home_Page/Country.html

Part V
Southern Africa

CHAPTER 11

Development, Family Change, and Community Empowerment in Malawi

Agnes M. Chimbiri

INTRODUCTION

Policy, socioeconomic, and sociocultural contexts create an environment in which individuals and couples make decisions that affect their families' lives. Until recently, theories, paradigms, policies, and program implementation strategies have been driven by Western ideologies and have narrowly matched the African context. In this chapter, we postulate that changes in development theories, paradigms, policies, and program strategies, mediated through social interactions, will cause changes in social organizational structures, their functions, and power relationships and vice versa. This chapter presents the shifts that have taken place within the conceptualization of development as a process of social change and how these shifts have in turn affected family dynamics. Underlying this study is the assumption that an understanding of family dynamics is crucial in policy processes.

The discussion in this chapter demonstrates three aspects of development as a process of social change. First, the conceptualization of development has historically been more focused on structural than on functional changes in a society. Structural changes are related to patterns of organization of social institutions, whereas functional changes are related to the roles and behaviors of members of those social institutions, which in turn make those institutions functional. Second, the acceptance of particular development paradigms has led to a failure to understand the importance of the dynamics of the family, the failure to understand the significant role of the forces of social interactions in development, and the failure to incorporate these into policy research, planning, and implementation. Third, the lack of recognition of the role of social interactions in development-related studies has led to the omission of changing communication and power relationships among lineage members and between spouses.

This chapter presents demographic, ethnic, religious, ecological, and socioeconomic profiles of Malawi, provides a brief political history, and discusses the conceptual issues related to shifts in development discourse since the 1950s and issues related to the role of indigenous African family traditions, Christian/European traditions, and Islamic/Arabic traditions in development processes in Malawi. Finally, issues related to the well-being and status of the family at the micro level are also discussed. The discussion shows how these issues are causing social change, which is in turn changing the identities of reproductive decision makers and the paths of reproductive decision making in Malawian communities.

DEMOGRAPHIC, POLITICAL, AND HISTORICAL PROFILES

Malawi is a landlocked country situated in Southern Africa, with a total surface area of 119,484 square kilometers, 20 percent of which is covered by water (Government of Malawi, 1987). Administratively, the country is divided into three regions (North, Center, and South). The total population is 9.8 million, with fewer males than other countries in Africa (Government of Malawi, 2000, 2002). The age-sex structure has a disproportionate distribution, with higher ratios of men in urban areas (Government of Malawi & United Nations, 1993; Government of Malawi, 1994, 2000, 2002).

Malawi's population is composed of more than 20 ethnic groups that migrated into the country between the 15th and 19th centuries. The major ethnic groups are the Tumbuka, the Ngoni, and the Tonga in the Northern Region; the Chewa and the Ngoni in the Central Region; and the Yao, the Lomwe, the Sena, and the Manga'nja in the Southern Region (Pachai, 1973). Currently found in the north, the Tumbuka originated in the northwest (Zambia and Tanzania) and settled in parts of Mzimba and Rumphi toward the end of the 15th century. The Tonga migrated into northern Malawi around the 18th century and occupied the western lakeshore area (Karonga and Nkhatabay). The Ngoni originated in South Africa and arrived in Malawi after the 1820s (Thompson, 1998). The Yao originated in Mozambique and migrated into most parts of the Mangochi, Machinga, and Chiradzulu districts (Pachai, 1973). The Lomwe also originated in Mozambique and settled in Mulanje, Thyolo, and parts of the Chiradzulu and Nsanje districts. The Sena, also from Mozambique, are mostly found in the Chikwawa and Nsanje districts. The Manga'nja, originally found in the Central Region, migrated southward into parts of the Chiradzulu, Chikwawa, Nsanje, and Thyolo districts.

All ethnic groups in the north practice patriliny, a system whereby descent is traced through the father and sons. Sons or male relatives inherit property. Marital residence is patrilocal. Bride price payment serves as compensation to the bride's parents for the loss of their daughter and as a guarantee that the husband will fulfill his obligations. Bride price is tendered in material goods such as livestock or money. As a result, divorce is not encouraged for fear of paying back the bride price. However, divorces are common in Malawi (Mitchell, 1971; Zulu, 1996; Kaler, 2001; Chimbiri-Kavinya, 2002).

Polygynous unions, which are common among patrilineal as well as matrilineal groups, are the outcomes of preferential rules that allow men to marry more than one woman and govern the marriage of widows. Levirate rules, for example, prescribe the inheritance of widows by a brother of the deceased husband (Murdock, 1959). Today, levirate rules are less likely to be applied because of the worsening HIV/AIDS and economic crises. In fact, there is anecdotal evidence that these practices are on the decline or are slowly being modified (Department for International Development, 2003).

In the Central Region, the two major ethnic groups (the Chewa and the Ngoni) practice different cultural systems. The Chewa practice matriliny, a system whereby descent is traced through the mother and daughters and property is passed on to daughters. However, in practice, it is the brother of the mother who owns and controls the inherited property and any significant family resources, including land (Phiri, 1983). In the past, material gifts for marriage were tendered in the form of a bride service, such as the husband building a house for the parents of the bride. The Ngoni practice patriliny and patrilocal marital residence. Due to intermarriage between the Chewa and the Ngoni, a mixed cultural system has developed and the matrilineal system has become weaker. In the south, the Yao, Lomwe, and Manganja are predominantly matrilineal and matrilocal. Although three-quarters of the Yao are Muslims, Yao traditions have persisted and coexist with Islamic traditions. Only the Sena in the South have a strong patrilineal system.

Freedom of worship has prevailed in the country since colonial times. However, members of the Jehovah's Witnesses were persecuted under postindependence one-party rule of Dr. Hastings Kamuzu Banda. Currently, 79.9 percent of the total Malawi population are Christian, 12.8 percent are Muslim, 3.1 percent belong to other faith groups, and 4.3 percent practice traditional religion (Government of Malawi, 2002). The coexistence of these faith-based organizations (FBOs) has been characterized by a mix of competition, tension, conflict, fear, and struggle over spheres of influence.

Malawi became a British protectorate (called Nyasaland Protectorate) in 1891 through the influence of British Christian missionaries who came into the country as early as the 1870s (Pachai, 1973; Thompson, 1998). Catholic and Presbyterian churches instituted schools throughout the country either independent of or in collaboration with the government. Thus, missionaries and the colonial government became equal partners in development and this relationship has persisted in postcolonial times. With the influx of Swahili slave traders starting in the 1840s, Islam started being propagated along the southern shores of Lake Malawi.

Postcolonial Malawi was governed by one-party rule under the Malawi Congress Party (MCP) led by Dr. Banda (1964–94) and by a multiparty government under the United Democratic Front (UDF) led by Dr. Bakili Muluzi from 1994 to the present. In the colonial period of the Nyasaland Protectorate, the British used indirect rule and the organization of government structures was based on the traditional leadership structures of chiefdom. In the postcolonial government structure, the head of state occupies the office of the president and the chair of the cabinet. Under the cabinet are the Regional Administrative Offices, the Traditional Local Authorities, and village chiefs.

The one-party regime regarded national unity as a priority. Chichewa was declared the national language and a medium for instruction. English became the official language. Today, approximately 50 percent of the population speaks Chichewa as a first language and the rest speak other indigenous languages (Government of Malawi & United Nations Children's Fund, 1998). Through multiparty elections in 1994, a democratic government was put in place under the leadership of Dr. Muluzi, a Muslim. The multiparty government introduced Yao, Tumbuka, Lomwe, Sena, and Ngonde as other languages of communication on the national radio, specifically for news coverage.

DEVELOPMENT ISSUES AND THE CHANGING FAMILY CONCEPT

Conceptually, neoliberal and postmodernist development perspectives assumed that the household in developing countries consisted of a nuclear family (husband, wife, and children) and that within each household there was a clear division of labor with a male breadwinner and a female homemaker (Brohman, 1996). Some authors have argued that the terms *family* and *household* are used interchangeably (Caldwell, 1982; Kabeer, 1994). This usage is based on the microeconomic model of the household, which treats the household as an altruistic collective of individuals, in essence assuming that a household acts like an individual.

In the Malawian context, household and family are different concepts. A household, which is locally known as *nyumba* or *khomo*, is a physical structure that accommodates extended, polygynous, or monogamous family structures. An extended family comprises two or more families of different generations united by kinship ties, common residence, or a single head. A polygynous family comprises a man and two or more wives, whereas a monogamous family comprises a man with one wife (Murdock, 1959, pp. 25–26; Phiri, 1983). Therefore, in the Malawian context a household is a physical entity, whereas a family is a social structure within a household.

Apart from the liberal development theorists, liberal feminists have also influenced policy approaches and intrafamilial power/gender relations. They have argued that because women are as rational as men, they must be recognized as equal citizens, empowered to control their own fertility, and given rights to land and other resources (Tinker, 1997). The theoretical path advanced by liberal feminism was elucidated in the Women in Development (WID) and Women and Development (WAD) approaches. These were driven by Boserupean thinking that women's roles as traditional workers and producers need to be recognized in policy because they contribute to economic and social changes (Boserup, 1989).

In Malawi, a women's organization called *Chitukuko Cha Amayi M'Malawi* (CCAM), which literally means Women's Development in Malawi, influenced the government to review its policies. The government had to ensure that women had equal rights with men and access to public choices, including protection, respect, and survival (National Commission on Women in Development, 1993). The demands by CCAM reflected women's empowerment through a gender-relations approach that recognizes the need to enhance women's power relative to men. The gender-relations approach is embedded in traditional social organizational structures in which dependency relationships are rooted. In these structures, men depend on their women for labor and women depend on their men for social and economic security.

Contemporary development discourse has focused on the empowerment approach, and is defined in economic and social terms. From an economic perspective, empowerment refers to the pooling of resources (including material, financial, ideological, and intellectual) and the consequent achievement of a collective capability to survive (Brohman, 1996). From a feminist and sociological perspective, empowerment entails access to and control of both material and informational resources to bring about structural and functional change (Batliwala, 1994; Labourie-Racape & Locoh, 1998), and the transformation of structures that perpetuate gender and social inequalities.

Women's empowerment is central to development in Malawi. Empowerment requires the pooling of resources to enable the poor and powerless, particularly women, to develop the capability to make rational economic and reproductive decisions that will improve their status and well-being. Within contemporary development thinking, empowerment is stressed in alternative development paradigms known as "participation" and "gender and development" (GAD). Proponents of the participatory development approach, who still follow the neoliberal principles of public choice and rationalization, promote the role of the community in policy planning and implementation (Boserup, 1989; Brohman, 1996).

Neoliberal feminists, however, expanded the participatory view of development and called for researchers and policy makers to first recognize the reproductive and productive roles of women and second, the relationship between family life and the organization of political and economic structures (Kabeer, 1994). Through their advocacy of GAD, the neoliberal feminists influenced development theorists and policy makers to incorporate aspects of gender relations in their approaches. GAD introduced a gender-relations approach to development suggesting the treatment of women as change agents (Kabeer, 1994) and consequently the transformation of power relations between men and women (Visvanathan, Duggan, Nisonoff, & Wiegersma, 1997).

Although the analysis in this chapter is grounded in development principles that focus on structural change, the assumption here is that structural and functional changes are symmetrical because structural change, which involves reorganization of the elements constituting those structures, leads to the disruption of gender, power, and communication relationships. Consequently, the functions of those organizational structures change because they have to adapt to the new situation. For example, when husbands migrate to cities in search of wage employment or for trading, they are no longer available to provide labor for agricultural production in the village. Thus, changes occur in the structure of the labor force within the lineage and the neonuclear family. It then falls to the women (and children) to produce both cash and food crops, which constitutes a functional change. But as the women have child care and household work to do, the level of agricultural production decreases (Phiri, 1983). The result is a food shortage at the household level, which produces an unhealthy labor force that perpetuates the impoverishment of families and the country as a whole.

The structural consequences of feminist, participatory, and GAD paradigms are likely to lead to changes in structures and functions of social institutions including gender, productive and reproductive roles of members of those institutions, and communication and power relationships. Although development studies and analyses have often focused on macro-level structural changes, meso- and micro-level structural and functional changes have taken place simultaneously. But little or no attention has been given to the consequences of these changes in development. The functional changes in community structures, such as the lineage and the neonuclear family, will affect the conjugal roles of men and women, and their respective participation in decision making and consequently in development. Therefore, functional as well as structural changes at the micro level are important components in processes of planning and implementing development-related research, policies, and programs.

LINEAGE STRUCTURES AND THE DILUTION OF LINEAGE POWER

Societies in Malawi comprise two distinct traditional lineage systems, termed matriliny and patriliny. A matrilineage is a system designed to maintain property rights within a kinship group. A daughter marries and her brother becomes the head of her family with control over all assets. If he dies, her son or her male relatives assume control. Matrilineal societies in Malawi (the Chewa, Yao,

Lomwe, and Mang'anja) emphasized *chikamwini*, meaning a matrilocal (uxorilocal) marriage, whereby the husband joined his wife and provided bride service (building a house, cultivating the garden, or making various handicrafts) for his parents-in-law. This also involved matrilineal inheritance of children (i.e., laborers) and family wealth (Schoffeleers & Litt, 1968; Phiri, 1983). Women and children were sources of human capital and investment for the matrilineage, and the women and children depended on the lineage for protection and survival.

In Chewa matrilineal families, the locus of productive and reproductive decision-making power lay with the woman's relatives (Phiri, 1983). Therefore, the matrilineage defined the rights and obligations of the individual family or household, gave it the sense of belonging, provided it with both social and material security, and defined its status within the larger community (Marwick, 1965). The women constituted the *mbumba* (members of the lineage) and the men acted as the *nkhoswe* (surety). This type of relationship made women dependent on male kinsmen (Schoffeleers & Litt, 1968; Phiri, 1983) through the creation of a hierarchical pattern of gender relations reinforced by rules of marital residence.

Patriliny is a parallel system to matriliny. It also exists to maintain property rights within a kinship group. In patriliny, control of the husband's lineage assets lies with the husband. If the husband dies, control passes to his son or his brother. Common characteristics of patriliny include patrilineality, patrilocality (virilocality), and the practice of polygynous or levirate marriages. Traditional societies in Malawi were overwhelmingly matrilineal. However, with social change over time, the Tumbuka, the Ngoni, and the Tonga have assumed patrilineal systems. The shift from matriliny to patriliny in the Northern Region is associated with the invasion by the Ngoni. In the Central Region, the shift from a strong matriliny to a weak one was due to intermarriages particularly with the Ngoni (Schoffeleers, 1973; Phiri, 1983). In the Southern Region, matriliny has persisted.

RELIGION, ETHNICITY, AND SOCIAL CHANGE

Changes have occurred from matrilineal/matrilocal to patrilineal/patrilocal lineage systems (van Valsen, 1960; Vaughan, 1987) and from extended families to monogamous neonuclear families (Kandawire, 1979; Phiri, 1983). The social system of the first settlers in the Northern Region, the Tumbuka (Young, 1932), was derived from avunculocal marriage. Under this system, residence was matrilocal (uxorilocal) which demanded that a man return to his mother's natal home at puberty or at marriage (Fox, 1967).

Prior to 1780, the Tumbuka adhered to matrilineal descent, inheritance, succession, and bride service, and matrilocal (uxorilocal) residence. In the late 1870s the Ngoni, who have a strong patrilineal system, migrated from South Africa and invaded Tumbuka lands. The Tumbuka then adopted the full-fledged

South African *lobola* (bride price) (Murdock, 1959). Today, the Tumbuka have strongly rooted patrilocal (virilocal) kinship structures and patrilineal systems. Similarly, the Tonga, who were formerly matrilineal, experienced many changes in their matrilineal rules, so that patrilateral kin came to play a pivotal role in kinship production and reproduction relationships (van Valsen, 1960).

Confirming the occurrence of family changes in Malawi, van Valsen (1960), Vaughan (1987), Kandawire (1979), and Phiri (1983) found that lineage systems have undergone changes in structures with consequent changes to gender roles and power relations. These changes are associated with the influence of intruding ethnic groups, the introduction of new religions, the institutionalization of colonial administration, and the modern capitalist economy.

The influence of Christianity on social change has been felt since it was introduced in Malawi in the 1870s. Islamic influence was nonexistent because following the abolition of slave trade, there was total breakdown of communication between the Malawian Islamic community and the Arabic communities. Consequently, the Islam that gained roots in Malawi was adapted to the local Yao culture and social structure. Even the Quran was translated into Yao language. This was mainly because it was propagated by local agents.

Western values, passed on through Christianity and colonial government, only challenged abuses in traditional structures but did not abolish the structures. To date, the structure of Christian churches is still patriarchal and therefore women are marginalized in decision making (Phiri, 1996, 1997, 1998). Competition over spheres of influence was strictly among Christian churches because Islam was associated with oriental values and was therefore not considered relevant to the socioeconomic and political setup of the country (Chakanza, 2002). During colonial times, Christians superseded Muslims in power and influence because missionaries provided social, economic, and religious services with little or no subsidy from the government.

In the past three decades, Islam has been recognized as a religion that is relevant and compatible with changing times. Consequently, Muslims have moved into spheres of influence. Since the wave of Islamic resurgence aimed at restoring the credibility and respectability of Islamic orthodoxy hit Malawi, Muslim communities in the country have been receiving financial and ideological support from Asian Muslim communities within Malawi and from Middle Eastern countries and South Africa. Scholarships for young Muslims to study in Islamic educational institutions worldwide are now available (Chakanza, 2002), and some Islamic institutions now provide health and education services.

The younger generations of Muslims in Malawi now have access to secular education, Islamic teachings and orthodoxy through madrass, and scholarships to Arabic and other Islamic countries. This has created an elitist group of Muslims and conflict has arisen between them and the traditional Islamic leaders. Because of their understanding of Arabic language, the former feel they are superior and that they understand Islam more than the traditional Muslim leaders. Under the multiparty regime, more Muslim scholars are demanding influential positions that will allow them to participate in national decision-making processes.

Indeed, the struggle for power and influence has been evident at institutional levels and has trickled down to the micro level. This process has eroded the decision-making power and influence of Malawian traditional systems. According to Kandawire (1979), the matrilineal system ceased to exist as a viable social and economic unit as early as the 1960s. The nuclear family (father, mother, and children) became the basic unit of production and consumption. But Kandawire's views ignored the continuing role of the family in processes of social reproduction. Kaler (2001) described the changing family structure in terms of changes in the social reproduction institution of the family (marriage), which she viewed as a "degenerate institution."

The observed changes in family structures may be consistent with Goode's argument that as societies develop (modernize) most social groups gradually become incorporated into modern economies (predominantly patriarchal) and matrilineal systems slowly diminish (Goode, 1970). In the case of Malawi, it has been observed that the presence of Christianity may have diluted the traditional practice of polygyny and instilled the concept of monogamy, but polygyny is still widely practiced (Government of Malawi, 2000; Kaler, 2001; Chimbiri-Kavinya, 2002).

Emerging from this review is the fact that changes have not only occurred in family structures and their functions but also in relationships between members of the lineage. Apart from its control over social reproduction, the lineage was also important for social production in traditional societies. As is the case in other African societies, the lineage in Malawi has lost much of its direct control over production, although it still regulates the inheritance of property and forms the basis of family enterprises. Lineage relationships were, and still are, central to processes of division of labor, reproduction of the labor force, and distribution of resources. Kin relationships have negative and positive effects on women in that, although they contribute to women's subordination, female-kin ties improve women's position through networks of mutual economic and moral support (Whitehead, 1975).

Traditionally, kin relations were for marriage, procreation, inheritance of property, and the reproduction of the lineage labor force. An individual was held in a tight network of vertical and horizontal communities that bound and supported him or her through their collective nature. The weakening of the lineage has consequently produced disjointed family units. The members are united by descent but operate as single production and reproduction units for the survival of individuals and the neonuclear family. These disjointed families are 'neonuclear families' because they maintain kinship ties. Neonuclear families are characteristic of contemporary Malawian communities.

The wealth flows theory suggests that the movement toward a capitalist economy causes a decline in the importance of familial production, a growth in internal family egalitarianism, and a reversal of intergenerational support flows from the traditional young-to-old to the modern old-to-young (Caldwell, 1982, p. 338). These changes are accompanied by changes in societal attitudes toward male-female and parent-child relationships. Due to the pressure from the forces of social and economic change in society, emotional relations between spouses become stronger with consequent agreement that the needs of children come first (Caldwell, 1982).

A recent study on Intergenerational Transfers in Malawi confirms Caldwell's theory. It found that currently intrafamilial material transfer relationships are more frequent with parents and siblings than with other lineage members (Weinreb, 1999). Contrary to expectations, the role of the neonuclear family has been strengthening while that of the lineage in community development has been weakening. Weinreb's findings suggest that traditional support flows in Malawi have not yet reversed. The modern support flows are a network type that combines vertical and horizontal flows. The flow is still overwhelmingly from young to old but includes siblings and some members of the lineage.

The shrinking support flow from children to lineage heads (paternal aunt and maternal uncle) and the strengthening support flow from children to parents and sibling to sibling are signs of the transition in family structures and functions. This marks the beginning of the process of nucleation of the family in Africa (Kandawire, 1979; Phiri, 1983; Weinreb, 1999; Kaler, 2001) but no adequate evidence of this transition yet exists (Locoh, 1997; Vignikin, 1997). According to Phiri (1983), migrant labor facilitated the beginning of the nucleation of the family in that when migrant husbands took their wives away to the city with them, the husbands had the sole responsibility to take care of their wives and children. Partial nucleation was also facilitated when migrant husbands took their wives to their own natal home on return to the village. This partial nucleation also marked the beginning of the shift of the locus of family decision making and the empowerment of individual men but not women.

URBANIZATION, MODERNIZATION, AND THE CHANGING FAMILY STRUCTURE

There is a cause-and-effect relationship between processes of social change, empowerment, and reproductive/economic decision making in Malawi. Social change has caused fragmentation of the traditional lineage system, which has led to power devolvement from lineage heads to couples and individuals, who now make reproductive as well as economic decisions mainly in their own interest and partially in the interest of the neonuclear family.

Social changes affecting Malawian society include schooling, a decline in mortality, urbanization, migration, and the food crisis. More recently, the environmental crisis (Cassen, 1994), the refugee influx, the economic crises (Locoh, 2000), and democratization (Ross, 1996) have reinforced these changes. Schooling has led the educated to migrate from villages to find wage employment in cities within and outside Malawi. Decline in mortality has resulted in population growth, thus putting pressure on family resources. Urbanization has exposed migrants to new ideas and reduced lineage control. The food crisis has arisen from reduced productivity caused by environmental degradation as a result of population pressure. The economic crisis has produced high inflation rates, low employment opportunities, and low earnings. The influx of refugees has put pressure on already limited resources. The environmental crisis has led to the reduction of landholding capacity, and consequently a reduction in subsistence productivity. Democratization has brought about popular demand for egalitarian decision making, particularly the participation of women, young people, and the poor.

Since the lineage head no longer has the resources to bestow on neonuclear family members, migration has become a means of survival for neonuclear families. Most of the gifts or support (money or material items) that migrants send back to villages now go to their village-based family members, with smaller amounts going to the lineage heads (Weinreb, 1999). The support that gets sent home maintains land rights, kinship links, and a share of control over lineage wealth, and becomes part of the donor's survival strategy. The lineage dependency relationship is therefore not expected to completely disappear because it may serve to ameliorate the economic, environmental, food, and HIV/AIDS crises.

Social changes have consequently empowered individuals (women as well as men), couples, and neonuclear families. Individuals, couples, and neonuclear families have taken over economic and reproductive decision making from the lineage heads. As Locoh (1997, 2000) has observed, the lineage structures have been fragmented leading to changes in women's conjugal roles and the disruption of traditional marital power relationships. These changes include atomization, a shift of the locus of decision-making power about nuptiality away from the circle of elders to young couples (Kaler, 2001). Some elderly women lament that:

Long ago, if you wanted to marry, there were some customs here at home: When you found a partner, people from your relatives could go to that girl's relatives and there they find *ankhoswe* to witness the marriage, and if there was chicken they could slaughter it and eat it together to celebrate the marriage.... And the parents said, "Our child should marry this person," based on the work that the family was doing (i.e., evaluating how hard working their prospective in-law appeared to be). And that marriage would last longer, that one which the parents chose.[1]

Due to the fragmentation of the traditional family structure, power and gender structures, including the communication networks inherent within traditional lineage systems, have become weaker, whereas those between spouses, female kin, and children and their biological parents have become stronger. The outcome is a multiplicity of paths and loci of reproductive and economic decision making, suggesting that nowadays the locus of decision making lies in the neonuclear family. An elderly man explains that

These days, a husband marries and takes away the wife to his village the same day. When he has children, the wealth that he accumulates is for him and his children. When he dies, the children are the ones who decide where to go but they inherit the wealth. As for their mother, the late father's lineage members set her free to go back to her home. If the lineage members cause trouble, these days children consult the courts.[2]

In this chapter we argue that policy changes drive family dynamics. Colonial government in Malawi drove intrafamilial changes by interventionist development policies. Postcolonial government, which was autocratic in nature, drove these changes using trickle-down and structural adjustment development policies. The one-party regime provided population incentives while advocating child spacing. Since the introduction of democratic multiparty politics, however, poverty alleviation/reduction policies and advocacy for reproductive health are exerting pressure on intrafamilial power and gender structures. This implicitly means that as the lineage lost its authority, the state gained more control over family decision-making processes, until recently when individuals and couples have asserted more control. The attractiveness of population incentives has diminished in the face of current crises. Nevertheless, the population policy of Malawi promulgates population disincentives. Chiefs are not rewarded for their population numbers, and the Malawi Public Service Regulations (MPSR) no longer provide tax exemptions for male public servants with large families. Furthermore, female public servants are not allowed more than one paid maternity leave in a three-year period.

Also, the shift from a familial subsistence system to a capitalist production system has led to changes in production relationships, the division of labor, and the assignment of new roles between husbands and wives. The introduction of crop production changed women's status and disrupted spousal power relations. Women were relegated to the domestic activities and subsistence farming, while men were encouraged to seek wage employment away from the village, and consequently women became more dependent on men (Phiri, 1983; Vaughan, 1987; Locoh, 1997). As the rural economic situation has worsened and survival has become more difficult each day, more men and women (single and married) have migrated to cities and other places where economic activities are concentrated.

The neoliberal, public choice, and free-market principles that have been translated into restructuring, structural adjustment, and poverty reduction policies have further reinforced these rural-urban circular movements as people struggle to survive. As a result, separations between husbands and wives, between parents and children, and between members of the lineage have increased. Conflicts between spouses, between kinship members, and between the old (parents) and the young (children) have also increased (Schoffeleers & Litt, 1968; Phiri, 1983: Kaler, 2001). One of the outcomes is an increase in marital instability (FAO & Government of Malawi, 1992; Kaler, 2001), which has led to a rise in the proportion of de facto female-headed households and a rise in levels of vulnerability particularly among women and children (Government of Malawi & United Nations, 1993). Along with this, there is an increase in autonomous decision making about when to get married and who to marry.

When exposed to new ideas and lifestyles in cities, migrants lose their sense of traditional norms and sanctions. They make decisions independently, or jointly with their wives, to leave their wives and children in the village. This is because either they cannot afford large families in cities or towns due to low wages (FAO & Government of Malawi, 1992) or they want to maintain their lineage links (van Valsen, 1960). The village-based wives and children are engaged in subsistence farming, which subsidizes the husband's remittances if any are sent. Sometimes migrant husbands remarry where they reside or their village-based wives also remarry. This increases their responsibilities. For example a woman in her forties recounts that:

Some five years ago, a truck came to pick our men to go to work in a tobacco estate in Kasungu (this is a district in Central Malawi). My husband went. I wanted to go with him. But the owner of the truck told us that they would come back to collect the wives and children. The truck never came back. For a few years, my husband communicated. He sent some MK 50.00 [the equivalent of almost $0.70 U.S. today] once. But I have never heard from him since. I suspect that he remarried. I have also remarried since.[3]

Therefore, while empowering men (married or single) social change has also empowered women (as individuals or groups). Village-based wives of migrant husbands make independent economic and reproductive decisions in order to cope with the economic hardships in the village while their husbands are away and unable to send adequate support. As noted in a poverty analysis reports for Malawi (Government of Malawi, 1993), these women struggle to survive and therefore engage in small-scale businesses. As Vaughan (1987) and Locoh (1997) observed among the Manganja and Yao in Southern Malawi, solo women identify women's networks with female kin as one of the survival strategies in times of economic and food crises. The female kin networks are a source of support (moral, manual, and material) and potential partners for small businesses (e.g., brewing beer, distilling *kachasu* (local gin), and selling local produce). This type of women's networking is also likely to take place in urban centers.

Migration, on which most Malawian individuals and families have for a long time depended for their economic survival, has become a major cause of social crises in Malawi and many countries in Africa. Coupled with the economic crisis, migration has not only changed lineage and spousal relations but has also eroded traditional moral values. Millions of men as well as women, and more especially teenage women in Africa, are caught up in sexually active lifestyles as a mechanism for economic survival (Okomma, 2000). This behavior trend fuels the spread of HIV/AIDS (Munthali & Chimbiri, 2003).

The HIV/AIDS Crisis and Family Change

Malawi reported its first AIDS case in 1985. By 1996, it had become the leading cause of death among adults aged 15–49 (Kanjaye, 1999). HIV prevalence is almost twice as high in urban areas (25 percent) as in rural areas (13 percent). The national prevalence rate for adults (age 15–49) is estimated at 15 percent, translating into almost 740,000 adults living with HIV/AIDS (National AIDS Commission, 2003). More than half of the new HIV infections are occurring in young people between 15 and 24 years (National AIDS Commission, 1999). Annual deaths due to HIV/AIDS are estimated at over 80,000, amounting to 555,000 deaths since 1985 (National AIDS Commission, 2003).

HIV/AIDS prevalence levels differ by gender, age, and residence. Girls between 15 and 24 years of age are five to six times more likely than their male counterparts to contract the virus. Furthermore, urban areas (especially the cities of Blantyre, Lilongwe, and Mzuzu) record much higher prevalence levels (22.5 percent) than semiurban (21.1 percent) and rural areas (10.7 percent) (National AIDS Commission, 2002). This creates the impression that AIDS is an urban and women's problem, but the high mobility of the Malawi population puts the rural population at an equal risk with the urban population.

The impact of the HIV/AIDS crisis on the individual, the family, the community, and the nation as a whole has not been sufficiently researched. However, there are indications that HIV/AIDS may have unevenly affected key social indicators such as a rise in adult mortality rates, a reduction in life expectancy, large numbers of HIV/AIDS patients occupying hospital beds (50 percent), an increase in attrition rates of personnel in key sectors (agriculture, education, health, media), and an increase in orphans (National AIDS Commission, 2003). Consequently, the labor force has been substantially reduced, directly affecting the basic productive unit (the family) and indirectly the nation. The traditional lineage system, which was a social manifestation of collectivism in the form of mutual caring and support that ensured individual well-being, is slowly losing this functional capacity, especially in this era of HIV/AIDS. Child fostering, for example, is no longer a lineage responsibility but has become more of a neonuclear family affair. Although there is a widespread mushrooming of institutionalized orphan care, the majority of orphans are taken care of by members of the neonuclear family (siblings, single mothers, stepmothers) and grandparents.

The feminization of Malawi's HIV/AIDS epidemic is not restricted to young people as older women are also vulnerable to infection. For example, poor and single mothers in particular are challenged to identify survival strategies that are HIV/AIDS risk free. Women often find themselves in the dilemma of making choices that determine life or death: abstinence or unsafe sex, childbearing or family planning. Unfortunately, negotiating sex is very difficult for Malawians because discussion of sexual and reproductive issues between men and women is not the norm in Malawian societies (FAO & Government of Malawi, 1992; Chimbiri-Kavinya, 2002).

In 1996, the government and its development partners initiated a number of evaluation, assessment, and capacity building efforts to determine the impact of HIV/AIDS control programs and activities. As a follow-up to these efforts, the National AIDS Commission embarked on community mobilization activities aimed at (1) strengthening the capacity of individuals and communities to understand and discuss the nature of the HIV/AIDS epidemic; and (2) strengthening the capacity of decision makers, program staff, technicians, activists, and advocates to understand and effectively address the key issues raised in Malawi by the HIV/AIDS epidemic.

Since the mid-1990s, Malawi has witnessed a marked decline in discipline and moral responsibility among the youth attributed to a misinterpretation of democracy and a relaxation of censorship. This weakens the social control and guidance functions of the family, the schools, and religious institutions. In addition, youth do not seem to have appropriate role models to emulate. The national response to this type of moral decay has been the formulation of new policies (National Gender Policy, National Youth Policy, Reproductive Health Policy, and National AIDS Policy), the review of some existing policies and legislation, and the introduction of legislation to address gender issues such as inheritance, rape, age at first marriage, and so on, which are currently pending parliamentary review.

Sexual and Reproductive Health and National Development Programs

In 2001, the government of Malawi undertook an assessment of the impact of HIV/AIDS on human resources in the public sector with the purpose of establishing the levels of attrition. Findings from this study provided evidence that the country is experiencing an erosion of human resource capacity, a higher rate of death among female employees, institutional vulnerability due to the lack of a national AIDS policy, and huge expenditures on the sick and funerals (Government of Malawi & UNDP, 2002). In an attempt to curb the spread of AIDS in Malawi and reverse this trend, the National AIDS Commission in collaboration with other stakeholders formulated a National AIDS Strategy, a Behavior Change Strategy, and a National AIDS Policy (Government of Malawi, 2001, 2002, 2003).

At the community level, the institutional response to the HIV/AIDS epidemic has been slow but dynamic. Faith-based organizations emphasize marital fidelity and abstinence. They preach against the use of condoms. They argue that condom use is a license to promiscuity and that it is not safe and that it gives false security. Nevertheless, religious groups are aware of the disadvantage that women have in matters of making choices regarding sexual and reproductive life. Government commitment to community mobilization about HIV/AIDS prevention is concentrated on service providers who openly talk about condom use and other preventive measures. NGOs are working closely with government service providers in advocating women's empowerment and condom use.

Politicians and other local leaders rarely talk about condom use. Therefore, community dialogue about sex, HIV/AIDS, and condoms is limited. However, recent studies show that there is extensive discussion about AIDS within families and communities (Chimbiri, 2003). Recently, churches have realized that people relate the epidemic to promiscuity and therefore subject AIDS victims to stigmatization. In response to this, churches are now fighting against stigmatization of people living with HIV/AIDS.

CONCLUSIONS

The discussion in this chapter has revealed how the classical and the contemporary theoretical paradigms of development and gender were instrumental in the formulation of public policies in Malawi, but failed to empirically consider important meso- and micro-level issues when planning and implementing research and policy. Four major issues have emerged out of this discussion. First is the fact that to date neoliberal paradigms, which are based on neoclassical economics, principles of public choice, and the free market, have remained the dominant paradigms. Although these paradigms were focused on macro-level issues, analogous micro-level theories that addressed issues related to the neonuclear family also coexisted. Competing with these theoretical paradigms were the neoliberal feminist theories that questioned the prevalent economic and social order of state structures and the lack of participation of women.

Second, the dominant and critical development paradigms tended to focus on structural changes and gave little attention to the nature of the internal dynamics and functional changes of the community-based structures (i.e., the lineage). It has been argued that structural and functional changes are symmetrical, and therefore have a role to play in development processes. This is because any change within an organizational structure is likely to lead to change in the functions of that structure as well as its elements. In this chapter we have seen how the traditional gender and power structures, including conjugal roles, have been transformed over time despite the parallel male-dominated control of both matrilineal and patrilineal systems.

Third, social changes—Christianization, Islamization, schooling, increase in adult mortality, and urbanization, including the economic, food, environmental, and HIV/AIDS crises—have an influence on social institutions. A variety of factors interact and cause changes in family dynamics leading to changes in communication and power relationships between spouses and members of the neonuclear family or the lineage and members of the community in general. These types of changes bring about additional changes in economic, reproductive, and political decision-making paths with religious groups acting as power brokers (Catholic Institute for International Relations, 1993; Ross, 1996).

Social changes therefore empower both men and women to fully justify their autonomous economic, reproductive, and political decisions, free of external control. For example, while kin ties often strengthen lineage ideologies they also improve women's status. Women capitalize on kin-based empowering elements such as gender-based kin ties and traditions (e.g., child spacing) that allow women to make decisions. This empowerment is also extended to women whose husbands have migrated away who take on men's responsibilities as providers and role models for their children. Conjugal and gender roles are then reversed. Individual spouses (migrant or nonmigrant, urban resident or rural resident) and single women strive to ensure their individual survival, as well as that of members of the neonuclear family including their siblings and lineage heads.

Apart from autonomous decision making, the other effects of social change are the strengthening of spousal communication and gender-based networks. The strengthening of spousal communication leads to joint decision making in the absence of which autonomous decision making takes place. Gender-based networks are also likely to mediate an individual's autonomous decision making.

Fourth, the omission of the nature of family dynamics from policy research and formulation is likely to lead to inappropriate development policies. A clear understanding of changes in family dynamics can help researchers and policy makers explain some of the puzzles surrounding the coexistence of high fertility, high adult mortality, high rates of HIV/AIDS infections, poverty, and low levels of development. Through this chapter, we have seen how the coexistence of faith-based groups, traditional customs, and government regimes directly affect the family structures and functions. As a result, migration, intermarriages, divorces, freedom of speech, freedom of association, and capitalism have affected families.

Churches want families to become nuclear. This is in line with church structures, which are patriarchal and unilateral. This view is within the modern capitalist approach to development, which moves toward individual achievements. Contrary to expectations, the conventional development approach, which is based on Western cultural setting, has not fitted the African context. Western traditions, Christian traditions, and African customs have coexisted but with little or no change in traditional values. Development policies have not worked because they have advocated change from outside (vertical change) and have overlooked change from within society (horizontal change). Development agents have always perceived change to be a process that involves competitive forces and not complementary factors. The competition over spheres of influence by government, Christian churches, and Islamic revivalists is a reflection of this type of thinking. Christian and secular education has been the norm until recently when the Islamic community has shown, through combining secular and Islamic education systems, that Western, Christian, Islamic, and African traditions can coexist.

Resistance to change is evident. Although the economic, education, environment, and HIV/AIDS crises have forced individuals, couples, families, communities, and nations to review their survival strategies, traditional values have remained intact. The efforts of Islamic groups have raised suspicions and fears among Christians that the programs are aimed at converting Christians to Muslims (Chakanza, 2002). Yet the earlier missionary groups have not changed any traditional values. Despite large numbers of converts and widespread secular education, traditional values still drive people's social lives. Christian groups still resist the involvement of women in church leadership roles. Even with the deadly killer HIV/AIDS around, communities are slow to appreciate the need to change or reform traditional practices because they claim that they have no power to change ancestral practices and if they change them, misfortunes would befall them. Western values, faith-based cultural beliefs, and traditional beliefs will continue to coexist. Policies and program formulators and implementers will therefore need to take into consideration the fact that this coexistence has an impact on family dynamics including its structure and functions and its members' roles.

The discussion in this chapter has shown that families and communities have been rational in their responses to policies. They have chosen to adopt strategies that will ensure their survival in the changing world but have stuck to their traditional beliefs, norms, customs, and values. This means that the Western, Christian, and Islamic values have just been layered over traditional values. They are just a silver or gold coating that can fade anytime, while the traditional values remain intact. Thus, policies that aim to effect change in people's behavior will require a participatory approach that helps individuals, couples, families, and communities identify and appreciate the need for change. Otherwise, any externally driven change will remain foreign in Malawian communities.

NOTES

1. Quoted in Kaler, 2001. These are interviews Kaler had conducted on marriage in Malawi between 1998 and 2000.

2. This was an interview the author conducted in 1990 with the younger brother of the late Traditional Authority Mkanda in Mchinji. He was 80 years old. He experienced the first settlement of the Chewa in central region and the coming of colonial rulers.

3. This interview was conducted by the author in Mulanje district in 1990 under the sponsorship of United Nations Population Fund (UNFPA) of Family Life Education Project.

REFERENCES

Batliwala, S. (1994). The meaning of women's empowerment: New concepts from action. In Gennain, S. G. & Chen, L. C. (Eds.), *Population Policies Reconsidered: Health, Empowerment, and Rights* (pp. 127–138). New York: International Women's Coalition.

Brohman, J. (1996). *Popular development: Rethinking the theory and practice of development*. Great Britain: T. J. Press.
Caldwell, J. C. (1982). *Theory of fertility decline*. London: Academic Press.
Cassen, R. (1994). *Population and development: Old debates, new conclusions*. Washington DC: Transaction.
Catholic Institute for International Relations. (1993). *Malawi: A moment of truth*. London: Russel Press.
Chakanza, J. C. (2002). Christian-Islam co-existence and development. *African Ecclesial Review (AFTER) 44 (3 & 4)*, 153–168.
Chimbiri, A. (forthcoming). The condom is an "intruder" in marriage: Evidence from rural Malawi. Center for Reproductive Health, College of Medicine, University of Malawi, Blantyre, Malawi. Under review for *Social Science and Medicine* publications.
Chimbiri-Kavinya. (2002). *Women's empowerment, spousal communication and reproductive decision-making in Malawi*. Unpublished doctoral dissertation, University of Waikato, New Zealand.
Department for International Development. (2003). Report on cultural beliefs and practices influencing sexual and reproductive health, and health-seeking behavior in Malawi. Lilongwe.
Food & Agriculture [FAO] & Government of Malawi. (1992). Transcripts of focus group discussions. Lilongwe: Ministry of Information.
Fox, R. (1967). *Kinship and marriage*. London: Penguin Books.
Goode, W. J. (1970). *World revolution and family patterns*. New York: Free Press.
Government of Malawi. (1987). *Malawi population and housing census 1987 analytical report*. Zomba: Government Printer.
Government of Malawi. (1993). *Situational analysis of poverty*. Lilongwe: Government Press.
Government of Malawi. (1994). *Malawi population and housing census 1987 analytical report*. Zomba: Government Printer.
Government of Malawi. (2000). *1998 Malawi population and housing census report of final census results*. Zomba: Government Printer.
Government of Malawi. (2001). *Malawi population and housing census analytical report*. Zomba: Government Printer.
Government of Malawi. (2002). *1998 Malawi population and housing census analytical report*. Zomba: Government Printer.
Government of Malawi. (2003). *Malawi population and housing census analytical report*. Zomba: Government Printer.
Government of Malawi & United Nations. (1993). *Situation analysis of poverty in Malawi*. Lilongwe: Government Press.
Government of Malawi & UNICEF. (1998). *Free primary education, the Malawi experience: A policy analysis*. Lilongwe: Ministry of Education.
Government of Malawi & UNDP. (2002). *The impact of HIV/AIDS on human resources in the Malawi public sector*. Lilongwe.
Kabeer, N. (1994). *Reversed realities: Gender hierarchies in development thought*. London, New York: Verso.
Kaler, A. (2001). Many divorces and many spinsters: Marriage as an invented tradition in southern Malawi, 1946–1999. *Journal of Family History 26(4)*, 529–556.
Kandawire, J. A. K. (1979). Thangata: Forced labor or reciprocal assistance? *Journal of African History 24*, 257–274.

Kanjaye, H. (1999). *Health-Malawi: Breaking the silence on HIV/AIDS epidemic*. Inter-Press Service. http://www.aegis.com/news/ips/1999/ IP991102.html. Retrieved: June 13, 2005.

Labourrie-Racape, A., & Locoh, T. (1998). *Genre et demographie: nouvelles problematiques ou effet de monde?* Dossiers et recherches #65, Paris.

Locoh, T. (1997). Changements des structures familiales et leurs consequences en Afrique. *Congres International de la Population*. Beijing: Union Internationale pour l'Etude Scientifique de la Population, vol. 3, 1107–1109.

Locoh. T. (2000). Genre, population et development dans les pays du sud, etat des lieux et perspectives. In Bozon, M. & Locoh, T. (Eds.), *Rapports de genre et questions de population II: Genre, population et développement* (pp. 1–34). Dossiers et recherches #85.

Marwick, M. G. (1965). *Sorcery in its social setting: A study of the northern Rhodesia Chewa*. Manchester, Eng.: University of Manchester Press.

Mitchell, J. C. (1971). The Yao village: A study in the social structure of a Malawian people. Published on behalf of the Institute for African Studies, University of Zambia. Manchester, Eng.: Manchester University Press.

Munthali, A., & Chimbiri, A. M. (2003). *Adolescent sexual and reproductive health: A synthesis report for Malawi*. New York: Allan Guttmacher Institute.

Murdock, G. P. (1959). Africa: Its peoples and their cultural history. New York: McGraw Hill.

National AIDS Commission. (1999). *National strategic framework on HIV/AIDS: 2000–2004 (NSF)*. Programs and Services for National AIDS Control Program of Malawi. http://www.aidsmalawi.org.

National AIDS Commission. (2002). *Behavior change communication strategy*. Lilongwe.

National AIDS Commission. (2003). *Joint review of the national HIV/AIDS strategic framework and operations of the National AIDS Commission. A consolidated report*. Lilongwe.

National Commission of Women in Development. (1993). *Women and the law in Malawi*. Lilongwe: National Center for Literacy and Adult Education.

Okommah, A. D. (2000). *HIV-AIDS epidemic in Africa*. Foundation for Democracy in Africa homepage. http://www.democracy-africa.org/hivaids.htm.

Pachai, B. (1973). *Malawi: The history of the nation*. London: Longman.

Phiri, I. A. (1996). Marched, suspended and stoned: Christian women in Malawi 1995. In Ross, K. R. (Ed.), *God, people and power in Malawi: Democratization in theological perspective* (pp. 63–106). Limbe: Assemblies of God Press.

Phiri, I. A. (1997). *Women, Presbyterianism and patriarchy: Religious experience of Chewa women in central Malawi*. Limbe: Assemblies of God Press.

Phiri, I. A. (1998). The initiation of Chewa women of Malawi: A Presbyterian women's perspective. In Cox, J. L. (Ed.), *Rites of passage in contemporary Africa* (pp. 129–144). Great Britain: Cardiff Academic Press.

Phiri, K. (1983). Some changes in the matrilineal family systems among the Chewa of Malawi since the nineteenth century. *Journal of African History 24*, 257–274.

Ross, K. R. (1996). The transformation of power in Malawi 1992–94: The role of the Christian churches. In Ross, K. R. (Ed.), *God, people and power in Malawi: Democratization in theological perspective* (pp. 15–40). Limbe: Assemblies of God Press.

Schoffeleers, J. M., & B. Litt. (1968). *The lower Shire Valley: Its ecology, population distribution, ethnic divisions, and systems of marriage*. Blantyre, Malawi: Montfort Press.

Schoffeleers, M. (1973). Towards the identification of Proto-Chewa culture. *Journal of Social Science (Malawi) 2*, 47–60.
Senghor, L. S. (1964). *On African socialization.* New York: Praeger.
Thompson, T. J. (1998). The sacramental conventions of the Ngoni of Northern Malawi: Conscious interaction or happy coincidence? In Cox, J. L. (Ed.), *Rites of passage in contemporary Africa* (pp. 1–14). Great Britain: Cardiff Academic Press.
Tinker, I. (1997). The making of a field: Advocates, practitioners and scholars. In Visvanathan, N., Duggan, L., Nisonoff, L., & Wiegersma, N. (Eds.), *The women, gender and development reader* (pp. 33–42). London: ZED Books.
Van Valsen, J. (1960). Labor migration as a positive factor in the continuity of Tonga tribal society. *Economic Development and Cultural Change 8(3)*, 265–278.
Vaughan, M. (1987). *The story of an African famine: Gender and family in twentieth century Malawi.* London: Cambridge University Press.
Vignikin, K. (1997). *Evolution des structures familiales en Afrique et consequences demographiques et socio-economiques.* Congres International de la Population (vol. 3, pp. 1139–1154). Beijing: Union Internationale pour l'Etude Scientifique de la Population.
Visvanathan, N., Duggan, L., Nisonoff, L., & Wiegersma, N. (1997). The women, gender and development reader. London: ZED Books.
Weinreb, A. A. (1999). *Was Goode right? New data on the nucleation of family ties in rural Malawi.* Paper presented at the Annual Meeting of the Population Association of America, New York.
Whitehead, A. (1975). *Women and men, kinship and property: Some general issues.* Oxford: Clarendon.
Young, T. C. (1932). *Notes on the history of the Tumbuka-Kamanga peoples in the northern province of Nyasaland.* London: Religious Tract Society, repro (1970). London: Frank Cass.
Zulu, E. M. (1996). *Social and cultural factors affecting reproductive behavior in Malawi.* Unpublished doctoral dissertation. University of Pennsylvania, Philadelphia.

CHAPTER 12

Family Life in Soweto, Gauteng, South Africa

Sylvia N. Moeno

INTRODUCTION

Soweto is a large black residential area a few kilometers southwest of Johannesburg. It is located in Gauteng, one of South Africa's nine provinces. Landlocked, it is the smallest province in area, occupying only about 1.4 percent of the country's landmass. The term *Soweto* is an acronym for the South Western Townships, which consist of 26 suburbs or townships. Soweto's population include a diverse group of indigenous African ethnic and cultural groups from South Africa (e.g., the Naledi, Mapetle, Tladi, Moletsane, and Phiri; the Basotho, Batswana, and Bapedi group; the Tsonga and Venda-speaking people; and the Dhlamini, Senaoane, Zulu, Xhosa, and Ndebele people). It is important to note that in the Sowetan situation, all these groups have been brought together and live in close physical and social proximity to each other, thereby influencing each other, and also exchanging many aspects of their cultures with one another.

An interesting thing about Soweto is that a large proportion of its population (41.6 percent) is unemployed (Morris, 1999). As in other townships of Gauteng, most Sowetans belong to several Christian churches established by white missionaries in the early days of the white settler occupation. Some of the largest congregations, as indicated in Pauw's (1973) study of East London (1973), are Methodists, Anglicans (who are also known as members of the Church of the Province of South Africa), Presbyterians, Roman Catholics, Baptists, and members of the Assemblies of God and the Dutch Reformed

Church. In addition, there are also a number of independent or separatist movements not affiliated with white missionary churches, the largest of which is the Zionist Christian Church which is composed of Bishop Lekganyane's followers. More recently, the presence of Muslims has also been felt in the province.

Johannesburg is the capital city of Gauteng Province, with Soweto housing its black workers 15 kilometers away. During the surge of industrial expansion that took place after the mid-1930s, Johannesburg became the main center for job seekers from far and wide. By 1948, about two-thirds of Soweto's population was composed of immigrants, who had taken residence in the Johannesburg/Soweto Complex (Bonner, 1998). Bonner and Segal (1998, p. 10) describe Johannesburg and its environs as a desolate landscape with only bare veldt in 1880. Before the discovery of gold in 1886, it had only a handful of African homesteads and Boer farmhouses. After the discovery of gold, this desolate high-veldt area became a mining camp, with mine dumps forming dusty grey-white hills throughout the Witwatershed, as Gauteng was then called, with a touch of green grass and some brown bushes for color.

In discussing such aspects of Soweto as ecological and geographical variations, reference must be made to past historical factors that have helped to shape the present situations. For example, Hammond-Tooke (1993, p. 14) writes that there are four major groupings into which present-day Bantu-speaking populations are divided—the Nguni, Sotho, Tsonga, and Venda—can be squarely located in four major geographical and ecological regions. These, in his opinion, can be grouped into two wider regions, the East and West, defined essentially as the coastal strip and the central plateau. Thus, the Sotho and Venda were associated with the central plateau, and the Nguni and Tsonga with the Indian Ocean littoral.

Kuper (1982) sees three sets of factors as responsible for variations in local bride wealth systems, as a consequence of adaptation to various local circumstances: the relative importance of pastoralism as opposed to agriculture; the marriage rules, for example, different forms of cross-cousin marriages; and the influence of social stratification. For example, with groups for whom agriculture was the main subsistence activity, like the Tsonga and Venda, bride wealth payments were high, but when agriculture was less significant, as among the Tswana and Nguni, payments were low. Even differences in cosmological systems can be traced to the pervasive influence of settlement patterns. Hammond-Tooke (1993, p. 21) concludes that there was indeed a broad connection between environment and the ways in which ethnic groups modified their cultures in an effort to achieve successful adaptation.

Therefore, whether this thesis can be applied to present Sowetans—who are the direct descendants of the Sotho, Tsonga, Nguni, and Venda people—and whether the differences in their culture can still be explained in these terms of reference remains to be seen.

HISTORICAL BACKGROUND

The Precolonial Era

Leonard Thompson (1985) states that the myth that white settlers occupied an empty land reflects the values of the white ruling group under apartheid, not a demographic fact. This view is supported by others. For instance, in the opening pages of *The Roots of Black South Africans*, Hammond-Tooke (1993) boldly states that their roots (black South Africans) lie, of course, in black Africa (p. 23).

The origin of the Bantu-speaking peoples occurred in the centuries immediately before the beginning of the common era, and was closely associated with the beginnings of the Iron Age, and seemingly occurred south of the equatorial forests in the savannah highlands of Katanga (in present day Zambia, and the region of the Great Lakes). By the 1st century CE, they had reached the Limpopo river, and moved into what is today South Africa (Hammond-Tooke, 1993, p. 24).

Before this time the country south of the Limpopo was inhabited by hunter-gatherers, using late Stone Age tools and inhabiting the entire sub-continent. In the lowveld and bushveld of the former Transvaal, there emerged settled communities engaged in agriculture, working and sometimes smithing and smelting iron metal. What is clear is that South Africa's first farming communities were established at least by the end of the third century. They were cultivating Pennisetum (millet). . . . By the fifth century populations were established in large villages of pole and thatch houses with plastered walls and floors. It is certain that most east Iron Age communities had at least some cattle . . . herded in central byres. (Hammond-Tooke, 1993, pp. 26–27)

Differences between the four major Bantu-speaking groupings—Nguni, Sotho, Venda, and Tsonga—appear to be caused by a combination of two very early traditions which date back to the early Iron Age: environmental influences stemming from later Iron Age dispersal into the highveld plateau until about the 14th century, and the 17th-century elaboration of cultural differences among the four groups, especially the establishment among highveld Sotho of aggregated settlements.

For the Nguni, dating is not so certain, Hammond-Tooke explains, because of the relative absence of discovered Iron Age sites in Natal and the Transkei. However, historical documents show that Nguni speakers were settled south of the Mthatha River well before the end of the 16th century, while oral traditions suggest that they were in the foothills of the Drakensburg as early as 1300 CE.

The Colonial Period

Our recorded South African history begins with the arrival of Europeans in 1652 at the Cape Colony. They settled in the southern tip of Africa to provide a way station for replenishing Dutch merchant ships on the way to and from the East Indies. This began the long saga of conquests by white settlers who came with guns and their bibles to trade where it was useful or profitable and to take over the land. The Khoisan, and subsequently other Bantu-speaking people, were either pushed off their land or were absorbed into the white settlement as conquered labor (Wilson & Thompson, 1969). This long process of conquest finally culminated in the notorious Land Act of 1913, which prohibited Africans from purchasing land outside the reserves, which was less than 14 percent of the total country.

Slavery was the second historical fact of conquest that further added to the dispossession of black South Africans. In this regard, Wilson and Thompson (1969) explain that the first white settlers, bringing with them the habits of established colonial power, were soon calling for slaves to meet their labor needs. However, the majority of the blacks in South Africa were never enslaved. Accordingly, the first shipment of slaves for private ownership landed in this country in 1658 from West Africa, Angola, Guinea, Madagascar, and Southeast Asia.

In 1760, slaves were required to carry passes when moving between rural and urban areas. By 1775, an indenture system for the offspring of male slaves and Khoikhoi women until the age of 25 had also been developed. The abolition of slavery in 1828 brought about the enactment of a further series of pass and vagrancy laws. These were then directed at controlling the movement into and within conquered groups of Nguni- and Sotho-speaking Africans. The many pass and vagrancy laws that developed during the 19th century became the foundation and structure of the migratory labor systems which became the distinguishing feature of South African industrialization. In 1872, the first of the Industrial Pass Laws to control the movement of mine labor was enacted.

The impact of these laws, which were passed to control and oppress the black majority in this country, was greatly felt throughout Southern Africa. The laws led to rural-urban migration in which many young men in the prime of life left their rural homes to work and live in towns and cities. In turn, the migration led to a breakdown of family ties and loyalties, as well as the moral fiber of black communities. Family "breakups" became rampant as women and children remained in rural homes, while traditional heads of families left to live in hostels and compounds. Because most of the migrant men never returned, their wives went to look for them and look for work. Families in rural communities were left to fend for themselves. This led to a breakdown of family norms and values in both rural and urban areas, with traditional family norms and values being replaced by Western norms and values.

The Contemporary Situation

South Africa has recently emerged from its dark history of apartheid into a new democratic era, which began with the release of Nelson Mandela from 27 years of captivity. Mandela went on to become the first democratically elected president of South Africa in 1994. Unfortunately, the pervasive and long-lasting effects of the apartheid system will continue to have an impact on the lives of the majority of South Africans, well into the 21st century. Indeed, the apartheid system was a prime example of institutional racism whose function was to deepen racial inequalities through systematic discrimination and oppression of other racial groups, especially the Africans, by a white minority group.

The institutionalization of apartheid meant that laws governed and regulated the forms of social relationships that existed between the oppressed racial groups. Separate institutional facilities were provided for the different racial groups. These policies were aimed at maintaining the greatest possible degree of social, residential, and political separation of the races, which led to differential treatment and inferior institutional facilities being provided for blacks. The system served to protect white political and economic interests, and gave whites a disproportionate share of the land, wealth, and power. Separate institutional facilities also tended to institutionalize social distance between groups and to entrench inequalities in South African society (Wilson & Ramphele, 1989).

The pervading patterns of inequality and discrimination were supported and reinforced by myriad laws and regulations that affected all areas of life—housing, family life, transportation, health, social services, public safety, insurance, and social security. We can see that such laws, in making existing norms and practices more rigid and authoritative, made discrimination, inequality, and status distinctions so utterly pervasive that these characteristics have penetrated deep into the consciousness of both black and white South Africans (Wilson & Ramphele, 1989).

FAMILY LIFE IN INDIGENEOUS AFRICAN AND EUROPEAN CULTURES

The African family in South Africa is a social institution that has weathered many storms. It has been subjected to various challenging and changing social situations throughout the different historical periods: from the traditional African family before contact with Western European influences of colonization, Christianity, capitalism, industrialization, and urbanization; through apartheid and its impact; to its present form. Its strength, tenacity, and resilience are a demonstration of the family's ability to change and adapt, as well as its importance as a central institution in African society. It has survived and adapted, assuming different forms and shapes as dictated by the various sociopolitical circumstances in which it existed, and it will continue to survive as long as society exists.

The shaping of Sowetan families evolved from the influences of the indigenous and European Christian cultures as there has been little, if any, contact between the indigenous African culture and the Islamic faith. It is only recently, since 1994, that we notice indications of conversions to the Islamic faith by Africans in Soweto.

Marriage and Family in Indigenous African Culture

Marriage was an important social institution among the southern Bantu. Despite differences in the manner in which marriages were arranged, there were some basic marriage rules. Preston-Whyte (1974) reports that a woman could only have one spouse while a man might have more than one wife at a time; and that marriage could only be effected by the transfer of *lobolo* (bride wealth).

The Nguni had strict rules of clan exogamy. Any girl with the same clan name as a man was excluded from consideration as a marriage partner. Whoever was married was a stranger, as she came from a different descent group (Hammond-Tooke, 1993). Among the Sotho and Venda, there was the expectation that a young man would marry a cousin, either a cross cousin or a parallel cousin. Marrying a parallel cousin meant that no bonds of alliance were formed with strangers, nor was it strictly necessary to transfer *bohadi* (bride wealth in Sotho). This kept bride wealth in the family.

Among the Southern Bantu, the passing of bride wealth (*bohadi* or *lobolo*) in the form of cattle was the essential act in legalizing a new union. It further conferred to the husband the rights of fatherhood over the children born out of the union. It transferred the capacity of a woman to bear children from her family to that of her husband's. Hammond-Tooke (1993) maintains that it had the effect of transposing certain rights over a girl, up to now vested in her father or guardian, to her husband and her family, linking the two family groups rather than the individuals. This meant that if a woman was barren, her sister would be sent "to put a child in the womb" of the barren woman. Similarly, in the event that a wife died without giving birth, a substitute could be sent to "raise up the house that has fallen." This led to the saying that "cattle beget children" (Hammond-Tooke, 1993).

The amount of *lobolo* differed from group to group. Among the Nguni, the amount was subject to considerable bargaining, and could be paid off in installments over the years. Among the Sotho, especially the Pedi and Tswana, the full amount was required before marriage. Among South Sotho, the amount was negotiable and the husband's people offered what they considered to be fair or affordable. Marriage negotiations could be opened by the parents of either the boy or girl, although it was common for the boy's parents to take the initiative and ask for the girl's hand in marriage.

After the passage of the *lobolo/bohadi*, wedding ceremonies followed including the actual physical movement of the bride from her father's home to her husband's. Kuper (1982) states that the essence of the southern Bantu marriage was the exchange of brides for cattle. There were slight differences between groups: the Sotho-Tswana emphasized *bohadi* payment, while among the Nguni the important element was the transfer of the bride.

The extended family was the prevalent family structural form, which represented the ideal level of development. An extended family might contain about a dozen relatives. Nzimande (1987) confirms that common extended family structures were either vertical as in a multigenerational family, or horizontal as in polygynous marriages. According to Nzimande (1987), the extended family's characteristics are as follows: a wider circle of people who are related by blood or marriage, who identify themselves as family, and who support each other. It is more durable as a social unit than the nuclear unit, as it moves through different development cycles, and acts effectively as a social support system, or social welfare system, by providing care and support to its dependents.

The Shaping of Family by the European Culture

As reported earlier, the contact between Africans and Europeans has affected African marriages and family life tremendously. Christianity played a critical role in this regard, as Christian teaching implied a radical change in the manner of life for early converts. Family relationships and the political structure were radically changed by the condemnation of polygyny. The British missionaries were the first to arrive in the Cape, under the rule of Sir George Grey in the 19th century. These missionaries expected African converts to wear Western-style clothing; to build square rather than round mud houses in villages around the church and school; and to abandon ancient traditional practices, such as the traditional initiation dances. The missionaries condemned *lobolo* as the "sin of buying wives." The Christian gospel became a destructive agent used to propagate the expansion of capitalism or cultural imperialism (Wilson & Thompson, 1969).

Colonization and Christianity, followed by industrialization and urbanization, were strong agents of social change that wreaked havoc on African society throughout the continent. In the South African situation, these social forces were also accompanied by a number of laws, which were passed to control and oppress the African majority in rural and urban areas alike. The discovery of diamonds, followed by gold in the 1860s, led to rural-urban migration, in which many young men left their rural homes to work in the mines and the other industrial centers of Gauteng (Witwatersrand region in the Transvaal Province).

The migratory labor system, influx control regulations, and the pass laws led to a breakdown of black family ties and loyalties, and adversely affected the moral fiber of the black communities from which these young black men were recruited. As mentioned earlier, family breakups resulted when the traditional heads of families left women and children behind in the rural areas. The men went to live in hostels and compounds in cities, which were prevented by the pass laws from accommodating women and families. Most of the men never returned to the rural areas. Instead, they married or formed new partnerships with single unmarried women in the towns and cities.

The migrant men were later followed by young women, who left their children and elderly parents to go look for their husbands and also to find work in the cities in order to support themselves, their children, and elderly relatives.

These migratory patterns, then, led to a further breakdown of family norms and values, as the rural and urban communities were unable to do anything to stop the situation. These influences resulted in many challenges, changes, and adaptations in the South African family.

CONCEPTUALIZATION OF BLACK SOUTH AFRICAN FAMILIES

Many early accounts of the organization of sexual and parental relationships stress the existence of certain biological imperatives, namely, the necessity of procreation to the survival of the human species, the lengthy physical and psychological dependence of children, and the need for security in sexual relationships. They also assume that these imperatives merge to produce a biological group, the nuclear family (Elliot, 1986, p. 16). The ordering of sexual relationships, reproduction, child rearing, and economic support of family members are closely interrelated tasks and are therefore best performed if fused within a single institution—the family (Elliot, 1986, p. 17).

The Western legal definition of family life usually clashes with the traditional African family norms and values, leading to:

1. The adoption of the nuclear family as the acceptable ideal to conform to, as opposed to the extended family concept of the African
2. A rejection of the custom of *lobolo* as an integral part of African marriage
3. The adoption of the Western Christian form of marriage—a church wedding—as the Western legal form
4. The rejection of customary African practices like the initiation ceremonies that prepared the youth for adulthood responsibilities and married life, per se
5. The adoption of the Western notion of family as a union between two individuals, rather than between families (kinship groups)
6. The rejection of cross-cousin marriages, which were practiced by some Southern Bantu groups, for example, the Sotho-Venda people
7. The rejection of the ancestral worshipping beliefs, based on the role played by family members even after their death; and consequently, the rejection of all rites and rituals grounded in these beliefs regarding the powers of the ancestors. (Dlamini, 1987)

The implications of the above are immense, as they mean the total rejection of who and what the African is, his/her past and history, and his/her land and cultural heritage. Bozzoli (1983) argues that in urban areas of South Africa, the black family has by no means taken on a capitalist character:

If it is assumed that [the] archetypal patriarchal nuclear family is a concomitant of capitalism, urban black families may retain certain general patriarchal characteristics, which represent continuity with rural patterns . . . extended family obligations persist where the father, if present, assumes the role of household head. So, while many families remain patriarchal, many others become matrifocal. In cases where they have been divorced, deserted, or never married, it is they who provide not only the income for the family, but the source of stability and ideological continuity. The capacity of these women to develop a viable independent family form, and to sustain extended family links to support them in so doing, is a dimension of "domestic struggle" which has too often been bypassed in analyses of capitalism's assumed requirements for a nuclear family. (Bozzoli, 1983, p. 165)

SOCIAL CHANGES AND FAMILY DYNAMICS IN BLACK SOUTH AFRICA

Due to the racially segregated nature of South African society, and the legacy of the apartheid system, there was and still is a tendency to regard and refer to the African family, in urban and rural areas, as dysfunctional and not worth studying. Researchers have concentrated more on its abnormalities, while using Western standards to support these sentiments of the superiority of Western ways over indigenous traditional African norms and practices. The truth is that South African society, as a whole, has been subjected to far-reaching changes, which have caused mounting tensions in family life of the various population groups and making the family increasingly vulnerable.

This is supported by the significant increase in family breakdowns, with its negative consequences for society in general and for personality development in particular. Therefore, to develop social policy to strengthen marriage and family life in South Africa, an integrated approach to the study of family in South Africa has to focus on all population groups in order to reveal any similarities, differences, and peculiarities. Research must discover why "good" or "bad" characteristics exist in some groups but not in others; and also develop strategies to improve the quality of family life for all South Africans. For example, the White Paper on Social Welfare, which was approved by the Cabinet on November 15, 1995, acknowledged family as the basic unit of South Africa, and stated that family life was to be strengthened and promoted through family-oriented policies and programs. The paper showed that the government was committed to giving the highest priority to the promotion of quality family life and to the survival, protection, and development of all South Africa's children (Ministry for Welfare and Development, 1995).

Mate Selection and Customary Marriage Types

Among the Southern Bantu peoples, the development of girls from childhood to adulthood consisted of a series of marked stages, each of which brought about increased status and greater responsibilities. The onset of puberty was followed by initiation, rituals, and other rites of passage to prepare youth for marriage and adulthood. This was followed by the public recognition of the girl's marriageable state. During this stage, the girls were controlled by a group of older girls, who taught, supervised, advised, and guided the younger girls through the process of courtship.

Male circumcision was also practiced by the Southern Bantu, and young men of the same age were enrolled in circumcision schools to teach them and prepare them for adulthood. This was followed by courtship. Among the Zulu beadwork was used as a form of communication, whereby young girls presented boys whom they fancied with beads as an expression of love. Different colors of beadwork symbolized different meanings; for example, white beads were the symbol of love, pink signified poverty, and yellow signified wealth in cattle. Thus, a single string of white, yellow, and pink read: "My heart is full of love, but you have no cattle to marry me with" (Krige, 1950, p. 118).

Courtship was followed by formal marriage negotiations, initiated by the boy's family to ask the girl's parents for permission to marry her. *Lobolo* was then settled in the form of the number of cattle, and agreed on during the marriage negotiations. This cemented the friendship between the two families, who would then be bound together by marriage ties (Ashton, 1952).

The choice of a marriage partner depended on personal factors such as physical attraction, personality, and the social status of the girl's family. For example, the Tswana had a wide choice of what type of cousin marriage to follow, which allowed for the development of strategies as ways to use marriage for economic and political advantage. Whereas, among the Sotho and Venda, cross-cousin or parallel cousin marriages were arranged and preferred, and couples were supposed to approve of the choice made by their respective families. Infant betrothal occasionally occurred, arranged by families who were friends. Parallel cousin marriage among the Tswana was particularly favored by their nobility, whereas among the Nguni strict rules of exogamy applied (Hammond-Tooke, 1993, pp. 118-119).

Urban Marriages in Soweto

The urban African situation is different from what typically takes place in the rural areas. There is a tendency toward marriage based on individual choice of partners with considerable variation within the different levels or strata, ranging from tradition-orientated ways to more modern urban ways. As a result of the breakdown of traditional social control mechanisms in Soweto and other urban townships, there is a prevalence of premarital sexual relations between young adults, who regard such behavior as normal during courtship. This behavior is not explicitly sanctioned. Pauw (1973) maintains that the widespread practice of premarital sex and the common occurrence of pregnancy among unmarried young people reflect a behavior pattern conflicting with both traditional ethical notions and the Christian norm of complete chastity before marriage.

The large portion of migrant laborers in Soweto also led to extramarital sex and the use of concubines. Mayer (1962) and Longmore (1959) explain the prevalence of extramarital sex and cohabitation in urban African areas in terms of sociopolitical and economic factors. It was a response to the pressure exerted by and the frustration caused by the many apartheid laws that led migrant workers to resort to cohabitation with urban girls so as to qualify for urban residence. In such situations, a man became the legal head of one rural family and also the domestic head of another urban family. He might end up staying in the city for good and having a family of town children, without legal paternity.

Dlamini (1987) also argues that urbanization has had an effect on marriage and family stability. For example, the extended family participated in mate selection so that a person who shared the same values and lifestyle would be chosen. It was important that the approval of the family be obtained because the family would be involved in the resolution of conflicts in marriage. When the family was not involved in selection, the traditional mechanism of conflict management within the family was severely undermined (Dlamini, 1987, p. 655).

In traditional African society, *lobolo/bohadi* constituted the main ingredient of a valid customary marriage. Although *lobolo* still continues to play a function of transferring the woman's reproductive capacity from her family to that of her husband's family, it has been incorporated into the Western forms of marriage (Dlamini, 1987; Moeno, 1969; Simons, 1968).

Polygynous marriages are on the decline in urban areas like Soweto, because of polygyny's unsuitability to the urban situation for economic reasons and the influence of Western, Christian, and legal practices. Although it continues to exist, it is economically burdensome and is also incompatible with the monogamous nature of a civil marriage—which incidentally is the only legally recognized marriage in South Africa. It is important to note that while a civil marriage is essentially monogamous, a customary union is potentially polygynous. And, although the economic situation discourages polygyny, as do Western education and religion, some black South African marriages still remain polygynous (Dlamini 1987, pp. 656–657).

Civil and Christian Marriages

As indicated earlier, the early colonists often felt that it was part of their "civilizing mission" to alter the indigenous customs and beliefs of Africans until they conformed to the laws of the colonial power. This was based on the assumption that colonial law was superior to customary law. As a result, Western forms of marriage were introduced and strictly enforced in urban areas of the country during the apartheid era through the application of such laws as influx control regulations, pass laws, and housing and work permits. Pauw (1973) maintains that the most common form of marriage is by Christian rites. In his East London survey sample, the majority of all marriages were by Christian rites, while a minority was by civil rites. He, however, explains that in spite of the large-scale acceptance of these marriage types, it is significant to note that they are mostly accompanied by *lobolo*. The adherence to *lobolo* in conjunction with Christian/civil marriage has been interpreted as an attempt to bolster the institution of marriage among urban Africans. Customary and traditional marriage have also remained an important and prominent part of the Sowetan lifestyle. Of the women who are or have been married, 91.6 percent had *lobolo* paid for them (Morris, 1999, p. 32).

Postponement of Marriages

There is a growing trend among young people to postpone marriage until a later age. Many of them remain single into adulthood. These young adults may raise their own or other family member's children. This practice is common in Gauteng and other parts of South Africa, as a result of the extended family system, the low socioeconomic status of women in traditional society, and the resulting poverty of many black South African families. This has led to a variety of family forms and structures.

Many upwardly mobile black families are customarily expected by their families to raise and educate relatives' and other close family members' children. This is owing to the fact that there have always been fewer schools and technical and tertiary educational institutions in rural areas. Therefore, as a form of social security provided by the family, members who live in urban metropolitan centers are obligated to live with and educate their younger relatives or other family members' children whose parents lack the economic means to educate them.

The customary practice of *bohadi* has contributed to the growth of single-parent households and extended families in Gauteng (Moeno, 1969, 1977). In contemporary society, the continuous rise of the cost of living also exacerbates the situation. It is important to realize that as the cost of living has risen, the cost of *bohadi* has also continued to escalate. Furthermore, while other customary practices have been eroded and abandoned as a result of urbanization and modernization, the custom of *bohadi* has resisted change by adjusting itself to modern economic pressures and realities.

In traditional times, there was a close association attached to the concept of cattle and children in African cultural terms. Even though money is now used to transfer this childbearing capacity from a woman's family to her husband's family during *bohadi* transactions, the families still negotiate in terms of cattle and not money. Once an agreement has been reached as to how many cattle the woman's family requires for their daughter, the value of the cattle is translated into monetary terms. Finally, it is important to highlight the fact that due to the great importance that is placed on women having children, many couples prefer to have children before finally committing themselves to marriage. This may be a way of confirming that the woman is able to bear children.

Levels of Childbearing

Children were and still are highly desired among the southern Bantu, and no marriage is considered complete without them. It was essential to have sons to ensure continuity of the descent group, to look after one in old age, and to sacrifice to one's spirit after death. Barrenness was greatly feared and potent medicines were used to cure the condition. Special dolls to promote fertility were used by the southern Nguni and southern Sotho. *Lobolo*, which transferred cattle to the bride's family, was designed to legalize the children of the union and thus secure the continuity of the group and the handing of property (Hammond-Tooke, 1993, pp. 129–131).

In a self-sufficient economy, supported by large extended family households, the rearing of children was not problematic, as Hammond-Tooke (1993) explains. However, things are different now, because of the expense of bringing up children and the traditional emphasis on improving the quality of life of the family. This leads to the clash of traditional beliefs with modern practical realities. For example, in the study of Wattville Township, Moeno (1969) came across a new trend of having a child(ren) before marriage (i.e., while *lobolo* was being paid or until a certain acceptable portion of it was settled). This trend was perhaps brought about by changes that resulted from using money instead of cattle to settle *lobolo*.

South Africa recorded an average of 27 births per 1,000 women in 1999, comparable to such countries as Bangladesh and Mexico. The rate of 27 was low compared to other southern African countries. The crude birth rate of Africans was 32.2; Indians, 18.5; whites, 13.3; and coloreds, 20.1. The fertility level in South Africa was 2.9 children per woman in 1998, with sizable differences between urban and nonurban women. The total fertility rate for women living in nonurban areas was almost double that of urban women. Among African women living in nonurban areas, the rate was 4.0 children per woman, while the rate among urban African women was 2.4 (South Africa Survey, 2001–02, p. 53).

The Soweto Survey (Morris, 1999) measured childbearing patterns only among these women who were and had been married. Of these, 8.5 percent were childless, 40 percent had their first child before turning 20, and 75 percent had a child by the age of 24. Unfortunately, this excluded those women who were unmarried but had children, especially as this group of women also had to prove their worth as potentially marriageable by producing—or rather proving that they were capable of producing—children, while their partners were working and saving up for *lobolo*.

Intergenerational Ties

Strong family ties still exist in Soweto and the other African townships as a result of the persistence of the extended family form despite the apartheid laws designed to enforce the adoption of the Western-style nuclear family type. Apartheid's discriminatory practices against black people of South Africa have helped to reinforce social class inequalities between races, so that the majority of Sowetans are working-class people, with very few in the middle class.

At the time of the Soweto Survey, Soweto's middle class was still small due to apartheid's education policies and employment practices. Only 15.4 percent of Sowetan households had monthly incomes income above 3,000 Rands—an equivalent of about $460 (Morris, 1999). This has led to the strengthening of family ties because economic dependence is highest in lower-income families. When members of a family are employed and in a good financial position, they tend to live with other family members and relatives. In the Soweto Survey, only 45.7 percent of the households were nuclear families, the rest were extended households in varying forms including a higher proportion of multi-generational household forms.

WOMEN'S STATUS AND THE CHANGING FAMILY DYNAMICS

It has been argued (Moeno, 1977) that black South African women's participation in the workforce is not a recent phenomenon. They have traditionally performed most of the tasks necessary for the survival and subsistence of their families such as tilling the fields, weaving cloth, building homes, milking cows, and generally helping to provide for their families. This was possible because their roles as wives and mothers were easily accommodated in their communities, as their work was centered around the homestead.

The arrival of white settlers, the discovery of gold and diamonds, and other interrelated factors led to the beginning of industrialization within the country, which in turn led to a whole range of societal changes. As a result, African men from all corners of the Southern African region left their rural homes and their traditional way of life to work and live in South African cities and towns. They left their wives, children, parents, and communities for short and long periods. This meant that the women had to learn to assume roles that were the main domain of their husbands and manage on their own. They practically ran their communities without the help, guidance, and support of their male counterparts. Through this they became independent and resourceful, learning to depend on themselves or on each other.

In this vein, Wolpe (1980) applied a structuralist interpretation of the genesis and functions of the native reserve economies over the decades since the discovery of gold. He argues that as the demands of the capitalist mode of production for labor increased, men were drawn into capitalist production, while women performed the functions of reproducing, maintaining, and sustaining in times of sickness and old age the cheap labor forces required by the mines. The weakness of this Marxist form of explanation is that it fails to provide "fruitful ground for discourse about the struggles between men and women within; or the struggles between the family as a social unit, and the wider system in which it is located" (Bozzoli, 1983, p. 144).

The independence that women enjoyed in the rural traditional situation, which resulted from the absence of their husbands due to the migratory labor system, slowly and subtly eroded the patriarchal system of their society. This empowered them as they became the temporary heads of their families while their husbands were away. They were still wholly responsible for the immediate (nuclear) unit in the absence of their husbands and had to provide and look after this unit fully.

Women who went to the urban areas worked as domestic servants, factory workers, liquor brewers and sellers, and washerwomen. Most women did not end up in the main industrial and mining sector because at the time of their arrival those sectors did not use black female labor. They therefore avoided getting incorporated into the proletarian factory labor system and were able to use their relative economic autonomy to establish an independent base within the urban family (Bozzoli, 1983, p. 164).

A functionalist approach, which seeks to explain the position of urban women in terms of the functions they perform for society, would identify the kind of occupations in which women came to be involved as "reproductive." They tend to be concerned with maintaining the reserve labor force; providing leisure outlets for workers in the city; or "reproducing" the white family through domestic labor and laundry work. This explanation is insufficient because it fails to explain why and how it was that women ended up doing this, neither does it enrich our understanding of how these women are active participants in shaping their destinies, which are often in conflict with capitalism.

Urban black families may retain certain general patriarchal characteristics, which represent continuity with rural patterns. The division of labor within the home remains unequal between males and females. The daughters of the home are obliged to help with domestic labor and extended family obligations; whereas the father assumes a place as head of household when he is present. Even though some families may remain patriarchal, generating and reproducing a conservative familial ideology, many of them become matrifocal. In cases in which women have been deserted, divorced, or never married, they provide the income for the family, as well as stability and ideological continuity. Consequently, the central feature of the emerging position of black women in South Africa is the prolongation of their incorporation into capitalism, and their assertion of a position of comparative power and strength within the domestic sphere in both urban and rural areas (Bozzoli, 1983, p. 163).

African women in the workforce are still highly discriminated against due to traditional cultural attitudes and practices, and their natural biological reproductive functions, as well as racist laws and practices. These attitudes and practices discouraged parents from educating girls in earlier times, as it was considered a waste of money. Thus, girls were relegated to performing jobs at the lowest rung of the occupational structure. However, as they have joined the labor force in greater numbers they are gradually moving into the professional, technical, and managerial fields such as teaching, nursing, social work, and physiotherapy. Nevertheless these professions tend to limit their future growth and mobility in the open labor market, and reinforce the stereotypes of a woman's traditional role in society.

Regarding the legal status of black women in South Africa, there have been major strides forward in improving their position in the country. In an attempt to reverse the history of women's discrimination and marginalization, traditionally and during the apartheid era, the current government has adopted a number of laws to promote equality between women and men regardless of race, class, disability, and sexual orientation. These laws protect the interests of women and men in the family and throughout most of social life (Office on the Status of Women, 2000).

This legal framework has empowered women and promoted gender equality; however, the implementation of these laws has been difficult given that many of these rights are still inaccessible to women, and many women don't have the knowledge and skills required to access legal avenues. The national gender policy elaborates the new legislative framework that must be activated to ensure that these measures are felt by women. Despite this, there remain gaps in the legal framework such as the practice of African customary law, which was based on the Black Administration Act 35 of 1927, that disinherits women.

It has been difficult to change the inherent traditional attitudes toward women and children. Male chauvinism continues in the socialization processes, which relegates African women to the lowest positions in society. Attitudes take a long time to change and will only be affected by formal and informal socialization processes, as more social changes occur due to globalization and improved communication technology both within and outside South Africa.

South African black women played leading roles in the liberation struggle in general and in the dismantling of the pass laws in particular. The first big protest against the pass laws took place in October 1955. Protests sprang up all over the country and culminated in a mass demonstration at the Union Buildings, Pretoria, on August 9, 1956, with a petition presented to the prime minister. Hundreds of thousands of signatures on petition forms were deposited at the office of the prime minister. The success of this massive protest by the women led to the designation of August 9 as Women's Day in South Africa. Since 1956, this day is celebrated as a national holiday to remind the world of the contribution made by women to society, and to acknowledge the challenges and prejudices many women still face in their fight for equal rights.

THE HIV/AIDS CRISIS AND THE BLACK SOUTH AFRICAN FAMILY HEALTH

The human immunodeficiency virus (HIV) and the acquired immunodeficiency syndrome (AIDS) epidemic poses a serious threat to African family life in both urban and rural areas of South Africa. The situation is especially critical in Gauteng as a result of its well-developed transportation systems, which serve as excellent corridors for accelerating infection throughout the country. Gauteng attracts a vast number of people from all over Southern Africa and the continent.

The first two HIV/AIDS cases in South Africa were diagnosed in 1982, with the first recorded death occurring in 1985. By the end of 1995, some 9,000 cases had been reported, of whom 8,000 were still alive; by 1999, some 4.2 million people were infected with HIV (Calitz, 2000). According to the Department of Health (1995), life expectancy will drop by almost 14 percent between 1996 and 2016. It would begin to increase between 2017 and 2026.

Gauteng Province and HIV/AIDS

Gauteng province has been hardest hit by the HIV/AIDS epidemic because of its economic position in South Africa and its high population density. African women in Soweto are a high-risk group, especially those in the lower socioeconomic strata who have multiple sexual partners. As a result, Calitz (2000) predicts the following: the figure for adults living with AIDS will increase from approximately 20,000 in 1996 to approximately 760,000 in 2010; AIDS orphans, that is, children whose parents both die of AIDS, are expected to increase from 50,000 in 1996 to 1,900,000 in 2010; and while other deaths are expected to stabilize around 400,000 per annum, AIDS deaths will increase from 390,000 in 1996 to 1,000,000 in 2010.

South Africa could lose 20 percent of its workforce in the next seven years. In the mining sector, 7 percent of workers have full-blown AIDS and productivity varies between 0 percent and 10 percent. Therefore, mines will have to employ 20 percent more workers over the next few years to maintain normal production levels by replacing the expected losses in the workforce. Furthermore, the HIV infection rate for the highly skilled labor force was forecasted to peak at 13.1 percent in 2004, compared with the infection rates of 22.8 percent for the skilled and 32.8 percent for the semiskilled and unskilled sectors; while the infection rate of the economically active population would peak at about 25.5 percent in 2006, well above the 16.7 percent maximum infection rate for the total population.

Furthermore, most people who die from AIDS are in the sexually active group of between 15 and 49 years of age. The labor market therefore loses many trained people with experience, which weakens the backbone of the economy.

Calitz (2000) adds that when AIDS entered the transportation industry, the disease became mobile throughout Southern Africa. As a result, AIDS is not just a South African problem, and the infection rate in the region provides an indication of how the subcontinent has been worst hit by the epidemic. At the present rate that the HIV/AIDS infection is spreading, the cost of health is expected to escalate tremendously. One recent study in the Gauteng region predicted a cost increase of 600 percent.

Financial constraints are identified as a core problem by Calitz (2000). Public hospitals lack the capacity and infrastructure to cope with the growing demand for health services. Hospital officials cite the provision of free primary health care and treatment of children under 5, as well as the demand for abortion, as sources of greater pressure on the system because of increased patient numbers and costs. The high HIV/AIDS infection rates have no doubt exacerbated this crisis situation in health care. Calitz (2000) explains that hospitals cannot currently cope with the number of HIV/AIDS patients, and the health budget cannot provide the medicines necessary for the needy. Pressures on the education and welfare systems have just begun to surface.

Impact of HIV/AIDS on Family Life

As was mentioned earlier, HIV/AIDS kills the breadwinners of families. This creates a society with large numbers of orphans (Calitz, 2000). The urban African family in Gauteng has already started experiencing this impact, because the majority of its workers fall in the lower ranks of the occupational ladder. They tend to have little education, are poorly skilled, and economically disadvantaged. Thus, the majority in this group are unemployed due to the present poor economic conditions.

Using the Statistics South Africa and a strict definition of the economically active population (EAP) measuring yardstick, the labor force participation rate in 1999 was 68 percent among whites; 63 percent among coloreds; 61 percent among Indians/Asians; and 47 percent among Africans. However, when using the expanded definition of unemployment, the following picture emerges: 57 percent of African women were unemployed in 1999, compared to 6 percent of white men, 7 percent of white women, and 37 percent of African men (South Africa Survey, 2001–02, p. 338). What this means is simply that the majority of the economically active population of black South Africans are unemployed and consequently poor. They are unable to compete on an equal basis with members of other racial groups for scarce resources such as jobs. Furthermore, the poor are usually hardest hit by epidemics such as HIV/AIDS, and lack the necessary resources to maintain themselves and their families.

CONCLUSION

South African society has experienced far-reaching changes since World War II, which have resulted in mounting tensions in families of various population groups. The new political situation, as well as the abolition of the influx control regulations of 1986, have also caused significant structural changes, the effects of which on family structures and support systems cannot yet be measured. Increased rural-urban migration and high levels of urbanization among African people, as well as legal and illegal immigration from other African countries and other parts of the world, necessitate increased research to advance our understanding of the dynamics of South African families.

As a result of the effects of apartheid on African family life, new forms of family life have emerged, and therefore require special attention. Since 1994 a new and very advanced Constitution guarantees, protects, and entrenches democratic principles and rights for all South African citizens and others who reside in the country. Apartheid was a ruthless, dehumanizing, and violent system of oppression, which produced and embedded a culture of violence and intolerance in all facets of society. This could be partly responsible for the present state of affairs that indicates a lack of social control mechanisms to protect the weaker and more vulnerable members of society. As a result, the following areas require special and urgent attention:

1. Child abuse and all forms of violence against children, including rape and incest
2. Rape, battering, and other forms of violence against women, as well as family murder
3. Single parenthood and teenage pregnancy, and their implications on black family life
4. HIV/AIDS—its prevention, its impact on black family life, and what strategies should be developed to control and manage its increase
5. Unemployment and its negative consequences on family life

The future prospects of the urban and rural African family in South Africa after HIV/AIDS seem bleak considering the devastation this epidemic has already caused. It is sad that such an easily preventable disease has caused so much death and devastation in South Africa and the rest of the continent. As the family is the most important and basic unit of society, it is important to channel all available resources and strengthen this important institution in our communities so that it can continue to survive, socialize, protect, and support the present and future generations of the country and continent.

Community programs that strengthen the family should be prioritized and developed so that the pervasive destructive forces inherent in a system of such extreme inequalities are eradicated. Such programs will educate and inform the public, and will raise their levels of consciousness on many of these matters. An increase in the level of formal education will empower people to make informed decisions regarding matters pertinent to their well-being and welfare.

In 2000, a legal framework was adopted to address existing gender inequalities across race and class. The document presented a vision of women's empowerment and gender equality based on national and international principles. It also provided an institutional and intersectoral coordination framework, as well as guidelines for monitoring and evaluating progress toward gender equality.

The Department of Health has continued its efforts to fight the HIV/AIDS epidemic. This has culminated in the development of an HIV/AIDS Strategic Plan for South Africa 2000–05. The strategic plan considers the availability and affordability of Azidothymidline (AZT), especially its cost implications (South Africa Survey, 2001–02).

The National Policy on HIV/AIDS for students and educators in public schools and training institutions bans compulsory disclosure of HIV/AIDS status by HIV-positive students and teachers; provides protection of confidentiality, nondiscrimination, and equality of students and teachers with HIV/AIDS; and promotes a safe school environment for HIV/AIDS education at all levels.

The Department of Education also launched the Implementation Plan for *Tirisano* (a Tswana slogan meaning "working together"). For the next five years, *Tirisano* will provide guidance for the department's activities in the areas of HIV/AIDS; school effectiveness and educator professionalism; literacy; further and higher education; and organizational effectiveness of the national and provincial departments (South Africa Survey, 2001–02). A National Literacy Agency was also established in October 2000 by the Ministry of Education to be responsible for implementation and overseeing the South African National Literacy Initiative, particularly in rural and informal settlements. The Adult Basic Education and Training Bill was also passed in 2000 (Survey South Africa, 2001–02, pp. 295–297).

All of these policies are sources of optimism, as well as the fact that the HIV/AIDS infection rate among girls aged 15–19 decreased from 21 percent in 1998 to 17 percent in 1999. Once all these educational and health policies are implemented effectively, South Africa as a country will become a leader in dealing with the HIV/AIDS epidemic. These policies, programs, and strategies will raise the standard of living for all South Africans, helping to eradicate poverty and social inequality. Improving the status of women inside and outside the home, increasing the public level of awareness, and generally improving the formal educational standards, as well as the living standards and quality of life in society, will go a long way in strengthening the family in Soweto, and indeed throughout South Africa.

REFERENCES

Ashton, H. (1952). *The Basuto.* London: Oxford University Press.
Bonner, P., & Segal, M. (1998). *Soweto: A history.* Cape Town: Masker Miller Longman.
Bozzoli, B. (1983). Marxism, feminism and South African studies. *Journal of Southern African Studies 9(2)*, April.
Calitz, J. M. (2000). Provincial population projections, 1996–2021: High HIV/AIDS impact: Pretoria: Development Bank of South Africa.

Department of Health. (1995). *Sixth national HIV survey of women attending antenatal clinics of the public health services in the Republic of South Africa (RSA) October–November 1995.* Pretoria: Department of Health.

Dlamini, C. R. M. (1987). The need for research in the social sciences for family laws. In Steyn, A. F., Strijdom, H. G., Viljoen, S., & Bosman, F. J. (Eds.), *Marriage and family life in South Africa.* Pretoria: Human Sciences Research Council.

Elliot, F. R. (1986). *The family: Change or continuity?* London: Macmillan Education.

Hammond-Tooke, W. D. (1993). *The roots of Black South Africa.* Johannesburg: Jonathan Ball.

Krige, E. J. (1950). *The social system of the Zulus.* Pietermaritzburg: Shuter & Shooter.

Kuper, A. (1982). *Wives for cattle: Bridewealth and marriage in Southern Africa.* London: Routledge & Kegan Paul.

Longmore, L. (1959). *The dispossessed.* London: Jonathan Cape.

Mayer, P. (1962). *The sociological aspects of labor migration.* Durban: University of Natal, Institute for Social Research.

Ministry for Welfare and Development. (1995). *Draft white paper on social welfare.* Pretoria: Government Printers.

Moeno, S. N. (1969). *The urban African family disorganization with special reference to the problem of illegitimacy.* Unpublished dissertation, University of South Africa, Pretoria.

Moeno, S. N. (1977). Illegitimacy in an African urban township in South Africa: An ethnographic note. *African Studies 36*, 43–47.

Morris, A. (Ed.). (1999). *Change and continuity: A survey of Soweto in the late 1990s.* Johannesburg: Department of Sociology, University of the Witwatersrand.

Nzimande, S. V. (1987). Family structure and support systems in Black communities. In Steyn, A. F., *Marriage and family life in South Africa.* Pretoria: Human Sciences Research Council.

Office on the Status of Women. (2000). *South Africa's national policy framework for women's empowerment and gender equality.* Pretoria: Office on the Status of Women.

Pauw, B. A. (1973). *The second generation: A study of the family among urbanized Bantu in East London.* Cape Town, New York: Published on behalf of the Institute of Social and Economic Research, Rhodes University, by Oxford University Press.

Preston-Whyte, E. (1974). Kinship and marriage. In Hammond-Tooke, W. D. *The Bantu-speaking peoples of Southern Africa.* London: Routledge & Kegan Paul.

Simons, H. J. (1968). *African women: Their legal status in South Africa.* London: Hurst.

South Africa Survey. (2001–02). *South Africa survey.* Johannesburg: South African Institute of Race Relations (SAIRR).

Thompson, L. (1985). *The mythology of apartheid.* New Haven, CT: Yale University Press.

Wilson, F., & Ramphele, M. (1989). *Uprooting poverty: The South African challenge.* Cape Town: David Phillip.

Wilson, M., & Thompson, L. (Eds.). (1969). *The Oxford history of South Africa, Vol. I: South Africa to 1870.* Oxford: Oxford University Press.

Wilson, M., & Thompson, L. (Eds.). (1969). *The Oxford history of South Africa, Vol. II: South Africa 1870–1966.* Oxford: Oxford University Press.

Wolpe, H. (1980). Capitalism and cheap labor-power in South Africa: From segregation to apartheid. *Economy and Society 1(4),* 1972.

Part VI
Conclusion

CHAPTER 13

The Study of African Families: Concluding Remarks

Baffour K. Takyi and Yaw Oheneba-Sakyi

> The African family is the most authentic social institution in the post-colonial era. In a continent steeped in artificiality, the African family is more real than many of our countries which were colonially made... more real than our economies most of which are mere shadows. You know, in most of our languages, including my own, there is no such a word as cousin because the children of my uncles and aunts are considered to be my brothers and sisters; there is no such a word as niece or nephew because I consider the children of my sister or the children of my brother as my children. You see, the family in Africa is vibrant in its emotions, compelling in its loyalties. It is alive and well, living right across the continent.
> —Mazrui (1986)

This volume of essays on the African family emerged from our desire, among other things, to provide an overview of family processes and also document some of the emerging trends in family processes on the continent. Given our objectives, we asked our authors to use a similar approach to provide us with some insights on family dynamics in their selected country of specialization and interest. While we must admit that the reliance on a suggested format reflecting on historical framework and certain themes may have limited our authors in what they could write, the approach provides the reader with some comparative and cross-cultural material for a wide array of countries. Overall, the family continues to be at the center of African social institutions, thereby making it a focus of investigation by family scholars, anthropologists, and sociologists over the past several years. Despite this interest, most of these studies have overemphasized reproductive behavior to the neglect of other aspects of family processes on the continent.

Even though the papers in this volume suggest that family and married life are central to African social organizations, we also cannot ignore the fact that profound transitions have occurred in family structure and processes since the postcolonial period. In this regard, we point to some of the documented transformations in African family life, including, for example, the changing modes of decision making due to the establishment of a cash crop economy (Oppong, 1970, 1977, 1981), nuptiality patterns (Aryee, 1985; Bledsoe, 1990), changing maternal roles (Oppong & Abu, 1984), an increasing age at marriage and declining fertility (Cohen, 1998; Lesthaeghe, 1989), a growing number of households headed by women (Lloyd & Gage-Brandon, 1993), an increase in the rate of marital instability and dissolution (Bruce, Lloyd, & Leonard, 1995; Takyi, 2001), and changing patterns of mate selection and family relations (Takyi, 2003; Takyi et al., 2003; Takyi & Oheneba-Sakyi, 1994). African traditional social obligations of sharing, caring, and child fostering may also have been compromised due in large part to the growing HIV/AIDS epidemic across the continent. In addition, there is the growing problem of intimate partner violence, which some scholars have argued may have been exacerbated by the ongoing HIV/AIDS epidemic (Piott, 1999; Martin & Curtis, 2004).

While acknowledging that changes have occurred in the traditional African family, and that these changes will definitely continue in the coming years, researchers differ on the causes of these transitions. In this debate on causation, two central theoretical orientations have become dominant in the discourse on the African family. Indeed during the past four decades, the research community has been debating on the question of whether African families are changing and the reasons behind the changes. At one end of this discourse are those who point to the inherent weaknesses within African social institutions themselves as providing the catalyst for recent changes to family and married life (see, e.g., Caldwell, Caldwell, & Quiggin, 1989; Lesthaeghe, 1989; Lockwood, 1995). In contrast, proponents of the external-induced or structural thesis focus on "modernization," or "Westernization," and its disruptive effects on the African traditional institutions including familial life and processes (Little, 1965; Pool, 1968; Oppong, 1970; Boateng, 1995).

Africa's contact with Europe and North America through the slave trade, colonialism, commodity trade, and migration has resulted in significant structural changes. While the introduction of Christianity brought in different belief systems some of which were counter to traditional beliefs, Western formal education increased autonomy among women, work outside the home in formal settings, a rapid rate of urbanization, and a sense of individualism that reduces kin and extended family ties. One can argue that the indigenous African family structure has also been influenced to a large extent by the continent's long relations and contact with its neighbors in the Arabic/Islamic world in Arabia and the Asian subcontinent. Equally important is Africa's link to the international community as a result of globalization, which is in turn altering family processes and dynamics on the continent.

Thus, in this volume, we reflect on the challenges to contemporary family life in Africa that have caused many families and households to make rapid adjustments in both structure and function. Regardless of where one stands on the debate as to the source(s) of family transitions (cultural versus structural transformations) in postcolonial Africa, we need to acknowledge that the changes which have occurred so far are not uniform across the continent, but vary from region to region and from one country to another. Moreover, given the trends we have identified in this volume, it seems likely that these changes will continue. The authors of the various chapters in this volume point to the fluidity of the African family despite the stresses that have come about as a result of Africa's continued contact with the outside world.

Of note also is the fact that the variations in family processes which have been pointed out in this book reflect in large part the different historical and postcolonial experiences between and within the countries in Africa. The impact of what Mazrui (1986) calls the "triple-heritage"—the justaposition of African indigenous, Arabic/Islamic, and European/Christian cultures—has not been uniformly felt throughout the continent. The infusion of foreign religions such as Islam and Christianity and their accompanying ideologies had differential impact on the African indigeneous cultures. For instance, while adherence to the Muslim faith did not effectively undermine the polygynous marriage system, Christianity with its insistence of monogamy might have turned out the phenomemon of "outside wifeship" (Karanja, 1994).

Some African countries have been able to survive effectively under the aegis of globalization, rural-urban and international migration, and HIV/AIDS, but the same cannot be said about others who have seen their societies under intense stress as a result of these social processes. HIV/AIDS poses a major threat and challenge to African families in the foreseeable future. Besides the health implications, the disease could potentially alter relations among family members. Not only is the disease afflicting women in large numbers, and influencing marital and childbearing patterns, but HIV/AIDS also has the potential to alter intrahousehold and kin relations. Moreover, recent reports linking the growing problem of intimate partner violence and other forms of abuse to HIV/AIDS implies that the disease has a potential to create havoc for family life and dynamics on the continent.

Similarly, as we alluded to earlier, African culture itself has been neither homogeneous nor stable as increasing economic decline, political instability, poor health care, and high levels of illiteracy have all had an impact on family processes and dynamics on the continent. A case in point is the observation that since the 1980s, and as a result of the World Bank and the International Monetary Bank (IMF) structural adjustment programs, family developments and processes have been affected in many ways, leading to an increase in poverty, the neglect of kin folks in some cases, and an increase in marital instability.

We conclude by arguing that throughout the latter part of the last century, social scientists have questioned the stability of the African family as a result of modernizing social processes. While it is true that the traditional family has changed in many ways and African families are confronted with new challenges, we need to point out that being a dynamic institution, the African family continues to adapt to the emerging structural changes. This is not to say that all is well within the family. Far from it, for as we enter the first decade of the new millennium, we see a host of issues and challenges that have the potential to weaken or threaten the survival of the traditional African family as we know it today.

For most of the latter half of the last century, high birthrates on the continent created a situation in which most families had a lot of young children. With the recent report of a decline in birthrates in some countries, which has been compounded by the HIV/AIDS epidemic that seems to disproportionately afflict the young and able-bodied people in Africa, there is a small but growing elderly population. In an atmosphere of declining governmental support, the situation of older families has become somewhat troubling. How the postcolonial family reacts to these threats and challenges has the potential to either maintain or undermine its role as a major organizing institution in Africa.

Also, due in large part to the IMF and World Bank–induced structural adjustments programs of the 1980s that emphasize privatization of social services, the limited support that governments provided to families has been reduced or eliminated completely. In the absence of a growing economy, families have increasingly become burdened with school fees, rising health care costs, and taxes.

In the end, we suggest a number of things as we reflect on the contemporary challenges and the future of African families. First, there is the need for more empirically based studies that test old and new theories about African family processes. This is necessary because our knowledge of African families, to date, has been gained primarily from anthropological literature. Second, family theories continue to evolve and change. Yet, it appears that existing research studies on African families have often relied on either the cultural or social disruptive arguments in their analyses of what is happening on the continent. Research that employs other theoretical frameworks (e.g., life course approaches) could also yield significant insight into family dynamics in Africa.

Third, there is need for comparative studies that go beyond ethnic and country boundaries as a way of providing cross-cultural information that can be used to either prove or disprove existing theories about family change and family processes in Africa. By virtue of the availability of data from recent national surveys such as the Demographic and Health Surveys, this is happening with demographic studies on the continent. Fourth, we believe that it is crucial for

African family scholars to go beyond their overemphasis on popular topics such as reproductive behavior to document other aspects of family processes that have received little or limited scholarly attention in contemporary and changing Africa. Thus, we suggest, for example, studies that investigate issues pertaining to dyadic relationships in postcolonial Africa, cohabitation, interethnic relations and marriage, family interaction, intimate partner violence, marital dissolution, and the role of religion in family processes. Fifth, as Bianchi and Casper (2005) have pointed out family change takes place within a specific time and place, meaning family scholars need to be aware of the historical and contextual factors that influence family processes. We think this suggestion is also true with respect to research on African families.

Sixth, the increase in international migration, and rural-urban migration (spatial movements) in Africa have also introduced a complex set of issues pertaining to family and social relations among the new immigrant/diasporan Africans. Even though the family will remain with us, it is quite certain that these spatial processes have altered family and kin relations in ways that we never thought of. Thus, we call on the research community to document some of these new developments in the African family, both on the continent and among the recent African diasporan communities in Europe and North America as well.

REFERENCES

Aryee, F. (1985). Nuptiality patterns in Ghana. In Singh, S., et al., (Eds.), *Demographic patterns in Ghana: Evidence from the Ghana Fertility Survey 1979–80* (pp. 17–48). Voorburg, Netherlands: International Statistical Institute.

Bianchi, S., & Casper L. M. (2005). Explanations of family change. In Bengston, V. L., Acock, A. C., Allen, K. R., Dilworth-Anderson, P., & Klein, D. M. (Eds.), *Sourcebook of Family Theory and Research*. Thousand Oaks, CA: Sage.

Bledsoe, C. (1990). Transformations in sub-Saharan African marriage and fertility. *The Annals of the American Academy of Political and Social Science 510*, 115–125.

Boateng, D. (1995). The changing family and national development in Ghana. In Ardayfio-Schandorf, E. (Ed.), *The changing family* (pp. 1–20). Accra: Ghana Universities Press.

Bruce, J., Lloyd, C., & Leonard, A. (1995). *Families in focus: New perspectives on mothers, fathers and children*. New York: Population Council.

Caldwell, J., Caldwell, P., & Quiggin, P. (1989). The social context of AIDS in sub-Saharan Africa. *Population and Development Review 15(2)*, 185–233.

Cohen, B. (1998). The emerging fertility transition in sub-Saharan Africa. *World Development 26(8)*, 1431–1461.

Karanja, W. W. (1994). The phenomenon of "outside wives": Some reflections on its possible influence on fertility. In Bledsoe, C. & Pison, G. (Eds.), *Nuptiality in sub-Saharan Africa: Contemporary anthropological and demographic perspectives* (pp. 194–214). Oxford: Clarendon.

Lesthaeghe, R. (1989). Production and reproduction in sub-Saharan Africa: An overview of organizing principles. In Lesthaeghe, R. (Ed.), *Reproduction and social organization in sub-Saharan Africa* (pp. 13–59). Berkeley: University of California Press.

Little, K. L. (1965). *West African urbanization: A study of voluntary associations in social change*. Cambridge: Cambridge University Press.

Lloyd, C., & Gage-Brandon, A. (1993). Women's role in maintaining households: Family welfare and sexual inequality in Ghana. *Population Studies 47(1)*, 115–131.

Lockwood, M. (1995). Structure and behavior in the social demography of Africa. *Population and Development Review 21(1)*, 1–32.

Martin, S., & Curtis S. (2004). Gender-based violence and HIV/AIDS: Recognizing links and acting on evidence. *The Lancet 363(9419)*, 1410–1411.

Mazrui, A., & Levine, T. K. (1986). *The Africans: A reader*. New York: Praeger.

Oppong, C. (1970). Conjugal power and resources: An urban African example. *Journal of Marriage and the Family, 32*, 676–680.

Oppong, C. (1977). A Note from Ghana on chains of change in family systems and family size. *Journal of Marriage and Family 39(3)*, 615–621.

Oppong, C. (1981). *Middle-class African marriage*. London: Allen & Unwin.

Oppong, C., & Abu, K. (1984). *The changing maternal role of Ghanaian women: Impacts of education, migration and employment*. Program Working Paper, #143, ILO Population and Labor Policies, Geneva.

Piot, P. (1999, March). *HIV/AIDS and violence against women*. Commission on the Status of Women (Forty-third Session) Panel on Women and Health. New York: United Nations.

Pool, I. (1968). Conjugal patterns in Ghana. *Canadian Review of Sociology and Anthropology 5*, 241–253.

Takyi, B. K. (2003). Tradition and change in family processes: Selecting a marital partner in modern Ghana. In Hamon, R. R. & Ingoldsby, B. B. (Eds.), *Mate selection across cultures* (pp. 79–94). Thousand Oaks, CA: Sage.

Takyi, B. K. (2001). Marital stability in an African society: Exploring the factors that influence divorce processes in Ghana. *Sociological Focus 34*, 77–96.

Takyi, B. K., & Oheneba-Sakyi. (1994). Customs, practices, family life and marriage in contemporary Ghana, West Africa. *Family Perspective 28(4)*, 257–281.

Takyi, B. K., Miller, N. B., Kitson, G. C., & Oheneba-Sakyi, Y. (2003). Marital choice in sub-Saharan Africa: Comparing structural and cultural influences in contemporary Ghana. *Comparative Sociology 2*, 375–391.

Appendix A: Contemporary Map of Africa

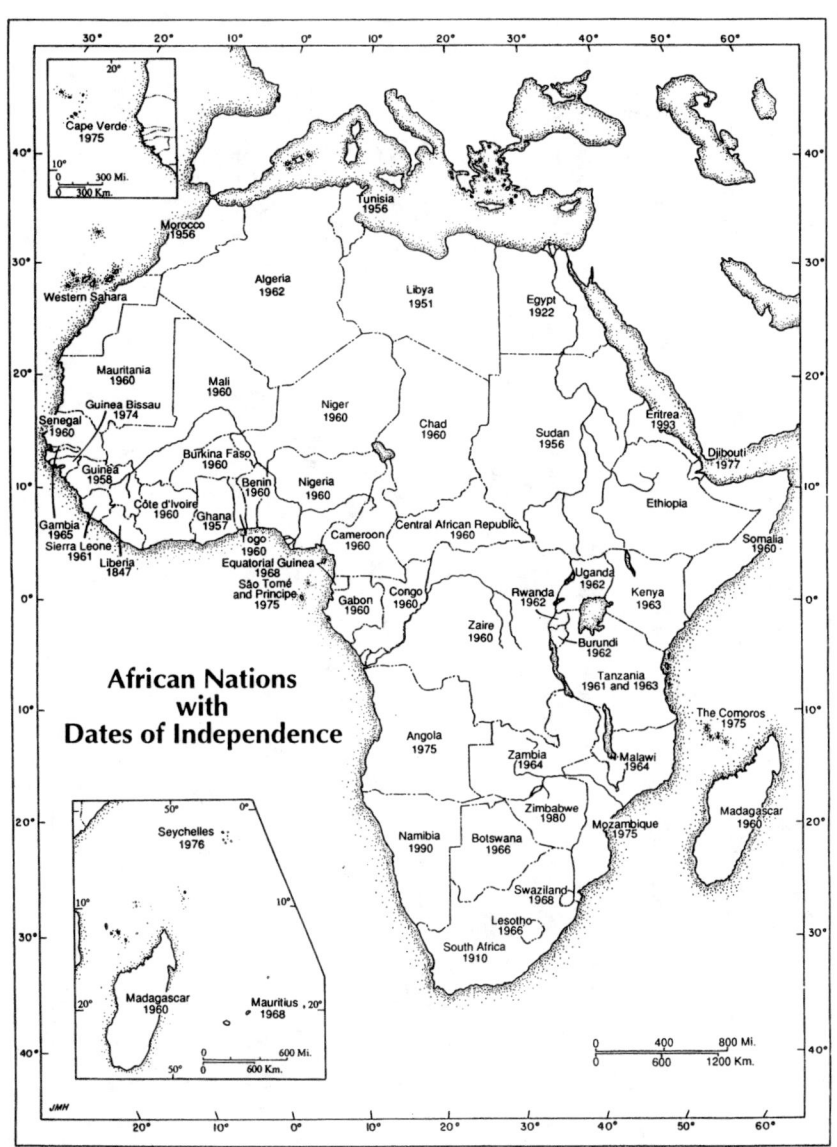

Source: Reprinted by permission of Indiana University Press. Copyright © 1995.

Appendix B: Basic Information about Selected Countries

Country (Independence)	Area[1]	Population (2004)	Capital	FCC[2]	Major Languages	Urban/Rural	Sex Distribution	TFR[4]	AHS[5]
Tunisia (1956)	63,170	9,975,000	Tunis	France	Arabic (O)[3] French	63/37	Male 50.3% Female 49.7%	1.8	4.7
Egypt (1922)	385,229	69,261,000	Cairo	Britain	Arabic (O) English	45/55	Male 50.46% Female 49.54%	3	4.7
Sudan (1956)	967,495	39,148,000	Khartoum	Britain Egypt	Arabic (O) English various Sudanic languages	37/63	Male 50.64% Female 49.36%	5.1	6.1
Senegal (1960)	75,955	10,339,000	Dakar	France	French (O) Wolof Pulaar Serer Mandé	47/53	Male 49.09% Female 50.91%	4.9	8.7
Côte d'Ivoire (1960)	123,863	16,897,000	Abidjan	France	French (O) Akan Kru Mandé Senufo Dioula Abidji	45/55	Male 50.28% Female 49.72%	5.6	7.8

(continued)

Basic Information about Selected Countries (continued)

Country (Independence)	Area[1]	Population (2004)	Capital	FCC[2]	Major Languages	Urban/Rural	Sex Distribution	TFR[4]	AHS[5]
Ghana (1957)	92,098	20,732,000	Accra	Britain	English (O)[3] Akan (Twi) Mossi Ewe Ga-Adangme	43/57	Male 49.46% Female 50.54%	3.3	4.3
Nigeria (1960)	356,669	128,254,000	Abuja	Britain	English (O) Hausa Fulani Yoruba Ibo Tiv Kanuri	45/55	Male 50.59% Female 49.41%	5.4	4.9
Cameroon (1960)	183,569	16,064,000	Yaounde	Germany France Britain U.N. Trust-Territories	English (O) French (O) Fulani Bamileke Bulu Ewondo Kirdi Douala	50/50	Male 50.27% Female 49.73%	4.6	5.5
Kenya (1963)	224,961	32,022,000	Nairobi	Britain	English (O) Swahili (O) Kikuyu Luo	39/61	Male 50.11% Female 49.81%	5	3.4

Basic Information about Selected Countries (continued)

Country (Independence)	Area[1]	Population (2004)	Capital	FCC[2]	Major Languages	Urban/ Rural	Sex Distribution	TFR[4]	AHS[5]
Malawi (1964)	45,747	11,907,000	Lilongwe	Britain	English (O) Chichewa Lomwe Ngoni Yao Luhya Kamba Kalenjin	15/85	Male 49.39% Female 50.61%	6.1	4.3
South Africa (1994)	470,693	46,587,000	Pretoria/ Tshwane	Britain	Afrikaans (O) English (O) Ndebele (O) Pedi (O) Sotho (O) Swazi (O) Tsonga (O) Tswana (O) Venda (O) Xhosa (O) Zulu (O)	58/42	Male 47.82% Female 52.18%	2.4	3.8

1. Area is in square miles.
2. FCC—former colonial country.
3. O—official language.
4. TFR—total fertility rate (average births per childbearing woman, 2003).
5. AHS—average household size.

Sources: Encyclopaedia Britannica 2005 Book of the Year. Chicago, IL: Encyclopaedia Britannica, Inc.; *Black Africa: A Comparative Handbook*, 2nd edition, by Donald George Morrison, Robert C. Mitchell, and John N. Paden. New York: Paragon House, 1989.

Author Index

Abu, K., 22, 278
Abwunza, J. M., 221
Achebe, N., 166
Adamu, F., 166
Addai-Sundiata, H., 150
Adeyokunnu, T. O., 166
Agence France Presse, 157, 166
Aina, O. I., 167
Ainsworth, M., 126
Ajayi, A. J., 167
Ake, C., 167
Akuffo, A. D., 18
Akuffo, F. O., 18
Alexandre, P., 189
Ali, N. M. M., 79
Amadiume, I., 167
Amoateng, Y., 18
Anarfi, J., 19, 150
Anderson, L., 45
Ansari, S. J., 189
Antoine, P., 101, 126
Antubam, K., 150
Apt, N. A., 150, 189
Ardayfio-Schandorf, E., 150–152, 277
Aryee, F., 19, 150, 277
Asante, M. K., 19

Ashton, H., 268
Assié-Lumumba, N. T., 126
Assimeng, M., 19
Atangana, E., 189
Awe, B., 167
Awusabo-Asare, K., 19, 150
Ayad, M., 102
Ayisi, E., 189
Ayittey, G. B. N., 167

Bâ, M., 94, 101
Bahoken, J., 189
Balepa, M., 189
Bangha, M. W., 189–190
Barakat, H., 45, 68
Barrère, B., 189, 191
Barrere, M., 126–127
Bass, L. E., 101
Batliwala, S., 244
Beckwirth, C., 19
Belhassen, S., 45
Ben Mrad, M. al-Salih, 45
Beneria, L., 190
Ben-Jochannan, Y., 190
Benneh, G., 150
Berquo, E., 190
Bessis, S., 45

Bianchi, S., 277
Biddlecom, A. E., 19
Blanc, A. K., 19
Blavo, E. Q., 150
Bledsoe, C., 19, 21, 101, 151, 191, 277
Bleek, W., 19
Boahen, A. A., 19
Boateng, D., 277
Bodman, H. L., 45
Bongaarts, J., 190
Bonner, P., 268
Borowiec, A., 45
Borrmans, M., 45
Boserup, E., 19
Botman, S., 68
Bourguiba, H., 45
Bourqia, R., 45
Bozzoli, B., 268
Brabin, L., 19
Bradley, C., 23, 167, 221, 223–224
Brand, L. A., 46
Brass, W., 221
Britannica, 174, 176–177, 190
Brohman, J., 245
Brown, C. K., 19, 150
Brown, L., 22
Bruce, J., 19, 277
Buah, F. K., 151
Bukh, J., 151
Burnham, P. C., 190

Cadigan, R., 19
Cain, M. T., 19
Caldwell, J. C., 19, 22, 150–151, 245
Caldwell, P., 19, 190, 277
Calitz, J. M., 268
Callaway, B., 101
Camara, F., 101
Carael, M., 151
Casper L. M., 277
Cassen, R., 245
Cattell, M., 221
Chakanza, J. C., 245
Chamari, A. C., 46
Charmie, J., 151
Charrad, M. M., 45–46

Chater, S., 46
Chelala, C., 68
Chen, C., 190
Chiabi, E., 190
Chimbiri, A., 245–246
Chimbiri-Kavinya, 229, 235, 240, 245
Chow, R., 167
Clark, G., 20
Clignet, R., 126
Cochrane, S. H., 46
Cohen, B., 20, 277
Cohen, D. W., 221
Cohen, R., 20
Colombo, R., 19
Cooksey, B., 190
Cosford, W., 19
Courbage, Y., 46
Cowgill, D. O., 190
Creevey, L., 101
Cross, A. R., 222
Curtis S., 278

Dasgupta, P., 20
Date-Bah, E., 20
Davidson, B., 151
Davis, K., 190
Davison, J., 222
De Vos, S. M., 190
DeLancey, M. W., 190
DeLancey, M. D., 190
Dinan, C., 20, 151
Diop, A. B., 101
Diop, C. A., 20, 101
Dixon, J., 190
Dizard, J., 190
Dlamini, C. R. M., 269
Doenges, C. E., 190
Dorjahn, V. R., 20
Dow, T. E., 222
Dreyer, J. T., 190
Du Bois, W. E. B., 2–3, 6–7, 20

Easterline, R. A., 191
El-Baz, S., 68
Elliot, F. R., 269
El-Obid, N. A. M., 79
Eloundou-Enyegue, P. M., 191
Eltis, D., 191

Enel, C., 101
Etienne, P., 127
Etounga-Manguelle, D., 167
Eze, E. C., 20

Fapohunda, B., 20
Farrell, G., 102
Feldstein, H., 22
Ferchiou, S., 45–46
Fernea, E. W., 45–46, 68
Fiawoo, D. K., 20
Fisher, A., 19
Fluehr-Lobban, C., 79
Folbre, N., 20
Forde, D., 20, 23, 151
Fortes, M., 20, 151
Fotso, M., 189, 191
Fox, R., 245
Frank, O., 127
Friedlander, D., 151

Gadlin, H., 190
Gage, A., 20
Gage-Brandon, A., 21, 127, 151, 278
Gage-Brandon, A. J., 127, 151
Gaisie, S. K., 151
Gallagher, N., 45
Gastellu, J-M., 101
Gatabaki, N., 222
Gibbs, J. L., 20
Giddens, A., 151
Gituto, B. M., 222
Glick, P., 23
Gluckman, M., 20
Goheen, M., 191
Goliber, T., 20
Goode, W. J., 191, 245
Goody, J., 20, 151
Gordon, A., 222–223
Graham, W., 192
Greenberg, J., 191
Greenstreet, M., 21
Grieco, M., 150
Gruenbaum, E., 79
Guilkey, D. K., 46
Guillaume, A., 126
Gurak, D. T., 21

Haddad, T., 46
Hagan, G., 21
Hammel, E., 191
Hammond-Tooke, W. D., 269
Harden, B., 222
Harrison, S. M., 127
Hart, K., 21
Hatem, M., 68
Heaton, T., 18
Hedinger, R., 191
Hermassi, E., 46
Herry, C., 126
Hite, A., 192
Hollings, E., 19
Holmes-Eber, P., 46
Hoodfar, H., 68
Hutchison, S., 21

Johnson, W., 191
Jolly, C., 221
Joseph, S., 46

Kabeer, N., 245
Kabira, W. M., 222
Kaler, A., 245
Kalu, O., 167
Kandawire, J. A. K., 245
Kanjaye, H., 246
Kañji, S., 101
Karam, A., 68
Karanja, W. W., 21, 191, 277
Kashif-Badri, H., 79
Kaudjis-Offoumou, F., 127
Kayongo-Male, D., 21
Kenyatta, J., 222
Khalil, K., 47
Khapoya, V. B., 21
Khasiani, S. A., 222
Khurshid, A., 101
Kielmann, K., 222
Kilbride, J. C., 222
Kilbride, P. L., 23, 167, 221–224
Kinsella, K., 191
Kizito, P., 222
Kludze, A. K. P., 151
Knipp, M., 167
Konotey-Ahulu, F., 151
Korboe, D., 151

Kouassigan, G., 101
Krieger, N., 167
Krige, E. J., 269
Kritz, M. M., 21
Kuenyehia, A., 21
Kumari, V., 191
Kuper, A., 269
Kuria, G. K., 222
Kurian, G. T., 222

Labourrie-Racape, A., 246
Lacombe, B., 191
Lambert, S., 127
Lapidus, I. M., 68
Laslett, P., 191
Launay, R., 127
Lee, J., 168
Lefebvre, M., 101
Lenton, C., 68
Leonard, A., 19, 277
Lesthaeghe, R., 21, 192, 278
Levasseur, A. A., 127
Levine, T. K., 21–23, 152, 278
LeVine, V., 191
Levy, M. B., 191
Little, K. L., 278
Lloyd, C. B., 19, 151
Lockwood, M., 21, 278
Locoh, T., 246
Logue, B., 192
Longmore, L., 269
Lorimer, F., 21, 191
Lumumba-Kasongo, T., 126
Ly, M., 102

Macleod, A. E., 68
Mafeje, A., 101
Mann, K., 21
Marck, J., 19
Margo, G., 167
Martin, L., 191, 193
Martin, S., 68, 167, 278
Marwick, M. G., 246
Mason, K. O., 21
Mayer, P., 269
Mazrui, A., 21–23, 127, 151–152, 223, 278
Mba, C. J., 192

Mba, N., 167
Mbamaonyeukwu, J. C., 192
Mbithi, J., 222
Mboup, G., 101
Mbugua, W., 22, 192
McCall, J. C., 222
Meekers, D., 127
Meinzen-Dick, R., 22
Mensa-Bonsu, H., 151
Mernissi, F., 68
Mikell, G., 22–23, 151
Mitchell, J. C., 246
Moeno, S. N., 269
Mohamed, N. F. O., 79
Mol, A. P., 192
Moloo, P. W., 222
Morey, M. J., 23
Morgan, R. W., 22
Morris, A., 269
Muhammad, B. B., 79
Mundt, R. J., 127
Munthali, A., 246
Murdock, G. P., 246
Myntti, C., 47

N'Cho, S., 127
Nagashima, N., 222
Nanitelamio, J., 101
Ndiaye, S., 102
Neher, W., 167
Nelson, N., 222
Ngubane, H., 222
Njoh, A. J., 192
Nkrumah, K., 22
Nnaemeka, O., 167–168
Ntozi, J., 19
Nukunya, G. K., 22, 152
Nyamnjoh, F. B., 192
Nyamwaya, D., 21, 191, 222–223
Nzimande, S. V., 269

O'Connor, A., 152
Obbo, C., 222
Obermeyer, C. M., 47
Obiora, A. L., 167
Oboler, R. S., 223
Obungu, W., 222
Ocholla-Ayayo, A. B. C., 167, 223

Odhiambo, A. E. S., 221
Oheneba-Sakyi, Y., 19, 22, 278
Okommah, A. D., 246
Okonjo, K., 167
Olaniyan, R., 152
Ollenu, N. A., 152
Omari, P. T., 152
Onyango, P., 21
Opoku, C., 152
Opoku, S. K., 150
Oppong, C., 18–22, 151–152, 223, 278
Orubuloye, I. O., 19
Osili, U. O., 167–168

Pachai, B., 246
Pala, A., 102
Palloni, A., 192
Panhuys, H., 102
Pappoe, M., 152
Parkin, D., 21, 191, 222–223
Pauw, B. A., 269
Phiri, I. A., 246
Phiri, K., 246
Piel, M., 152
Piot, P., 278
Pison, G., 21, 101, 151, 191–192, 277
Poh, K., 152
Pool, I., 278
Pool, J., 22
Popenoe, D., 168
Potter, R. G., 190
Poukouta, P., 126–127
Prazak, M., 223
Preston-Whyte, E., 269

Quiggin, P., 19, 277
Quisumbing, A., 22

Radcliffe-Brown, A. R., 20, 23, 151
Ramphele, M., 269
Rattray, R. S., 23, 152
Ray, D., 152
Reinwald, B., 102
Reynar, A., 23
Riza, R., 47

Roberts, T., 192
Robinson, D., 23
Robinson, W. C., 223
Robirosa, M. C., 192
Romaniuc, A., 192
Ross, K. R., 246
Ruel, M. J., 223
Rutenberg, N., 20
Rwomire, A., 223

Sai, F. T., 23
Said, E., 68
Salem, B. L., 45
Sangree, W. H., 223
Sarr, I., 102
Schacht, J., 68
Schapera, I., 223
Schoepf, B. C., 23
Schoffeleers J. M., 246
Schoffeleers, M., 247
Schuster, I., 223
Seck, O., 102
Segal, M., 268
Sène, S., 102
Senghor L. S., 247
Seppala, P., 223
Shaw, S. M., 168
Shenton, R. W., 168
Sherif, B., 68
Siegel, B., 223
Simons, H. J., 269
Singerman, D., 68
Singh, R. D., 23
Skinner, E. P., 23, 152, 223
Slyomovics, S., 46
Sofola, Z., 168
Solivetti, L. M., 168
Sombo, N., 126–127
Sow, F., 102
Stamp, P., 223
Steady, P., 102
Sudarkasa, N., 168
Sutton, J. E. G., 223

Taj, A. M., 21
Takyi, B. K., 22, 152, 278
Tetteh, P. A., 152
Thiongane, A., 102

Thompson, L., 269
Thompson, T. J., 247
Timaeus, I. M., 23
Tinker, I., 247
Todd, L., 192
Tohidi, N., 45
Tosh, J., 152
Toubia, N., 79
Treas, J., 192
Tucker, J., 68
Turner, B., 224

Ubaidullah, M., 191
Uchendu, V., 168

van de Walle, E., 23
Van Valsen, J., 247
Vantini, G., 79
Vaughan, M., 247
Velkoff, V., 191
Vellenga, D. D., 152
Vignikin, K., 247
Vimard, P., 127
Visvanathan, N., 247

Waines, D., 68
Wakam, J., 127
Warnes, A. M., 193
Weekes-Vagliani, W., 193
Weeks, J. R., 23
Weinreb, A. A., 247
Weisner, T. S., 23, 167, 221, 223–224
Welch, C., 23
Were, G. S., 224
Westoff, C. F., 127
White, L., 224
Whitehead A., 247
Wilson, F., 269
Wilson, M., 269
Wolf, D. A., 193
Wolpe, H., 269
Wortham, R., 224

Xenos, P., 190

Yeboah, I. E. A., 152
Young T. C., 247

Zulu, Eliya M., 247

Subject Index

Abidjan, 120, 124–127, 280
Abidji, 107, 280
Abouré, 107–108
Abron, 107
Abuse:
   child, 144–145
   spousal, 144, 161, 238–239
Acts, 38, 62, 105, 110, 171, 181, 230, 255
Adioukrou, 107
Adoption, 37, 105, 109, 111, 114, 124–125, 131, 135, 144, 173, 179, 203, 256, 262
Affinities (cultural), 106
Africanity, 5, 10, 203, 208, 215
Afrique Occidentale Française (AOF), 105–106, 115
Afro-Asiatic, 79, 174
Agni, 107
Agriculture, 13, 78, 140, 157–158, 166, 183, 201, 238–239, 251
Aguza, 54
Ahfad, 77–79
Ahliyyat, 54
Akan, 106–108, 111, 117, 122, 127, 131, 143, 152, 280–281

Ali, Ben, 36
Ancestors, 3, 103, 147, 185, 199, 202, 206, 256
Anglophone, 172, 175
Apartheid:
   effects on African family, 253, 255–256, 257
   effects on labor, 252–253
Arab Republic of Egypt, 49
Arab; Arabic; Arabian, 3–4, 132–133, 275
Arab-Islamic Heritage, 39
Assets, 14, 62, 108, 114, 116, 126, 165, 212, 232–233
Assimilation, 110, 201
Attié, 107

Ba, Mariama, 94, 101
Bait, 56
Banda, Kamuzu, H. (Dr.), 229–230
Bantu, 173–174, 191, 199–201, 224, 254, 256–258, 261, 269
Baoulé, 107, 114, 117, 127
Bapedi, 249
Basotho, 249
Batswana, 249

SUBJECT INDEX

Berber or Bedouin, 4, 49–50
Berlin Conference of 1884–1885, 4, 105
Bété, 107
Bilateral, 107–108
Birthrate, 50
Black(s), 252–253
Blantyre, 240, 245–246
Blood descent, 208
Bohadi or Lobolo, 254, 259–260. *See also* Bride wealth.
Borders, 4, 103, 105, 126, 174, 200
Bourguiba, Habib, 30
Brain drain, 118, 188, 193
Bride:
   price, 74, 210
   -to-be, 156–157
   wealth, 74–75, 206–207, 210
Burkina Faso, 105–106, 115–116, 130

Cameroun, République Unie du, 171–193
Capitalism, 60, 72, 115–118, 168, 198, 204–205, 211, 220–221, 243, 253, 255–257, 263, 269
Caste(s), 84, 87
Catholic Institute for International Relations, 242, 245
Catholicism; Catholic missionaries, 242–244
Census, 70, 84, 102, 107, 115, 129, 151, 166, 172, 176, 184, 191, 198, 223, 245
Central Africa, 169–193
CFA Franc, 176
Change (Structural), 103–127, 232
Chewa, 228–229, 232–233, 244, 246
Child care, 14, 134, 141, 156, 216–217, 232
Child fostering, 17, 126, 134, 240, 274
Childbearing, 12–13, 65–66, 95, 139, 182–184, 212–216, 261
Christian; Christianity:
   access to resources, 154, 205, 212
   early influences of, 4–5
   role in marriage, 259–260

Circular, 111, 206, 238
Civil Code of Côte d'Ivoire, 110
Cocoa Belt, 116–117
Code of Personal Status:
   and amendments, 39
   and feminists, 37
   and Islamic fundamentalism, 36
   and kinship structure, 37
   and state building, 39
   substance of, 36–39
Colonial borders; colonial boundaries, 69–71, 72, 73
Colonialism, colonial era; colonial influences; Colonialist(s), 70–73, 77, 88–89, 100, 110, 115, 121, 133–134, 149, 155, 160–161, 204, 251–252, 274
Commercial sex workers, 146
Condom use, 98, 241–242
Conjugal, 4–5, 8, 13, 22, 33, 140–141, 162, 179, 182, 187, 218, 232, 237, 242–243, 278
Consanguinity, 90–91, 208. *See also* Blood descent.
Conservatism on Family, 34
Contemporary, 14–15, 252–253
Continuity, 12, 27–28, 45, 103–127, 139, 153, 159–160, 164–166, 187, 204, 223, 247, 256–257, 261, 263, 269
Contraception, 7, 17, 42–44, 183
Convention Against Discrimination in Education, 96
Coptic, 49–51, 63
Co-residence, 180, 217
Côte d'Ivoire, 103–112, 115–116, 118–122, 124–127, 130–131, 184, 280
Co-wife, 206
CREDI (Centre de Recherche, de Documentation, et d'Information sur la Femme), 46
Cross cousin, 254
Cushitic, 199
Customary law, customary marriage, 10, 11, 73–74, 94, 136–137, 140, 144, 149, 161, 163, 203, 208, 211, 222, 257, 259, 264

Dakar, 89, 92–93, 101–102, 120, 126–127, 192, 280
Darfur, 71, 78
Death by stoning, 163
Decision maker; decision-making, 20, 114, 233, 235, 237–238, 242, 245
Delocalization, 205, 216
Demographic and Health Surveys (DHS), 7, 23, 77, 172, 178, 181–182, 184, 220, 276
Department of Health, 265, 268–269
Development:
   classical, 71, 124, 242
   macro-level, 232, 242
   meso-level, 232, 242
   theories, 3, 171, 227, 242, 276
Direction National du 2éme RGPH Cameroun, 172, 184, 190
Dislocations, 16, 155, 164–165
Division of labor, 8, 13, 63, 71, 140, 212, 230, 235, 238, 263
Divorce, 11–13, 15–16, 18, 20–21, 27, 29, 31–32, 35, 37–39, 46, 53, 57, 64–65, 67, 72, 83, 86–88, 91–93, 100, 105, 111–114, 119–120, 137–138, 155, 161–164, 168, 181, 184, 214, 229, 278
Domestic servants, 58, 263
Dynasty; dynasties, 50–51

East Africa; Eastern Africa, 195–224
Ebrié, 107
Echo, 98, 101, 156
Economic Community of West African States (ECOWAS), 125
Education, 4–10, 12–16, 18, 21–22, 32, 35, 41, 50–53, 56, 63, 72, 77–79, 84–89, 93–96, 99–100, 107, 110, 115–118, 120, 122–124, 126–127, 134, 138–141, 145–149, 154–156, 166–167, 171, 181–183, 185–187, 190, 198–201, 205–206, 210, 221, 224, 234, 240, 243–246, 259, 262, 266–269, 274, 278. *See also* Schooling.
Egypt, 3–4, 16, 32, 49–53, 55–68, 71–72, 132, 173, 280

Elite(s), 65, 70, 167, 217
e-mail, 49
Encyclopedia Africana Project, 299–302
Endogenous, 102–112, 114
Endurance, 118–123
Enduring, 105, 119, 205
English, the, 72–73, 207
Epidemic, 17, 153–154, 265, 275
Ethnic groups, ethnicity, 84–85
Ethos, 103–104, 107, 118, 126
Euro-Christian, European Christianity, 2–3, 4–5, 8, 11–12
Europeans, 1, 4, 106, 110, 130, 133, 199, 202, 251, 255
Evolution, 60, 103, 105, 108, 142, 164, 172, 178, 187, 247
Exogamous, 159
Extended kinship:
   and social forces, 141–142
   strength of, 18, 77, 141, 168, 197, 217

Family:
   code, 86–88
   defined, 2
   extended, 14, 18
   health, 16–17
   nuclear; nucleation, 9, 220, 236, 247
   law, 28–31, 112–115
   planning, 7, 13, 19–21, 42–44, 47, 65–66, 79, 192, 193, 212, 222–223, 228, 231–232, 240, 242
   research, 60–61, 91–93, 204–205
   rural, 14–15
   size, 39–44
   stability (instability), 15–16, 58–59, 216–219
   types, 2–3, 8, 96, 108, 123, 135, 142–143, 155, 161, 166, 179, 242, 257, 260
   urban, 14–15
   value(s), 14, 64–66, 103, 106, 108–111, 121, 123–125, 134, 139, 140, 172–173, 197, 198, 211–213, 259, 260

Family Law:
  and colonialism, 3–4, 17, 72–73
  and feminism, 28
  and Islamic fundamentalism, 36
  and Maliki School, 28–29
  and nationalism, 28
  and state building, 36
Farming, 13, 78, 140, 157–158, 166, 183, 201, 238–239, 251
Farmworker, 14–15
Female-headed households, 119, 139, 144, 149
Feminism:
  and Code of Personal Status, 37–39
  liberal, 30
  western, 36–39
Feminist, 32–33, 75, 77, 89, 101, 168, 231–232, 242
Fertility:
  level, 41–43, 45, 65–67, 84, 87–88, 91–96, 99, 140, 173, 185–186, 210, 212, 241, 261, 267
  rate, 42–43, 66, 83–84, 89, 93, 95, 99, 139, 172, 182–183, 186, 198, 212, 240–241, 261, 265–266
First World War, 106
Food and Agriculture (FAO), 245
Food crisis, 236–237
France, 4, 28, 83, 89, 105–106, 125, 157, 166, 189, 191, 281–282
Francophone, 51, 172, 175, 184
French, 2, 28–32, 35, 44, 50–52, 88, 98, 104–106, 110, 115, 122, 172–175, 280–281
French law, 28
Fulani, 132, 153, 155–158, 167, 174, 177, 282. *See also* Hausa; Hausa-Fulani.
Functionalist; functionalism, 103, 263
Fundamentalist Islam, 28, 35–38, 51
Funerals, 99, 111–112, 117, 241

Gagou Godié, 107
Gauteng, South Africa, 249–269
Gender:
  relations, 13, 53–54, 61–63, 96–98, 112–115, 139–141
  roles, 13, 53–54, 61–63, 96–98, 112–115, 139–141
Germany, 4, 201, 281
Ghana:
  Demographic and Health Survey (GDHS), 130
  Government of, 129–130
  Living Standards Survey (GLSS), 130
  Republic of, 130
  Statistical Service (GSS), 130
Gida, 156
Gift, 64, 181, 210
Globalization, 2–3, 49, 55, 62, 89, 100, 150, 155, 159, 164, 192, 198, 264, 275
Goods, 97, 107–110, 116, 122, 147, 182, 210, 221, 229
Gouro, 107
Government of Malawi, 228–230, 235, 238–241, 245
Government of Senegal, 86–88, 97, 101, 102
Gowon, Yakubu, 154
Groom, 9, 63–64, 91, 95
Guéré, 107

Haddad, Tahar, 46
Hajj, 72
Hal Pulaaren, 84–85, 93–94, 100
Half-century, 27, 45
Harmful customs, 73
Hausa; Hausa-Fulani, 131, 155–158, 162–164, 166–168, 281. *See also* Fulani.
Hauwa Abubakar, 163
Haves/have-nots, 197
Healthcare, 75
Heritage (cultural), 103, 135, 178, 256
Hijab (veil), 53–54
Historical framework, 1, 273
HIV/AIDS:
  and condom use, 98, 241–242
  and family change, 240, 275
  awareness, 99, 220, 268, 275
  control of, 13, 31, 51, 75, 88, 132, 160, 183, 204, 211, 231, 233, 242
  crisis, 275

SUBJECT INDEX

epidemic, 17, 153–154, 265, 275
impact of, 266, 275
prevalence of, 75, 275
prevention, 44, 125, 189, 220, 222, 241, 267
rates of infection, 43–44, 59, 78, 98–99, 145, 153–154, 219–220, 240–241, 265–266
risk of infection, 43–44, 59, 78, 98–99, 145, 153–154, 219–220, 240–241, 265–266
spread of, 59, 219–220
Homosexual practices; homosexuality, 59
Household:
  defined, 2
  economics, 8, 83, 126, 152, 242
  membership, 8, 13, 91, 103, 107, 111, 116, 118, 121, 136, 165, 175
  size, 12, 18, 22, 39, 42, 44, 61, 69, 77, 107, 114, 120, 126, 139, 142, 144, 153, 184, 220, 278, 282

Igbo, 153, 155, 157–158, 161–162, 167–168
Iju ase, 161
Immigration; immigrant, 40–41, 85, 115–116, 146, 165, 177, 179, 267, 277
Indigenous, 253, 254–255
Industrial Pass Laws, 252
Industrialization, 8, 12, 40–41, 144, 171, 252–253, 255, 262
Inheritance:
  property, 4–5, 9–11, 16, 22, 29, 54, 59, 74, 87–88, 97, 129, 132, 136–137, 140, 145, 149–151, 160, 181, 204–206, 214, 217, 229, 232–235, 247, 261
  widow, 5, 11, 137, 145, 206, 208
Intergenerational:
  relationships, 14
  ties, 66–67, 141–142, 212–216, 261–262
International Labor Organization (ILO), 20, 22, 181, 191, 278

International Monetary Fund (IMF), 5, 188, 191, 275–276
International Women's Conference, 16
Intestate Succession Law, 137, 150
Irioba, 202
Iron Age, 200, 251
Islam, Islamic:
  access to resources, 154, 205, 212
  early influences of, 2, 3–4
  fundamentalism, 28, 35–38, 51
  role in marriage, 11
Islamic, 2, 3–4, 11, 35–38, 51, 73 132, 149, 154, 177, 205, 212, 242
Islamic Tendency Movement, 37
Islamization, 73, 132, 149, 177, 242

Jehovah Witness, 229
Jihad movement, 156
Jihan's Law, 65
Johannesburg, 249–250, 269
Joola, 84–85, 88–89, 93–94, 101
Journal Officiel, 101, 110
Jumhuriyat Misr al-Arabiyah, 49

Kaberry Research Center (KRC), 174, 179, 183–184, 191
Kendakes, 71
Kenya, 197–224
Kenya Demographic and Health Survey (KDHS), 209, 219, 223
Kër, 90
Khutba, 64
Kin; Kinship; Kin folks; Kin network, 39, 57–58, 90–91
Kin-based patriarchy, 27, 29, 32–33, 38
King Menes, 50
Koulango, 107
Krou, 106
Kru, 107, 280
Kunya, 157

La Presse (Tunisia), 39, 46–47, 280
Labor force, 12, 52, 62–63, 70, 77, 180, 188, 190, 206, 232, 235, 240, 263–266
Labor intensive, 180, 238–239
Lagunaire, 106–107

Land Act, 252
Law(s), 54–55
Legislation, 32, 35, 44, 63, 85, 96–97, 207, 241
Levirate rules, 229
Life, cycle of, 19, 54, 142
Lilongwe, 240, 245–246, 282
Limpopo, 251
Linas-Marcoussis Agreement, 125
Lineage, 108, 232–233. *See also* system of descent.
Literacy, 50, 158, 246, 268
Living arrangement(s), 40, 91, 139, 141, 157, 162, 180, 187, 190, 192
Lobi, *Loi*, 46, 107
Local authorities, 230
Lomwe, 228–230, 233, 282
Lord Kitchener, 72
Lower Egypt, 56, 65–66

Maghrib, 27–29, 44, 46
Mai gida, 156
Malawi, 186, 227–247, 282
Male circumcision, 258
Male domination, 2
Maliki school, 28–29
Malinké, 106–107, 113
Mamelukes, 51
Mandé, 106–107, 114, 122, 280
Mandela, Nelson, 252
Mang'anja, 233
Marriage(s):
  African, 9–10
  child, 209–211, 257–258
  Christian, 11, 259–260
  civil, 11
  conceptions of, 108, 134, 136
  Consensual Unions, 11
  forcé, 113
  Islamic, 11
  mixed, 106, 201, 229
  Muslim with non-Muslim, 11
  Multiple, 10–12, 64–65, 94–95, 162, 206, 211–212. *See also* Polygyny.
  systems, 10–12
  Traditional, 11
  woman to woman, 11

Marxists, 34
Mate selection, 9–10, 63–64, 94, 138, 181–182, 209–211, 257–258
Matrilineal, 16, 22, 70–71, 87, 94, 107–111, 113–115, 122, 135, 139–140, 145, 185, 229, 232–235, 242, 246
Matrimonial Causes Act, 163
Mbumba, 233
Micro International, Inc (MI), 151, 223
Migrants, 38, 58, 90, 116–117, 123–124, 165, 200, 237, 239
Migration, 115–118, 274
Migratory labor system, 255, 263
Military Coup, 73, 125
Ministry of Girl Child Education, 145
Ministry of Women and Children Affairs, 145
Missionary activity, 202, 205
Mobility, 138, 144, 166, 173, 217, 240, 264
Modernity; Modernize, Modernization, role of, 15–16, 58–59, 184–187, 216–219, 236–239
Modes of production, 99, 212–215, 274, 278
Mogya, 136
Monogamy, 10–12, 64–65, 86, 94–95, 104, 105, 119, 122, 162, 206, 211–212, 235, 275
Moral codes; morality, 6, 31, 78, 147, 197
Mortality:
  infant/child, 75
Mourou, Abdelfattah, 37
Mrad, Ben, 31, 45
Multiethnic, 70, 79
Multigenerational, 107, 154, 158–159, 198, 204, 255, 262
Multinational, 15
Multiracial, 70
Muluzi, Bakili (Dr.), 230
Muslim Brotherhood, 35, 73
Muslim *Ulama*, 156
Muslim(s), Non-Muslims, 4, 41, 51, 62, 70, 74–75, 95, 130, 177, 203, 229, 234, 244, 250

SUBJECT INDEX

Naming, 99, 105, 111, 113, 131, 133, 175
Napoléon, 51
Nassar, Gamal Abdel, 252
National AIDS Commission, 146, 240–241, 246
National Commission of Women in Development, 246
National Union of Tunisian Women, 36, 38, 41, 47
Nationalism, 28, 53, 145, 190, 205
Nation-state, 28, 103, 111
Ndebele, 249, 282
Neo-liberal(s), 30, 231
Ngai, 202
Ngoni, 228–229, 233, 247, 282
Nguni, 250–251, 254, 258, 261
Niger-Congo, 174
Nigeria, 21, 23, 71, 153–168, 174–175, 177, 191–192, 281
Nile Delta/Nile Valley, 50, 56, 72, 78–79
Nilo-Saharan, 174
Nilotic, 70, 74, 199–200, 214
Nkhoswe, 233
Non-relatives, 14, 18
North Africa; Northern Africa, 25–79
Ntoro, 136
Nubian, 49–51, 71, 79
Nuclear family; nuclearization, 14

Obasanjo, Olusegun, 154
Office on the Status of Women, 264, 269
Online, 49
Open Door Policy, 52
Orientalist, 61
Otieno, 217–218, 222–223
Ottoman Empire, 51
Ottoman Turkish, 72
Out-migration, 115–118, 274
Outside Wifeship, 10, 12, 143, 184, 275

Pastoral; Pastoralism, 71, 74, 78, 156, 200
Patriarchy, 27, 29, 32–33, 37–38, 69, 87, 96, 140, 205, 212–213, 246

Patrilineal; patrilineage, 39, 74, 159
Patriliny; Patrilocal, 70, 73–74, 107–108, 113, 121, 143, 229, 232–234
Persian Gulf, 76
Personal Status Law, 54–55, 59, 65
Pharaohs; Pharonic, 50
Philosophical consciencism, 3
Policy; Policymakers, 6, 10, 12–13, 16, 19–21, 29, 31–36, 46, 52, 63–65, 73–75, 99–101, 108–112, 120–124, 132–134, 151, 192, 202, 227–228, 231, 238, 241–245, 257, 264, 269
Polygyny, 3, 5–6, 10, 12–13, 16, 19–21, 29, 32–34, 37, 64–65, 74–75, 83–84, 86–87, 89–93, 95, 99–101, 104, 108–112, 121–123, 132, 134, 136–137, 143, 145, 151, 158, 161–162, 164, 183–184, 188, 192, 203, 205–206, 208–209, 214–215, 235, 255, 259
Population Council, 7, 13, 19–20, 22, 162, 277
Population Reference Bureau, 13, 15, 23, 42, 47, 84, 102, 172, 192
Post-colonial; postindependence, postindustrial, 70–71, 73, 109–112, 119, 124, 129, 137, 172, 192, 229, 273
Precolonial; Precolonial Africa, 251
Pre-Islamic, 71, 86, 100
Price (Bride, Wealth), 74–75, 206–207, 210. *See also* Bride price; bride wealth.
Private polygyny, 10, 12, 143, 184, 275
Pro-choice, 9
Pro-family and marriage ideology, 9
Promiscuity, 75, 241–242
Protestant, 5, 200, 203
Provincial National Defence Council (PNDC), 137, 145
Ptolemaic, 50
Purda, 156

Quran; Quaranic, 3–4, 11, 35, 55, 62, 64, 66, 85, 87–88, 97–98, 156, 234

Racial segregation; racially segregated, 257
Racist attitudes, 6
Rain forest, 69
Raison d'etre
Rassemblement Démocratique Africain (RDA), 106
Recto-Vaginal Fistula (RVF), 156–157
The Red Cross; Red Crescent, 44
Religion; religious, 3–5, 10–11, 31–32, 50, 51, 73, 98, 104–106, 130–134, 154–156, 176–178, 202, 233–234
Religious diversity, 67, 130
Remittances, 90, 165, 168, 185, 198, 239
Republic of Kenya:
 Central Bureau of Statistics Central Bureau, 223
 National Council for Population and Development, 223
République Tunisienne, Institut National de la Statistique (INS), 28, 32–34, 40, 42–43, 46–47, 126–127
Rift Valley, 199–200
Roman Empire, 50
Rural-urban, 142–144

Sadat, Anwar, 52
Sahelian, 106
Sarakuna, 156
Schooling, 5, 10, 13, 67, 94, 110, 205, 212, 236, 242. *See also* Education.
Self-acquired property, 9, 136
Semiarid; semiurban, 69, 119, 199–200, 240
Sena, 228–230
Senegal, 83–99, 101–102, 105, 116, 120, 156, 189, 280
Senegal Family Code, 86–88
Sénoufo, 107, 111
Sereer, 84–85, 87–88, 93–95
Sexual behavior, 75, 103, 188, 219
Sexually-Transmitted-Diseases (STDs), 164. *See also* HIV/AIDS.
Shabba, 54
Shabka, 64

Shari'a, 3, 11, 28–29, 33–34, 36–37, 52, 55, 65–66, 73, 163, 203
Sinai Peninisula, 50–53
Slavery, 17, 78, 145, 252, 274
So Long a Letter, 7, 94, 100–101, 167
Social:
 capital, 34, 70–71, 99, 120, 131, 134, 172, 175, 217, 233, 250, 280–282
 change, 257
 class, 56–57
 institutions, 1, 3, 5, 17, 72–73, 104–106, 131, 133, 135, 176, 210, 220–221, 227, 232–234, 260, 268, 273–274
Sociocultural; socioeconomic, sociogeographic, 5, 103–105, 116, 120–121, 136, 140, 147, 149, 158, 163, 171–172, 179, 182, 183, 212, 221, 227, 234, 260, 265
Social Security Benefits, 14
South Africa Survey, 261, 266, 268–269
South Africa; Southern Africa, 225–269
Sowetan, 249, 253, 260, 262
Soweto, 249–269
Spiritual, 103–104, 131, 154, 197, 202
Street Children, 146–147, 150–151
Structural Adjustment, 85, 238, 275
Subcontinent, 201, 266, 275
Sub-Saharan Africa, 17, 19–23, 49, 59, 86–87, 101, 127, 133, 151–152, 166, 190–192, 197, 222, 277–278
Sudan, 4, 50–51, 69–79, 131–132, 155, 174, 189, 200
Sudan Demographic & Health Survey (SDHS), 77, 79
Suez Canal Zone, 52
Sunni, 50, 70
Supernatural powers, 3
Swahili slave traders, 230
Syndicat Agricole Africain (SAA), 106
System of descent, 108

Thebes, 71
Theories:
 development, 1, 5–6, 16, 18–23, 39, 42, 44, 46, 50–52, 77–79, 101–102, 108, 120, 132, 139–140, 150–151,

160, 165–168, 175, 178, 187–188, 192–193, 217, 234–239, 241–243, 245–247, 254–258
  economic, 1–5, 16, 18–19, 22–23, 38–40, 42, 44, 46, 50–52, 76–77, 79, 99–101, 108, 117–126, 131–133, 139–147, 152, 162, 165, 172–176, 187–190, 192–193, 216–222, 234–239, 242–244, 247, 253, 257–258, 265–266, 269, 275
  social, 1–3, 14–19, 21, 23, 36–37, 39–46, 56–58, 60–68, 76–77, 95–101, 103–110, 119–122, 138–145, 147–152, 164–165, 171–173, 185–190, 203–206, 220–224, 230–237, 239–247, 249–250, 253–255, 257–258, 262–264, 267–269, 273–278
Third World, 20, 70, 76, 222
Trade; traders:
  Arab, 1, 4, 7, 11, 27, 30, 32, 39, 44–45, 49–51, 53, 60, 68, 79, 199, 201
  commodity, 214, 274
  slave, 1, 3, 6, 70, 72, 75, 84, 133, 156, 178–179, 191, 203, 230, 234, 274. *See also* Trans-Atlantic Slave Trade.
Three v's (voiture, villa, virement), 184
Tonga, 228, 233–234, 247
Total Fertility Rate (TFR), 12, 42, 50, 76, 139, 182, 212, 261, 282
Township, 261, 269
Townships, 249, 258, 261
Tradition; Traditional; traditionalism, 2–3, 5–14, 16–19, 30–31, 37–40, 57, 75, 101, 109, 113–114, 121, 133–138, 158–162, 167, 176–187, 189–191, 242–245, 252–253, 255–264, 274, 276, 278
Traditional belief system(s), 148, 202, 244, 261, 274
Traditional Gender Role Expectations, 13
Traditional-modern dichotomy, 5
Trans-Atlantic Slave Trade, 1, 191
Trans-Saharan, 1, 132
Transvaal, 252, 253

Triple Heritage, 3, 10, 18, 71–73, 85–86, 88–89, 100, 105, 127, 134, 151–152, 176–179, 202–203, 223
Trokosi, 147–148
Tumbuka, 228, 230, 233–234
Tunisia, 27–47, 280
Tunisian External Communication Agency and National Union of Tunisian Women, 47

Unilineal, 108, 158
United Nations:
  AIDS (UNAIDS), 23, 193
  Children's Fund (UNICEF), 23
  Demographic Yearbook, 23
  Institute for Training and Research (UNITAR), 188, 193
  Office for the Coordination of Humanitarian Affairs (OCHA), 125, 193
  Population Fund (UNFPA), 192
United States:
  Bureau of the Census, 84, 102
  Central Intelligence Agency (CIA), 79, 224
Upper Egypt, 50, 65–66
Urbanization; urbanize, 15–16, 58–59, 90, 144, 216–219, 236–239

Vertical solidarity, 92
Vesico-Vaginal Fistula (VVF), 156–157
Village chiefs, 87, 230
Voltaïque, 106–107, 122

Wali, 162
War, 4, 33, 37, 51–52, 69–70, 73–74, 76–79, 106, 154, 175, 189, 266
Website, 199, 202
Well-being, 17, 83, 111, 114, 121, 179, 228, 231, 240, 267
West Africa; Western Africa, 83–168
Westernization, 12, 49, 55, 89, 103–104, 107, 110–111, 161, 177, 215, 220, 274
White(s), 253, 261, 266
Will, 16, 97–98
Witch Camps, 148

Witwatersrand, 255, 269
Wolof, 84–85, 87, 89–91, 93–94, 98, 100–101, 280
Women; women's:
  economic participation, 62
  empowerment, 16, 79, 227–229, 231, 233, 235–237, 239, 241–245, 247, 267, 269
  in Development, 21–22, 150–167, 227–229, 231–232, 242, 245–246
  movement, 6, 30–31, 33–35, 37–38, 49, 52–54, 69, 72, 75, 77–78, 89, 106, 115, 125, 156, 235, 252, 254
  property rights, 16, 22, 59, 88, 97, 232–233
  status, 16, 21–23, 59, 87–88, 96–98, 231, 233, 238, 243, 268–269
  working, 18–22, 41–42, 44, 49, 59, 61–62, 65, 68, 70, 76, 84, 88–89, 93, 101, 114
Workforce, 12, 70, 76, 100, 262–263, 265
World Almanac Education Group, 199–201, 224
World Bank, 5, 42–43, 47, 127, 172, 176, 186–188, 191, 193, 275
World Conference on Education, 16
World Fertility Surveys (WFS), 7, 172, 182
World Health Organization (WHO), 17, 23, 43–44, 47, 99, 102
World War I/World War II, 4, 52, 175, 266
Worldview, 15

Yao, 228–230, 232, 234, 239, 246, 282
Yaounde, 172, 175, 185–186, 281
Yom Kippur War, 52
Yoruba, 19, 21, 153, 155, 157–159, 162, 167, 281
Youssef, Ben, 32, 34, 42
Youthful age structure, 84

Zulu, 20, 229, 247, 249, 258, 282

About the Contributors

ELIZABETH ARDAYFIO-SCHANDORF is Professor in Geography and former head of the Department of Geography and Resource Development, University of Ghana, Legon. She holds a B.A. (Honors) from the University of Ghana, Legon, a Ph.D. from the University of Birmingham, UK, and a Post-Doctoral Studies in Women, Public Policy and Development, University of Illinois. She is the West African Representative of the Commonwealth Geographical Bureau. She is also the Director of the Family and Development Program and a Fellow of the Ghana Academy of Arts and Sciences. Her published books include *Bridges of Development: A Compendium of Gender and the Ghanaian Family* (2004) and *The Changing Family in Ghana* (1996).

N'DRI THÉRÈSE ASSIÉ-LUMUMBA is Associate Professor in the Africana Studies and Research Center, Cornell University, where she is also a member of the graduate fields of Education, International Development, and International Agriculture and Rural Development. She earned her Ph.D. in Comparative Education from the University of Chicago, two master's degrees from Université Lyon II, Lyon, France, with part of her academic training at Université d'Abidjan (Côte d'Ivoire) and Université Laval (Québec, Canada). She is also Chercheur Associé at Centre de Recherches Architecturales et Urbaines (C.R.A.U.) at Université de Cocody in Abidjan (Côte d'Ivoire), and Research Affiliate in the Institute for Higher Education Law and Governance of the University of Houston. She is cofounder and Associate Director of Pan-African Studies and Research Center in International Relations and Education for Development, Abidjan (Côte d'Ivoire).

MARTIN W. BANGHA is the Project Manager for the African Census Analysis Project (ACAP), Population Studies Center at the University of Pennsylvania. Prior to joining ACAP in 2001, he served the Union for African Population Studies (UAPS) in various capacities including as Interim Executive Secretary; Coordinator of the UAPS Small Grants Program on Population and Development; as well as Managing Editor of the journal *African Population Studies.* He has written articles and contributed to book chapters. His research interests are mainly in the areas of reproductive behavior, health conditions, and health care strategies in sub-Saharan Africa.

LORETTA E. BASS, an Associate Professor at the University of Oklahoma, focuses her research on children and stratification issues in West Africa and the United States. Her recently completed book *Child Labor in Sub-Saharan Africa* (2004) presents a comprehensive, systematic study of this social issue and offers a window on the lives of Africa's child workers, drawing on research and demographic data from 43 countries. Her research has been supported by grants from the U.S. Agency for International Development, the U.S. Census Bureau in cooperation with the Joint Center for Poverty Research, and internal grants at the University of Oklahoma.

MOUNIRA M. CHARRAD is Associate Professor of Sociology at the University of Texas–Austin. She received her undergraduate education at the Sorbonne in Paris and her Ph.D. at Harvard University. Her publications in French and in English address state formation, culture, women's rights, and Islamic law. She is the author of *States and Women's Rights: The Making of Postcolonial Tunisia, Algeria and Morocco* (2001), which received several awards including the 2004 Distinguished Scholarly Publication Award for the Outstanding Book in Sociology from the American Sociological Association.

AGNES M. CHIMBIRI is the Director of the Center for Reproductive Health of the Malawi College of Medicine in the Department of Community Health. She holds a Ph.D. from University of Waikato, New Zealand. Her research experience focuses on sexual and reproductive health behaviors in relation to the structures and functions of government and traditional social systems. Since the early 1990s, she has been involved in a longitudinal study on the role of social networks in family planning and HIV/AIDS behavior, and gender dynamics in condom use patterns of sexual and reproductive health behaviors of young people in Malawi.

CAROLYN FLUEHR-LOBBAN is Professor of Anthropology and African Studies at Rhode Island College. She received her B.A. and M.A. degrees from Temple University and her Ph.D. from Northwestern University. She has spent years living and conducting research in the Sudan, Egypt, and

Tunisia. Her research subjects have covered such topics as Islamic law and Islamic society, women's social and legal status in Muslim societies, ethics and anthropological research, human rights and cultural relativism, and comparative studies in law and society. She is a founder and twice past president of the Sudan Studies Association. Her publications include *Islamic Society in Practice* (1994) and *Islamic Law and Society in the Sudan* (1987), which has been translated into Arabic and published in 1999.

ALLYSON B. GOEKEN graduated from the University of Texas–Austin in May 2002 with a master's degree in Middle Eastern Studies. She received her bachelor of arts in History from Idaho State University. Her interests center on gender and education, labor, and politics with a focus on Tunisia and Algeria.

CHUKS J. MBA is the Deputy Director and Senior Lecturer at the Regional Institute for Population Studies, University of Ghana, Legon, Ghana. He is a graduate of universities in Nigeria and Ghana and was a postdoctoral Research Fellow for the African Census Analysis Project (ACAP) at the Population Studies Center, University of Pennsylvania, supported by the Andrew W. Mellon Foundation grant. He has to his credit many publications on population aging, population policies, and adolescent reproductive behavior in several peer-reviewed journals.

SYLVIA N. MOENO is Senior Lecturer at the Department of Sociology, University of Johannesburg, Soweto Campus, Guateng Province, South Africa. She received her Ph.D. in Sociology from York University, Toronto, Canada, and was a Postdoctoral Fellow at Yale University in 1990–91. She has lectured at various institutions in the United States, South Africa, Swaziland, and Canada and has done research for the Population Research Laboratory, University of Southern California, Los Angeles, and the City Council of Johannesburg. Her research includes the study of family life in South African Townships.

OBIOMA NNAEMEKA is Professor of French, Women's Studies, and African/African Diaspora Studies and Director of the Women's Studies Program at Indiana University, Indianapolis. She is also the President of the Association of African Women Scholars and the recipient of numerous national and international awards. She has published extensively on literature, Women's/Gender Studies, human rights, development, and African/African Diaspora Studies.

YAW OHENEBA-SAKYI is Professor and Head of the Africana and American Indian Studies Program at California State University, Fresno. He received his B.A. (Honors) from the University of Ghana, Legon; his M.A. in Africana Studies from the State University of New York (SUNY) at Albany; and his Ph.D. in Sociology from Brigham Young University. The author of

Female Autonomy, Family Decision Making and Demographic Behavior in Africa (1999), he has also published several articles in noted journals. He has conducted research and study tours throughout Africa. He is the recipient of the SUNY Chancellor's Distinction Award for Scholarship and Research in the Humanities, Arts, and Social Sciences and the Chancellor's Award for Excellence in Teaching. His scholarship has been supported with grants from U.S. Department of Education, Rockefeller Foundation, National Endowment for the Humanities, Nuala McGann Dresher Fellowship, and the London School of Economics and Political Science.

MIROSLAVA PRAZAK is Professor of Anthropology at Bennington College. She received her Ph.D. in Anthropology from Yale University with a thesis titled *Cultural Expressions of Socioeconomic Differentiation among the Kuria of Kenya*, and has been conducting longitudinal research on inequality in rural Kenya for nineteen years. She has presented papers and published articles and chapters on family, demography, adolescence, gender, education, and economy. She is currently working on a monograph titled *Negotiating Identity: Circumcision and Witchcraft in Kuria Life*.

BAHIRA SHERIF-TRASK is Associate Professor of Individual and Family Studies at the University of Delaware. She has a B.A. degree in Political Science from Yale University and a Ph.D. in Cultural Anthropology from the University of Pennsylvania. Her research centers on issues of cultural diversity, gender, work, and intergenerational relations. She has conducted fieldwork on these topics in the United States, Europe, Islamic North Africa, and the Middle East and has published extensively on these issues. She edited a volume on the lives of Middle East women for the *Greenwood Encyclopedia of Women's Issues* (2003). She is currently working on a new study on cross-cultural perceptions of the intersection between marriage and work.

FATOU SOW, a Professor at the University Cheikh Anta Diop of Senegal, focuses her research on family life, women's position, and gender issues in West Africa. She also holds a distinguished researcher position with the Institut Fundamental d'Afrique Noire (IFAN), associated with the University Cheikh Anta Diop. She has widely published her research and technical findings in scholarly journals, and is a consultant with the United Nations Food and Agriculture Organization on rural women's position in sub-Saharan Africa.

BAFFOUR K. TAKYI is an Associate Professor of Sociology at the University of Akron, Ohio. He received his Ph.D. and M.A. in Sociology from the State University of New York (SUNY) at Albany, and his B.A. (Honors) from the University of Ghana, Legon. His varied research interests include reproductive-related behavior, family dynamics, and African immigrants in the United States. He has published extensively on the family in such journals as the *Journal of Marriage and Family*, *Social Science and Medicine*, *Journal of Comparative Family*, *Journal of Family and Economic Issues*, *Sociological Focus*, *Family Perspectives*, *African Journal of Reproductive Health*, *Ethnic and Racial Studies*, and *Western Journal of Black Studies*.

African Families at the Turn of the 21st Century